Clashing Views
on Controversial
Economic Issues

5th edition

Clashing Views on Controversial Economic Issues

5th edition

Edited by

Thomas R. Swartz
The University of Notre Dame

and

Frank J. Bonello
The University of Notre Dame

The Dushkin Publishing Group, Inc.

This book is dedicated to the thousands of students who have persevered in the "Bonello/Swartz-B.S." introductory economics course sequence at the University of Notre Dame. It is also dedicated to our children and grandchildren. In order of their birthdates, they are:

Mary Elizabeth, Karen Ann, Jennifer Lynne, John Anthony, Anne Marie, Rebecca Jourdan, David Jospeh, Stephen Thomas, and Chelsea Margaret.

Library of Congress Catalog Card Number: 89-81549

Manufactured in the United States of America

Fifth Edition, First Printing
ISBN: 0-87967-859-3

The Dushkin Publishing Group, Inc.
Sluice Dock, Guilford, CT 06437

PREFACE

> Where there is much desire to learn, there of necessity will be much arguing.
>
> —John Milton (1608–1674)
> English poet and essayist

Presented here are twenty debates on important and compelling economic issues, which are designed to stimulate critical thinking skills and initiate lively and informed discussion. These debates take economic theory and show how it is applied to current, real-world public policy decisions, the outcomes of which will have an immediate and personal impact. How these debates are resolved will affect our taxes, jobs, wages, educational system, etc.; in short, they will shape the society in which we live.

It has been our intent throughout each of the five editions of *Taking Sides: Clashing Views on Controversial Economic Issues* to select issues that reveal something about the nature of economics itself and something about how it relates to current, everyday newspaper headlines and television news stories on public policy issues that deal with economic considerations (and almost all do these days). To assist the reader, we begin each issue with an *issue introduction*, which sets the stage for the debate as it is argued in the YES and NO selections. Each issue concludes with a *postscript* that briefly reviews the arguments and makes some final observations. The introduction and postscript do not preempt what is the reader's own task: to achieve a critical and informed view of the economic issue at stake. Certainly, the reader should not feel confined to adopt one or the other of the positions presented. The views presented should be used as starting points, and the *suggestions for further reading* that appear in each issue postscript offer additional resources on the topic. At the back of the book (beginning on page 338) is a listing of all the *contributors to this volume*, which provides information on the economists, policymakers, political leaders, and commentators whose views are debated here.

Changes to this edition In this edition, the most significant changes are in Part 2: Macroeconomic Issues. As we leave the 1980s and enter the decade of the 1990s, we confront a new set of policy concerns: *Should the Government Take Action to Increase the Savings Rate?* (Issue 11); *Should the Capital Gains Tax Be Lowered?* (Issue 12); *Is Workfare a Good Substitute for Welfare?* (Issue 13); *Do Federal Budget Deficits Matter?* (Issue 14); *Is the Financial Institutions Reform, Recovery, and Enforcement Act of 1989 the Solution to the Savings and Loan Crisis?* (Issue 15). We have added a new debate in Part 1 on the wisdom of college education vouchers that can be earned for "national service" (Issue 3). And we've updated the readings of some of the existing issues. As with all of the previous editions, the issues can be used in any sequence and are designed to stand alone, although the general organization of this book loosely parallels the sequence of topics often found in standard introductory economics textbooks.

A word to the instructor An *Instructor's Manual with Test Questions* (multiple-choice and essay) is available through the publisher. The manual includes a grid that correlates the individual issues in this edition of *Taking Sides* with chapters of ten standard textbooks often used in introductory economics courses. And a general guidebook, called *Using Taking Sides in the Classroom*, which discusses methods and techniques for integrating the pro/con approach into any classroom setting, is also available.

Acknowledgments We have received many helpful comments and suggestions from our friends and readers across the United States and Canada. Their suggestions have markedly enhanced the quality of this edition of *Taking Sides*. If as you read this book you are reminded of an essay that could be included in a future edition, we hope that you will drop us a note. We very much appreciate your interest and help and would be pleased to hear from you.

Our thanks go to those who responded with suggestions for the fifth edition: John D. Abell, University of North Carolina-Charlotte; Leo M. Corbaci, University of Notre Dame; Frank Falero, California State College-Bakersfield; Pat Humston, Bee County College; Rebecca Judge, St. Olaf College; Lois Ann McElroy Lindell, Wartburg College; Michael McCully, Ohio Wesleyan University; Paddy Quick, St. Francis College; Peter W. Replogle, Orange County Community College; Edward Saueracker, Hofstra University; Robert L. Sherry, Keene State College; and Daniel G. Varty, West Valley College. We are also indebted to Mimi Egan, our editorial advisor at the Dushkin Publishing Group. She provided excellent council, suggested material and topics for this edition, and gave us much needed support as we approached our publication deadlines. Those who suffered most in the preparation of this manuscript are our typists: Frank J. Bonello, Margaret Jasiewicz, Nancy Kegler, Cheryl Reed, and Sherry Reichold. They rarely complained about Swartz's tortured handwriting. Finally, we owe much to our graduate assistants at Notre Dame: Kevin Brunson, Reynold Nesiba, and Karin Wells. They were always willing to drop whatever they were doing to run off to the Hesburgh Library for us. To all these folks we owe a huge debt, many thanks, and none of the blame for any shortcomings that remain in this edition of *Taking Sides*.

TRS/FJB
Notre Dame, Indiana

CONTENTS IN BRIEF

CONTENTS

Free-market economist Milton Friedman contends that the sole responsibility
of business is to increase its profits. Business school professor Thomas
Mulligan maintains that businesses can pursue a policy of social responsibility without generating the costs outlined by Friedman.

Dorgan, a U.S. representative from North Dakota, fears that public policy has
become too concerned with the interests of the large corporate farms while
ignoring the small family farm that has "made agriculture one of the few
American industries still competitive in international markets." Columnist
Chapman argues for "rugged individualism." He asserts that: "If Americans
still believe in the virtue of hardy self-reliance, they should tell Washington to
get out of the way and let farmers practice it."

Representative McCurdy of Oklahoma argues that earning college education vouchers through community or armed forces service will reinstill in the nation's youth a sense of civic pride and responsibility. University president Altman finds that, if implemented, the National Service Act would revoke the nation's commitment to postsecondary educational opportunities.

Social critic Hackett argues that comparable worth would put to an end the "laws of supply and demand or other economic principles that determine wage rates for different kinds of work." Labor economist Needleman contends that pay differentials between men and women cannot be traced to differentials in "human capital." She concludes that these differentials result from discriminatory practices and attitudes.

Political science professor Houseman asserts that the economic rewards reaped by Wall Street takeover artists come at the expense of workers, stockholders, and the general public. Business economists Paulus and Gay argue that the corporate restructuring of the 1980s is a direct result of the need to increase productivity in the face of declining U.S. competitiveness.

Economist Weidenbaum asserts that government decision makers should face the same economic constraints that business executives do in the private sector. They must insist that the benefit of their actions at least match the cost of their actions. The editors of *Dollars and Sense* contend that although benefit-cost analysis seems to have a "certain simple logic," it is neither simple nor objective. Rather, they believe benefit-cost analysis and the related cost-effective approach are fatally flawed by an inherent social bias.

Professors Bluestone and Harrison assert that large modern corporations (particularly conglomerates) systematically milk profits from healthy firms, mismanage them, fail to maintain them, and then shut them down on the grounds that they are inefficient. Professor McKenzie argues that, in a healthy market economy, it is natural and necessary for some firms to move and others to close in order to achieve the benefits of economic efficiency.

Congressional supporters of legislation to permit and enforce parental leave maintain that there is a "growing conflict between work and family" that can be corrected and resolved by guaranteeing workers the "right to unpaid family leave." The dissenting members of the House Committee on Education and Labor argue that H.R. 4300 may be "well-intentioned," but it is also "rigid and inflexible."

The editors of *Nation's Business* insist that support for the minimum wage is based on eight myths that ignore the fact that minimum wage legislation "hurts the very employees it is intended to help." Economist Ghilarducci maintains that both "advocates and detractors of the minimum wage" have ignored the impact it has had on the economic well-being of "women workers."

Former Treasury secretary Simon argues that government has gone too far in its efforts to provide "cradle-to-grave security." According to Simon, wealth can only be created through the free operation of markets, and it is imperative that productivity and the growth of productivity be given the highest economic priority. Harvard economist Galbraith believes that the services provided by government contribute as much to the well-being of society as those provided by the private sector. Although taxes may reduce the freedom of those who are taxed, the freedom of those who benefit from the tax-financed programs is enhanced.

Economics professors Ferleger and Mandle find that the "decrease in domestic savings in conjunction with a constant rate of investment" has increased U.S. international dependency and, therefore, "it would be desirable to raise the level of domestic saving." Conservative economist Friedman argues that it is virtually impossible to determine exactly what is the "right" amount of saving. As a consequence, "the government has no business meddling in our family planning: whether about how many heirs we have or how much wealth we choose to leave them."

Senator Kasten, from Wisconsin, believes a reduction in the tax rate on capital gains would provide three benefits to the economy: it would increase governmental revenues, stimulate investment, and put the United States in a position that is more consistent with its international competitors. Professor Miller argues that lowering the capital gains tax would reduce federal tax revenues and is just a "bonanza for the rich."

Professor of politics Mead finds that "work" is the key ingredient in solving poverty and dependency in the United States. Attorney Sklar's experiences suggest that workfare is not cost-effective for those it can help and, unfortunately, there are many a workfare program simply cannot help.

Federal Reserve chairman Greenspan believes that there is a pressing need to reduce federal government budget deficits, for they have "begun to eat away at the foundations of our economic strength." Morris, a freelance writer who writes frequently about national affairs, argues that many of the economic problems usually associated with budget deficits, including higher interest rates, lower savings and investment rates, and greater trade deficits, cannot be supported by an examination of the empirical evidence.

Michigan senator Riegle believes that governmental action to resolve the savings and loan (S & L) crisis is desperately needed. He argues for the proposed S & L legislation because it addresses the major problems confronting the thrift industry by creating a new regulatory and insurance structure, it curbs excessively risky lending, and it provides for the future of a very important part of the financial system. North Dakota senator Conrad also sees the need for government action to bail out the thrift industry and admits that the proposed legislation contains several good points. But he opposes this particular piece of legislation on the grounds that it will be too costly to taxpayers.

Columnist Kuttner writes that "comparative advantage" is determined by exploitative wage rates and government action; it is not determined by free markets. Social critic Kinsley replies that we do not decrease American living standards when we import the products made by cheap foreign labor. He claims protectionism today, just as it did in the eighteenth century, weakens our economy and only "helps to put off the day of reckoning."

Economist Bauer argues that Third World debtor nations could meet their obligations if they were pressed by political and commercial interests. Journalist Stokes maintains a great deal of luck will be needed for the Third World to repay its financial obligations.

Robert Mugabe, prime minister of Zimbabwe, argues that the black African community is prepared to bear the costs of sanctions in order to rid South Africa of apartheid. Helen Suzman, a long-time member of the Progressive Federal Party in the South African Parliament, argues that economic sanctions will ruin the South African economy for all, destroying the "inheritance that blacks . . . will one day share."

Katharine L. Bradbury, an economist with the Federal Reserve Bank of Boston, believes that the middle class is shrinking; that is, there was a decline in the percentage of families with middle class incomes between 1973 and 1984. Frank Levy, an economist at the University of Maryland, sees substantial stability in the distribution of income over time.

McUsic, a former researcher at the Federal Reserve Bank of Boston, examines the behavior of output, employment, and productivity in U.S. manufacturing and finds that manufacturing has maintained its relative share of U.S. total production. Perna, an economist with General Electric, is pessimistic about recent changes in the structure of the economy, and he identifies several symptoms of ill health in manufacturing.

INTRODUCTION

Economics and Economists: The Basis for Controversy

Thomas R. Swartz

Frank J. Bonello

> "I think that Capitalism, wisely managed, can probably be more efficient for attaining economic ends than any alternative system yet in sight, but that in itself it is in many ways extremely objectionable."
> —Lord John Maynard Keynes, *The End of Laissez-Faire* (1926)

Although more than sixty years have passed since Lord Keynes penned these lines, many economists still struggle with the basic dilemma he outlined. The paradox rests in the fact that a free-market system is extremely efficient. It is purported to produce more at a lower cost than any other economic system. But in the process of producing this wide array of low-cost goods and services, problems arise. These problems—most notably a lack of economic equity and economic stability—cause problems for some economists. Other economists choose to ignore or minimize these issues. These problems form the foundation of this book.

If the problems raised and analyzed in this book were merely the product of intellectual gymnastics undertaken by "egg-headed" economists, then we could sit back and enjoy these confrontations as theoretical exercises. Unfortunately, we are not afforded that luxury. The essays contained in this book touch each and every one of us in tangible ways. They are real-world issues. Some focus upon the current state of the U.S. economy and examine the underlying causes, effects, and cures for inflation, unemployment, and recession. Another set of issues deals with "microeconomic" topics. We refer to these issues as "micro" problems not because they are small problems, but because they deal with small economic units, such as households, firms, or individual industries. A third set of issues concerns international aspects of economic activity. This area has grown in significance as the volume of international transactions has grown and as U.S. society has come to realize the importance of international interdependence. The final set of issues touch on our future directly, and force us to consider whether or not we should consider fundamental changes in our economic policy.

For each of the twenty issues considered in this book we have isolated those areas that currently generate the most controversy among economists.

In a few cases, this controversy represents a confrontation between extreme positions. Here, the views of the "free-market economist" are contrasted with the views of the "radical reformist economist." In other cases, the conflicts are not as extreme. Rather they represent conflicts between one extreme and economists of more moderate persuasions. Finally, we could not ignore the conflicts that occur among economists who, on other issues, generally agree. Economists, even economists who identify strongly with a given philosophical perspective, rarely agree on all issues. Thus, these otherwise like-thinking economists sometimes differ on specific topics.

The underlying reason for this apparent conflict and disagreement among economists can be explained, at least in part, in terms of Lord Keynes' 1926 remark. How various economists will react to the strengths and weaknesses found in an economic system will depend upon how they view the importance of efficiency, equity and stability. These are central terms, and we will define them in detail in the following pages. For now the important point is that some economists may view efficiency as overriding. In other cases, the same economists may be willing to sacrifice the efficiency generated by the market in order to ensure increased economic equity and/or increased economic stability. Determining when efficiency should be given a high priority and when efficiency should give way to other considerations occupies a large portion of the professional economist's time.

Given this discussion of conflict, controversy, and diversity, it might appear that economists rarely, if ever, agree on any economic issue. We would be most misleading if we left the reader with this impression. Economists rarely challenge the internal logic of the theoretical models that have been developed and articulated by their colleagues. Rather, they will challenge either the validity of the assumptions used in these models or the value of the ends these models seek to achieve. For example, it is most difficult to discredit the internal logic of the microeconomic models employed by the "free market economist." These models are elegant and their logical development is most persuasive. However, these models are challenged. The challenges typically focus upon such issues as the assumption of functioning, competitive, markets and the desirability of perpetuating the existing distribution of income. In this case, those who support and those who challenge the operation of the market agree on a large number of issues. But they disagree most assuredly on a few issues which have dramatic implications.

This same phenomenon of agreeing more often than disagreeing is also true in the area of economic policy. In this area, where the public is most acutely aware of differences among economists, these differences are not generally over the kinds of changes that will be brought about by a particular policy. Again, the differences more typically concern the timing of the change, the specific characteristics of the policy and the size of the resulting effect or effects.

ECONOMISTS: WHAT DO THEY REPRESENT?

Newspaper, magazine and TV commentators all use handy labels to describe certain members of the economics profession. What do the headlines mean when they refer to the "Chicago School," the "Keynesians," the "Antitrusters," or the "Radical Economists"? What do these individuals stand for? Since we too use our own labels throughout this book, we feel obliged to identify the principal groups or camps in our profession. Let us warn you that this can be a most misleading venture. Some economists, perhaps most economists, defy classification. They float from one camp to another, selecting a gem of wisdom here and another there. These are practical men and women who believe that no one camp has all the answers to all the economic problems confronting society. As a consequence, they may be ardent supporters of a given policy recommendation of one philosophic group but vocal critics of other recommendations emanating from the same philosophic group.

Recognizing this limitation, four major groups of economists can be identified. These groups are differentiated on the basis of several criteria: how they view efficiency relative to equity and stability; what significance they attach to imperfectly competitive market structures; and how they view the evolution of an economic society. Before describing the views of the four groups on these criteria, it is essential to understand the meaning of certain terms to be used in this description.

Efficiency, equity, and stability represent goals for an economic system. Efficiency reflects the fact that the economy produces those goods and services which people want and that it does so without wasting scarce resources. Equity in an economic sense has several dimensions. It means that income and wealth are distributed according to an accepted principle of fairness; that those who are unable to care for themselves receive adequate care; and that mainstream economic activity is open to all persons. Stability is viewed as the absence of sharp ups and downs in business activity, in prices, and in unemployment. In other words, stability is marked by steady increases in output, little inflation, and low unemployment.

When the term market structures is used, it refers to the number of buyers and sellers in the market and the amount of control they can exercise over price. At one extreme is a perfectly competitive market where there are so many buyers and sellers that no one has any ability to influence market price. One seller or buyer obviously could have great control over price. This extreme market structure, which we call pure monopoly, and other market structures which result in some control over price are grouped under the broad label of imperfectly competitive markets. That is, imperfect competition is a situation where the number of market participants is limited and as a consequence the participants have the ability to influence price. With these terms in mind, we can begin to examine the various schools of economic thought.

Free-Market Economists

One of the most visible groups of economists and perhaps the easiest group to identify and classify is the "free-market economists." These economists believe that the market, operating freely without interferences from government or labor unions, will generate the greatest amount of *well being* for the greatest number of people.

Economic efficiency is one of the priorities for free-market economists. In their well developed models, "consumer sovereignty"—consumer demand for goods and services—guides the system by directly influencing market prices. The distribution of economic resources caused by these market prices not only results in the production of an array of goods and services which are demanded by consumers, but this production is undertaken in the most cost-effective fashion. The free-market economists claim that at any point, some individuals must earn incomes which are substantially greater than other individuals. They contend that these higher incomes are a reward for greater efficiency or productivity and that this reward-induced efficiency will result in rapid economic growth which will benefit all persons in the society. They might also admit that a system driven by these freely operating markets will be subject to occasional bouts of instability (slow growth, inflation, and unemployment). However, they maintain that government action to eliminate or reduce this periodic instability will only make matters worse. Consequently, government, according to the free-market economist, should play a minor role in the economic affairs of society.

Although the models of free-market economists are dependent upon functioning, competitive markets, the lack of these competitive markets in the real world does not seriously jeopardize their position. First, they assert that the imperfect competition found in the real world allows a firm to produce at an efficient level and these savings in turn provide for even greater efficiency since costs per unit of output are lower. Second, they suggest that the benefits associated with the free operation of markets are so great compared to government intervention that even a "second best solution" of imperfectly competitive markets still yields benefits far in excess of government intervention.

Lastly, the free-market economists clearly view the market as the highest form of economic evolution. The efficiency of the system, the simplicity of the system, the power of the system, and above all, the personal freedoms inherent in the system demonstrate its superiority.

These advocates of the free market have been given various labels over time. The oldest and most persistent label is "classical economists." This is because the classical economists of the eighteenth century, particularly Adam Smith, were the first to point out the virtues of the market. Smith captured the essence of the system with the following words:

> Every individual endeavors to employ his capital so that its produce may be of greatest value. He generally neither intends to promote the public interest nor knows how much he is promoting it. He intends only his own security, only

his own gain. And he is in this led by an invisible hand to promote an end which was no part of his intention. By pursuing his own interest he frequently promotes that of society more effectively than when he really intends to promote it.

—Adam Smith, *The Wealth of Nations* (1776)

Since free-market economists, and those who echo their views, resist most forms of government intervention, they are also sometimes referred to as "conservatives" or "libertarians." These labels are as much political labels as they are economic characterizations. It must be recalled that the classical economists of the eighteenth century not only embraced the political philosophy of laissez-faire (roughly translated to: leave it—the economy—alone), but developed a set of economic theories that were totally consistent with this political theory. These "political-economists" were, as a result, called libertarians because they espoused political and economic policies that maximized personal freedoms or liberties. The nineteenth-century libertarians are not to be confused with twentieth-century liberals. Modern-day liberals, as we shall explain shortly in more detail, are often willing to sacrifice some freedoms in the marketplace in order to ensure the attainment of other objectives.

Still other labels are sometimes attached to the free-market economists, such as "monetarists," "The Austrian School," "Public Choice Economists," "Chicago School Economists," "Rational Expectations," or "Friedmanites." Here the reference is to the modern-day practitioners of free-market economics. Most notable among this group is the Nobel laureate Milton Friedman, formerly of the University of Chicago. He and others argue that the government's attempts to promote economic stability through the manipulation of the money supply actually causes more instability than would have occurred if the government had not intervened. As a consequence, these scholars advocate a policy that would allow the money supply to grow at a reasonable, steady rate.

In the 1980s, a new group of free-market economists was formed, called the "supply-siders." These economists, led by Arthur Laffer, also believe strongly in the market. What makes them unique is the specific proposals they offer to reduce government intervention in the economy: They contend reductions in marginal tax rates will stimulate private activity.

Before turning our attention to the other major camps of economists, we should note that the free-market economists have been very successful in influencing the development of economics. Indeed, most introductory economic textbooks present major portions of the basic theoretical concepts of the free-market economist. It is because of this influence in many areas of both microeconomics and macroeconomics over long periods of time that so many labels are used to describe them, so much is written about them, and so much is written by these conservative economists. In the twenty issues that are considered in this book, the free-market position is represented in a substantial number.

Liberal Economists

Probably the single largest group of economists in the United States in one way or another can be classified as "liberal economists." Liberal in this instance refers to their willingness to intervene in the free operation of the market. These economists share with the free-market economists a great respect for the market. However, the liberal economist does not believe that the explicit and implicit costs of a freely operating market should or can be ignored. Rather, the liberal maintains that the costs of an uncontrolled marketplace are often borne by those in society who are least capable of bearing them: the poor, the elderly, the infirm. Additionally, liberal economists maintain that the freely operating market sometimes results in economic instability and the resultant bouts of inflation, unemployment and slow growth. Thus, although liberal economists believe that economic efficiency is highly desirable, they find the attainment of economic efficiency at any cost to be unacceptable and perhaps even "extremely objectionable."

Consider for a moment the differences between free-market economists and liberal economists at the microeconomic level. Liberal economists take exception to the free market on two grounds. First, these economists find a basic problem with fairness in the marketplace. Since the market is driven by the forces of consumer spending, there are those who through no fault of their own (they may be aged, young, infirm, physically or mentally handicapped) may not have the wherewithal to participate in the economic system. Others, however, perhaps because they are extremely lucky or because they have inherited wealth, may have not only the ability to participate in the system, but they may have the ability to direct the course of that system. Second, the unfettered marketplace does not and cannot handle spill-over effects or what are known as "externalities." These are the third-party effects that may occur as a result of an economic act. Will a firm willingly compensate its neighbors for the pollutants it pours into the nearby lake? Will a truck driver willingly drive at 55 MPH and in the process reduce the highway accident rate? Liberal economists think not. These economists are therefore willing to have the government intervene in these and other, similar cases.

The liberal economists' role in macroeconomics is more readily apparent to the layman. Ever since the failure of free-market economics during the Great Depression of the 1930s, Keynesianism (still another label for liberal economics) has become widely known. Lord John Maynard Keynes's 1935 book *The General Theory of Employment, Interest, and Money* laid the basic groundwork for this school of thought. Keynes argued that the history of freely operating market economies was marked by periods of recurring recessions, sometimes very deep recessions, which we call depressions. He maintained that government intervention through its fiscal policy—government tax and spending power—could eliminate, or at least soften these sharp reductions in economic activity and as a result move the economy along a more stable growth path. Thus for the Keynesians, or liberal economists, one of the "extremely objectionable" aspects of a free-market economy is its inherent instability. Their call for active government participation is in sharp contrast to the policies of the free-market economists who argue that economic stability (growth, employment, and prices) can be achieved only if government intervenes less and not more.

Liberal economists are also far more concerned about the existence of imperfections in the marketplace than are their free market counterparts. They reject the notion that imperfect competition is an acceptable substitute for competitive markets. These economists may agree that the imperfectly competitive firms can achieve some savings because of their large size and efficiency, but they assert that since there is little or no competition the firms are not forced to pass these cost savings on to consumers. Thus liberal economists, who in some circles are labeled "antitrusters," are willing to intervene in the market in two ways. In some cases they are prepared to allow some monopolies, such as public utilities, to exist, but they contend that these monopolies must be regulated by government. In other cases they maintain that there is no justification for monopolies and they are prepared to invoke the powers of antitrust legislation to break up existing monopolies and/or prevent the formation of new monopolies.

Unlike the free-market economist, the liberal economist does not believe that the free marketplace is the highest form of economic evolution. By definition, the liberal economist asserts that the highest form of economic evolution is a "mixed economy"—an economy where market forces are tempered by government intervention. These economists do not advocate extensive government planning and/or government ownership of productive resources. But, they are not always willing to allow the market to operate on its own. They maintain that the immense power of the marketplace can be controlled with government intervention and the benefits generated by the unfettered market can be equitably distributed throughout society.

We can conclude this section by making a hazardous guess. It would appear that during the 1940s, 1950s, 1960s and up to the middle 1970s, liberal economics dominated economic policy in the United States. In the late 1970s, there was a reemergence of free-market economics, which for nearly forty years had played an important but clearly secondary role. In the 1980s, free-market economics dominated public policy decisions, but policymakers employing these classical models will encounter some stubborn economic problems. This will cause the pendulum to swing once again. The resting point of the pendulum may be liberal economics, but it might also swing past this point and stop in the domain of "institutional economics" or "radical reformist economics." These two schools of thought are the subject of the next sections.

Institutional Economists

One of the most difficult groups of economists to classify and, as a consequence, one of the most misunderstood groups of economists is the "institutionalists." The difficulty in understanding and classifying this school of economists stems from the fact that institutional economics has no single body of theories. Institutional economists are vocal critics of traditional economics—the economics espoused by free-market economists and liberal economists. They maintain that the models that are constructed by these economists may explain how economic actors would behave *if* these actors behaved in a rational, self-interested manner and *if* they lived in a competitive world. However, they assert that consumers, business firms, and other economic actors do not always act in a rational, self-interested fashion. They also see the world in which we live as a dual-economy world. One part of that world is competitive. Another part of that world is dominated by a few firms that have the power to set prices. The institutional economists, as a consequence, find traditional economics to be an eloquent theory that does not conform to reality. Unfortunately, to date, institutional economists have not developed their own set of integrated economic propositions or laws which they can offer as a substitute for traditional economics.

This does not mean, however, that the institutionalists have nothing to offer. In their attempts to make economics conform to the reality they claim to explain and predict, institutional economists have shed light on many diverse topics. For example, some members of this school of thought have concentrated their efforts on the structure of corporations, particularly multinational corporations, as economic institutions. These economists, sometimes referred to as structuralists, examine the economic planning these large economic units undertake, the impact they have on the system, their influence on inflation, unemployment, income distribution, and efficiency, and the role they play in international affairs. Other institutional economists take a broader perspective. Since they generally believe that large corporate entities engage in massive economic planning that affects the whole of society, some institutional economists analyze alternative forms of regional and national economic planning that can be undertaken by the government. The basic point is that institutional economists work in many, seemingly unrelated, areas. Since they have no integrated theory to tie all these pieces together, and since many of their ideas such as utility regulation, antitrust action, price controls, etc., have been accepted as public policy, it is at times difficult to keep in mind that Thorstein Veblen on financial capitalism, John Kenneth Galbraith on industrial structure, and many economists in between are all part of the institutional school of economics.

On the basis of our first criterion, institutional economists differ dramatically from free-market economists and liberal economists. By rejecting the assumptions of rationality and self-interest, they maintain that whatever you set as your highest priority—be it efficiency, equity, or stabilization—you cannot achieve it by using the abstract models of the market economists. Indeed, their analysis indicates that the market as it exists in its concentrated form today leads to inefficiency, inequity, and inherent instability.

The second and third criteria further distinguish the institutional economists from the other schools of economics. For the institutionalist, economics is in a constant state of evolution. (The importance of evolution for the institutional economists is best underscored by noting that this school is also referred to as evolutionary economics.) At one time, perhaps when Adam Smith and his fellow classical economists were formulating their basic models, the economy could be legitimately characterized as competitive. At that moment, free-market economics reflected reality and therefore could explain that reality. At this time, functional competition does not exist and a new body of theorems and concepts must be developed to explain this reality. At some future date, still another set of economic institutions will exist and still another body of theorems and concepts will be needed. Consequently, the institutional economist does indeed attach a great importance to the existence of imperfect competition and to the process of economic evolution. The institutionalists know that new theories must be developed to explain today's reality of imperfect competition, and they know that the economy is always in a constant state of evolution. What they don't know with certainty is which direction future evolution will take our current reality.

To confuse the issue further, there is yet another group within the structuralist-institutionalist camp. These economists call themselves the post-Keynesians. They are post-Keynesians because they believe that they are closer to the spirit of Keynes than is the interpretation of Keynes that is used to support the liberal economists' position. As some authors have suggested, the key aspect of Keynes's work as far as the post-Keynesians are concerned is his assertion that "expectations of the future are not necessarily certain." On a more practical level, post-Keynesians believe, among other things, that the productivity of the economic system is not significantly affected by changes in income distribution, that the system can still be efficient without competitive markets, that conventional fiscal policies cannot control inflation and, that "income policies" are the means to an effective and equitable answer to the inflationary dilemma. (This listing is drawn from Alfred S. Eichner's "Introduction" in *A Guide to Post-Keynesian Economics*, White Plains: M.E. Sharpe, Inc., 1978.)

Radical Reformist Economists
As we move further and further away from the economics of the free market, we encounter the "radical reformist economists" or the "left." These economists, who actually spring from several theoretical foundations, share a belief that the market and the capitalist system, no matter how well disciplined, is fatally flawed and doomed to eventual failure. Out of the ashes of this system, which is guided by the "invisible hand" of self-interest, will rise the "visible hand" of public interest. That is, the fundamental institutions of private ownership will slowly fade and be replaced by government ownership of productive resources.

This does not mean that all private ownership will cease to exist at some distinct moment. Rather, many radical reformists maintain that it is the ownership of the one thousand largest firms which cause the basic problems for the "capitalist economy." It is the operation of these highly concentrated economic entities for the benefit of a few which cause the basic problems and it is the private ownership of these one thousand firms which must eventually fade away. As a result, not all property must be owned collectively. Only the most radical of the left would go that far.

As was the case with our other three broad clusters of economists, there is much diversity within this fourth cluster of economists. One group of economists within this cluster contains the radical, political economists who often focus upon microeconomic issues. They are concerned with issues such as the abuses that may result from "administered prices"—prices that can be administered or set by a firm because of the firm's monopoly influence in the marketplace. Another identifiable subgroup is the "Marxists." Their lineage can be traced to the nineteenth-century philosopher-economist Karl Marx. Ironically, Marx himself shares his economic roots with the free-market economists. Before writing his most impressive work, the three volumes of *Das Kapital*, Marx studied the work of the classical economists and incorporated a basic tenent of those works—David Ricardo's "labor theory of value"—into his own work. But unlike free-market economics, which Marx prophesied would fall of its own weight, Marx laid the foundation for "socialism." Socialism, where some form of public ownership of the means of production is substituted for private ownership, is far more prevalent throughout the world than is capitalism. Thus, we in North America cannot afford to ignore this group of economists.

Note that socialism may take many forms. It varies from the democratic socialism of the United Kingdom to the radical Eastern European socialism, which underwent massive reform in 1989 and early 1990. The one common characteristic is public ownership of the means of production. However, the extent of this public ownership varies dramatically from one socialistic country to another.

Although it may be difficult to classify the different subgroups of radical reformist economists, we can differentiate them from the other broad classifications of economists on the basis of our three criteria. In terms of the first criterion—the relative importance of economic efficiency, equity, and stabilization—they are clearly set apart from their non-radical counterparts. Not only do they set a much higher value on equity and stability when compared to the free market economists, (a posture they share with the liberal and institutional economists) but they have developed a set of economic models that attempts to ensure the attainment of equity and stability. The radical reformist economists assert that not only is the economic efficiency which is supposed to exist in a market economy an illusion, but the market system is fundamentally flawed. These flaws, which result in unacceptable inequities and recurring bouts of economic instability, will eventually lead to the market's demise.

The radicals are concerned by the existence of imperfect competition. For them the current reality is an immense concentration of economic power which is a far cry from Adam Smith's world of competitive markets. Today, in their view, the market economy operates to benefit a few at the expense of the masses. Firms with monopoly power control the economy. They administer prices. They are the invisible hand that guides the economy to their benefit.

So strong is their aversion to the market economy that they predict its demise as we know it. Indeed, if we look to the Marxist camp, they see capitalism as one step, a necessary step, in the evolution of economic systems. Capitalism is needed to raise the economy out of the chaos of a feudal society. But after capital has been accumulated and a modern economy is developed, the basic inequities and instabilities will bring the market economy to its knees and socialism will emerge. Socialism itself is not the end of the evolutionary process. Socialism will eventually give way to communism—where government is non-existent and everyone will work "according to their ability" and receive "according to their need."

Of course, not all radical reformist economists are Marxist. However, most radicals do share a desire for some form of socialism. Unlike their Marxist colleagues, most do not see socialism as evolving automatically, and they certainly do not see communism emerging at the end of an evolutionary process. Rather, these economists see a need to explicitly encourage the development of some form of socialism for North America. The socialism that results is then considered to be the likely end of the evolutionary process.

Before we turn to the next section, we must warn you again to interpret these labels with extreme care. Our categories are not hard and fast. There is much "grayness" around the edges and little that is "black and white" in these classifications. This does not mean, however, that there is no value to these classifications. It is important to understand the philosophical background of the individual authors. This background does indeed color or shade their work. This is best demonstrated by examining several of the issues included in this volume.

However, before discussing a few of the issues, it is useful to repeat several of the themes developed in the preceding section. First, there is much disagreement among economists and others on economic problems. There is, however, rhyme and reason to this disagreement. In large measure the disagreement stems from various ideologies or basic philosophies that these individuals may espouse. Indeed, the differences which exist between economists and groups of economists can be most sharply defined in terms of their respective views of efficiency, equity, and stability; on the relative merits of imperfect competition; and on the place of the current economy in the evolutionary process peculiar to economic systems.

Second, the identification of causes, effects, and cures for economic problems must be undertaken at the practical level. At this level, sharp distinctions tend to disappear, and actions may be recommended by certain individuals which seem inconsistent with their ideology. Here the economist must sacrifice "ideological purity" for practical solutions. The science of economics must deal with real-world problems or it loses its meaning for most people.

THE ISSUES

It is not difficult to identify major problems in the American economy. Each month the news media discuss in detail the newly released statistics that reveal the success or failure of policies designed to reduce inflation and unemployment. For example, the 1984 political platforms were very concerned with economic issues. In addition to the issue of tax cuts, the Democratic and Republic platforms outline general principles as well as specific actions that should be undertaken to spur productivity, to stem the rising tide of automobile imports, and to make the American economy dynamic and vital. Each day it seems that some businessman, some labor leader, some consumer advocate, or some public official releases a new proposal that will remedy pollution, improve the quality and the safety of products or the workplace, restore health to the Social Security system, or halt and reverse the decay of our cities. Thus the difficulty in developing this book was not in identifying real and important economic problems or in locating alternative views on those problems. Rather, the difficulty was one of selecting only twenty issues from what, at times, appears to be an endless list of both problems and views on those problems.

We have resolved this difficulty by attempting to provide a broad coverage of the conflicts that society faces. We have provided this generality in three different ways. First, the twenty issues represent six macroeconomic, nine microeconomic, three international, and two issues dealing with the future. Second, within these sets of issues, the range of topics is broad. For example, within the macroeconomic set there are issues that represent basic disagreements among economists on specific policy topics, such as the desirability of reforming the current federal taxation of capital gains, as well as disagreements that can be characterized as basic philosophical conflicts, such as the appropriate size of government. The third dimension concerns the ideologies of the views that are presented. The list of authors includes well-regarded academic economists, politicians, journalists, business leaders, and labor leaders. These individuals represent the far right, the far left, and many positions in between. Although ideology is sometimes tempered by practical considerations, the basic ideological positions remain apparent.

A summary of several of the issues may serve to indicate the extent of this generality. This discussion will also demonstrate the interplay that exists between basic philosophy and practical considerations in arriving at a real-world solution or position on an economic problem.

One of the macroeconomic issues is: *Is Workfare a Good Substitute for Welfare?* Free-market economists generally believe that we have gone too far with our anti-poverty programs, and they contend that we have made these programs so attractive that people may choose not to work and instead stay at home and receive benefits available under several different welfare and income security programs. The solution to this "economic distortion of incentives" is apparent to the free-market economist: make the welfare recipients work or prepare for work as a condition of their welfare payment; thus, they would substitute workfare for welfare. In taking this position, the free-market economists stress individual self-interest. They maintain that the problem with our welfare system is that we as a society have made *not* working so attractive that it is in the self-interest of the poor to drop out and become "dependent" on those who are hardworking.

Liberal economists, on the other hand, argue that the free-market position oversimplifies the problem. All welfare recipients are not "welfare loafers." Many are children and too young to work. Others are aged and too old to work. Of those who remain, half find jobs and leave welfare after a brief stay in the program. Thus, for the liberal economist, the impact of workfare would be restricted to the seven percent or so of all welfare recipients who are long-term users of welfare. In the liberal view, the question is whether or not these hard-core welfare recipients, who are often lacking in job skills and deficient academically, can best be motivated by short-term work experiences or comprehensive training programs. They find that the latter is far more expensive in absolute dollars but far more cost-effective in the long run.

Of course, institutionalists and radical reformers have taken positions on this issue. The institutionalists would probably side with the liberals but argue that it might be more appropriate to attack poverty through institutional change rather than through the current maze of anti-poverty programs. While institutional changes are being made (such as improving the educational system and increasing labor mobility), it would be better to be too generous rather than not generous enough, they say. To the radical reformer, the whole question is an example of the inherent contradictions of a market economy. And in a class society, poverty programs are a means by which the dominant class can maintain its position. Radical reformers might even join conservatives in an effort to eliminate poverty programs. However, for the radical reformer, the motivation for opposing these programs is not greater efficiency, but rather an effort to polarize the class struggle and bring ever-closer the day of revolution.

Should the Federal Government Deregulate American Business? is one of the nine microeconomic issues. Again we can associate a position on this issue with each of the four basic economic philosophies. Clearly conservatives would strongly oppose government regulation. In support of their position they would cite the self-regulating nature of a free-market capitalist system.

No rational individual would buy products of inferior quality or products which are unsafe if alternatives were available at competitive prices. No rational individual would work for a firm that maintained an unsafe job site unless that individual found that job to be to his or her economic advantage. On the question of pollution or other so-called externalities, regulation, the conservatives might suggest, should be undertaken, but only if the benefits of regulation clearly are greater than the costs of the regulation.

Liberals of course, are much more tolerant, indeed supportive, of government regulation. In part, this follows from their emphasis on equity, but also because they may have a different measurement of both the costs and the benefits of regulations. Liberals generally estimate the costs lower and the benefits higher than their conservative colleagues. The institutionalists would also support the notion of regulation. Their support of regulation follows from their view that the structures and institutions of free-market capitalism have changed in such a way that safe and high quality products and safe job sites are no longer assured. In the absence of perfect competition, regulation of industry is in order. It is necessary, to prevent abuses by both buyers and sellers.

The radical reformists believe that most current regulation, to the extent that it exists, benefits the power structure; that regulation by definition serves the regulated. They attack the basic notion of cost-benefit analysis as a method of determining the appropriate amount of regulation. After all, they ask, how can one measure the worth of the benefits of saving a single life by making a job site safer?

In selections addressing this issue, the emphasis is on the usefulness of cost-benefit analysis as a technique for determining the proper level of government regulation. One selection suggests that the use of cost-benefit analysis implies that government regulation is excessive. The other selection attacks the very heart of the cost-benefit procedure, laying bare all the implicit assumptions which such procedures make. In this sense the selections can be viewed as an argument between the conservative position and the radical reformist position.

We should mention an apparent paradox with respect to regulation policy. The above discussion implies that liberals should be more supportive of regulation than conservatives. However, deregulation or decontrol was a basic policy stance of the Carter administration. The Democratic Congress passed, and the Democratic executive branch signed into law, legislation that deregulated the airline industry, the trucking industry, and financial intermediaries. Again, practical considerations rather than basic philosophies often determine specific policy actions. Reality and philosophical considerations make strange bedfellows.

One of the three international issues concerns the policies of the white-dominated government of the Republic of South Africa: *Can Strict Economic Sanctions Help End Apartheid in South Africa?* This issue represents a clash between two liberals. On the one side of this debate is Helen Suzman, a long-time member of the Progressive Federal Party in South Africa who has been a vocal critic of the white South African policy of apartheid. She argues that the good intentions of those who support the imposition of economic sanctions and disinvestment threaten the economic welfare of those whom the sanctions are intended to help. The opposing view is captured in Robert G. Mugabe's essay. Here, the prime minister of one of South Africa's most important neighbors, Zimbabwe, argues that we must raise the economic cost of maintaining the political system of apartheid.

It is important to note that both essays in this issue assume that markets work. Indeed, they assume that markets have yielded huge economic rewards for some in the economy. Both essays also recognize the injustices that result from the white monopoly power that characterizes South Africa. In essence, they only differ on how and when economic power should be wrested away from the white monopolists.

This debate could be joined by conservatives, institutionalists and radical reformists. Conservatives would take their traditional position to the right of Ms. Suzman. They would maintain that the market is proving its value by generating incomes in South Africa which are well above the incomes of neighboring countries. They would go on to argue that the only way to improve the well-being of the black majority would be to improve the well-being of the economy at large. That is, as John F. Kennedy asserted, "a rising tide raising all boats." In this case the rising tide would raise the economic boat of the black worker. Finally, they would agree with Helen Suzman's assertion that interfering with the market would only hurt those whom the liberal community hopes to protect.

The institutionalists, as usual, would position themselves between the liberals and the radical reformists. They would argue that the colonial-type institutions that dominated the southern tip of Africa for the past 150 years must give way to the political reality of a black majority. In short, the white community can no longer ignore and manipulate 73 percent of the population. It must provide them with the economic rights that a modern-day society provides all members of the community.

Finally, radicals would take their position on the far left by asserting that the crisis in South Africa reflected the corruption that is an inherent part of a market economy. They would remind us that 27 percent of the population controls the majority population. Those who hold that power will exercise it for their own benefits. Indeed, those who maintain the monopoly stranglehold on the black community will continue to brutalize that community until the only option that remains is revolution.

SUMMARY

It is clear that there is no shortage of economic problems. These problems demand solutions. At the same time there is no shortage of proposed solutions. In fact, the problem is often one of oversupply. The twenty issues included in this volume will acquaint you or, more accurately, reacquaint you with some of these problems. And, of course, there are at least two proposed solutions for each of the problems. Here we hope to provide new insights regarding the alternatives available and the differences and similarities of these alternative remedies.

If this introduction has served its purposes, you will be able to identify common elements in the proposed solutions to the different problems. For example, you will be able to identify the reliance on the forces of the market advocated by free-market economists as the remedy for several economic ills. This introduction should also help you understand why there are at least two proposed solutions for every economic problem; each group of economists tends to interpret a problem from its own philosophical position and to advance a solution that is grounded in that same philosophical framework.

Our intention, of course, is not to connect persons to one philosophic position or another. We hope instead to generate discussion and promote understanding. To do this, people must see not only a proposed solution, they must also be aware of the foundation that supports that solution. With greater understanding, meaningful progress in addressing economic problems can be achieved.

PART 1

Microeconomic Issues

Our lives are profoundly affected by economic decisions made at the microeconomic level, and all the issues debated here relate to microeconomic concerns.

Are Profits the Only Business of Business?

Should We Try to Save the Family Farm?

Is National Service the Wave of the Future?

Is "Comparable Worth" Worthless?

Are There Too Many Hostile Takeovers?

Should the Federal Government Deregulate American Business?

Do Firms Exploit Workers and Local Communities by Closing Profitable Plants?

Should Congress Guarantee U.S. Workers the Right to Parental Leave?

Was It a Mistake to Increase the Minimum Wage?

1

ISSUE 1

Are Profits the Only Business of Business?

YES: Milton Friedman, from "The Social Responsibility of Business Is to Increase Its Profits," *New York Times Magazine* (September 13, 1970)

NO: Thomas Mulligan, from "A Critique of Milton Friedman's Essay 'The Social Responsibility of Business Is to Increase Its Profits,' " *Journal of Business Ethics* (1986)

ISSUE SUMMARY

YES: Free-market economist Milton Friedman contends that the sole responsibility of business is to increase its profits.
NO: Philosopher Mulligan insists that a commitment to social responsibility is not a "fundamentally subversive doctrine in a free society."

Every economic society—whether it is a traditional society in Central Africa, one of the fossilized planned economies of Eastern Europe, or a wealthy capitalist society found in North America, Western Europe, or the Pacific Rim—must address the basic economic problem of resource allocation. These societies must determine *what* goods and services they can and will produce, *how* these goods and services will be produced, and *for whom* these goods and services will be produced.

The *what, how,* and *for whom* questions must be answered because of the problem of scarcity. Even if a given society were indescribably rich, it would still confront the problem of scarcity—in this case, "relative scarcity." It might have all the resources it needs to produce all the goods and services it would ever want, but it couldn't produce all these things simultaneously. Thus, it must set priorities and produce first those goods and services with the highest priority and postpone the production of those goods and services with lower priorities. If time is of the essence, *how* should these goods and services be produced? And since this society cannot produce all it wants instantly, *for whom* should the first bundle of goods and services be produced?

Few, if any, economic societies are indescribably rich. On the other hand, there are many examples of economic societies that face grinding deprivation daily. In these societies and in all the societies that fall between poverty and great affluence, the *what, how,* and *for whom* questions are immediately apparent. Somehow these questions must be answered.

In some societies, such as the Amish communities of North America, the answers to these questions are found in tradition. Sons and daughters follow in their parents' footsteps. Younger generations produce *what* older generations produced before them. The methods of production—the horsedrawn plow, the hand-held scythe, the use of natural fertilizers—remain unchanged; thus, the *how* question is answered in the same way that the *for whom* question is answered—by following historic patterns. In other societies—for example, self-sustaining religious communities—there is a different pattern of responses to these questions. In these communities, the "elder" of the community determines *what* will be produced, *how* it will be produced, and *for whom* it will be produced. If there is a well-defined hierarchical system, it is similar to one of the stereotypical command economies of Eastern Europe.

Although elements of tradition and command are found in the industrialized societies of Western Europe, North America, and Japan, the basic answers to the three questions of resource allocation in these countries are determined by profit. In these economic societies, *what* will be produced is determined by what will yield the greatest profit. Consumers, in their search for maximum satisfaction, will bid for those goods and services that they want most. This consumer action drives the price of these goods and services up, and, in turn, these higher prices increase producers' profits. The higher profits attract new firms into the industry and encourage existing firms to increase their output. Thus, profits are the mechanism that ensures consumers get what they want. Similarly, the profit-seeking behavior of business firms determines *how* the goods and services that consumers want will be produced. Since firms attempt to maximize their profits, they select those means of production that are economically most efficient. Lastly, the *for whom* question is also linked to profits. Wherever there is a shortage of goods and services, profits will be high. In the producers' attempts to increase their output they must attract factors of production (land, labor, and capital) away from other economic activities. This bidding increases factor prices or factor incomes and ensures that these factors will be able to buy goods and services in the open marketplace.

Both Mulligan and Friedman recognize the merits of a profit-driven economic system. They do not quarrel over the importance of profits. But they do quarrel over whether or not business firms have obligations beyond making profits. Friedman holds that the *only* responsibility of business is to make profits. He argues that anyone who maintains otherwise is "preaching pure and unadulterated socialism." Mulligan, on the other hand, contends that Friedman's argument rests on a questionable paradigm, a false premise, and a logic that sometimes lacks cogency.

YES · Milton Friedman

THE SOCIAL RESPONSIBILITY OF BUSINESS IS TO INCREASE ITS PROFITS

When I hear businessmen speak eloquently about the "social responsibilities of business in a free-enterprise system," I am reminded of the wonderful line about the Frenchman who discovered at the age of 70 that he had been speaking prose all his life. The businessmen believe that they are defending free enterprise when they declaim that business is not concerned "merely" with profit but also with promoting desirable "social ends; that business has a social conscience" and takes seriously its responsibilities for providing employment, eliminating discrimination, avoiding pollution and whatever else may be the catchwords of the contemporary crop of reformers. In fact they are—or would be if they or anyone else took them seriously—preaching pure and unadulterated socialism. Businessmen who talk this way are unwitting puppets of the intellectual forces that have been undermining the basis of a free society these past decades.

The discussions of the "social responsibilities of business" are notable for their analytical looseness and lack of rigor. What does it mean to say that "business" has responsibilities? Only people can have responsibilities. A corporation is an artificial person and in this sense may have artificial responsibilities, but "business" as a whole cannot be said to have responsibilities, even in this vague sense. The first step toward clarity in examining the doctrine of the social responsibility of business is to ask precisely what it implies for whom.

Presumably, the individuals who are to be responsible are businessmen, which means individual proprietors or corporate executives. Most of the discussion of social responsibility is directed at corporations, so in what follows I shall mostly neglect the individual proprietor and speak of corporate executives.

In a free-enterprise, private-property system, a corporate executive is an employee of the owners of the business. He has direct responsibility to his employers. That responsibility is to conduct the business in accordance with their desires, which generally will be to make as much money as possible while conforming to the basic rules of the society, both those embodied in law and those embodied in ethical custom. Of course, in some cases his employers may have a different objective. A group of persons might establish a corporation for an eleemosynary purpose—for example, a hospital or a school. The manager of such a corporation will not have money profit as his objective but the rendering of certain services.

In either case, the key point is that, in his capacity as a corporate executive, the manager is the agent of the individuals who own the corporation or establish the eleemosynary institution, and his primary responsibility is to them.

Needless to say, this does not mean that it is easy to judge how well he is performing his task. But at least the criterion of performance is straightforward, and the persons among whom a voluntary contractual arrangement exists are clearly defined.

Of course, the corporate executive is also a person in his own right. As a person, he may have many other responsibilities that he recognizes or assumes voluntarily—to his family, his conscience, his feelings of charity, his church, his clubs, his city, his country. He may feel impelled by these responsibilities to devote part of his income to causes he regards as worthy, to refuse to work for particular corporations, even to leave his job, for example, to join his country's armed forces. If we wish, we may refer to some of these responsibilities as "social responsibilities." But in these respects he is acting as a principal, not an agent; he is spending his own money or time or energy, not the money of his employers or the time or energy he has contracted to devote to their purposes. If these are "social responsibilities," they are the social responsibilities of individuals, not of business.

What does it mean to say that the corporate executive has a "social responsibility" in his capacity as businessman? If this statement is not pure rhetoric, it must mean that he is to act in some way that is not in the interest of his employers. For example, that he is to refrain from increasing the price of the product in order to contribute to the social objective of preventing inflation, even though a price increase would be in the best interests of the corporation. Or that he is to make expenditures on reducing pollution beyond the amount that is in the best interests of the corporation or that is required by law in order to contribute to the social objective of improving the environment. Or that, at the expense of corporate profits, he is to hire "hard-core" unemployed instead of better-qualified available workmen to contribute to the social objective of reducing poverty.

In each of these cases, the corporate executive would be spending someone else's money for a general social interest. Insofar as his actions in accord with his "social responsibility" reduce returns to stockholders, he is spending their money. Insofar as his actions raise the price to customers, he is spending the customers' money. Insofar as his actions lower the wages of some employees, he is spending their money.

The stockholders or the customers or the employees could separately spend their own money on the particular action if they wished to do so. The executive is exercising a distinct "social responsibility," rather than serving as an agent of the stockholders or the customers or the employees, only if he spends the money in a different way than they would have spent it.

But if he does this, he is in effect imposing taxes, on the one hand, and deciding how the tax proceeds shall be spent, on the other.

This process raises political questions on two levels: principle and consequences. On the level of political principle, the imposition of taxes and the expenditure of tax proceeds are governmental functions. We have established elaborate constitutional, parliamentary and judicial provisions to control these functions, to assure that taxes are imposed so far as possible in accordance with the preferences and desires of the public—after all, "taxation without representation" was one of the battle cries of the American Revolution. We have a system of checks and balances to separate the legislative function of imposing taxes and enacting expenditures from the executive function of collecting taxes and administering expenditure programs and from the judicial function of mediating disputes and interpreting the law.

Here the businessman—self-selected or appointed directly or indirectly by stockholders—is to be simultaneously legislator, executive and jurist. He is to decide whom to tax by how much and for what purpose, and he is to spend the proceeds—all this guided only by general exhortations from on high to restrain inflation, improve the environment, fight poverty and so on and on.

The whole justification for permitting the corporate executive to be selected by the stockholders is that the executive is an agent serving the interests of his principal. This justification disappears when the corporate executive imposes taxes and spends the proceeds for "social" purposes. He becomes in effect a public employee, a civil servant, even though he remains in name an employee of a private enterprise. On grounds of political principle, it is intolerable that such civil servants—insofar as their actions in the name of social responsibility are real and not just window-dressing—should be selected as they are now. If they are to be civil servants, then they must be selected through a political process. If they are to impose taxes and make expenditures to foster "social" objectives, then political machinery must be set up to guide the assessment of taxes and to determine through a political process the objectives to be served.

This is the basic reason why the doctrine of "social responsibility" involves the acceptance of the socialist view that political mechanisms, not market mechanisms, are the appropriate way to determine the allocation of scarce resources to alternative uses.

On the grounds of consequences, can the corporate executive in fact discharge his alleged "social responsibilities"? On the one hand, suppose he could get away with spending the stockholders' or customers' or employees' money. How is he to know how to spend it? He is told that he must contribute to fighting inflation. How is he to know what action of his will contribute to that end? He is presumably an expert in running his company—in producing a product or selling it or financing it. But nothing about his selection makes him an expert on inflation. Will his holding down the price of his product reduce inflationary pressure? Or, by leaving more spending power in the hands of his customers, simply divert it elsewhere? Or, by forcing him to produce less because of the lower price, will it simply contribute to shortages? Even if he could answer these questions, how much cost is he justified in imposing on his stockholders, customers and employees for this social purpose? What is the appropriate share and what is the appropriate share of others?

And, whether he wants to or not, can he get away with spending his stockholders', customers' or employees' money? Will not the stockholders fire him? (Either the present ones or those who take over when his actions in the name of social responsibility have reduced the corporation's profits and the price of its stock.) His customers and his employees can desert him for other producers and employers less scrupulous in exercising their social responsibilities.

This facet of "social responsibility" doctrine is brought into sharp relief when the doctrine is used to justify wage restraint by trade unions. The conflict of interest is naked and clear when union officials are asked to subordinate the interest of their members to some more general social purpose. If the union officials try to enforce wage restraint, the consequence is likely to be wildcat strikes, rank-and-file revolts and the emergence of strong competitors for their jobs. We thus have the ironic phenomenon that union leaders—at least in the U.S.—have objected to Government interference with the market far more consistently and courageously than have business leaders.

The difficulty of exercising "social responsibility" illustrates, of course, the great virtue of private competitive enterprise—it forces people to be responsible for their own actions and makes it difficult for them to "exploit" other people for either selfish or unselfish purposes. They can do good—but only at their own expense.

Many a reader who has followed the argument this far may be tempted to remonstrate that it is all well and good to speak of government's having the responsibility to impose taxes and determine expenditures for such "social" purposes as controlling pollution or training the hard-core unemployed, but that the problems are too urgent to wait on the slow course of political processes, that the exercise of social responsibility by businessmen is a quicker and surer way to solve pressing current problems.

Aside from the question of fact—I share Adam Smith's skepticism about the benefits that can be expected from "those who affected to trade for the public good"—this argument must be rejected on grounds of principle. What it amounts to is an assertion that those who favor the taxes and expenditures in question have failed to persuade a majority of their fellow citizens to be of like mind and that they are seeking to attain by undemocratic procedures what they cannot attain by democratic procedures. In a free society, it is hard for "good" people to do "good," but that is a small price to pay for making it hard for "evil" people to do "evil," especially since one man's good is another's evil.

I have, for simplicity, concentrated on the special case of the corporate executive, except only for the brief digression on trade unions. But precisely the same argument applies to the newer phenomenon of calling upon stockholders to require corporations to exercise social responsibility (the recent G.M. crusade, for example). In most of these cases, what is in effect involved is some stockholders trying to get other stockholders (or customers or employees) to contribute against their will to "social" causes favored by the activists. Insofar as they succeed, they are again imposing taxes and spending the proceeds.

The situation of the individual proprietor is somewhat different. If he acts to reduce the returns of his enterprise in order to exercise his "social responsibility," he is spending his own money, not someone else's. If he wishes to spend his money on such purposes, that is his right, and I cannot see that there is any objection to his doing so. In the process, he, too, may impose costs on employees and customers. However, because he is far less likely than a large corporation or union to have monopolistic power, any such side effects will tend to be minor.

Of course, in practice the doctrine of social responsibility is frequently a cloak for actions that are justified on other grounds rather than a reason for those actions.

To illustrate, it may well be in the long-run interest of a corporation that is a major employer in a small community to devote resources to providing amenities to that community or to improving its government. That may make it easier to attract desirable employees, it may reduce the wage bill or lessen losses from pilferage and sabotage or have other worthwhile effects. Or it may be that, given the laws about the deductibility of corporate charitable contributions, the stockholders can contribute more to charities they favor by having the corporation make the gift than by doing it themselves, since they can in that way contribute an amount that would otherwise have been paid as corporate taxes.

In each of these—and many similar—cases, there is a strong temptation to rationalize these actions as an exercise of "social responsibility." In the present climate of opinion, with its widespread aversion to "capitalism," "profits," the "soulless corporation" and so on, this is one way for a corporation to generate goodwill as a by-product of expenditures that are entirely justified in its own self-interest.

It would be inconsistent of me to call on corporate executives to refrain from this hypocritical window-dressing because it harms the foundations of a free society. That would be to call on them to exercise a "social responsibility"! If our institutions, and the attitudes of the public make it in their self-interest to cloak their actions in this way, I cannot summon much indignation to denounce them. At the same time, I can express admiration for those individual proprietors or owners of closely held corporations or stockholders of more broadly held corporations who disdain such tactics as approaching fraud.

Whether blameworthy or not, the use of the cloak of social responsibility, and the nonsense spoken in its name by influential and prestigious businessmen, does clearly harm the foundations of a free society. I have been impressed time and again by the schizophrenic character of many businessmen. They are capable of being extremely far-sighted and clear-headed in matters that are internal to their businesses. They are incredibly short-sighted and muddle-headed in matters that are outside their businesses but affect the possible survival of business in general. This short-sightedness is strikingly exemplified in the calls from many businessmen for wage and price guidelines or controls or incomes policies. There is nothing that could do more in a brief period to destroy a market system and replace it by a centrally controlled system than effective governmental control of prices and wages.

The short-sightedness is also exemplified in speeches by businessmen on social responsibility. This may gain them kudos in the short run. But it helps to strengthen the already too prevalent view that the pursuit of profits is wicked and immoral and must be curbed and controlled by external forces. Once this view is adopted, the external forces that curb the market will not be the social consciences, however highly developed, of the pontificating executives; it will be the iron fist of Government bureaucrats. Here, as with price and wage controls, businessmen seem to me to reveal a suicidal impulse.

The political principle that underlies the market mechanism is unanimity. In an ideal free market resting on private property, no individual can coerce any other, all cooperation is voluntary, all parties to such cooperation benefit or they need not participate. There are no "social" values, no "social" responsibilities in any sense other than the shared values and responsibilities of individuals. Society is a collection of individuals and of the various groups they voluntarily form.

The political principle that underlies the political mechanism is conformity. The individual must serve a more general social interest—whether that be determined by a church or a dictator or a majority. The individual may have a vote and a say in what is to be done, but if he is overruled, he must conform. It is appropriate for some to require others to contribute to a general social purpose whether they wish to or not.

Unfortunately, unanimity is not always feasible. There are some respects in which conformity appears unavoidable, so I do not see how one can avoid the use of the political mechanism altogether.

But the doctrine of "social responsibility" taken seriously would extend the scope of the political mechanism to every human activity. It does not differ in philosophy from the most explicitly collectivist doctrine. It differs only by professing to believe that collectivist ends can be attained without collectivist means. That is why, in my book "Capitalism and Freedom," I have called it a "fundamentally subversive doctrine" in a free society, and have said that in such a society, "there is one and only one social responsibility of business—to use its resources and engage in activities designed to increase its profits so long as it stays within the rules of the game, which is to say, engages in open and free competition without deception or fraud."

NO

Thomas Mulligan

A CRITIQUE OF
MILTON FRIEDMAN'S ESSAY

In this famous essay, Milton Friedman argues that people responsible for decisions and action in business should not exercise social responsibility in their capacity as company executives. Instead, they should concentrate on increasing the profits of their companies.[1]

In the course of the essay, he also argues that the doctrine of social responsibility is a socialist doctrine.

The purpose of this paper is to assess the merit of Friedman's arguments. I shall summarize his main arguments, examine some of his premises and lines of inference, and propose a counter-argument.

FRIEDMAN'S ARGUMENT: CORPORATE EXECUTIVES SHOULD NOT EXERCISE SOCIAL RESPONSIBILITY

Friedman argues that the exercise of social responsibility by a corporate executive is:

(a) unfair, because it constitutes taxation without representation;
(b) undemocratic, because it invests governmental power in a person who has no general mandate to govern;
(c) unwise, because there are no checks and balances in the broad range of governmental power thereby turned over to his discretion:
(d) a violation of trust, because the executive is employed by the owners "as an agent serving the interests of his principal";
(e) futile, both because the executive is unlikely to be able to anticipate the social consequences of his actions and because, as he imposes costs on his stockholders, customers, or employees, he is likely to lose their support and thereby lose his power.

These conclusions are related.

Points (b) and (c) depend on (a), on the ground that "the imposition of taxes and the expenditure of tax proceeds are governmental functions." Point

From Thomas Mulligan, "A Critique of Milton Friedman's Essay 'The Social Responsibility of Business Is to Increase Its Profits,' " *Journal of Business Ethics*, vol. 5 (1986). Copyright © 1986 by D. Reidel Publishing Co., Dordrecht, Holland, and Boston, U.S.A. Reprinted by permission of Kluwer Academic Publishers.

(d) also depends on (a), because it is precisely in imposing a tax on his principal that this executive fails to serve the interests of that principal. Point (e) depends, in part, on (d), since it is the executive's failure to serve the interests of his principal which results in the withdrawal of that principal's support.

Point (a) is thus at the foundation of the argument. If (a) is false, then Friedman's demonstration of the subsequent conclusions almost completely collapses.

Is it true, then, that the executive who performs socially responsible action "is in effect imposing taxes . . . and deciding how the tax proceeds shall be spent"?

To make this case, Friedman argues by depicting how a company executive would perform such action.

He first introduces examples to illustrate that exercising social responsibility in business typically costs money. He mentions refraining from a price increase to help prevent inflation, reducing pollution "beyond the amount that is in the best interests of the corporation" to help improve the environment, and "at the expense of corporate profits" hiring 'hardcore' unemployed.

To establish that such costs are in effect taxes, he argues:

1. In taking such action, the executive expends "someone else's money"—the stockholders', the customers', or the employees'.
2. The money is spent "for a general social interest".
3. "Rather than serving as an agent of the stockholders or the customers or the employees . . . he spends the money in a different way than they would have spent it".

The first two premises suggest a similarity between this money and tax revenues, with respect to their sources and to the purposes for which they are used. However, an expense is not yet a tax unless it is *imposed* on the contributor, irrespective of his desire to pay. Only Friedman's third premise includes this crucial element of imposition.

This third premise reveals the essential character of the paradigm on which Friedman bases his whole case.

FRIEDMAN'S PARADIGM

In the above examples of socially responsible action and throughout his essay, Friedman depicts the corporate executive who performs such action as a sort of Lone Ranger, deciding entirely by himself what good deeds to do, when to act, how much to spend:

> Here, the businessman—self-selected or appointed directly or indirectly by the stockholders—is to be simultaneously legislator, executive and jurist. He is to decide whom to tax by how much and for what purpose.

On this paradigm, the corporate executive does not act with the counsel and participation of the other stakeholders in the business. This is the basis of Friedman's claim that the executive is *imposing* something on those other stakeholders—unfairly, undemocratically, unwisely, and in violation of a trust.

But does Friedman's paradigm accurately depict the socially responsible executive? Does it capture the essential nature of socially responsible action in business? Or has he drawn a caricature, wrongly construed it as accurate, and used it to discredit the doctrine it purportedly illustrates?

A COUNTER-PARADIGM

Friedman's paradigm is valid in the sense that it is certainly possible for a corporate executive to try to exercise social responsibility without the counsel or participation of the other stakeholders in the business.

Friedman is also correct in characterizing such conduct as unfair and as likely to result in the withdrawal of the support of those other stakeholders.

Yet Friedman insists, at least with respect to the executive's employers, that the socially responsible executive "must" do it alone, must act in opposition to the interests of the other stakeholders:

> What does it mean to say that the corporate executive has a "social responsibility" in his capacity as a businessman? If this statement is not pure rhetoric, it must mean that he is to act in some way that is not in the interest of his employers.

There is no good reason why this remarkable claim must be true. The exercise of social responsibility in business suffers no diminishment in meaning or merit if the executive and his employers both understand their mutual interest to include a proactive social role and cooperate in undertaking that role.

I propose a different paradigm for the exercise of social responsibility in business—one very much in keeping with sound management practice.

A business normally defines its course and commits itself to action by conceiving a mission, then proceeding to a set of objectives, then determining quantified and time-bound goals, and then developing a full strategic plan which is implemented by appropriate top-level staffing, operating procedures, budgeted expenditures, and daily management control.

Many stakeholders in the business participate in this far-reaching process.

Founders, board members, major stockholders, and senior executives may all participate in defining a mission and in setting objectives based on that mission. In so doing, these people serve as "legislators" for the company.

Top management's translation of these broad directions into goals, strategic plans, operating procedures, budgets, and daily work direction brings middle management, first-line management and, in some companies, employee representatives into the process. This is the "executive branch" of the business.

When the time comes to judge progress and success, the board members and stockholders serve as "jurists" at the highest level, and when necessary can take decisive, sometimes dramatic, corrective measures. However, the grassroots judgment of the court of employee opinion can also be a powerful force. More than one company has failed or faltered because it did not keep a course which inspired and held its talented people.

In sum, a business is a collaborative enterprise among the stakeholders, with some checks and balances. In general, this system allows to any one stakeholder a degree of participation commensurate with the size of his or her stake.

For a business to define a socially responsible course and commit to socially responsible action, it needs to follow no other process than the familiar one described in the preceding paragraphs.

On this paradigm, if socially responsible action is on the corporate executive's agenda, then it is there because the company's mission, objectives and goals—developed collaboratively by the major stakeholders—gave him license to put it there and provided parameters for his program. Lone Ranger executives are no more necessary and no more welcome in a socially responsible business than in one devoted exclusively to the maximization of profit.

This paradigm conforms more accurately than Friedman's to the reality of how action programs—socially responsible ones or otherwise—are conceived and enacted in a strategically managed business. The corporate executive in this process, in contradistinction to Friedman's corporate executive, does not impose unauthorized costs, or "taxes", on anyone. On this account, he usurps no governmental function, violates no trust, and runs no special risk of losing the support of the other stakeholders.

THE PROBLEM OF KNOWING FUTURE CONSEQUENCES

The preceding argument addresses most of Friedman's objections to a corporate executive's attempts to exercise social responsibility.

Friedman, however, provides one objection which does not rest on his paradigm of the Lone Ranger executive. This is the objection that it is futile to attempt socially responsible action because the future social consequences of today's actions are very difficult to know.

Suppose, he writes, that the executive decides to fight inflation:

> How is he to know what action of his will contribute to that end? He is presumably an expert in running his company—in producing a product or selling it or financing it. But nothing about his selection makes him an expert on inflation. Will holding down the price of his product reduce inflationary pressure? Or, by leaving more spending power in the hands of his customers, simply di-

vert it elsewhere? Or by forcing him to produce less because of the lower price, will it simply contribute to shortages?

The difficulty of determining the future consequences of one's intended good acts has received attention in the literature of philosophical ethics. G. E. Moore, in his early twentieth century classic *Principia Ethica*, writes of "the hopeless task of finding duties"[2] since, to act with perfect certainty, we would need to know "all the events which will be in any way affected by our action throughout an infinite future".[3]

Human life, however, requires action in the absence of certainty, and business people in particular have a bias toward action. They do not wait for perfect foreknowledge of consequences, but instead set a decision date, gather the best information available, contemplate alternatives, assess risks, and then decide what to do.

Decisions about socially responsible actions, no less than decisions about new products or marketing campaigns, can be made using this "business-like" approach. The business person, therefore, has even less cause than most moral agents to abstain from social responsibility out of a sense of the futility of knowing consequences, since he is more practiced than most in the techniques for making action decisions in the absence of certainty.

SOCIAL RESPONSIBILITY AND SOCIALISM

Some of Friedman's most emphatic language is devoted to his position that the advocates of social responsibility in a free-enterprise system are "preaching pure and unadulterated socialism".

He asserts this view in the first and last paragraphs of the essay, and concludes:

> The doctrine of "social responsibility" . . . does not differ in philosophy from the most explicitly collectivist doctrine.

Friedman's argument for this conclusion is located roughly midway through his essay, and it too rests on his paradigm of the socially responsible executive "imposing taxes" on others and thereby assuming governmental functions:

> He becomes in effect a public employee, a civil servant. . . . It is intolerable that such civil servants . . . should be selected as they are now. If they are to be civil servants, then they must be elected through a political process. If they are to impose taxes and make expenditures to foster "social" objectives, then political machinery must be set up to make the assessment of taxes and to determine through a political process the objectives to be served.
>
> This is the basic reason why the doctrine of "social responsibility" involves the acceptance of the socialist view that political mechanisms, not market mechanisms, are the appropriate way to determine the allocation of scarce resources to alternative uses.

I shall raise three objections to this line of reasoning.

First, this argument rests on the paradigm which has already been called into question. If we accept the counter-paradigm proposed above as truer to the nature of a socially responsible corporate executive, then there is no basis for saying that such an individual "imposes taxes", becoming "in effect" a civil servant.

Second, it is not apparent how the propositions that, under the doctrine of social responsibility, a corporate execu-

tive is "in effect" imposing taxes and "in effect" a civil servant logically imply that this doctrine upholds the view that political mechanisms should determine the allocation of scarce resources.

To the contrary, as Friedman points out, his paradigmatic executive is not a true political entity, since he is not elected and since his program of "taxation" and social expenditure is not implemented through a political process. Paradoxically, it is Friedman who finds it "intolerable" that this agent who allocates scarce resources is not part of a political mechanism. Nowhere, however, does he show that acceptance of such a political mechanism is intrinsic to the view of his opponent, the advocate of social responsibility.

Third, in order to show that the doctrine of social responsibility is a socialist doctrine, Friedman must invoke a criterion for what constitutes socialism. As we have seen, his criterion is "acceptance of the . . . view that political mechanisms, not market mechanisms, are the appropriate way to determine the allocation of scarce resources to alternative uses".

The doctrine of social responsibility, he holds, does accept this view. Therefore the doctrine is a socialist doctrine.[4]

However, this criterion is hardly definitive of socialism. The criterion is so broad that is holds for virtually any politically totalitarian or authoritarian system—including feudal monarchies and dictatorships of the political right.

Further, depending on the nature of a resource and degree of its scarcity, the political leadership in any system, including American democracy, is liable to assert its right to determine the allocation of that resource. Who doubts that it is appropriate for our political institutions, rather than market mechanisms, to ensure the equitable availability of breathable air and drinkable water, or to allocate food and fuel in times of war and critical shortage?

Therefore, Friedman has not provided a necessary element for his argument—a definitive criterion for what constitutes socialism.

In summary, Friedman's argument is unsound: first, because it rests on an arbitrary and suspect paradigm; second, because certain of his premises do not imply their stated conclusion; and, third, because a crucial premise, his criterion for what constitutes socialism, is not true.

Although he complains of the "analytical looseness" and "lack of rigor" of his opponents, Friedman's argument has on close examination betrayed its own instances of looseness and lack of rigor.

CONCLUSION

I have considered Friedman's principal objections to socially responsible action in business and argued that at the bottom of most of his objections is an inaccurate paradigm. In response, I have given an account of a more appropriate paradigm to show how business can exercise social responsibility.

Friedman is right in pointing out that exercising social responsibility costs money. If nothing else, a company incurs expense when it invests the manhours needed to contemplate the possible social consequences of alternative actions and to consider the merit or demerit of each set of consequences.

But Friedman is wrong in holding that such costs must be imposed by one business stakeholder on the others, outside the whole collaborative process of strategic and operational business management. He presumes too much in intimating through his imagined examples that the business person who pursues a socially responsible course inevitably acts without due attention to return on investment, budgetary limitations, reasonable employee remuneration, or competitive pricing.

My purpose has been to provide a critique of the major lines of argument presented in a famous and influential essay. The thrust has been to show that Friedman misrepresents the nature of social responsibility in business and that business people *can* pursue a socially responsible course without the objectionable results claimed by Friedman. It would be another step to produce positive arguments to demonstrate why business people *should* pursue such a course. That is an undertaking for another occasion.

For now, I shall only observe that Friedman's own concluding statement contains a moral exhortation to business people. Business, he says, should engage in "open and free competition without deception or fraud". If Friedman does not recognize that even these restrained words lay open a broad range of moral obligation and social responsibility for business, which is after all one of the largest areas of human interaction in our society, then the oversight is his.

NOTES

1. Milton Friedman, 'The Social Responsibility of Business Is to Increase Its Profits', *New York Times Magazine*, 13 September 1970, 32 ff. Unless otherwise noted, all quotations are from this essay.
2. G. E. Moore, *Principia Ethica*, Cambridge, 1979, p. 150.
3. *Ibid.*, p. 149.
4. In the concluding paragraph of his essay, Friedman states, "The doctrine of 'social responsibility' taken seriously would extend the scope

of the political mechanism to every human activity". "Every human activity" certainly seems at least one extra step beyond the set of activities involved in "the allocation of scarce resources to alternative uses". Unfortunately, Friedman's essay contains no explication of the reasoning he used to make the transition from the language of his argument midway through the essay to the grander claim of this concluding paragraph.

POSTSCRIPT

Are Profits the Only Business of Business?

Economist Friedman dismisses the pleas of those who argue for socially responsible business action on the grounds that these individuals do not understand the role of the corporate executive in modern society. Friedman points out that these executives are responsible to the corporate owners, who expect these executives to do everything in their power to earn the owners a maximum return on their investment. If the corporate executive takes a "socially responsible" action that reduces the owners' return on their investment, he or she has spent the owners' money. This, Friedman maintains, violates the very foundation of our political-economic system: individual freedom. He believes that no individual should be deprived of his or her property without his or her permission. If the corporate executives wish to take socially responsible actions, they should use their own money; they shouldn't prevent the owners from spending their money on whatever social actions they might wish to support.

Business professor Mulligan challenges the Friedman essay argument by argument. First, he finds a serious weakness in a key premise of the Friedman article, which is that social responsibility is taxation without representation. Next, he objects to Friedman's assertion that it is "futile to attempt" acts that are socially responsible because the future is "very difficult to know." Finally, Mulligan is unmoved by Friedman's insistence that those who advocate social responsibility are "preaching pure and unadulterated socialism."

Perhaps no one topic is more fundamental to microeconomics than the issue of profits. Many articles have been written in defense of profits, such as Milton and Rose Friedman's *Free to Choose: A Personal Statement* (Harcourt Brace Jovanovich, 1980), Ben Rogge's *Can Capitalism Survive?* (Liberty Fund, 1979), and Frank H. Knight's classical book *Risk, Uncertainty, and Profits* (Kelley Press, 1921). There are a number of books that are highly critical of the Friedman-Rogge-Knight position, including James Robertson's *Profit or People? The New Social Role of Money* (Merrimack Book Service, 1978), Sam Aaronovitch's *Political Economy of Capitalism* (Beekman Publishers, 1977), and Sherman Howard's *Radical Political Economy: Capitalism and Socialism from a Marxist Humanist Perspective* (Basic Books, 1972). Mulligan has two other essays on this topic: "Two Cultures in Business Education," *Academy of Management Review,* vol. 12 (1987) and "Justifying Moral Initiative by Business," *Journal of Business Ethics* (Spring 1990).

We should also note that there are many professional journals that deal with ethics and business. Best known among these publications is the *Journal of Business Ethics,* where the Mulligan essay appeared in 1986. Other journals that are important in this area are: *Business and Professional Ethics Journal; Philosophy and Public Affairs;* and *Business and Society.*

ISSUE 2

Should We Try To Save the Family Farm?

YES: Byron Dorgan, from "America's Real Farm Problem: It Can Be Solved," *The Washington Monthly* (April 1983)

NO: Stephan Chapman, from "The Farmer on the Dole," *Harper's Magazine* (October 1982)

ISSUE SUMMARY

YES: Representative Dorgan of North Dakota fears that public policy has become too concerned with the interests of the large corporate farms while ignoring the small family farm that has "made agriculture one of the few American industries still competitive in international markets."

NO: Columnist Chapman argues for "rugged individualism." He asserts that: "If Americans still believe in the virtue of hardy rural self-reliance, they should tell Washington to get out of the way and let farmers practice it."

Agriculture is a highly competitive sector of the economy, and it is particularly susceptible to wide swings in profitability. When times are good, profits are very good, but, when times are bad, they are very bad. This vulnerability can be traced to two factors, which are ultimately related to the nature of competitive markets: First, if market prices fall, the small producers, who are already operating on a tight budget because of debt obligations, respond out of desperation by increasing supply. They do not bring less to the market; they bring more. Their acts of desperation drive market prices down further. Second, although the majority of farmers have little or no control over the price at which they sell their products, the goods and services they must buy from the non-agricultural community often come from firms that do have monopoly power. (The petrochemical industry, the farm implement industry, and the money markets are hardly "competitive" in a textbook sense.) Over time, the profits the farmers receive for their output are much lower than the prices they must pay for their inputs. The net result is that the farmers' relative income falls.

This phenomenon is exaggerated during periods of recessions. Indeed, during the Depression of the 1930s, the disparity between farm income and non-farm income became so great that the United States inaugurated its first farm price support program: the Agricultural Adjustment Act of 1933. This legislation, based on the notion of *parity* (the notion that the value of farm output be maintained relative to the value of non-farm output), became the mainstay of U.S. agricultural policy in the 1930s, 1940s, and 1950s. In short, this policy was designed to protect the small family farm by reducing the supply of agricultural commodities that found their way to the marketplace. This reduced supply, increased agricultural prices, and, in turn, increased incomes in the agricultural community.

During the 1960s and 1970s, agricultural policy was refocused. The opening of world markets and the presence of poor harvests in many parts of the world meant that the demand of U.S.-produced food and fiber were at all-time high levels. As a result, public policy shifted toward improving the operation of agricultural markets and reducing the cost of producing agricultural products, rather than supporting agricultural prices.

In the 1980s, farmers were buffeted by a number of events that were largely out of their control. First, the economy was gripped by "stagflation." The prices of inputs (non-agricultural products) that farmers had to buy skyrocketed, while at the same time the domestic demand for agricultural products slackened. Second, the monetary authority dramatically raised interest rates. In the agricultural sector—which is dependent upon loans to pay for its seed, fertilizer, and equipment—this represented a major financial blow. Third, the bubble burst on agricultural land speculations. In the face of a very deep recession, land prices leveled off and began to fall. Since farmers are land-intensive, the value of their major asset seemed to disappear before their eyes. Lastly, world demand for United States-produced food and fiber fell sharply. This was the result of a world recession, bumper crops throughout the world, and U.S. grain embargoes, which were imposed for political purposes. The net result was falling agricultural prices and incomes.

Farm price support programs automatically came to the rescue of the ailing farm community. Indeed, for fiscal year 1983, United States farm programs cost taxpayers approximately $21 billion or seventy-five percent more than the previous year. But even in the face of these huge dollar expenditures, farmers—particularly small farmers—were facing bankruptcy proceedings at a rate unmatched since the Depression of the 1930s.

Congressman Dorgan is shaken by the prospect of losing the family farm. He argues that the "invisible hand" of the market can "end up shooting farmers in the foot." Free-market advocate Chapman replies that if we want to preserve the "cherished American tradition" that is embodied in the notion of a family farm, we should "tell Washington to get out of the way" so farmers can do their jobs.

YES

Byron Dorgan

AMERICA'S REAL FARM PROBLEM: IT CAN BE SOLVED

Recent scenes from America's farm belt seem like a grainy film clip from the thirties. Young families putting their home and farm machinery on the auction block. Men, choked with emotion, breaking down in tears as they describe their plight. Angry farmers organizing, getting madder and madder.

It's not as bad as the thirties yet; no governor has called out the National Guard to stop the foreclosures, the way North Dakota's William "Wild Bill" Langer did in 1933. But the pain is running deep. Losing a farm is not like have a new Chevrolet or a color TV repossessed. In many cases, what's lost is land that's been in the family for generations—and a way of life that for many is the only one they've ever known or wanted.

It's not that other victims of the recession deserve less sympathy. But there's an important difference between the plight of the farmer and that of other producers. What's happening in the farm belt is a far cry from what's happening in Pittsburgh and Detroit. Nobody is berating our farmers for falling behind the foreign competition and losing their edge, like the auto and steel industries. Nobody is shoving books on Japanese management into their faces. To the contrary, American farmers are our all-star economic performers. When other countries want to find out how to improve agriculture, they don't send their delegations to Tokyo. They send them to Iowa and Kansas and the Dakotas.

And the farmers' reward? Most North Dakota wheat farmers are getting $4 for a bushel of wheat that costs them $5.50 to grow. Farmers are making less in real income today than they did in 1934. Creditors are foreclosing in record numbers; the Farmers Home Administration alone reports that at least 4,000 of its borrowers were forced out of business in 1982.

From Byron Dorgan, "America's Real Farm Problem: It Can Be Solved," *The Washington Monthly* (April 1983). Copyright © 1983 by The Washington Monthly Co., 1711 Connecticut Avenue, NW, Washington, DC 20009. (202) 462-0128. Reprinted by permission of *The Washington Monthly*.

RURAL MYTHS

Agriculture is a $140 billion-a-year industry, our nation's largest, far bigger than steel, automobiles, or any other manufacturing enterprise. Farming and food-related businesses generate one out of five jobs in private industry and account for 20 percent of our GNP. Sooner or later the problems on the farm catch up with the rest of us, as the laid-off employees of International Harvester already know too well. Students of the Depression will also recall that it was long *before* the 1929 crash—while the market was still revving up—that farm income began falling. The troubles on the farm were a large part of the weight that ultimately dragged the entire economy down into the Depression.

If you read the editorial columns of *The Wall Street Journal*, you know that some people have a simple explanation for the farmers' plight. Too much production is the problem, they say, and if government would only stop subsidizing overproduction by keeping prices artificially high, the free market would work its will and weed out the inefficient producers. What's more, many conservatives and liberals alike believe farmers are only getting their just deserts, having grown fat and happy on government price supports and double-digit inflation. You've seen the caricatures on "60 Minutes"—farmers driving big Cadillacs, spending their winters in Boca Raton—and still complaining that the government doesn't pay them enough *not* to grow certain crops.

Those aren't the farmers I know. But with less than four percent of all Americans now living on farms, it's little surprise people have so many misconceptions about our farm program. Start with the "overproduction" argument. There are

children and older people in this country who still don't have enough to eat, and roughly 450 million people in the world who go hungry most of the time. That people talk about "overproduction" rather than "underdistribution" is rather telling in itself. But more to the present point: almost from the time the early settlers planted their first row, American farmers have been growing more food than the nation could consume. The tendency toward producing surpluses is a perennial problem. It hardly explains the extraordinary difficulties our farmers now face.

As for the "60 Minutes" caricatures, they are just that—caricatures. Last year (1982) the federal government paid farmers $1.5 billion in direct subsidies (it loaned another $11.4 billion that farmers must repay). Money from these federal programs came to about two percent of total receipts in 1982 for the average farmer, whose farm netted just $8,000. Add in what he and his family earned away from the farm, and his household still made less than a GS-11 civil servant and about half as much as a young lawyer on Wall Street. That's for working from morning to night and doing what many Americans no longer do—produce something the rest of us need.

But this is no blanket apology for the nation's farm policies—far from it. There are some farmers who get more than they deserve from the government, and nobody gets madder about that than the vast majority of farmers who bear no resemblance to them. Egregious abuses do exist, and it's time that representatives from the farm states (of which I'm one) begin to eliminate them. If we ignore such problems or dismiss them as inevitable, they will continue to act as lightning rods for attacks on all farm programs. Representatives of farm states must clean their own house for if they don't, I'm afraid, someone else will do it—hurting farmer and non-farmer alike.

The nation needs a federal farm program; to think otherwise in today's highly competitive international economy is self-defeating and naive. But we need the *right* kind of farm program, one that not only meets the test of fairness, but that promises to keep American agriculture second to none.

Unfortunately, that's not the kind of farm program we now have. Approaches that were fine in the thirties are no longer doing the job. In fact, what began as survival programs for family farmers are becoming the domain of extra-large producers who often elbow aside the very family farmers for whom these programs were originally intended. Congress must bear much of the blame for this. We continue to target most farm assistance not according to the circumstances of the individual farmer but largely according to the volume of the commodity he grows. While these federal programs have all been done in the name of the family farmer, the interests of the various commodity groups have not always been identical to those of the nation's family farmers.

This is not to criticize these groups, for everyone is entitled to his say. But it is to suggest that we in Congress have talked too much about programs for feed grains and wheat and corn and assorted "market prices" and "loan rates"—and not enough about the kind of agriculture that's best for the country. And we've done more than waste money in the process. For if our agricultural policy continues largely unchanged, I'm concerned the criticisms that now so tragically apply to the nation's automakers—that they became too big, too inflexible,

and too inefficient to compete—may one day be appropriate for America's agriculture.

FARM ECONOMICS

To understand the failings of existing farm programs, it's important to understand the roots of the current farm crisis. At the heart of the problem is money—how much there is and how much it costs to borrow.

A farmer is a debtor almost by definition. In my own state, it's not unusual for a wheat farmer with 1,000 acres to owe several hundred thousand dollars for land and machinery. In addition to making payments on these loans, it's common for such a farmer to borrow about $40,000 each spring to cover fertilizer, diesel fuel, seed, and other operating expenses. The months before the harvest will be anxious ones as the farmer contemplates all the things that could bring financial hardship: bad weather, crop disease, insects, falling commodity prices. If he has a good year, the farmer can repay his loans and retain some profit; in a bad one, he can lose his whole farm.

Money thus becomes one of the farmer's biggest expenses. Most consumers can find some refuge from high interest rates by postponing large purchases like houses or cars. Farmers have no choice. In 1979, for example, farmers paid $12 billion in interest costs while earning $32 billion; last year they paid $22 billion in interest costs, while earning only $20 billion. In a business in which profit margins are small, $4,000 more in interest can mean the difference between profit and loss. Since 1975, 100,000 family farms have disappeared, and while interest rates have fallen recently, they still imperil the nation's farmers.

This is why the most basic part of our nation's farm policy is its money and credit policy—which is set by Paul Volcker and the Federal Reserve Board. The Federal Reserve Board's responsibility for nearly ruining our economy is well-known. What's often overlooked is how the board's policies have taken an especially devastating toll on farmers. While high interest rates have increased farm expenses, they've also undermined the export market farmers have traditionally relied on. High interest rates, by stalling our economic engines, have been a drag on the entire world's economy. Developing and third-world nations have been particularly hard hit; struggling just to meet interest payments on their loans from multinational banks, they have had little cash left over to buy our farm products.

Even those countries that could still afford our farm products abandoned us for other producers. Our interest rates were so high they attracted multinational bankers, corporations, and others who speculate on currencies of different countries. These speculators were willing to pay more for dollars in terms of pesos, yen, or marks because those rates guaranteed them such a substantial return.

The news commentators called the result a "strong dollar," which gave us a rush of pride. But what did this strong dollar really mean to the farmer? It meant people in other countries found themselves suddenly poorer when they went to buy something made or grown in America. In 1981, for example, West Germans paid 21 percent more for American soybeans, even though our farmers were getting 11 percent *less* for those very same soybeans than they had the previous year. Overall, our "strong dollar" has been jacking up the price of American farm exports by a full 25 percent, biting our potential foreign customer with a 25 percent surcharge the moment they start thinking of buying American. No wonder these exports have dropped for the first time in 12 years. This isn't a strong dollar, it's a big banker's dollar—and with a central bank like the Federal Reserve Board, who needs soil erosion, grasshoppers, or drought?

To be fair, interest rates aren't solely responsible for undercutting our farmers' export markets. President Carter's grain embargo did more than close the Russian market; it also drove away other foreign customers who wondered how dependable we were. Reagan has lifted the embargo, but to little avail, since he still refuses to sign a long-term grain contract with the Soviet Union. Meanwhile, our foreign competitors have quickly stepped into the breach, supporting their farmers with generous subsidies that make ours look miserly by comparison. Last September, for example, wheat from the U.S. and the Common Market countries was selling for almost the same price on the international market. But while the U.S. farmer was getting about $3.40 a bushel, his Common Market counterpart received $5.37.

Both the Federal Reserve Board's market-skewing policies and the hefty subsidies that foreign agriculture receives illustrate an important point. Those who say America should go back to a "free market" in agriculture are asking our farmers to go back to something that no longer exists. In today's world there's no free market in agriculture, just as there is none in steel, automobiles, or other major industries.

We learned during the Depression that agriculture, by its very nature, requires a moderating hand to smooth out the violent cycles that otherwise could destroy even the best farmers. No other producers have to confront the sudden price shifts with which farmers regularly contend. Automakers, for example, don't have to worry that prices for their product may drop 50 percent, as wheat prices did from 1974 to 1977. This is why even that bastion of free-market orthodoxy, the Heritage Foundation, concedes the need for a government role in agriculture.

HOME-GROWN DEPRESSION

For the nation's first 150 years, there was no farm program as such. The Department of Agriculture wasn't created until 1862, and when President Lincoln proposed it to Congress he could applaud the nation's farmers as a "great interest so independent in its nature as to not have demanded and extorted more from government." For the next 70 years the department limited itself largely to statistics and research. Farmers received little in the way of subsidies; like all other consumers, they helped subsidize manufacturers through the tariffs they paid on imported goods.

Contrary to popular belief, the Depression hit our farms long before the Okies started their desperate treks across the dust bowl in their sputtering Models T's. During World War I Europe bought our food like it was going out of style. Prices rose to record heights; farmers expanded their operations and borrowed heavily to do so.

Then the war ended. Export markets quickly dried up as European countries started to rebuild their own agriculture. American farmers watched helplessly as prices plummeted, leaving many with huge debts to repay and no income with which to pay them. A rash of foreclo-sures followed, rehearsing a cycle that bears an eerie similarity to the current one. By 1932 farm income was less than one-third of what it had been in 1919. During this period, more than 1.5 million Americans left the farm. (The exodus was reversed during the Depression, when many returned to the farm in order to survive.)

Then, as now, the conventional economists and their camp followers in Congress and the press found little alarming in this hardship. The "invisible hand," they said, would force farmers to produce less until prices returned to normal levels. The "weak" and the "inefficient" might be cut down in the process, but that was the way the free market was supposed to work. It didn't.

Unfortunately, someone forgot to tell the nation's farmers about the economic etiquette that professors and journalists expected of them. As prices continued to fall, the farmers didn't produce less—they produced more. It's not hard to understand why. Farmers have certain set costs—such as debt—whether or not the plant a single seed. When prices dropped, many tried to produce more to make up the difference. Besides, to farm is to hope. The market may be terrible one year, but who knows what will happen next? Will there be drought in Europe? Blight in Russia? When you have to decide how much to plant in the spring, you have little idea what the market will really be in the fall. The worse things look, the more you pin your hopes on a sudden surge in prices. So you plant.

Those who put all the blame on government for today's excess production and low prices are long on theory and short on history. We produced "too much" throughout the twenties, when there was no farm program to speak of. And it wasn't the weak and the inefficient who tumbled then. It was just about everybody.

BLIND GENEROSITY

The New Dealers recognized that when it comes to agriculture, the invisible hand can end up shooting farmers in the foot. Their solution was straightforward—and effective. Remedies like the Agricultural Adjustment Act were begun to prop up the prices of certain commodities so that the farmers who grew them could count on at least a minimal return. The main approach was to link government assistance to the farmers' agreement to cut production, thus forcing prices to rise according to the laws of supply and demand.

These relief programs were not geared to the circumstances of individual farmers. They were aimed at regulating the supply and price of certain commodities. Still, the commodity approach amounted to a relief program for the family farm because there just weren't many other kinds of farms around. In 1932 one of four Americans lived on a farm, and for that reason the commodity programs were a major part of the whole New Deal relief effort.

Over the last half century, this commodity approach has remained relatively unchanged, while American agriculture has changed radically. The number of farms today is one-third what it was during the Depression, and just seven percent of these control over half the farmland and account for over half the sales. Yet while farming has become more concentrated, the government still dispenses federal aid with a blindfold on, treating a multi-thousand-acre agrifactory giant as if it were a bedraggled Okie with a handcrank tractor and a cow. As a result, 29 percent of all federal farm benefits go to the top one percent of our farmers.

The government distributes this largess in a variety of ways. Some programs amount to government-guaranteed prices. For a few crops—tobacco and peanuts, for example—the government sanctions an allotment system by which the marketing of these is strictly controlled. The government also provides crop insurance, disaster relief, and subsidized loans for such things as purchasing more farmland and meeting operating expenses.

The traditional mainstay of the farm program is the "commodity loan." Each year the government establishes a loan rate for major crops, including wheat, corn, barley, sorghum, and soybeans. The rate for wheat, for example, was $3.55 per bushel in 1982. Early in the year, a farmer must decide whether he is going to sign up for the program; if he does, he may have to agree to cut back his production to help keep surpluses down. If the eventual market price goes above the loan-rate level, the farmer simply repays the loan, takes back his wheat, and sells it on the open market. But if the market price is below the loan rate, the farmer may take the money and leave the wheat with the government. In addition to the commodity loan, there is a "deficiency payment" that supposedly helps bridge the gap between what the farmer earns in the market and what his crop costs to produce.

It's important to understand two things about this price-support program. First, a guaranteed price is not a guaranteed profit. The loan rates and deficiency payments do not necessarily return the farmer's cost of production, and in recent years they haven't. In 1982, for example, the target price for wheat was more than a dollar less than the farmer's cost of production.

More important, the way these programs work, the more you have, the more the government gives you. A wheat farmer with 250 acres producing 30 bushels per acre gets a support loan of $26,625. A farmer with 2,500 acres of similarly productive land gets approximately ten times that much. The deficiency payments work in pretty much the same way.

For deficiency payments there is a nominal $50,000 cap that in practice does not have much effect. For support loans, there is no limitation at all. Thus, while smaller farmers get a little help, the largest farms walk off with a bundle. In a recent editorial attacking all farm subsidies, *The Wall Street Journal* fumed about a midwestern wheat grower who received $68,760 last year from the government yet "rides around his 4,000-acre farm on a huge four-wheel-drive tractor with air conditioning and a radio."

I'll bet the editorial writers of *The Wall Street Journal* have air conditioning, radios, and a whole lot more in their offices; still, they do have a point. As Don Paarlburg, a conservative agricultural economist who toiled in the last three Republican administrations, has put it, the result of the present federal farm program is that "average farm income is increased by adding more dollars to those already well-off and adding little or nothing to those at the low end of the income scale."

This bias toward bigness runs through most of the federal government's farm program. One of the best illustrations is the Farmers Home Administration, a case study of how a federal program that began to help only those in need became a safety net for just about everybody else.

The FmHA was created in the depths of the Depression as a lender of last resort for small and beginning farmers who had a reasonable chance to survive. For most of its life, the agency did serve family farmers struggling to get their operation on its feet and unable to obtain credit elsewhere. But in the 1970s, Congress tacked on something called the Economic Emergency Loan program. To qualify for this new program you didn't have to be small, needy, or even a family farmer. You just had to be in economic trouble. Soon the "economic-emergency" loans were pushing aside the kinds of loans the FmHA was originally intended to provide. By 1980 FmHA was lending *four times* as much in such "emergency" assistance as it was in the so-called "limited-resource" loans for needy farmers who were now receiving less than ten percent of the agency's total. Ninety percent of these emergency loans went to bigger, more established farms, many of which were unlikely candidates for public philanthropy. One politician and judge with a net worth of $435,000 and a non-farm income of $70,000 a year received $266,000 in such low-interest "emergency" loans.

After "60 Minutes" exposed a $17 million emergency loan to a California agrifactory, an embarrassed Congress imposed a $400,000 limit on the program. Though this was an improvement, the still-generous limit enables the larger farms to eat up the bulk of FmHA's loan resources.

Showing nicely its concept of the "truly needy," the Reagan administration tried to abolish completely the limited-resource loan program that was targeted to the smaller farmers the agency was established to help in the first place. Congress wouldn't let it, so the Reaganites discovered the value of bureaucracy and gave it the redtape treatment. Nationwide, the FmHA in 1982 managed to lend only about half the money Congress had approved for these loans—this during the worst year for farmers in half a century.

In fairness, the administration has also stopped making economic-emergency loans. But that misses the point. Those loans should be made, but only to family farmers who need them. The FMHA's recent crackdown on delinquent borrowers, moreover, has fallen most heavily upon the smaller farmers. It's cruel irony: having lavished so much money on the largest farmers, at least some of whom could have gotten credit elsewhere, the government now has too little left for smaller farmers who have nowhere else to turn. Not surprisingly, many are going under.

Meanwhile, the Reagan administration has introduced a Payment-In-Kind program that gives farmers government surplus commodities they in turn can sell, if they agree to take acreage out of production. PIK is thus a variation on traditional New Deal programs. But while the PIK program offers many beleaguered farmers some genuine help, it also embodies the same most-for-the-biggest approach.

AGRICULTURAL BLOAT

Of course, some will argue there's nothing wrong with a farm policy that encourages bigger and bigger farms. This will only make them more efficient, so the argument goes, and past gains in agricultural productivity will continue indefinitely as farms get bigger.

To such people, a concern for the family-size farm seems a mushy and misplaced Jeffersonian nostalgia. In fact, it is anything but. Family farming is practical economics. Anyone who's looked recently at our automobile and steel industries knows that economies of scale stop beyond a certain point. When Thomas Peters and Robert Waterman examined successful American businesses for their book *In Search of Excellence*, what were

the qualities they found? Small work units. Lean staffs. A minimum of management bureaucracy. Managers who get their hands into what they manage. Enterprises that stick to their knitting instead of using their assets to flit from one business to another.

It sounds like a profile of the American family farm. It's also a description of what we *lose* when we allow factory-in-the-field agglomerations to gobble up individual family farmers.

There's growing evidence to suggest that in agriculture, as in other endeavors, the old "bigger is better" saying is a myth. A decade ago the Department of Agriculture was telling Congress the optimum size for a California vegetable farm was 400 acres, though 73 percent of the state's vegetables were already produced on farms much larger than that. A 1979 USDA study found that the average U.S. farm reaches 90 percent of maximum efficiency at just 314 acres; to attain 100 percent efficiency, the average size has to quadruple to 1,157 acres. Beyond that, farms don't get any better—they just get bigger. They may even become more bureaucratic and less efficient.

Consider, for example, the matter of debt. The very largest farms are twice as debt-prone as smaller family farms. This is of little consequence when times are flush. But when trouble hits, as it has with Mr. Volcker's interest-rate policies, it's like sending a fleet of large sailing ships heading into a gale with twice the sail they normally carry.

Just as a rope of many strands is more flexible and resilient than a single strand, a diverse agriculture of many relatively small units can adjust and change. Unlike the very largest operations, family farmers don't have so much capital tied up in what they did yesterday to keep them from doing what needs to be done tomorrow. Small farmers don't have to push paper through tedious chains of command. If they see a way of doing something better, they can do it right away. This kind of flexibility is important if sudden shifts in market conditions warrant different crops or production techniques.

There's also the question of rural communities. I grew up in Regent, North Dakota, a farming community of 400 people. Family farms were and are the economic bloodstream of that town. When such farms are eaten up by larger ones, towns like Regent wither, and the government finds itself with a tax-consuming social problem instead of a healthy and tax-providing community.

In short, there is a link between the *way* we have farmed—in traditional family-size units—and the extraordinary productivity of our agriculture as a whole. Yet our farm policies are pushing us towards a top-heavy agriculture that threatens to mimic the same problems we are facing in other areas of our economy. The high interest rates of the last two years have made the problem even worse: whether family farmers go bankrupt or simply decide to sell out, the trend toward concentration is hastened.

Even worse, this trend feeds on itself. The alteration of the FmHA is instructive. Having helped create large farms, the government felt compelled to keep them from failing. When a small family farmer bites the dust there may be a few condolences but nobody worries much. When a multi-thousand-acre agrifactory totters, its bankers and creditors get the jitters over the millions of dollars at stake. It's a prairie twist on the maxim familiar to international bankers: "Make a small loan and you create a debtor. Make a big loan and you create a partner."

Are we encouraging farms so big that we can't afford to let them fail? I fear we are and I think it's an ominous prescription for slowly but inevitably undermining the very things that have made agriculture one of the few American industries still competitive in international markets. Despite high interest rates, agriculture still contributed more than $40 billion in export sales last year, helping defray the costs of our unhappy dependence on imported oil and automobiles.

HELP FOR THE FAMILY FARMER

What does all this mean for our farm policies? Mr. Paarlburg recommends that we eliminate the current "tilt in favor of big farms" in our federal programs, and at least keep the playing field level. I agree with that, but would go a step further. For the reasons I've discussed, I think we should retarget the current programs toward family-size unites. For example, we should put a cap on the commodity price-support loans to eliminate the exorbitant amounts going to the very largest farmers, thus freeing up more for those who need it more. In 1981, for example, I proposed capping these loans at $150,000, which would have affected less than ten percent of all farmers but would have enabled us to increase the support price by about 35 cents per bushel for the rest. (This new level, incidentally, would have still been below production costs.) Farmers could become as large as they wanted—the federal government just wouldn't pay them for doing so.

We should alter the FMHA loan program in similar fashion, restoring this agency to its original purpose of providing economic opportunity to beginning and smaller farmers. In the present crisis, the money saved should be used to extend loan deferrals to family farmers who have fallen behind on their FmHA loans because of economic circumstances beyond their control. At the same time, we should alter other federal policies, such as tax laws that invite lawyers and doctors to invest in farms as tax shelters, driving up land prices to the detriment of the beginning farmer.

Of course, it would not be fair to pull the plug suddenly on these larger farm operations. Many are essentially family farmers who overextended themselves during the 1970s, with a good deal of encouragement (including subsidized loans) from the government. Some of these farms may need emergency loans; the question is the direction in which our farm program goes from here.

These are the broad outlines of a farm program that I think would dispense agricultural benefits more fairly while promoting the right kind of agriculture. But the high interest rates of the last two years should serve as a stark reminder that the best farm program in the world will not do a great deal when a Federal Reserve Board accountable to no one can unleash an interest-rate tornado that levels the economic landscape. The best thing the government can do for the nation's farmer is not to subsidize him, but to promote the kind of monetary policies that make credit available at a fair price. . . .

More than a century ago, President Abraham Lincoln warned us that "the money power of this country will endeavor to prolong its reign until all wealth is aggregated in a few hands and the Republic is destroyed." While its policies have moderated somewhat in recent months, the board has taken us in precisely this direction. Money and credit should serve production, not the other way around. Regaining control over them is of utmost importance not only to the family farmer, but to all independent businessmen as well—not to mention the rest of us.

NO

Stephen Chapman

THE FARMER ON THE DOLE

The family farmer is a durable feature of American folklore. From its beginning America was regarded by Europeans as a pastoral Eden, shielded from the corrosive influences of city and commerce. American soil was cultivated, not by serfs and peasants as in the Old World, but by self-supporting landowners, thought to be the soul of a healthy democracy. In 1797 the *Encyclopaedia Britannica* stated that "in no part of the world are the people happier . . . or more independent than the farmers of New England." Thomas Jefferson frequently cited the blessings of America's agricultural character. "Those who labour in the earth are the chosen people of God, if ever he had a chosen people, whose breasts he has made his peculiar deposit for substantial and genuine virtue," he wrote in *Notes on the State of Virginia*. "Corruption of morals in the mass of cultivators is a phaenomenon of which no age nor nation has furnished an example."

This vision of a nation of small farmers has always been largely mythical. Jefferson urged his fellow Americans, "Let us never wish to see our citizens occupied at a workbench, or twirling a distaff," lost in the "mobs of great cities." When he wrote those lines, one in three of his countrymen already lived away from the farm. Many of the rest were on slaveholding farms and plantations in the South, not exactly compatible with Jefferson's ideal.

Today, only 2.8 percent of the American population lives on farms, and fewer than half of these citizens depend on farming as their principal source of income. If independent family farmers are indeed the bedrock of the republic, that foundation has long since been eroded. But the idealization of the family farm persists, along with the impulse to preserve it at whatever cost. These sentiments know none of the usual ideological or partisan boundaries.

Democrat Jim Hightower, a self-styled populist . . . quotes approvingly this characteristically apocalyptic complaint from the National Farmers Organization: "The farmhouse lights are going out all over America. And every time a light goes out, this country is losing something. It is losing the precious skills of a family farm system. And it is losing free men." Over on the other side of the political spectrum, conservative senator Robert Dole strikes a similar pose. "Family farms represent the very essence of what this country is about," he says. "They are the backbone of America." Like Hightower, Dole is worried about the decline of the family farm. "The farms are getting fewer, and the time has come for Congress to act," he argues.

Such emotionally charged pleas tend to strike a responsive chord in Congress, which, in fact, has been acting to protect the family farm for half a century. The array of programs ostensibly designed to preserve the nation's stock of sturdy yeomen has made agriculture the most heavily subsidized sector of our economy. The expense of these programs has grown even as the importance of farms in the economy has inexorably declined— from nearly a tenth of the nation's income in 1933, when most of the existing farm programs were initiated, to 2.6 percent in 1980. Last year the government spent over $11 billion on various forms of farm assistance—virtually all of them justified by pitchforkfuls of "save the family farm" rhetoric.

Even critics of the government's farm policies usually accept the goal of family-farm preservation, tending only to question whether the programs really help the beleaguered family farmer rather than his larger corporate competitors, or arguing simply that the expense has become excessive in a tight-budget era. These concerns are well founded, but they ignore the more basic question: why, exactly, does the tiny fraction of our population that chooses to practice family farming deserve all this solicitude in the first place?

So potent is the traditional image of the family farmer, and so unacquainted are most Americans with the real thing, that his actual characteristics are often ignored. For one thing, farm families are not worse off than their fellow citizens. Fifty years ago, the per capita income of farm dwellers was only 33 percent of the figure for nonfarmers; but since 1971 the recorded income of farm dwellers has amounted to 97 percent of that for nonfarmers, with the average farm family taking home $23,822 in 1980.

But the official figures undoubtedly underestimate the financial health of family farmers, given their ability, as self-employers, to underestimate their income when reporting it to the authorities (not to mention the favorable tax treatment those authorities accord what income farmers do report). Also, statistics on farm income typically include the nearly two million farmers—often retirees or disenchanted urbanites—who farm more as a hobby than anything else. The average income of commercial farmers (those who actually do it for a living) is an impressive $34,000. And the typical farmer (even counting the hobbyists) has even greater wealth than income, largely because he owns, on average, 400 acres of land. That and other assets bring his family's net worth to about $300,000, approximately twice the average for other American households.

In short, today's family farmer is typically not a desperate homesteader, but a sophisticated, relatively prosperous businessman. His success—which is simply the success of American agriculture—should not be resented, but it hardly makes him an obvious candidate for massive government assistance.

Why do we hear so much, then, about the family farmer's decline? The most striking illustration of his plight, supposedly, is the continuing decrease in the number of farms and farmers. At the turn of the century, thirty million Americans lived on 5.7 million farms. By 1979, only 6.2 million people lived on 2.3 million farms. Projecting this trend far enough, it is easy to predict that soon there will be no farmers and no farms. This makes as much sense as assuming that because American fertility rates have declined steadily since the nation was founded, eventually no one will reproduce at all.

The decline of the farming sector is both perfectly natural and wholly beneficial. It reflects two welcome phenomena: the increasing productivity of American farms and the rising living standards of all Americans. Seventy years ago, 106 man-hours of labor and seven acres of land were needed to produce 100 bushels of wheat; today it takes only nine man-hours and three acres. Technological improvements in machinery, fertilizer, pesticides, and seed have made the difference. Hence fewer farmers cultivating roughly the same amount of land as in 1910 can feed a much larger number of people.

Then there is the effect of the growing affluence of the nation as a whole. In a modern economy, the demand for food grows only about as fast as the population—a reflection of the fact that nearly everyone is adequately fed. The demand for other goods and services grows much faster, meaning that more and more people have to work to provide everything from television sets to medical care, while fewer and fewer have to grow food. It says something about the usual picture of farmers being driven off the land by factors beyond their control that the migration accelerates during times of prosperity, not during slumps. (During the Great Depression, the direction of the migration was actually reversed.) A shrinking agricultural population, far from being a sign of decay, is almost invariably a by-product of material progress. The only economies in which farming is stable are the poorest and most primitive, where most people farm because otherwise they wouldn't eat.

By itself, the, the decline in the number of farms, or farmers, is no reason to worry. Some alarmists, however, blame it on the rise of big corporate farms—agribusiness, as the phenomenon is ominously labeled. Trued, farms have gotten bigger, as has nearly every other type of economic enterprise. They have done so in order to take advantage of the economies of scale offered by modern production techniques. Even so, the average farm has increased only 16 percent in size since 1969. There are still 2.4 million farms. In fact, only 8 percent of all U.S. farmland is farmed by corporations, set up mainly to avoid taxes. When you count only nonfamily corporations, the figure dips to one percent. So much for the fear that agriculture is being concentrated in a few corporate hands.

The number of federal programs directed at saving American farmers from extinction will come as a surprise to anyone familiar with the myth of the independent yeoman. Most farmers have their prices guaranteed by the federal price support program, which applies to wheat, corn, barley, oats, rye, sorghum, sugar, peanuts, soybeans, wool, rice, cotton, tobacco, and dairy products—just about everything, in fact. If the market price falls below the level set by the government, the Department of Agriculture in effect buys the farmers' crop. For many crops, it also provides an additional subsidy—"deficiency payments," which pay the farmer the difference between the market (or support) price and a higher "target price." This year, (1982) the support price for wheat is $3.55 a bushel. The target price is $4.05 a bushel. If the market price were $3.30 a bushel, the farmer could sell his crop to the government for $3.55, and then collect an additional fifty cents for each bushel. Most price subsidy programs also require farmers to "set aside" (that is, not plant) part of their land, in an attempt to hold prices up by restricting production.*

It is widely but mistakenly assumed that Washington has gotten tough with farmers since Ronald Reagan took office. Last year Congress *increased* the support price for nearly every farm commodity covered by USDA programs, and provided for additional increases in subsequent years. The wheat price rose from $3.20 to $3.55 a bushel, corn from $2.40 to $2.55, peanuts from $455 to $550 a ton. Congress also enacted a new system of price supports for sugar, supplementing the existing protectionist tariffs on sugar imports. Reagan did propose abolishing "deficiency payments," but these too were kept, and most of the "target prices" were raised. Even the price support program for tobacco—the least defensible subsidy of all—was left alone.

The 1982 budget, the vehicle for so many well-publicized Reaganesque spend-

*President Reagan's version of a "set aside" program is the PIK program introduced in 1983. PIK refers to Payment in Kind. This price support program offers farmers surplus agricultural products which are currently in storage. Farmers are given these surplus stocks if they agree to withhold land from production. It is anticipated that this program will have a double barreled impact on farm prices: surplus or past supplies are reduced and future supplies are reduced. This should result in a rapid increase in the price of agricultural products and of course an increase in the prices paid by consumers.—Eds.

ing cuts, actually raised the Agriculture Department's spending by 45 percent. Reagan's 1983 budget would reduce it by almost that much, but less because of newfound austerity than because his advisers expect higher market prices to reduce the direct cost of various commodity programs. That expectation will almost certainly be proved wrong. And Congress is likely to overrule the administration and provide extra dollars to farmers, who, like everyone else, are suffering the effects of the recession.

Aside from the basic programs designed to guarantee farmers comfortably high prices, the government performs dozens of smaller special favors. The USDA offers numerous loans to farmers—operating loans to buy seed, fertilizer, and machinery; real-estate loans to finance purchases of land; homeownership loans to help low- and moderate-income farmers buy houses; loans to help farmers recover from natural disasters, like droughts; loans to finance soil and water conservation projects; even loans to rural communities to pay for sewers. Most of these loans are made at subsidized interest rates. Farmers can also get direct payments (in addition to low-interest loans) to help them cope with disasters. They can buy crop insurance from the government, again at prices subsidized by the taxpayer. The Rural Electrification Administration, a relic of the Great Depression, still runs a $5 billion subsidized loan program. Farmers in most of the West get water from federal water projects at absurdly low rates. So the government spends billions making arid land fertile and then pays farmers to leave it idle.

Finally, the tax codes have often provided particularly rich soil for cultivating farmers. To avoid imposing administrative burdens on farmers, the tax law permits them to use the cash method of accounting. This allows the quick deduction of capital expenses, while much farm income—from the sale of cattle, for example—gets taxed as a long-term capital gain, at 40 percent of the normal rates. True, farmers once had to worry that the very land that made them wealthy might also subject them to high federal estate taxes when the property passed to the next generation—but their representatives in Washington have helped assuage these fears. Congress has decreed that the value of farmland, for estate tax purposes, may be computed according to a special "use value" formula, rather than by its ordinary market value. This formula cuts the value of a farm estate by more than half, on average. The law also lets farm heirs postpone payment of this reduced tax for up to five years, and then pay in ten installments, on which interest accrues at the luxurious rate of 4 percent.

The purpose of these provisions was to prevent family farmers from having to sell their land to pay taxes. But in 1980 Congress (spurred by farm-belt senators) repealed provisions in the income tax law that would have taxed farmers who *do* sell their inherited land on the full increase in its value since its purchase. (Now they need only pay taxes on any increase in value since the land was inherited.) Finally, in 1981—under pressure from farmers who persisted in complaining about their onerous tax burdens— Congress virtually eliminated the estate tax by creating a flat $600,000 exemption (effective in 1985).

This welter of subsidies and privileges constitutes not a safety net for farmers but a cocoon. Unfortunately, like recipients of most federal benefits (Social Security beneficiaries, veterans, students with guaranteed loans), farmers have come to regard them as something they're entitled to. When commodity prices fall below prosperous levels, farmers pour into Washington to demand action; in 1979 one militant group, the American Agricultural Movement, set fire to a tractor in front of the Agriculture Department in protest. AAM also organized an unsuccessful "farm strike" in 1978 in an effort to extract higher prices for their crops. The reaction to the recession of 1981–82 has been equally predictable, as farm defenders in Congress have introduced a "farm crisis" bill that would increase crop subsidies still further, while restricting production in order to force prices up.

Ironically, the most serious threat to the family farm may come from the measures designed to preserve it. For example, tax treatment of farms has become so favorable that high-bracket nonfarm taxpayers—doctors, dentists, lawyers, and the like—now purchase farmland as a tax shelter. Farmers who own their own acreage are tempted to sell it to such absentee landlords—hardly grounds for pitying the farmers who cash in, but still a threat to the owner-operated farm as an institution. Equally important, the absentee tax shelters frequently bid up the price of land so high that aspiring young farmers are unable to acquire it.

. . . [T]he bigger and wealthier the farmer, and the more distant from the traditional image of the family farmer, the more help he gets from the government. Thirty percent of all government payments go to the 11 percent of farmers with the largest farms, measured in annual sales. This is an especially well-off bunch, with an average household income of nearly $46,894 in 1980 (a bad year, by the way), more than double the median family income in the U.S.

The incentives built into these price support programs aggravate the very problem they are supposed to alleviate. Market prices are lower than farmers would like, mainly because of chronic overproduction. Low prices inform farmers that they are producing too much of a given commodity and encourage them to stop. The artificially high prices established by the Agriculture Department send exactly the opposite signal, stimulating farmers to do more of what got them into trouble in the first place. The government tries to address this contradiction by limiting the amount of land each farmer can plant with a particular crop.* But land is only one factor in the production equation. Each individual farmer can circumvent the acreage restrictions by cultivating the remaining acres more intensively. So when the government reduces the allowable cultivated land by 20 percent, it can normally expect to reduce total output by only half that much. Of course, the techniques of intensive cultivation that this system rewards—primarily the use of more machinery, water, pesticides, and fertilizer—are the very techniques in which larger farms are likely to enjoy an advantage over smaller farms.

Who pays to achieve these questionable goals? Price supports, the centerpiece of the farm programs, exact costs in two ways. Taxpayers have to bear the expense of whatever farm produce the Agriculture Department has to purchase when prices fall below the price support level. (In the last fiscal year, these purchases, along with "deficiency payments," cost more than $7 billion.) But that isn't the end of it. The whole point of the program is to "support" market prices—to keep them artificially high—so

*This is expressly the intent of PIK—Eds.

as to minimize or even eliminate direct government expenses. So consumers pay higher prices in the grocery store for everything from bread to milk to peanut butter. Unfortunately, not all consumers suffer equally. The higher prices act as a regressive tax—placing the heaviest burden on the poor and the lightest on the rich. This is because the lower your income, the greater the share of it you have to spend on necessities like food. It is not an exaggeration to say that, under the price support system, slum children in Harlem go without milk so that dairy farmers in Wisconsin may prosper.

Even if family farms were in danger of extinction, and even if federal farm programs served to preserve them, why should we? We don't try to preserve the family grocery store, the family pharmacy, or the family clothing store, and for good reason. In many industries and businesses, bigger has turned out to be better—better in the sense of providing more and better goods and services at a lower cost to consumers. In a relatively free market, large firms will drive out small ones only when their size allows greater efficiency. Such increases in efficiency are desirable because they raise living standards. If family farms were too inefficient to compete with huge corporate farms (which all evidence suggests they aren't), they would soon disappear in the absence of special aid. That might be unpleasant for family farmers. But it would increase the country's productivity, which tends to make everyone better off.

The usual rationale for aid to family farmers is that it preserves a cherished American tradition of self-sufficiency—a supposed contrast to the gray conformity of life in the corporate sector. But the farm programs preserve the tradition's form without its content. Whatever the hardship and rigors of rural life, farmers are no longer rugged individualists, responsible to no one but themselves. They have become welfare addicts, protected and assisted at every turn by a network of programs paid for by their fellow citizens. In exchange, most farmers allow Washington to dictate much of what they do. They have abandoned independence for security. Today's family farms are to Jefferson's vision what government consultants are to Horatio Alger. If Americans still believe in the virtue of hardy rural self-reliance, they should tell Washington to get out of the way and let farmers practice it.

POSTSCRIPT

Should We Try to Save the Family Farm?

Although the dollar costs of federal farm programs have reached an all-time record, Congressman Dorgan is concerned that too many of these dollars are being diverted from the family farm and ending up in the pockets of large corporate interests. He maintains that if this pattern persists, farms may become too much like our nation's automakers or steelmakers: they may become "too big, too inflexible, and too inefficient to compete" in the world marketplace. Thus, Dorgan argues that to keep our competitive advantage in agriculture, we must preserve the institution that has given us the competitive advantage; we must nurture and protect our family farmers.

Chapman responds that the "decline in the number of farms, or farmers, is no reason for worry," maintaining this is a natural course of events. He argues that farmers and other economic enterprises have gotten bigger so that they can take advantage of "the economies of scale offered by modern production techniques." He goes on to assert that "even if family farms were in danger of extinction"—a proposition he soundly rejects—"why should we try to preserve them?" He contends that in an economy that is driven by markets, inefficient farms, whether they are small family farms or large corporate farms, will be driven from the marketplace. According to Chapman, "that might be unpleasant" for those who go broke, but it "tends to make everybody better off."

Whether you believe the growing presence of corporate agribusiness is a sign of economic growth and vitality or whether you see this as a sign of future economic problems depends upon how you view the presence of imperfectly competitive firms in the marketplace.

The library is filled with books and articles that discuss United States farm policy. Partly, this large amount of literature reflects the importance that we, as a society, have placed upon the values embodied in a rural lifestyle. But, in part, the attention we have paid to agriculture reflects the importance that this sector has played and continues to play in our general economy. For an introduction into agricultural economics and United States agriculture policy, see the following three essays that appeared in the *Monthly Review*, which is published by the Federal Reserve Bank of Kansas City: C. E. Harshbarger and R. D. Rees, "The New Farm Program—What Does It Mean" (January 1974); M. R. Duncan, B. W. Bickel, and E. H. Miller, Jr., "International Trade and American Agriculture" (March 1976); and M. R. Duncan and C. E. Harshbarger, "A Primer on Agricultural Policy" (September/October 1977). Two additional articles addressing the unique problems of agriculture in the early 1980s are: Mary Strange, "Feeding the Farm Credit Crisis," *Food Monitor* (January/February 1983) and Harold F. Breimyer, "Agriculture: Return of the Thirties?" *Challenge* (July/August 1982).

ISSUE 3

Is National Service the Wave of the Future?

YES: David McCurdy, from "Statement by Representative David McCurdy—Committee on Education and Labor," *H.R. 660, The Citizenship and National Service Act* (March 15, 1989)

NO: Steven Altman, from "Testimony Prepared for Joint Hearing on National Service Legislation—Committee on Education and Labor," *H.R. 660, The Citizenship and National Service Act* (April 19, 1989)

ISSUE SUMMARY

YES: Congressman McCurdy co-sponsored H.R. 660 because he believes it will "instill" in the nation's young people "a sense of citizenship" and because it will offer them "educational opportunities."
NO: University president Altman commends the "spirit and intent" of national service, but he rejects H.R. 660 on the grounds that it would "revoke the national commitment to postsecondary opportunities."

In the spring of 1989, eight separate national service bills were introduced before Congress by such legislators as Senator Claiborne Pell (D-R.I.); Senator Barbara Milkulski (D-Md.); Representative Morris Udall (D-Ariz.); Representative Leon Panetta (D-Calif.); Senator Ted Kennedy (D-Mass.); and Senator Dale Bumpers (D-Ark.). Of these bills, none was more important than the Citizenship and National Service Act introduced by Senator Sam Nunn (D-Ga.) and Representative David McCurdy (D-Okla.), whose merits are debated in this issue.

The Nunn-McCurdy Plan would provide vouchers that could be used to offset the expenses of a college education or applied toward the down payment on a home. In order to earn these vouchers, the participant would be required to engage in one or two years of full-time "civilian service" or two years active plus six years reserve service in the "military." While in national service, the participant would earn a nominal income of $100 per week, which would include health insurance.

For fiscal year 1989, six million students in the United States received federal aid totaling approximately $9 billion. The Nunn-McCurdy bill directly challenges the premise of the existing system of educational grants and subsidized loans that are currently in place to provide equal access for all citizens to postsecondary educational opportunities with a minimum number of restrictions or conditions. The new system would explicitly tell high-school graduates that if they want a college education paid for by society, then they have to serve society. After a five-year phase-in period, education grants-in-aid would be conditional on national service.

President Bush has taken steps in the direction of national service by creating the White House Office on National Service. This office is to initiate a program that has been called "Youth Engaged in Service to America."

The bills introduced in Congress and President Bush's actions are a signal that national priorities may be changing. But should they? Should the federal government tie government financial support for higher education to national service? Certainly it appears that policymakers in the executive and congressional branches of government support this as a wise decision. However, many in the education community are concerned that the proposed legislation will undermine the national commitment to equal educational opportunities, even if they support the "positive aims" and "good intentions" of this legislation.

In assessing the merits or lack thereof of national service for young people, you might also want to see if you can relate what you may have already learned in your economics course about the operations of the labor market and about human capital theory to this debate.

YES

Dave McCurdy

STATEMENT BY REPRESENTATIVE DAVE McCURDY—COMMITTEE ON EDUCATION AND LABOR

MR. CHAIRMAN, I appreciate having the opportunity to testify today on H.R. 660, the Citizenship and National Service Act.

For the past several months, H.R. 660 has been the focus of a great deal of debate. It has gained so much attention because it is a radical departure from traditional service and education assistance programs. It addresses many social concerns in a direct and effective manner. It requires a fundamental change in the way Americans view their role in society. Most importantly, this plan offers citizenship and opportunity to our young people.

The results of this debate have been very positive. There has been useful input from community service groups, the educational community, and the military. On Monday, the U.S. Junior Chamber of Commerce endorsed this plan. We have had the opportunity to hear the criticisms and consider their value. I am well aware that no legislation as comprehensive as this is flawless when introduced. With these constructive criticisms, we are developing an effective proposal to best address the issue of national service.

National service presents a framework to effectively address many concerns. Among these are rising postsecondary tuition costs, the skyrocketing default rates on student loans, the declining pool of youth available for military recruitment, the decreasing ability of many young Americans to purchase homes, and the multitude of social needs to be met. This country faces concerns with care of the elderly, illiteracy, health care, child care, and conservation efforts, to name a few. The Citizenship and National Service Act is a way for individuals to serve their country's needs and earn something for themselves in return.

By serving for one or two years in community service or two years in the Armed Forces, an individual can earn vouchers to defray college expenses, to pay for vocational or job training, or to use as a down payment on a home. By

From "Statement by Representative David McCurdy—Committee on Education and Labor," H.R. 660, The Citizenship and National Service Act, 15 March 1989.

participating in a program such as this, a young person can gain a sense of pride and civic responsibility. These are very important considerations.

However, the debate surrounding this issue doesn't revolve around whether or not civic duty and service to the nation are vital tenets of our society. Rather, the debate rests on what the terms of that national service should be.

MR. CHAIRMAN, I want to spare the committee my stump speech on national service. Today, I would like to present and address some of the criticisms of this proposal.

One of the most frequently voiced concerns relates to the education title. Questions focus on the appropriateness of tying federal educational assistance to the performance of national service. We don't apologize for proposing a program of mutual obligation.

Democracy is the cornerstone of our great nation, but it is not free. For each right that is bestowed by democratic principles, there is an obligation owed in return. Federal aid for education should be an earned benefit, not an entitlement.

As an entitlement program, federal college assistance has created a dilemma for many students who otherwise can't afford college. Since 1980, college costs have risen by about 40%, while median family income has grown by only 5%. Simultaneously, the emphasis of federal aid has shifted from grants and work-study to guaranteed student loans, which account for 66% of all aid today as opposed to 21% in 1976. Since 1980, student indebtedness has increased by 60%. A new class of "indentured students" is being created.

There are those who would argue that we need to work for changes within the existing framework of financial aid programs, that the system in place is effective. However, in the face of budget constraints that threaten the very existence of federal educational assistance, it is time to seek a new solution. What we really need is a fundamental restructuring of the system. We have some real obstacles to overcome, and small adjustments aren't the answer.

H.R. 660 proposes a positive overhaul. By tying receipt of federal educational assistance to national service, this legislation allows students the possibility of financing their entire education without incurring debt. It makes educational assistance an earned benefit through service to the nation. This legislation requires a change in our fundamental perception of federal financial aid. I submit that it's time we made that change.

The current financial aid programs are not reaching all of those in need. From 1980 to 1986, the proportion of students from blue collar families enrolling in college dropped by one-fifth. Black enrollment dropped from 34% in 1976 to 25% in 1985; Hispanic enrollment declined from 36% to 27%. This trend must be reversed.

The Citizenship and National Service Act opens new doors of opportunity for these students. It affords many individuals the chance to gain a postsecondary education who might otherwise not be able to do so. At the same time, it increases the benefits available for those already planning to attend.

There have also been suggestions that this legislation targets low-income youths.

In addition to providing educational benefits for students from all economic backgrounds, the legislation also greatly improves opportunities for students from low- and middle-income families. The average Pell grant award for fiscal year 1989 is $1,459. This means that an individual eligible for such a grant is likely to receive only $6,000 for four years of college. That amount covers less than 29% of the average tuition bill. Any additional federal assistance would be in the form of loans. But the young people incurring this debt are those least able to repay. This is evidenced by the increasing student loan default rate. Last year, student loan defaults cost the federal government $1.6 billion.

There have also been concerns expressed regarding the possible hardships this bill might place on non-traditional students.

One important point to remember is the flexibility of the Citizenship and National Service Act. Tying federal student financial aid to national service is a constructive measure. It isn't meant to unfairly discriminate against non-traditional students. The bill contains language to allow individuals over the age of 25 the option of applying directly for guaranteed student loans without having performed national service.

There is also a provision to exempt individuals from service if they are deemed to show "compelling personal circumstances" or have a physical or mental handicap. Compelling personal circumstances include considerations for such things as age, family size or status, and income. For instance, if an individual is 18 years of age and has a child, then the Corporation for National Service would likely deem that person to have compelling personal circumstances. It would not be feasible for that young parent to perform national service and live on subsistence wages. This is just one example to show how the bill considers an individual's particular situation.

It is important to realize that this legislation doesn't eliminate all existing federal financial aid programs. It simply narrows the eligibility criteria for those who may receive the funds.

Another concern relates to the time frame for implementation of this program.

The transition period is an important provision of the legislation. It allows for a five year phase-in period, during which time the program will run on a graduating scale. During this period, national service positions in local communities will be created and filled with volunteer applicants as they are available. If a position is not available, then an individual can apply for federal assistance. This will be a period during which the program can build a strong base of support, and young people can plan ahead for participation in national service.

Many people have asked us: "What about those who don't intend to pursue any form of postsecondary education?"

These individuals are often referred to as the "forgotten half," and they have needs that are just as important. That issue is addressed through use of the voucher as a down payment on a home. Homeownership is one of the American dreams, but it is becoming less of a financial reality for many young Americans.

From 1973 to 1987, the percentage of those under age 25 owning their own home decreased from 23.4% to 16.1%. The Joint Center for Housing Studies of Harvard University in its publication, *The State of the Nation's Housing 1988*, stated that "lower homeownership rates for young adults are found in all regions of the country, not just the high-cost Northeast or West. The continuing high after-tax cash cost of homeownership and the growing rental payments burden are preventing renters in all regions of the country from accumulating the resources needed to make the down payment and meet the initial year carrying costs of homes of their own."

The Citizenship and National Service Act will make it possible for young Americans to overcome the greatest burden to homeownership. It will allow them to earn a voucher for a home down payment. The legislation is a mechanism to assist the "forgotten half" in achieving what may be their greatest hope in life. It will help them own a home. National service can help meet the needs of these young people, and the opportunity should not be missed.

Another of the most frequently heard concerns relates to the effects this legislation would have on the Armed Forces.

The potential benefits of this legislation for the military are enormous. As we enter into the 1990's and beyond, the Armed Forces will be faced with a declining pool of available youth. This means that the military will need to recruit increasingly higher percentages of the available young adult population.

The G.I. Bill has worked and will continue to work exceedingly well as a recruiting tool for the Armed Forces. H.R. 660 is not a replacement for that program. It is simply an additional enlistment benefit option. The military would be able to recruit larger numbers of young people in order to maintain and possibly strengthen its personnel needs.

MR. CHAIRMAN, national service is an idea whose time has come. The principle is a solid one. I offer complete support of initiatives to encourage volunteer participation in kindergarten through the twelfth grade. I believe that altruism is a quality which we must instill in our young people at an early age. Part-time

service also has its place. This legislation, however, goes one step further. It identifies sources of funding, which is the key to an effective piece of legislation. Unlike the other bills proposed here today, when asked where funding will come from, we can point to identifiable sources of funding. That's an important factor.

In order to deal effectively with the issues facing our nation today, a broad structural change must be affected. It is simply not enough to hope for change. We must cause it to happen. The Citizenship and National Service Act provides for the necessary motivating factor.

The Citizenship and National Service Act proposes an effective means to address the national service question. I would encourage you to consider it favorably.

NO

TESTIMONY PREPARED FOR JOINT HEARING ON NATIONAL SERVICE LEGISLATION—COMMITTEE ON EDUCATION AND LABOR

Mr. Chairman and Distinguished Members: I am Steven Altman, President of Texas A & I University. I appreciate the opportunity to present my views and those of the American Association of State Colleges and Universities on several legislative proposals for national and community service.

The message I intend to leave you with today is that we support the positive aims and good intentions of all these bills, to stimulate a sense of service to the nation and the community as an obligation of citizenship. This concept has been a basic tenet of American higher education throughout its history. As educators, we all seek ways to create and advance development—in people, in organizations and institutions, in communities, and in the nation—and so a program of national service can provide an excellent means to achieve these goals. We are proud of our role in establishing, early in the 19th century, teachers colleges to meet what was then described as an emerging need created by a burgeoning public school system committed to equal educational opportunity. Recognizing local and state public needs and acting responsibly to provide educational opportunity with assistance from federal and state sources is characteristic of the 374 AASCU state colleges and universities representing over two and one-half million students enrolled in higher education today.

Texas A & I is a good example of the type of institution created to service the public need. We were founded in 1925 as a teachers college to serve the needs of a large area of South Texas. Over the years our role expanded several times, and today we are a public, comprehensive institution enrolling over 5700 students. We offer a wide range of undergraduate and graduate degree programs. Our student body is 55% Hispanic and 5% Black, figures that exactly match the ethnic/racial profile of the region we serve. For many

From Steven Altman, "Testimony Prepared for the Joint Hearing on National Service Legislation—Committee on Education and Labor," H.R. 660, *The Citizenship and National Service Act*, U.S. House of Representatives, 19 April 1989.

years we have been among the country's top providers of Hispanic engineers, geologists, biologists, chemists, teachers and accountants.

However, South Texas is not only heavily Hispanic, but it is also poor—three of the poorest Metropolitan Statistical Areas (MSA's) in the country are located there. Over 70% of our students qualify for need-based aid, and most who qualify do not receive their full allotment because of restrictions on funds. A large portion of our students are "at-risk," meaning that regardless of intellectual ability, they are in jeopardy of not completing their education and either becoming a cost to society because of their social service needs, or being less than full contributors when the country needs them most. Our attrition rate is high; surveys conducted to determine why regularly indicate that financial problems, family problems, and poor academic preparation are the most frequent reasons for drop-outs. Yet, as a minority institution with strong programs we *are* contributing to the pool of minorities who will be leaders for the future. And we are doing so without the direct federal institutional support enjoyed by the historically black colleges, but our role is equally deserving and just as urgent to the national agenda.

The reason for the urgency is that the Hispanic population is the fastest growing minority group in the country and will continue to be in the foreseeable future. Hispanics are at the same time severely underrepresented in virtually all fields requiring a college degree, and therefore are unable to compete, or more importantly, contribute to the coming labor shortage. The demographic shift now evident in the country creates a situation wherein we must find ways to help these people advance as a matter of national security. The country's ability to compete in world markets can only be fulfilled with an educated workforce. Today, Hispanics do not have the same opportunities to be part of the solution we need. There is a population boom evident among the very young, and we can predict with a high degree of accuracy that the very large numbers of young boys and girls living in the Southwest will grow up! The question is whether we can prepare now for them to take their needed place in the American workforce. With continued high drop-out rates, high incidence of poverty and illness, and several obstacles to educational achievement, they certainly cannot. Given the projections that the U.S. will run out of white males to fill all the jobs we will need by 2005, we believe that Texas A & I, and many others, can do much to help, and we must continue to do so.

It is against this backdrop of the role of AASCU institutions, and some of the compelling national needs that we wish to evaluate and comment upon the issues posed by the Chairman. The several bills which have been introduced contain elements deserving of policy consideration. Framing an integrated omnibus national and community service piece of legislation is what we believe must be done. It must be sensitive to the increasingly diverse nature of our population, have a clear sense of the goals to be achieved, apply fairly and equally to all citizens, and be feasible within budget constraints. Some of the provisions proposed contain troubling elements, and these will be described in a moment. But, in general, the concept of national service can do much to benefit the nation, and support those of us in higher education to build a more educated population.

The following is an examination of the issues which we were requested to address.

1) *Tying service to student financial assistance programs.*

The student financial assistance system, which has been developed with bipartisan support over three decades, is designed to achieve the vital national purpose of assuring postsecondary opportunities to all students who have the ability, but lack the financial resources, to attend the institutions best suited to their needs.

One of the goals of these programs is to stimulate awareness very early in life that higher education is accessible to all able students, even if their families cannot provide the financial resources. Another goal is to enable those who desire short-term vocational programs and credentials other than a bachelor's degree to obtain the skills necessary to support themselves and their families. Millions of students, but most specifically the students at Texas A & I and their families, depend on the federal government to continue its commitment to these programs.

Under most of the legislative proposals, national service would complement the goals of the current student aid programs: volunteers who commit themselves to a term of service would earn benefits that could be used to help meet college costs. The Nunn-McCurdy bill, however, would phase out eligibility for current programs and make national service the sole criterion for assistance to most students. Not only does this single provision cause us to oppose the Nunn-McCurdy bill, it detracts from many of the more plausible aspects of the bill which deserve discussion. Implementing the phase-out of grant and loan financial assistance would revoke the national commitment to postsecondary opportunities established three decades ago, when President Eisenhower proposed legislation which became the National Defense Education Act of 1958. As he said at the time: "The security of the Nation requires the fullest development of the mental resources and technical skills of its young men and women. . . . We must increase our efforts to identify and educate more of the talent of our Nation. This requires programs that will give assurance that no student of ability will be denied an opportunity for higher education because of financial need."

The Nunn-McCurdy provisions would be disastrous for Texas A & I! It would limit enrollment to those few fortunate enough to pay tuition themselves. The forces operating among peers, families, and tradition would move the prospect of college off center stage for many of our students, and we would virtually have to start all over again to build the attitudes needed to prepare these people to attend college.

For those of you who are concerned about whether financial assistance programs are achieving their goals, I invite you to Kingsville to see that it is. Our students' first stop is not the Admissions Office, but rather the Financial Aid Office. This office is where the dream of higher education is matched up to reality. Federal financial assistance is *the* major vehicle for our students to keep their hopes alive, and for our students, and many others, it is working. Without it, the reality of providing true educational opportunity would simple never materialize.

Requiring national service as a precondition for federal student assistance would severely restrict postsecondary opportunities. The Nunn-McCurdy bill is designed to offer 700,000 volunteer positions a year; current federal programs assist some six million recipients, including over two million new students each year. If the program were to be conducted on a scale sufficient to accommodate all current recipients of student aid, it would cost in the range of $30 to $50 billion annually. Even if it was implemented on a smaller scale, my supposition is that most of my students would be cut out of the system because yet another barrier to getting into college would be present. Students today are looking for greater flexibility and more access not more barriers to college. We cannot afford to let that happen.

2) *How high school and college students can be encouraged to participate in youth service programs.*

There is ample evidence to suggest that the concept of national and community service is warmly supported and encouraged by American higher education.

Since 1985, when the Campus Compact was organized as a project of the Education Commission of the States, some 150 institutions in 38 states have joined this coalition to advance community service by sponsoring projects to combat adult illiteracy and tutor academically at-risk elementary and secondary students. Campus Compact recently established state compacts in California, Michigan, and Pennsylvania; others are being organized.

Another network, the Campus Outreach Opportunity League, launched by students in 1984, now numbers 450 colleges and 200 national and local nonprofit organizations. The League sponsors joint workshops, technical assistance, and an extensive variety of community service projects to make such opportunities more readily available to students.

The Partnership for Service-Learning, established in 1982, now numbers 40 colleges and universities whose programs unite academic study and community service, so that the service makes the study immediate and relevant, and the study relates to and supports the service.

Some colleges have established a community service requirement for graduation. In addition to the growing number of service opportunities in college, some private agencies provide Peace Corps-type experience after graduation. For example, some 354 volunteers from 115 public and private colleges are currently serving one-year terms in the Jesuit Volunteer Corps, performing social service work in 58 cities throughout the nation.

At Texas A & I, our students are encouraged and regularly participate in service activities through a variety of interest clubs, fraternal organizations and as a component of our social sciences curriculum.

We have learned a number of lessons from the experiences of institutions about how to encourage participation. Expanding this concept, we ask you to consider the following suggestions:

a) Any program of national service should be voluntary rather than mandatory. "Forcing" service undercuts the principle of volunteerism and ultimately creates resentment. Programs should be constructed which create a sense of value, opportunity, and fair play.

Successful programs rely on plausible incentives (i.e., loan forgiveness, college credit) for participation.

b) Any program of national service should provide supplementary benefits to those who participate. As noted earlier, we oppose a system which would make service a precondition for federal financial aid.

c) Any program of national service should encourage opportunities for service in a variety of forms, for citizens of all income levels.

The bills before the Committee offer a variety of models for addressing this criterion. The Nunn-McCurdy bill specifically includes retired citizens; the Mikulski-Bonior bill and the Kennedy bill in the Senate provide service incentives to citizens of all ages.

To the greatest extent possible, volunteer activities should encourage service-learning experiences which relate the educational process to the real world. Most of the current bills do not place specific emphasis on activities which encourage such a relationship between learning and working in a field relevant to the individual's future career (although the Kennedy bill requires all projects to include age-appropriate learning components for all participants).

Programs for disadvantaged pre-college youth should include a strong component of compensatory education to increase their chances of enrollment in, and successful completion of, postsecondary education. The Dodd-Panetta bill does this by requiring that 10 percent of project funds be earmarked for remedial educational programs while in service.

Academically at-risk students, and all who wish to pursue their education directly, should have options to perform their service after college and throughout their lifetime. Service during college, on weekends and vacation periods, should also be an option, and would appeal particularly to older and part-time students who make up a growing share of college enrollments. The Mikulski-Bonior bill provides such options in the form of service that could be performed two weekends a month and two weeks a year, or on a part-time basis. The Bumpers bill in the Senate offers another incentive for service after college by extending current provisions for loan forgiveness and repayment deferral for service.

d) Any program of national service should be implemented carefully and deliberately.

Several years of careful planning should be provided before a larger-scale program is established, to test the concept on a limited basis and determine how volunteers can be absorbed most effectively at the state and local levels, and what kind of activities are most appropriate.

The most telling example of the need for planning comes in attempting to address the answers to questions like:

1. What capacity does the nation, state, community possess to absorb national and community service recruits?

2. What skill level of training for recruits would be necessary before they engage in community service and who would train them?

3. What impact would having a second "citizen army" have on the nation's armed forces and their ability to recruit for the existing services?

Successful legislation will have to be well integrated to consider pre-college, college, post-college, senior citizens, and even yuppies. The more we think about it, the more complicated it gets. Imagine the consequences of losing public confidence in and support for national and community service because we started our program too quickly, were too ambitious, it cost far too much, and we had no solid evidence from pilot studies or models to show that it would work!

It is fair to ask what we could support as the next step in developing legislation for national and community service. The American Association of State Colleges and Universities and its Council of State Representatives (its elected policy making body) have taken positions on this question. We have stated a position which does support the development of a pilot program meeting these conditions heretofore stated and that the program be undertaken in a group of states representative of the nation. The pilot program should have specific and clear guidelines for implementation to assure equal and fair treatment in each state and should have a carefully designed evaluation component. The pilot program should not require state matching funds since some states that would likely be representative may not be able to afford the match. Finally, the pilot program should supplement rather than supplant federal financial aid programs.

In supporting a pilot program, we nonetheless call attention to the fact that this kind of a program does not address large segments of alienated and disenfranchised youth in our population who do not complete high school and hence would be ineligible to participate in a college-bound type of national service program.

The Pell-Garcia bill is a model for this criterion, offering a limited pilot program to establish a five-year test before considering further legislation. The Dodd-Panetta bill also provides a useful study by a national commission to evaluate the results of the program and make recommendations for changes.

e) Any program of national service should seek to build partnerships with the extensive community service activities already being conducted in the states and localities, educational institutions and public interest organizations.

The above approach will avoid excessive federal regulations and minimize the need for a new bureaucracy. Eligibility determination and oversight of community service programs would be conducted by a quasi-governmental entity with representation from the states and local governments, public and independent colleges, and the private sector.

Like most things in life, people respond, learn and are enthusiastic about activities which are meaningful and which are perceived to be well organized and purposeful. The bills before the committee are sensitive to these needs, and as such, will serve to encourage participation.

3) *How participation in such programs after high school may affect college attendance and persistence.*

Second only to the chilling prospect of supplanting financial assistance programs discussed earlier, this issue raises substantial trepidation for us in the academic community. It is of special concern for those of us serving large minority populations.

Recent research findings (from the National Center for Education Statistics) on college students show that the longer a student delays going to college after high school, the less the chance is that the student will ever enroll in college. Fully three-quarters of 1980 high school graduates who entered a four-year institution immediately and persisted full-time had earned a baccalaureate by 1986; only 21 percent of those who delayed entry had completed the degree by then. For low-income students (who tend to have poorer academic preparation), the completion rate was 8 percent; for high-income students, the rate was 34 percent.

Thus, requiring service before college would be especially damaging to low-income and minority students, who disproportionately come from disadvantaged backgrounds and who will constitute one-third of all school-age children by the year 2000. Creating such obstacles to successful postsecondary education for so many of our youth would also have serious consequences for the national economy: surveys indicate that the vast majority of new jobs created in the next two decades will require some kind of postsecondary education.

The matter is even more severe for Hispanic students. The pipeline is already very leaky. Not only do we face the prospect that 25 percent of high school students (and 45 percent of Hispanics) will not graduate, data from the Hispanic Association of Colleges and Universities (HACU) indicates that only 70 of every 1000 Hispanic students who enter the U.S. education system, on the average, will graduate from college.

Universities like mine are actively involved in pre-college preparation programs for minorities, especially in acute shortage areas like science, math and engineering. We are working hard to get students interested in college and what it means at early ages. And we are staying close to them to promote the transition to higher education by reducing the barriers they face. National service requirements after high school will dramatically undercut these efforts by interrupting the educational cycle.

The problem is serious enough already. For example, transfer rates from community colleges to four-year schools range from 5 percent to 15 percent for Hispanic students, yet 55 percent of all Hispanic students are enrolled in community colleges. The point is that even for those we can encourage to take the next step to a community college, we are still having a difficult time getting adequate persistence. Another interruption will reduce the participation rates even more.

Unfortunately, we daily confront the situation in families that do not share the act of faith that higher education is important for personal and career success. Poverty places a high premium on immediate economic returns, and when one comes from a tradition of doing without, the prospect of further sacrifice is repugnant.

Texas A & I is exerting its resources to attract, motivate and enroll students in activities which might improve the success for graduating students from high school and attracting students to our college. It takes all the resourcefulness we can employ and as many different ways as one can imagine to improve underrepresentation of Hispanic and other minority students in college.

Our research, as well as HACU's suggests that minority student role models are not the visible public officials, athletes, musicians, or even teachers or clergy. For this reason, and not unlike other colleges and universities, we are making great efforts to serve our own communities and families in them, and to direct our service activities there. Hence, volunteer programs in literacy, drug education, and the creation of positive values toward education occupy much of our time. To take students out of these situations and to interrupt the flow to college will have a negative effect on the investment we are making. New barriers and delay are tantamount to cancelling the dream for our prospective students.

4) *Existing service programs that might serve as models for a National Youth Service Policy.*

Several programs were mentioned earlier which provide elements for a national policy. In addition, programs of loan forgiveness for teachers and physicians who satisfy specific conditions have been effective in achieving certain policy goals. Programs which provide incentives and flexibility for the diverse nature of our population will be most successful.

We commend the spirit and intent of the various congressional bills regarding national service, recognizing thereby the value service has to the nation by its citizens, the maturing effect it can have on its youth, the lessening of dependency on loans by college students, and the potential for ingraining the concept of volunteerism as a meaningful aspect of one's life. We support these efforts and stand ready to help.

POSTSCRIPT

Is National Service the Wave of the Future?

Representative David McCurdy pleads with us to return to the traditional American value of service. However, in the McCurdy world, the reward for good citizenship is not left to chance. Rather, those who serve the needs of others earn a reward themselves: They earn a voucher that can be redeemed to offset the expenses associated with attending college or with purchasing a home. For McCurdy, linking federal aid for education with a service obligation is reasonable in a democratic society. Students are not "entitled" to this assistance; they must earn this benefit.

The higher education community does not share McCurdy's enthusiasm for education vouchers. They fear that, in the rush to encourage volunteerism, national service legislation will destroy the notion of equal educational opportunities for all members of society. In particular, they fear "service" will become mandatory for the poor, while the affluent will buy their way out of this national obligation.

Much has been written and will continue to be written about this issue as Congress continues to address it. One source of further information is a volume prepared by the Democratic Leadership Council (DLC), a group of conservative Democrats who are attempting to attract the political right back to their party. Their monograph *Citizenship and National Service: A Blueprint for Civic Enterprise* was published in May 1988. A second group to contact for information is the National Service Secretariat, a Washington, D.C., group that sponsors the Coalition for National Service. Since 1966, this nonprofit organization has acted as a clearinghouse for information and they sponsored the Wingspread Conference in July 1988, which articulated an action agenda for the 1990s. (See *National Service: An Action Agenda for the 1990s*, Washington, D.C.: The National Service Secretariat, 1988.) Other sources are the written statements prepared by those who have testified before the Committee on Education and Labor concerning the topic, "Citizenship and

National Service." These hearings were held during the spring of 1989. Additionally, coverage has appeared in the *Chronicle of Higher Education* (March 15, 1989), the *Wall Street Journal* (October 16, 1989), and, on a continuing basis, in *Experiential Education*—a publication of the National Society for Internships and Experiential Education. One other source might be of value: Charles C. Moshos's *A Call to Civic Service—National Service for Country and Community*. This very informative book was published by Free Press in 1988.

In response to new legislative efforts introduced in Congress in January 1990 that called for a national service corps, Janet Lieberman, a spokesperson for the U.S. Student Association, declared that the measures are a "step backward for student aid." The U.S. Student Association argues that measures to provide college students who volunteer for national service with vouchers for education expenses, or the purchase of a first home, discriminate against lower-income students. They charge that low-income students should be guaranteed access to college and they feel that the provision linking national service to student aid might discourage such students from attending college.

ISSUE 4

Is "Comparable Worth" Worthless?

YES: Clifford Hackett, from "Woman, Work, and the Question of 'Comparable Worth': Better from a Distance," *Commonweal* (May 31, 1985)

NO: Ruth Needleman, from "Pay Equity: Freeing the Market from Discrimination," *An Original Essay Written for This Volume* (January 1986)

ISSUE SUMMARY

YES: Social critic Hackett argues that comparable worth would put an end to the "laws of supply and demand or other economic principles that determine wage rates for different kinds of work."

NO: Labor economist Needleman contends that pay differentials between men and women cannot be traced to differentials in "human capital." She concludes that these differentials must result from discriminatory practices and attitudes.

The term "comparable worth" may be relatively new, but the problem it addresses is quite old: women are and have been paid less than men. Today the pay differential means that the average woman earns about 64 cents for every dollar earned by a man.

This is not a problem that has been ignored by public policy. As early as 1917, the federal government created the War Labor Board in part to handle charges of sex discrimination in the war industries. In the face of these charges, the Board ordered that the wages of women should equal the wages paid to men when the service rendered was equal. During World War II the War Labor Board again attempted to establish the basic concept of equal pay for equal work. This time the Board was less successful. A few corporations, notably Westinghouse and General Electric, persisted in setting different wages for men and women doing equal work.

Although women continued to lobby for federal legislation that would guarantee equal pay for equal work throughout the 1940s and 1950s, this right was not established by Congress until 1963 when the Equal Pay Act was passed. The following year Congress took yet another step toward closing the wage gap by enacting Title VII of the Civil Rights Act which broadly prohibited employment discrimination based upon race, color, national origin, religion, or sex. The net result of these two major legislative initiatives was to establish clearly the right of women to "equal pay for substantially equal work."

Yet more than twenty years after these laws were passed, large wage differentials between men and women still exist. The laws have eliminated most of the blatant discrimination where women and men doing the same jobs are paid different wage rates; but, the law did little to eliminate the alleged discrimination that exists because the vast majority of women hold jobs that are low-paying and traditionally considered to be female jobs.

Proponents of comparable worth argue that on the basis of objective criteria—job skill requirements, job responsibilities, education, training, and experience levels needed—many low-paying women's jobs are as demanding as some high-paying male-dominated jobs. These proponents go on to argue that the only way to correct these wage differences which reflect institutional sex discrimination is to objectively judge each job classification and correct any sex-biased differences that are uncovered.

In 1981, the Supreme Court issued a decision in the *Washington County v. Gunther* case which appears to make it possible to bring these cases to the courts. Additionally, thirty-three states have introduced or are attempting to introduce comparable worth legislation, while six states have implemented explicit forms of comparable worth programs for their public employees. Lastly, a number of trade unions are bringing this issue to the bargaining table.

This groundswell in support of comparable worth has alarmed many free-market economists. They insist, as Clifford Hackett insists, that "comparable worth destroys the link between work and its marketplace evaluation." Proponents of comparable worth, on the other hand, argue that the market reflects "discriminatory attitudes and practices" and these prejudices led to wage rates that are substantially lower in women-dominated occupations than they are in male-dominated occupations.

YES   Clifford Hackett

BETTER FROM A DISTANCE

Should women be paid for jobs on the basis of what men earn in entirely different jobs? The answer would seem to be yes following the federal equal-pay-for-equal-work law of 1963, which laid the ground for improved work opportunities for women. Yet the idea, called comparable worth, is finding it difficult to emerge, as some had predicted it would, as the "issue of the '80s" for women.

The appeal of comparable worth is considerable—especially from a distance. It seems to address a basic economic injustice: men earn more than women whether the measure is annual income, average hourly wages, starting salaries, or concentration in top-paying jobs. This differential also exists within jobs and professions, and persists even as women are moving into new job fields and upward in career tracks. Clearly, comparable worth defenders say, these discrepancies are unfair, perhaps illegal, and should be ended by law.

There is another broad appeal to justice related to the issue: the seeming inability of the free market economy to provide reasonable pay scales crossing vocational lines. Some of us are appalled by plumbers who get $40 for a house call; others are repelled by lawyers who earn $200 an hour. Johnny Carson and NFL football players prompt many to say, "No one can be worth that much!" An unstated comparison in our minds pits these "over-paid" exemplars against those of us who perform the hum-drum jobs which keep the economy going or who (and these are mostly women) undertake the most humane, compassionate, and bedeviling jobs in all societies: nursing, child care, and primary education—all low-paying labors. Is this pay disparity fair? Clearly not.

But the closer one looks at comparable worth, the more doubtful its real value appears. Instead of helping move women into new jobs as the equal-pay law did, comparable worth seems to give up that fight. It pleads for higher pay for women on two quite different, but equally dubious, bases: first, it argues that jobs women actually perform are undervalued and should be upgraded by law; second, it maintains that women's abilities, education, and experience are undervalued and they should get more money no matter *what* jobs they do.

Whatever happened to the premise of equal pay for women, that if women earned the same as men in a particular job category they would more surely compete for those jobs? For many reasons, women still do not always seek the same jobs men do. Comparable worth advocates conclude society must reevaluate the work women do choose. But this revaluing without regard to the job market is at the heart of the comparable worth dispute, the cause of dismay among almost everyone except those who think women would gain from a radical remaking of the economy.

Comparable worth entails assigning numbers to every important aspect of every paying job. Some incredible mechanism of government would then insure that everyone with the same numbers would get the same pay. Who assigns the numbers and weighs job skills against education, experience versus risks, and so on? A committee of personnel experts! But doesn't the open market already perform its own kind of valuation when people put their skills out for examination and competition? Yes, but unfairness results because women's work or women themselves are undervalued.

Let's be clear about what comparable worth is and isn't. It is not about the fact that football players and movie stars earn too much money, but that women make less money than men. Comparable worth is not concerned with the kinds of jobs women do, only how much they earn. Finally, comparable worth is not about job opportunity, job mobility, or job advancement, but about whether the open marketplace for jobs, with its flaws, should be abolished.

What is wrong with this new approach? First, it ignores the source of the problem: the labor pool has an over-supply of women who are available for too limited a number of entry-level jobs. Second, even admitting that economic life is not always fair, who is wise enough to evaluate continuously the varying worths which society applies to jobs? Who will decide, for instance, the worth of four years studying elementary education at a first-class university compared to four years studying engineering at a community college? Who will weigh the relative worth of a super-salesman who actually spends much of his time preparing for a few million-dollar sales a month and a senior secretary whose long hours and mental strain are usually endured under someone else's direct control?

The answer of comparable worth advocates is that these factors be judged by a committee of personnel experts who regularly analyze job content and make comparisons of skills and experience in large firms and within government. Yet such experts as Norman D. Willis, head of a personnel advisory firm which the state of Washington employed in one of the most famous comparable-worth cases, says he recoils at the possibility that his classifications, or anyone else's, should become law.

Even if large numbers of employers were persuaded to apply comparable worth, the concept could not be limited to women alone. It would have to apply to men's jobs as well. Would not church workers and writers, to take just two obvious examples of underpaid professions, have claims on higher pay based on the comparable worth of their education, skills, and contributions to society? It's not hard to see why private employers cannot take seriously the idea of actually setting pay by comparable-worth rules.

Private employers pay the lowest possible wages needed to stay in competition. As long as the competition remains relatively open, workers benefit by maintaining the mobility and skills to move into better paying or more interesting jobs. The two are not always the same, but moving up usually means more demanding work. It may include not only greater skills but longer or irregular hours, and sometimes higher risks. Firefighters are paid for risking their lives in a pattern which alternates boredom with real danger. Most workers do not desire such a life, and those who do are thus able to demand higher wages and earlier retirements. Often the demands consist of entrance hurdles, like bar exams, advanced degrees and other qualifiers. Comparable worth proponents are sometimes accused of "credentialism" for seeking more pay for those women, like nurses and librarians, who also face educational hurdles for qualifications. But the pay which women, as well as men, receive is based not only on the credentials but also on market competition. If women want higher wages, they soon learn to avoid jobs with many qualified competitors, whether men or women. Why should employers pay librarians as much as electricians when the supply of the former will produce ample numbers at little more than the minimum white collar wage, while electricians are almost always scarce and, therefore, expensive?

Facing great hostility in the private sector, comparable worth has moved with some success into closed markets like state and local government where worker and union pressures combine with trendy political constituencies. Minnesota, a progressive state by most standards, recently passed laws requiring a study of job characteristics of all government jobs, state and local, and set aside money to start applying the program. In San Jose,

California, a similar plan was initiated with $1.5 million for pay equity adjustments. What is wrong, then, with these plans, especially if they have public support?

The long-term problem is that comparable worth destroys the link between work and its marketplace evaluation. In the private sector, this linkage is vital to keep a company competitive. In government, paying secretaries without regard to their cost in the local job market destroys confidence in government's ability to match the efficiency of business. Eventually, elected officials will have to account for the pay of their secretaries and their plumbers. If the secretary earns premium pay in order to match the plumber's wage, private sector workers who pay the taxes will object. It is not possible, over the longer term, to have pockets of comparable worth in an otherwise competitive economy without problems.

Take the case of San Jose. It conducted a jobs study as the result of a strike over comparable worth. The study concluded that both librarians and electricians were worth $3,000 a month. In the local, competitive economy, however, librarians could be hired for much less while electricians in the area were paid more. The city must now pay electricians more than the study said they were "worth," while librarians are being paid above-market salaries. With victories like that, comparable worth will eventually fall of its own weight.

Behind all the arguments and the tactics of the comparable worth debate is the strong conviction that discrimination against women is a major factor in the labor market. But a careful look at female employment proves inconclusive on this point. Labor economists start by identifying known differentials on jobs and pay by sex, race, age, and occupational group. They weigh factors like intermittent and part-time work, interruptions for pregnancies, and other causes for lower pay for women. But because of the complexities in the job market there are always too many "other" or "unknown" factors of such analyses to explain the residual differential of lower pay for women. Yet, this inconclusive method of reductional analysis is at present the only "proof" of discrimination against women.

A recent article in a U.S. Labor Department journal by Janice Shack-Marquez, a federal economist, says, "Most of the studies of the pay disparity between men and women have been motivated by a desire to quantify the effects of discrimination in the labor market on women's earnings." Labor market discrimination, she notes, may be only one answer, of undetermined importance, in assessing women's lower pay. The pay difference, she says, is much smaller when narrowly-defined white collar jobs are compared for men and women than in broader studies. Ms. Shack-Marquez says "not enough is known" about individual earnings "to be confident that all the labor market variables in which men and women differ have been isolated."

No such caution animates the comparable worth advocates. Editors of a recent book *Comparable Worth and Wage Discrimination* (Temple University Press, $39.95, 311 pp.) note that the authors, mostly women, represent a "broad spectrum" of views on the issue. Yet they agree that salary disparities between male- and female-dominated jobs "are based in large part on discrimination."

For the women's movement itself, comparable worth seems a very depressing course to take. To back the principle that women must be paid more because

they are women implies a pessimism about the chances of full integration of women in the job market. If women can compete, this argument goes, they will; otherwise, they want to doctor the system so that the work they do gets more pay through government or judicial fiat.

Comparable worth advocates answer this argument in several ways, none fully cogent. First, they say, this competition of women in a men's job market will be enhanced if women in lower-paying jobs get the same pay as comparable men. Employers would then choose workers by merit, not gender. Second, the predominance of women in some low-paying jobs—retail clerking, secretarial and clerical work, child care and domestic work—has patterned so many women for so long that many are now too old to be retrained. Third, pay equity advocates say, these jobs are undervalued simply because women hold them. Why should women, who like to nurse or teach school, change jobs just to earn as much as men with comparable skills, education, and experience? Society is, in fact, subtly undervaluing jobs only because women perform them. And that, advocates say, is discrimination.

Correcting this discrimination will not bankrupt the country, proponents of comparable worth say, pointing to several cases where the system has been applied to government and private organizations. But these instances provide thin gruel to nourish the cause. While the only large-scale case, involving the state of Washington, is still in the courts, state taxpayers may have to pay over $1 billion if the suit prevails. The Washington state legislature's study of state jobs, which used the Willis scale, concluded that women's work was underpaid. Yet the governor's request for funds to implement the study was rejected in a budget crisis. The federal judge who heard the case decided that the state acted in bad faith by commissioning a study whose findings of pay discrimination were then not implemented. The state is certain to appeal the decision to the Supreme Court.

Even if the Washington state decision is sustained and the state government gets a huge bill for back wages, the case's impact on comparable worth remains unclear. Failure to pay, not the principles of comparable worth, are at issue here. Federal courts have, in several other cases, specifically excluded comparable worth from decisions about pay differences between men and women.

In a major decision in 1977 (*Christensen v. Iowa*), the Supreme Court cited the attempt to use the Civil Rights Act of 1964 as a basis for comparable worth. It rejected this approach saying: "We find nothing in the text and history of Title VII (of the Act) suggesting that Congress intended to abrogate the laws of supply and demand or other economic principles that determine wage rates for different kinds of work." Even in the 1981 *Gunther* case, cited most often by women as holding the door open for comparable worth actions, the Supreme Court said that the women prison guards' claim of lower pay because they were women "is not based on the controversial concept of 'comparable worth.'"

In order to make progress and to avoid another stalemate like the ERA, comparable worth advocates will have to either change the law or convince judges that existing laws require comparable worth interpretations. Neither the mood of the present Supreme Court, nor the explicit scorn of the Reagan administration is promising in this regard.

Over a dozen states have passed laws which refer to comparable worth, pay equity, or similar goals in their civil service systems, but most of these laws are too new or too vague to have established comparable worth up to now. Minnesota's 1982–83 laws on the subject were backed with an initial appropriation of $27 million to adjust state salaries. Until further studies are done, no one knows what the total cost to the state and its local governments, also covered, will be.

Comparable worth is like the parable of the golden egg. If its advocates insist on using political pressures to pay women in government more than wages in the private sector, cities and states will eventually react to increased costs by contracting much of "women's work" to the private sector.

In conclusion, if comparable worth seems such a mistaken solution for misconceived problems, here are several principles with which to insure that maximum benefits accrue to women in their search for true pay and job equity:

* *Not every difference between men and women in the job market comes from malevolent causes.* Even if we reach the most perfect system of job access and pay for women, there may still be important differences in both the jobs they hold and what they earn. The values that women share may always be different from those of men. Anticipation of motherhood, its arrival, and its consequences will always affect women in the job market. Women's values, and the jobs they embody, are important for society and for the women who perform them, even when the pay is not high.

* *Economic rewards are not the only measure of job value for women or men.* Many male-dominated jobs also pay less than others with lower investments of

skills, education, and experience. The churches, the universities, art, and the government often pay less than business and industry. But pay, for these lesser-paid workers, is fortunately not the only consideration in their jobs.

- *Choosing motherhood may not be fully compatible with other career choices.* This is such an old truth that it may *have* to be completely forgotten so we can learn it again. Yet many women know this before motherhood or shortly after. This fact of maternal life is not, in itself, unfair or a matter for the courts to handle. But motherhood should not bar the maximum participation a woman wants in the job marketplace. A genuine problem, worth some of the attention given to comparable worth, is how mothers of all ages can gain and hold such participation without sacrificing, jeopardizing, or postponing motherhood.

- *Comparable worth may have some benefits as an ideal if it leads toward better job integration.* Even if most plumbers will always be men and most day-care workers women, society benefits when rigid job segregation by sex is softened. First, most women do not want to be shunted away, by gender, from certain jobs even if they choose other work. Second, men and women complement each other in social values, temperaments, and sensitivities. This relation may help and almost certainly does not hinder any workplace, even if not all jobs are interchangeable.

- *Women should consider more selective and specific approaches to better pay and job integration.* In Colorado, nurses sought better wages through comparable worth action but lost in court. When they went on strike, however, they won. Job actions—whether in a single job, in one business or industry at a time, or nationwide—will probably command more attention and get more results in the long term than the murky concepts of comparable worth.

- *There will be no revolution in the workplace no matter what the strategy.* There have been important changes this century in women's wages which have risen faster than men's since 1900, according to a recent Rand Corporation study. The sixty cents a woman earns today, on average, to a man's dollar, will rise to seventy-four cents by the end of the next decade. But the competing interests of blacks, Hispanics, and others who want to change the job market according to their legitimate grievances will prevent a clear field for women. Black women, for example, have now closed the wage gap with white women. Black men, however, hold many of the male-dominated blue collar jobs which comparable worth proponents cite as examples of unfairly high pay. Further, the private sector has so far largely ignored the comparable worth approach as a frothy concoction of no import. If state or court actions move toward serious implementation of the concept, a fierce reaction to the perceived threat against the free market will come. This assault against comparable worth could make the ERA debacle look mild by comparison. To avoid this course, more measured, more confident, and more reasonable goals are needed for women.

One unspoken premise of the comparable worth fight is resentment against the male domination of the political, social, and economic life of our society. However, the appropriate response to this male dominance is a realistic demand for fairness to women in the job market, not a casually conceived and marginally tenable idea like comparable worth.

NO
Ruth Needleman

PAY EQUITY: FREEING THE MARKET FROM DISCRIMINATION

Why are women paid only 64 cents on the average for every dollar paid to men? Is this wage difference the inevitable result of a "free market" system at work? Or, on the contrary, have discriminatory attitudes and practices influenced wage-setting as they have influenced employment opportunities in general for minorities and women?

The controversy surrounding this question has centered on the issue of pay equity or comparable worth. These two interchangeable terms refer to the policy of equal pay for comparable work; a policy that holds that a job should be compensated based on objective criteria like skill, education, training, responsibility and work conditions and not on the race or sex of those who traditionally perform the job. The goal of pay equity is to eliminate sex and race-based wage discrimination from the labor market.

Consider this example of sex-based wage discrimination: The Department of Labor compiles a *Dictionary of Occupational Titles* (DOT) which includes ratings for each job category. Ratings are used in establishing wage scales. Dog pound attendants and zoo keepers, according to the DOT, are rated more highly than nursery school teachers and day care workers. Research undertaken to identify how the DOT ranked job-related skills found that the Department had not even counted skills associated with taking care of children. In contrast, skills associated with caring for animals had received high point scores. Why? Because the Department of Labor decided that knowing how to care for children is not a job-related skill, since it involves qualities intrinsic to being a woman.[1]

AT&T provides a second example. The company carried out a job evaluation study of all positions, including managerial. In assessing skills and attributing points, the company ranked "customer contact" extremely high for its managerial staff, but failed to count "customer contact" when it evaluated its telephone operators. As a result, the study ranked the operator's job low in points and recommended an equally low wage. Criticized for setting up two separate standards, one for a male-dominated profession and another for a female-dominated one, AT&T acquiesced and upgraded the job ranking and wages for its operators.[2]

Contrary to what opponents claim, pay equity does not demand that traditionally women's jobs be paid the same as men's regardless of the work performed and skills required. What pay equity addresses is the discrimination that has resulted from continued and pervasive sex segregation in the labor market. Despite civil rights legislation and the development of affirmative action programs, women have not made significant inroads into the male-dominated sectors of the job market. An overwhelming majority of women—nearly 80%—still work in jobs traditionally considered female; 55% are employed in two occupational groups alone, clerical and service. The Equal Pay Act of 1963 is designed only to eliminate discrimination in pay where women and men are employed to do the same or similar work. But most women perform different work, though often comparable in terms of requirements, responsibilities and tasks.

The fact is women's work has been systematically undervalued and wages *artificially* depressed. Why else would a nurse, with a college degree, responsible for human life, working weekends and rotating shifts, be paid only 75% of the salary, say, of a vocational education teacher, a job rated as equivalent by a Minnesota job evaluation study?[3] Less than 3% of all employed women earn over $50,000 a year, but more than 50% earn between $3,000 and $15,000 annually.[4] Pay scales for jobs held predominantly by women are across-the-board 20–30% lower than pay scales for male occupations.

WHAT ACCOUNTS FOR THE WAGE GAP?

Pay equity cannot and is not meant to eliminate all wage differentials. There are many legitimate factors involved in determining wage scales which have contributed to the earnings gap between women and men. Unionization is one of them. Membership in a labor organization generally insures a worker wages 30% above the industry average. Not as many women as men are unionized— although two-thirds of all new union members in the last decade are women— and those occupations traditionally dominated by women are among the least unionized. Nevertheless, since only 18% of the U.S. workforce is unionized, this particular factor has had only minimal impact on average earnings.

Human Capital Variables

Unquestionably, factors like education and training affect one's ability to earn money. Critics of pay equity, however, tend to attribute the wage gap almost entirely to human capital variables. Were it not for the differences in labor force attachment, education and skill levels, the argument goes, women's earnings would not lag behind men's. What's more, some opponents would add, women have chosen to enter the lower-paying jobs as part of a trade-off for other advantages like shorter hours, easier work and employment more "suitable" to a woman. It is worth examining each of these points to determine which factors actually contribute to the wage gap and which ones reflect gender-based myths and stereotypes.

Labor Force Attachment: For decades employers have viewed women as temporary workers, taking a job until marriage and then remaining at home throughout their child-rearing years. A Westinghouse manual on wages pointed to this pattern of female work behavior as the reason for the company's own lower and separate wage scales for women:

> The gradient of the women's wage curve is not the same for women as for men because of the more transient character of the service of the former, the relative shortness of their activity in industry, the differences in environment required, and extra services that must be provided, overtime limitations, extra help needed for the occasional heavy work, and the general sociological factors not requiring discussion herein.[5]

Although arguments such as these still have their adherents, they lack substance. Developments over the past two decades have radically altered women's labor force participation. In the last ten years alone, more than 11 million women have entered the job market. Women of childbearing age and mothers in particular have sought jobs outside the home in greater numbers than ever before. Forty percent of all new women workers since 1970 are mothers, and 58% of women with children under 18 work. As a result, women's average worklife is increasing dramatically. As recently as 1950, a 26-year gap separated the average worklife of a woman from that of a man. By 1960, however, the difference had closed to 21 years; by 1970, to 17, and by 1977 there was only a ten-year difference. For women entering the labor market today, their worklife expectancy is almost identical to men's.[6]

Are women more inclined than men to switch jobs? Statistics indicate that workers in low-paying and dead-end jobs are more likely to have higher turnover rates, but that this behavior is related to work status and not gender. Nonetheless, men in such jobs have demonstrated higher turnover rates than women, especially during their first years in the labor market.[7]

Education: Among the human capital arguments most commonly used to account for wage differentials are those related to educational levels and previous work experience. According to an editorial in one Indiana newspaper: "women with credentials and experience comparable to their male counterparts make at least as much on the average."[8] Nothing could be further from the truth. The Bureau of Labor Statistics estimates that the median income of a woman with postgraduate college experience is less than the median for a male with a high school diploma. More than half of all women college graduates earn *less* than a male high school dropout with eight years or less of education.[9] Even in cases where experience is also comparable, for example in entry-level jobs, the disparity is striking. A recent study of Harvard graduates sets the average salaries for male graduates of the School of Public Health at $37,800 a year and for women at $21,300.[10]

Former Secretary of Labor and economist Ray Marshall maintains that "less than half of the gross earnings differentials can be accounted for by such human capital factors as education, training, experience and skill requirements."[11] Average occupational earnings tend to vary inversely with the percentage of women among job-holders regardless of human capital factors.

The Free Market Argument

Discounting discrimination as a factor, pay equity opponents resort to a combination of "free market" theory and gender-based stereotypes to explain away the remaining wage gap. For example, the chairman of the University of Chicago's Economics Department recently argued that women selected jobs in areas like health care since they "appealed to women with homemaking responsibilities because they are less strenuous and provide more flexible hours than factory work."[12] In reality, this statement has very limited validity. Hospital work generally has worse hours and schedules than most factories. Weekend work and rotating shift schedules are extremely common. The work, moreover, is not only physically but emotionally strenuous, without much in the way of monetary compensation or other benefits.

Critics of pay equity are concerned, above all, with what they perceive as a threat to the free market system. They are wrong, in the first place, in assuming that a free market economy still exists. Second, it is equally incorrect to assume that the impersonal forces of supply and demand actually determine wage levels. Since the emergence of trusts and monopolies toward the end of the nineteenth century, accompanied by an increase in government regulation, a very *modified* market economy has replaced laissez-faire economics. Corporate price and wage-fixing and control over product markets occur routinely in the global marketplace. One example of wage-fixing surfaced during court hearings on a comparable worth suit in Denver: nurses introduced evidence proving that hospital administrators citywide had been meeting each year to decide wage rates.

Supply and Demand: The role of supply and demand in setting pay scales deserves more comment. Women receive lower wages in traditionally female jobs, according to the free market proponents, due to an oversupply of qualified workers. If a plumber, for example, receives more than a librarian, it is because the market places greater value on scarce resources, i.e., the plumber. But, if this were really the case, what then would account for the low wages of nurses and teachers, even during years of critical shortages? When the supply of nurses dipped far below the demand, hospital management did not boost salaries to attract additional job-seekers. Instead they worked through the media and educational institutions to lure more people into nursing careers, while, at the same time, relying on the government's help to encourage thousands of foreign-born nurses, particularly Filipinas, to accept jobs in the U.S. at even lower than market rates.

A similar manipulation of supply occurred during the 1950s, when industrial expansion absorbed large numbers of minority workers who had been farm laborers. Agribusiness did not allow wages to rise to draw these workers back into the fields; they pressured the government to negotiate a farm-labor program (*Bracero* Program) with Mexico to open the borders to immigrants during the harvest. Average wage levels declined as a result of the program. In both examples, sex and race discrimination interfered with how supply and demand set wages; pay equity, in contrast, would "free" the market from that kind of intervention.

Government Intervention
Equally central to the free market argument is the resistance to outside or government intervention. Employers have always opposed government reforms affecting labor markets. Despite protests, though, restrictions on child labor, as well as fair labor standards, minimum

wage and civil rights legislation have been passed to prevent employer abuses. With pay equity, many critics fear that "some incredible mechanism of government" will be established to dictate wage rates to private employers. More than other arguments, this one involves the gravest distortion of fact. No pay equity suit or advocate has called for government action in wage-setting in the private sector; nor has anyone suggested that wage rates should or could be established according to national standards.

Job Evaluation

One of the most common procedures for determining wage scales in the private and public sector is job evaluation and work measurement. Because employers value jobs differently, because jobs and requirements vary from one employer or industry to the next, no absolute standard would be feasible. Job evaluations are generally carried out by individual employers, involving two dimensions: 1.) an internal one looking at the relative value of jobs within a single firm; and 2.) an external one looking at the value of a job with respect to prevailing labor market rates. According to the National Research Council of the National Academy of Science:

> Paying jobs according to their worth requires only that whatever characteristics of jobs are regarded as worthy of compensation by an employer should be equally regarded irrespective of the sex, race or ethnicity of job incumbents.[13]

In cases where a job evaluation study has led to a pay equity settlement, it was the employer who commissioned the study. Perhaps the most famous case occurred in Washington State, where job evaluation studies were undertaken by the government. The results indicated that

female-dominated occupations were paid on the average 20–35% less than male-dominated occupations regardless of their evaluated worth. An LPN, for example, was rated equivalent to a campus policeman in terms of total points, based on skills, education, responsibility and work conditions. The jobs themselves were not compared. But an LPN earns only $739 a month, 69% of a campus policeman's salary. The gap, according to the study, was not due to any productivity-related job content or to supply and demand factors in the market. The gap resulted from sex-based wage discrimination.[14]

Legal Status

. . . As early as 1981, in *County of Washington v. Gunther*, the Supreme Court found that intentional sex-based wage discrimination was illegal under Title VII of the 1964 Civil Rights Act, and that similar cases could be brought under Title VII, since they did not meet the strict eligibility requirements of the Equal Pay Act. Those who argue that pay equity suits have no legal basis are relying on a distorted definition of pay equity/comparable worth, built on the idea of general across-the-board job comparisons rather than on concrete job evaluation studies. While it is true that federal court justices have refused to do job comparisons, because they lack both the authority and the expertise, they have consistently accepted employer job evaluation studies. In fact, they have ruled that a discrepancy between the evaluated worth of a job and its actual pay level constitutes evidence of intentional discrimination.

One further objection to comparable worth involves the cost; some employer groups are estimating a price tag of $2 to

$150 billion. Their assumption, however, is that all pay equity settlements would be made at one time. But, as has occurred with all social reforms, pay equity adjustments are being implemented gradually over many years. The Minnesota legislature, for example, appropriated 1.25% of its annual personnel budget for the *first phase* of a settlement. A formula for future allocations has been jointly negotiated by labor and management. Many of the current settlements have, in fact, been voluntarily agreed to through collective bargaining.

IS PAY EQUITY
ONLY A WOMEN'S ISSUE?

Although sex and race-based wage discrimination involves occupations historically dominated by women or minorities, all current employees in such jobs are affected. Not only have men benefitted from pay equity settlements, but the number of male beneficiaries is increasing as men are forced to seek work in traditionally female job areas. Over the past decade, with the decline in blue-collar manufacturing jobs, even more men are becoming telephone operators, nurses and public school teachers. For them, pay equity is no less a priority.

Pay equity is also a family issue. Faced with a deteriorating standard of living, many families could not have made ends meet without the addition of a woman's wage. Over 55% of married women are in the labor force. Yet 50% of all two-wage earner families have incomes *under* $25,000 a year. Families headed by women are in much greater financial trouble. Department of Labor figures place one-third of all these families below the poverty line; 80% of female-headed families earn under $15,000.[15] Any measure to reverse the effects of sex-based wage discrimination will have a long-term positive effect on the family.

Is equal pay for comparable work a viable policy? Not only is pay equity viable and an important vehicle for reducing discrimination in the job market, but it is currently being implemented. Thirty-three states have pay equity legislation passed or pending, and existing pay equity settlements are beginning to exert pressure on wage structures in surrounding labor markets. Pay equity is an idea whose time is already here.

NOTES

1. Witt, Mary and Patricia K. Naherny. *Women's Work: Up From 878—Report on the DOT Research Project.* Madison: Women's Educational Resources, University of Wisconsin-Extension, 1975.

2. Steinberg, Ronnie J. " 'A Want of Harmony': Perspectives on Wage Discrimination and Comparable Worth," in *Comparable Worth and Wage Discrimination,* ed. Helen Remick. Philadelphia: Temple University Press, 1984, p. 22.

3. Grune, Joy Ann and Nancy Reder, "Pay Equity: An Innovative Public Policy Approach to Eliminating Sex-based Wage Discrimination," in *Public Personnel Management,* 12, 4 (1983), p. 398.

4. U.S. Department of Labor, *Time of Change: 1983 Handbook on Women Workers.* Bulletin 298. Washington, D.C., pp. 51–57.

5. Steinberg, p. 8.

6. Smith, Shirley J. "New Worklife Estimates Reflect Changing Profile of Labor Force," in *Monthly Labor Review,* 105, 3 (March 1982), pp. 15, 17 & 18.

7. Kanter, Rosabeth Moss. "The Impact of Hierarchical Structures in the Work Behavior of Women and Men," in *Women and Work* ed. Rachel Kahn-Hut, Arlene K. Daniels and Richard Colvard. New York: Oxford University Press, 1982, pp. 234–35.

8. "Dangerous Policy Is on the Horizon," *The Times.* Hammond, Indiana (May 29, 1985).

9. *Time of Change,* p. 98.

10. Marshall, Ray. *Women & Work in the 1980's.* Washington, D.C.: Women's Research and Education Institute of the Congressional Caucus for Women's Issues, 1983, p. 16.

11. ibid.

12. Becker, Gary S. "How the Market Acted Affirmatively for Women." *Business Week* (May 13, 1985), p. 16.

13. Milkovich, George T. "The Emerging Debate" in *Comparable Worth: Issues and Alternatives* ed. E. Robert Levernash. Washington, D.C.: Equal Employment Advisory Council, 1980, p. 70.

14. Steinberg, p. 17.

15. Levitan, Sar A. and Richard S. Belous. "Working Wives and Mothers: What Happens to Family Life?" *Monthly Labor Review*, 104, 9 (September 1981), p. 29 and *Time of Change*, p. 19.

POSTSCRIPT

Is "Comparable Worth" Worthless?

Free-market supporter Clifford Hackett submits that comparable worth laws and regulations represent a direct attack upon the free market. He reasons that wages are low in some occupations because there is an excess supply of labor in those areas. If we were to artificially increase wage rates in these occupations, the problem would only be worsened. Even more women would gravitate to those occupations that are already overpopulated. This can only result in more downward pressure on the wage rate. Finally he is amazed that anyone would seriously think that "some incredible mechanism of government" could assign wage rates more efficiently and equitably than the time-tested and honored market mechanism.

Labor economist Ruth Needleman challenges the assertion that pay differentials between men and women are the result of differentials in human capital—skill, education and training levels. Although the free market is supposed to capture these differentials, the market simply fails when it comes to assigning appropriate wage rates in traditional women's occupations. Her survey of the empirical evidence in this field suggests that "earnings tend to vary inversely with the percentage of women among job holders regardless of human capital factors." Thus for Needleman there are a number of myths and misconceptions surrounding the causes of the wage gap: (1) human capital differences can't explain this gap; (2) women's worklife is now nearly as long as men's; (3) the market is really not free to set wage rates; (4) low wages in some occupations is not traceable to an oversupply of labor; and, (5) government intervention will not distort the free market.

Much has been written about the advisability and inadvisability of comparable worth. An excellent introduction to this topic by an advocate of comparable worth is in Helen Reinick, ed., *Comparable Worth and Wage Discrimination* (Temple University Press, 1984). The opposition's arguments are well argued in E. Robert Levernash, ed., *Comparable Worth: Issues and Alternatives* (Washington, D.C., Equal Employment Advisory Council, 1980). An extremely readable and informative set of Congressional hearings is found in U.S. Congress, Hearings before the Subcommittees on Human Resources, Civil Service, Compensation and Employee Benefits, Committee on Post Office and Civil Service, *Pay Equity: Equal Pay for Work of Comparable Worth*, 97th Congress, 2nd session, 1982.

ISSUE 5

Are There Too Many Hostile Takeovers?

YES: Gerald L. Houseman, from "The Merger Game Starts with Deception," *Challenge* (September-October 1986)

NO: John D. Paulus and Robert S. Gay, from "U.S. Mergers Are Helping Productivity," *Challenge* (May-June 1987)

ISSUE SUMMARY

YES: Political science professor Houseman asserts that the economic rewards that are reaped by Wall Street takeover artists come at the expense of workers, stockholders, and the general public.

NO: Business economists Paulus and Gay argue that the corporate restructuring of the 1980s is a direct result of the need to increase productivity in the face of declining U.S. competitiveness.

The wave of mergers and acquisitions in the 1980s raises many questions. What laws and court decisions control acquisitions and mergers? What is the difference between the current merger movement and the mergers and acquisitions that took place before the 1980s? And finally, do friendly mergers and acquisitions have the same economic consequences as unfriendly, or hostile, takeovers?

The answers to these questions are found in part in our economic history. Mergers and acquisitions have appeared in four waves. Just before the turn of this century the first great merger movement dominated the economy. The Whiskey Trust, the Sugar Trust, the Cotton-Oil Trust, the Standard Oil Trust were attempts to pull together small and larger firms into new business organizations that could act collectively to reduce supply and increase price. Since Congress concluded that these new business organizations could inflict abuses upon society, which were in direct conflict with the tenets of a free-market economy, Congress passed its first antitrust legislation, the Sherman Act of 1890.

But this act did not slow the approach of the second wave of mergers and acquisitions that appeared shortly after World War I. This wave had many of the same characteristics as the first wave. Business combinations were generally in the form of horizontal mergers (mergers of firms at the same stage of production within one industry, such as merging two steel manufacturers). At the same time, however, two new forms of mergers and acquisitions began to appear: vertical mergers (mergers of firms at different stages of production within one industry, such as merging a firm that manufactures shoes with another firm that is a retail chain) and conglomerate mergers (mergers between a firm in one industry and a firm in a totally different industry, such as the merger of an oil company with a department store chain). In the face of this second wave of mergers and acquisitions, Congress attempted to strengthen the Sherman Act by passing the Clayton Antitrust Act of 1914.

The third wave of mergers and acquisitions took place from 1948 to 1979. The Federal Trade Commission (FTC)—the federal agency that is responsible for assuring competitive markets in the U.S.—estimates that of the more than 2,000 large mergers in manufacturing and mining that occurred in this period, three-fourths of these mergers and acquisitions were conglomerate mergers.

Lastly, and of immediate importance for this issue, is the fourth wave of mostly hostile takeovers that began to appear more and more frequently in the 1980s. In these cases, the acquiring firm is able to complete the merger without the aid and cooperation of the acquired firm. This is usually accomplished by quietly buying a controlling quantity of the acquired firm's publicly held stock. Since the threat of a hostile takeover constitutes a direct challenge to the management of the acquired firm, management is forced into evasive action. In extreme cases, this results in the payment of green-mail—buying back the stock from the corporate raider at inflated prices. Thus corporate raiders such as Rupert Murdock, the Bass brothers, and T. Boone Pickens have made huge speculative gains by merely *starting* to acquire the stock of an unsuspecting firm.

In self-defense, firms have pushed their state legislatures for laws that would protect them from unfriendly advances. Currently, twenty-one states restrict unfriendly takeovers and more states are likely to follow since the Supreme Court has upheld in the Arvin Case (1987) the right of states to regulate takeovers. On April 21, 1987, in a 6 to 3 vote, justices from both the conservative and the liberal sides of the Court joined retiring Justice Lewis Powell in his majority opinion that state action in this area was not a burdensome infringement on interstate commerce.

The success in state legislatures has encouraged others to push for federal legislation that would protect firms in all fifty states from hostile takeovers. Even if this does not occur, some professionals, for example Gerald L. Houseman, maintain that much "could be accomplished without enacting any new laws." He argues that the present state of affairs demands that we utilize the antitrust tools that we already have at hand. Paulus and Gay would be horrified by the prospect of renewed antitrust action. They maintain that the "corporate restructuring" that has occurred in the 1980s represents our "best hope for resolving our current trade problems" and for keeping "inflation remarkably quiescent for the foreseeable future."

YES

Gerald L. Houseman

THE MERGER GAME
STARTS WITH DECEPTION

You've got perhaps ten men guiding the future of corporate America.
—Ivan Boesky, well-known merger investment specialist*

Mergers, acquisitions, and hostile take-overs are hot stuff. There are now some 3,000 a year taking place compared to 1,500 in 1980. The dollars involved were less than $20 billion a year in 1974, more than $40 billion a year in 1980, and approximately $173 billion in 1985. A more than fourfold increase in five years' time indicates that a major restructuring of corporations is now going on—and the end is nowhere in sight. Ivan Boesky, one of the best-known take-over artists, [in 1986] decided to increase his leveraging account from $200 million to $1 billion, and anyone [could have bought] into this deal for a cool million. With this money, he [would have stood] as a threat to many boards of directors and managements, and he [would have undoubtedly wreaked] havoc on workers threatened with unemployment; stockholders who want to stay with the corporate entity as is; the general public as it is increasingly faced with monopolistic or oligopolistic business practices; and the economy, which is already afloat in the junk bonds which threaten its growth and vitality. There are also taxation questions raised by such activity, and there is little question that the capital resources used up in such games has a deleterious effect upon research and development. There are at least indirect effects upon such global concerns as international trade and Third World development. And most importantly, the entrepreneurial myths in American capitalism tend to be exploded when the various tax incentives found in our laws and the much-trumpeted abilities to create product innovations and new jobs are lost in these money-shuffling and debt-creating machinations.

This combination process begins with deception. The Williams Act of 1968 requires disclosure of ownership of significant blocks of securities. If a take-

*Eds: This article was written and published shortly before Ivan Boesky was indicted on numerous counts of insider trading.

From Gerald M. Houseman, "The Merger Game Starts With Deception," *Challenge* (September/October 1986). Reprinted with permission of publisher, M.E. Sharpe, Inc., 80 Business Park Drive, Armonk, NY 10504.

over artist such as Carl Icahn or Victor Posner acquires as much as 5 percent interest in a company, this must be disclosed. When this information is provided to the Securities and Exchange Commission, it must be accompanied by an explanation. This explanation—sometimes reported on in the press—is invariably a statement that the acquirer has bought into the company for investment purposes only. Few knowledgeable observers believe this, particularly when the "investor" is a well-known take-over artist.

THE "INSIDER" ISSUE

Before such an item ever appears in the financial press, however, informed investors will have bought into the stock; for despite the rules against "insider" trading or disclosure, the tips will be out on Wall Street. This is shown by the almost invariable uptick in the price which occurs *before* the take-over artist's announcement is made. When the stock really begins to take off as a result of the buy-out expectations and the premium price that is anticipated, these "insiders" will take their profits. The biggest "insider" of all, of course, is the investor who has reported his 5 percent or greater interest; he or she can be expected to profit merely from buying into the company and staking out an interest. Since the stock goes up on this information in nearly all circumstances, the acquirer can determine his or her own profit in a way that is analogous to shooting fish in a barrel.

At this very outset of the takeover or merger process, then, there are ethical and legal questions to grapple with: whether deception has occurred; whether "insider" money-making is involved caused by the announcement; and whether the self-directed "insider" has an advantage in raising the price of securities merely by indicating an interest in them.

ANTITRUST VIOLATIONS AND NONENFORCEMENT

A second set of problems presented almost immediately by buy-out activity is found in antitrust considerations. In particular, this is the case in proposals for mergers or takeovers which are "horizontal"; that is, those which involve the combining of former competitors. There is still a major problem, however, when a "vertical" union is proposed—one in which the firms involved are not direct competitors. These arrangements can often be just as bad for the economy and for the general public as the "horizontal" deals. Centralization seems to produce no particular efficiencies; indeed, the economic evidence appears to be the contrary. (It is interesting to reflect upon the Reagan administration's attitudes about bureaucracy that seem to support an unlikely thesis that while government, in the nondefense sector, gains efficiency as it grows smaller, corporations gain efficiency as they grow larger.) In order to determine whether monopolistic or oligopolistic conditions are threatened by a proposed merger, the present administration has devised an "HHI Index" (named for its creators, Herfindahl and Hirschman) which, though it is a lax and watered-down guide to measuring monopoly or oligopoly, has the virtue of relying upon a simple formula. Unfortunately, the formula is observed in the breach as much as in application, so that, by and large, the administration has all but abandoned antitrust enforcement.

QUALMS GENERATED
BY BUY-OUT ACTIVITY

Receipt of the offer of purchase causes no particular worries in the board room or in top management if the offer is "friendly"; that is, if it is presumed that the buy-out forces do not plan to replace them. Employees, of course, may lose out even in a friendly merger. And it should be borne in mind that even a friendly merger is often an unproductive use of capital. The recent General Electric acquisition of RCA Corporation, for example, was regarded by many Wall Street observers as an uninspired use of $12 billion; and this was a cash deal, the kind which presumably does the least harm to the economy.

Unfriendly offers, which are assumed by the target company's leadership to mean the likely end of their careers with the firm, may be unanticipated and can cause a great deal of consternation. Will the firm continue to exist in some recognizable form or another? In the case of many companies, the answer clearly has been negative. What about existing labor contracts? And what will happen to middle management? Book company managements have been known to be replaced by broadcast people when the latter took over the book firm; it was explained that, after all, broadcast people, like book people, are in communications.

Experience shows that the very top-level people in a firm have nothing worse to fear than a "golden parachute" arrangement of pay and other conditions of severance which will make them rich even if they are no longer powerful.

All kinds of factors can obtain, of course, in a buy-out deal. It may be in the best interests of the top leaders of a firm, and even of its stockholders and employees, to acquiesce; or it may be best to fight. Sometimes it is possible to win by losing—by paying the take-over artist to leave the company alone.

GREENMAIL

Many offers to take over a company (so-called "tender offers") are made with little or no thought of actually taking it over. The objective in these cases is to threaten the board and management but, after a variety of financial and legal skirmishes, to withdraw—if the company will pay off with "greenmail." Greenmail, technically speaking, is the premium over market value paid by a company to the raider for its own stock in order to obtain withdrawal from a proxy fight (the fight for control of the firm). Let us assume a market value of $40 per share. The stock goes to $52 on the news of the take-over attempt. (Again, the reader is reminded that there is already a great short-term gain on the investment which has occurred only because the take-over artist decided to make it happen.) After considerable public and private maneuvering, let us assume that the take-over investor is prevailed upon (more likely, advised by the legal and financial staff at his disposal) to sell his interest in the company and to give up the thought of taking it over. When this occurs, a contract is drawn up which guarantees that the raider will not try to do this again for a set number of years. In exchange for this agreement, he sells his stock back to the company for a price of, say, $62. (The terms of the agreement outlined in this example are quite typical.) The take-over artist, or "broker," which is his usual title, has been well rewarded for notifying the SEC about buying into the company "for investment purposes" and for carrying out a war of nerves against the firm.

Most hostile take-over attempts result in greenmail; in other words, they are "unsuccessful" and, it is often alleged, are meant to be. The take-over investor would actually have to run the company if he won control, and that is not usually the object of this game. Greenmail amounts can be substantial. Some recent examples are $100 million paid to Sir James Goldsmith by St. Regis Paper; $163.3 million paid to Carl Icahn by Chesebrough-Ponds; $180 million given to Rupert Murdoch by Warner Communications; $325 million paid to Saul Steinberg by Walt Disney Productions; $471.7 million awarded to the famous (or infamous) T. Boone Pickens by Phillips Petroleum; and $178 million turned over to the Bass brothers by Texaco.

Greenmail payments can substantially weaken a corporation. In the Disney case, for example, the floating of a large amount of debt was necessary to pay off Steinberg and the company's debt-to-equity ratio was severely affected. This ratio is presently at near-record levels for all of corporate America, and much of the reason is found in these kinds of activities. Some companies sell off assets while others turn to the high-interest instruments known as "junk bonds." Whatever financial strategy is decided upon, the corporation can only come off badly from a take-over battle.

The game for the greenmailer, which is uninhibited by the law, goes on. There are thousands of available targets. Some companies have erected defenses against take-overs, but they are not impenetrable. One of the most pernicious of these defenses is the "poison pill," or the acquisition of debt (often in "junk bonds" form) in order to make the target firm less attractive. Needless to say, companies that involve themselves in this kind of activity weaken their capital structure and may also hurt the economy generally because of the increased floating of questionable instruments of indebtedness.

LEVERAGED BUY-OUTS

Most mergers, acquisitions, and hostile take-overs are leveraged buy-outs if they succeed. A leveraged buy-out is an acquisition of a company which leaves the acquired operating entity with a greater than traditional debt-to-equity ratio. There are varieties of leveraged buy-outs, to be sure. They can be aimed at asset acquisition or stock acquisition or both. They can be aimed at a division or part of a company such as those found in a conglomerate. And they can be fostered by arrangements involving secured or unsecured financing. The tendency today, in our increasingly loose and ungovernable financial markets, is toward the latter. "Junk bonds" are expected to do their magic.

A host of arrangements are available for a leveraged buy-out, but one particular form deserves special comment. This one, which is increasingly in vogue, involves only a small number of investors, bankers, and company officials who manage to take a company out of the stock market altogether. It "goes private." This has happened recently in the case of Beatrice, R. H. Macy, and other companies, some of them extremely large, with assets in the billion-dollar range. The primary actors in such a deal are the managements of public companies. These individuals may start out with relatively few shares. In the course of the buy-out, however, they acquire all of the company (with the help of a few select outside investors and a huge amount of debt, much or most of it in the form of "junk bonds"). Some of these deals leave the company with debt-to-assets ratios as high as 80 percent. Often there is conflict of interest set up by this arrangement, because the management, rather than representing the interests of the stockholders as imposed by their fiduciary relationship and responsibilities, may well be imperiling the company's financial stability. The argument that a discontented stockholder can always sell her or his shares begs the question of the long-term interests of the firm and the economy in general. The process of "going private" is, naturally, the ultimate defense against take-overs or, in the words of one merger lawyer, "the ultimate lock-up."

"JUNK BONDS"

"Junk bonds" have been overwhelmingly important engines of the merger, acquisition, and take-over activity of recent years. The brokerage industry prefers the term "high-yield" bonds, but "junk bonds" is the most descriptive of these admittedly shaky debt instruments.

These bonds have been around most of this century, but they have had no great importance in securities markets until about 1980. They are indeed high-yield, which reflects their stature in the world of securities and debt instruments. A further reflection is their rating: neither Moody's nor Standard and Poor's, the two bond-ranking services, gives them any rating at all. They are not AAA, AA, B, C or any other bond. They get no rating because they apparently deserve none.

The classic use of junk bonds has been to get a company "over the hump"; that is, to give it perhaps one last chance to become profitable again by allowing it to borrow at high rates of interest. The investors who buy such instruments realize that the purchase is risky.

No great threat was posed to the economy as long as junk bonds represented something like 3 or 4 percent of the debt instruments in the market. But today they comprise nearly 20 percent of the debt instruments floating around, and the reason for this is simple enough. They are the preferred vehicles for mergers, acquisitions, hostile take-overs, and all sorts of leveraged buy-outs. Their value, which is dubious, is premised upon the future sale of assets of the target firm. In other words, junk bonds are nothing, in most instances, except a promise to liquidate some of the assets of a company once a take-over attempt has succeeded.

This brings up an important point. Hostile take-overs and many or most leveraged buy-outs have *asset liquidation*—the selling off of company assets—in mind as the way out of the intensely leveraged debt situation they create. Ted Turner, for example, intended to float vast amounts of junk bonds, as many as he could print, in order to take over CBS. His intention, never unclear, was to sell off such company assets as rich local outlets or this or that division. His effort did not succeed for a variety of reasons, including prudent defenses established by CBS. There is no doubt that a smaller CBS would have been the result of these machinations if they had succeeded.

While it can be seen that unhealthy social, political, and economic effects can flow from the overuse of junk bonds, there is a critical factor today that may be overlooked. In the past, junk bonds were almost all held by banks. Banks are best equipped to invest in these instruments because they have the ability, after all, to be understanding if the bond-floating firm faces new hurdles. Since junk bonds have historically been held by banks, it has always been possible to alleviate some of their bad economic effects.

Now, however, junk bonds are found in every nook and cranny of the investment market. Not only banks, but thrift institutions (who buy many of them), insurance companies, investment funds, and brokerage houses are among the purchasers, and many individual investors are attracted to their high yields as well. This array of institutions and individuals cannot provide the same debt management advantages and help that the banks can. They can hardly be understanding about new problems or unanticipated developments faced by the debtor firm. The junk-bondholders of today, then, are brittle rather than flexible, rigid rather than liquid. If a junk-bond-floating company runs into trouble, there is a good chance that it will go under.

The implications are broad indeed. The next crash, in fact, could be a "junk-bonds crash," and this possibility is recognized even by many of the brokers who underwrite such instruments.

These concerns were unquestionably behind the recent proposal of Federal Reserve Board Chairman Paul Volcker to establish margin requirements on the floating of junk bonds. Until January 1986, it was possible to issue junk bonds on the strength of only 10 percent of their capital value. Volcker proposed that all junk bonds be issued with a margin requirement of 50 percent. The Reagan administration strongly objected, although its reasons were never very clear, for the most part befogged in platitudes about free enterprise. During the period of one month (early December 1985 to early January 1986) in which the Federal Reserve Board took opinions on the proposed rule, a compromise was worked out: a 50 percent margin is required in the event of a hostile take-over attempt; only 10 percent is necessary, however, in order to float these dubious instruments for the sake of a friendly mergers or acquisitions or leveraged buy-outs of most kinds. Since hostile takeovers represented fewer than 20 of the 2,500 mergers of 1985, this compromise was clearly an administration victory.

NOW AND FUTURE

There are some weak arguments presented from time to time in favor of all of this churning and empire-building. T. Boone Pickens and other take-over artists say that they can engage in their activities because their targets have stock that is priced too low, and that this low price reflects mismanagement. A *Business Week* article recently stated that, although we do not see the benefits at the present time, the wave of mergers, acquisitions, and take-overs will yield great—but unspecified—benefits to all of us.

In my view, apologists for this phenomenon are caught in any number of dilemmas when they accept the manic drive behind these power trips of managers and directors, brokers and financiers, proxy fighters and take-over specialists as the exercise of free enterprise. If making their argument to Adam Smith, they would have to do an over-arching amount of backing and filling to show how new conditions, or the anomalies of corporate structure, or the record of government intervention—or perhaps our astrological bearings!—have altered our classic understanding of the meaning of market competition.

All kinds of policy prescriptions suggest themselves as recent corporate history is surveyed. Simply removing the tax incentives, such as deductions for interest on debt for merger-acquisition-take-over activity would be a good start. Volcker's original margin requirement for junk bonds—50 percent for all of them, not just those used for hostile take-overs—is a worthwhile proposal. Better disclosure rules in corporate governance and especially in merger-acquisition-take-over activity would help to alert the public, stockholders, and various affected parties. The use of junk bonds should probably be restricted in various ways. Greenmail should probably be against the law, and both civil and criminal sanctions should be enacted. A much clearer statement of the real intentions of investors can be mandated. The stock exchanges should guarantee that firms they list treat all stockholders equally.

A great deal could be accomplished without enacting any new laws or regulations. The re-establishment of regulation, the renewal of antitrust enforcement, and a vigorous policy of requiring adherence to the law could all do a great deal to bring about a measure of social and financial (if not political) responsibility to the corporate world. The tools are already there on the law books. This is not to say that enforcement, or even the laws themselves, were adequate prior to the gross laxity of recent years; but it would be healthy for the American polity to return to a rule of law in matters of corporate organization and restructuring.

NO

John D. Paulus
and Robert S. Gay

U.S. MERGERS
ARE HELPING PRODUCTIVITY

The last few weeks of 1986 could well go down as a watershed period in the competitive struggle facing corporate America. General Motors, IBM, and AT&T—all giants without peer in U.S. industry—introduced significant restructuring programs aimed at restoring their preeminence as low-cost producers. This spate of announcements represents the frankest admission yet of America's international competitiveness problem, symbolized so dramatically by the soaring trade deficit.

The flip side of this shortfall, the dependence on foreign capital to finance the grade gap, implies that Americans presently are living beyond their means. Such a trend cannot continue, and thus the United States is finally facing up to the fact that it either will have to accept a lower standard of living or become more competitive by raising worker productivity.

The American competitiveness problem has its roots in the inflation of the 1970s. During that decade, productivity growth slipped badly, as ever-rising product prices protected inefficient production practices. Moreover, many workers represented by strong unions were able to extract wage gains which failed to reflect the slump in output per hour. In some industries—such as steel, autos, and trucking—wage premiums, or the excess of wages in a given industry over the national average, vaulted from the 30–40 percent range at the beginning of the 1970s to over 70 percent by the end of the decade.

The problem became increasingly obvious as import penetration rose substantially in the 1970s, even before the U.S. dollar skyrocketed during the first half of the 1980s. For example, the share of U.S. expenditures on manufactured goods devoted to imports roughly doubled from 1968 to 1981, rising from 4.3 percent to 8.4 percent. For some industries, the increase in penetration during this time frame was truly spectacular: for apparel, imports rose from 4.2 percent to 13.7 percent; for leather and leather products, from 8.9 percent to 24.7 percent; for steel, from 12.2 percent to 21.8 percent; for machine tools, from 14.6 percent to 29.4 percent; and for motor vehicles and parts, from 5.7 percent to 21.7 percent.

From John D. Paulus and Robert S. Gay, "U.S. Mergers Are Helping Productivity," *Challenge* (May/June 1987). Reprinted with permission of publisher, M.E. Sharpe, Inc., 80 Business Park Drive, Armonk, NY 10504.

The sharp rise in the dollar from 1981 to 1985 worsened the competitive disadvantage of U.S. firms and contributed to the burgeoning trade deficit. Thus, with high costs, increased import penetration, and a strong dollar, corporate America would have to undertake a massive adjustment program to repair the damage done to the nation's competitive position.

COPING THROUGH RESTRUCTURING

The United States has reacted to its competitive inadequacies largely (though not exclusively) by redeploying assets in configurations aimed at enhancing productivity. The popular term for this process is "corporate restructuring," which refers to such practices as closing inefficient plants and modernizing others, shedding businesses that require specialized management skills, granting wage concessions, and paring "fat" from bloated corporate bureaucracies. Even deregulation, as applied to the trucking and airline industries, for example, represents a form of restructuring, which, in turn, intensifies competition since new firms entering the industry operate at costs lower than those existing companies.

Playing an integral role in the overall restructuring are mergers, acquisitions, and leveraged buyouts, which facilitate transfers of ownership, and ultimately, changes in management and work practices. Moreover, the mere threat of such a change in ownership may induce senior managers to reshape their corporations before outside forces enter the picture. At the very least, financial restructuring is a natural by-product, and perhaps an important catalyst, in corporate America's struggle to regain its once preeminent competitive stature.

A precise measure of the extent of corporate restructuring is impossible. But the dollar value of merger and acquisition activity is certainly related to the degree of restructuring in the broader sense. Using this measure, it is possible to gauge the relationship between the amount of restructuring in a given industry and subsequent gains in productivity and cost control. Such analysis can help to answer the question: "What is corporate restructuring doing to the American economy?" Ultimately it also sheds light on the more important question: "Is America helping herself to improve competitiveness?"

HAS IT WORKED?

Merger and acquisition (M&A) activity began to take off in 1981, not by coincidence, a year when the realities of heightened import penetration began to hit home. The next surge began in 1984 and has continued ever since. Over the past six years a fairly stable proportion of M&A activity—between 50 percent and 65 percent—has occurred in manufacturing and mining, sectors that represent the bulk of our goods-producing infrastructure that has become increasingly vulnerable to foreign competition. In 1985, these two sectors accounted for about 25 percent of U.S. output.

What is particularly intriguing is that there has been impressive improvement in productivity in the manufacturing and mining sectors during the time M&A activity has accelerated. From the first quarter of 1980 to the present, productivity in the manufacturing sector has grown at an average annual rate of 3.3 percent, up significantly from an average of only 1.4 percent for the 1973–80 period, and higher even than the 3 percent average growth recorded during 1960–73.

Such a performance in output per hour in the 1980–86 period is especially impressive since production expanded slowly over those years—at an average rate of only 2.3 percent annually. And it is widely conceded that high rates of productivity growth are much easier to achieve during periods of rapid growth when resources are more intensively utilized.

Moreover, during 1980–86, productivity in manufacturing, where restructuring was especially intense, appears to have greatly outperformed that of the rest of the economy where restructuring was less intense. From 1948 to 1980 productivity growth in the industrial sector was about equal to that recorded for the nonfarm economy overall. However, with restructuring intensifying after 1980, the performance of productivity in manufacturing has been far superior to that of the nonfarm economy as a whole.

A LOOK BY INDUSTRY

If restructuring can, in fact, be linked to the solid improvement of productivity in manufacturing, those industries in which asset redeployment has been most intense should also show the largest gains in output per hour. To test this premise, we have developed a restructuring intensity measure (RIM)—the ratio of the share of M&A activity accounted for by each industry relative to the same industry's share of U.S. output.

For example, if an industry accounted for, say, 10 percent of financial restructuring in a given year, but only for 5 percent of GNP, then its RIM would be 2.0. Thus, if the RIM is greater than 1.0—that is, if

financial restructuring is proportionately greater than output for a given industry—that segment of the economy has been intensively restructured. On the other hand, if the RIM is equal to 1.0, restructuring intensity would be average, and if less than 1.0, below average.

Some stunning productivity success stories for industries that have undergone extensive restructuring are revealed in Table 1. Industry groupings that have RIM ratios greater than 1.0 have experienced substantial improvements in productivity growth in the 1980s, compared with the 1970s.

For example, after eking out very little, if any, productivity gains during the 1970s, industries such as metal mining, coal mining, sawmills, hydraulic cement, steel, primary copper, copper rolling, motor vehicles, tires, and railroad transportation have achieved impressive productivity gains of 5 percent or more annually during the 1980s. These dramatic turn-arounds are all the more remarkable because many of these industries have not enjoyed strong increases in output; indeed, virtually all the rise in production is due to higher productivity. Obviously, the firms involved have taken concerted actions to bolster their competitive position.

To be sure, not all industries have participated in the revival of productivity growth. A number of nondurable goods industries have experienced smaller gains this decade than during the 1970s. Indeed, average productivity performance in the nondurable goods sector (2.8 percent annually) has not been as high as that for durable goods (4.4 percent), perhaps because nondurables producers, in general, have not felt an urgency to revamp production techniques in the face of intense foreign com-

Table 1

Productivity Trends and Restructuring in Selected Industries

	Restructuring intensity measure 1980 to 1985	Average annual productivity		
		1973 to 1980	1980 to 1985	Change in trend
Metal mining	16.4			
Iron ore		1.4%	8.1%	6.7%
Copper		1.1	9.9	8.7
Coal mining	2.5	−1.6	6.5	8.1
Total manufacturing	1.6	1.2	3.7	2.5
Lumber and wood products	2.2			
Sawmills and planing mills		0.6	5.4	4.9
Stone, clay, and glass	0.9[1]			
Hydraulic cement		−1.9	8.7	10.6
Primary metals	1.5			
Steel		−0.5	6.1	6.6
Gray iron foundries		−0.6	3.8	4.3
Primary copper, lead, & zinc		1.3	13.0	11.7
Primary aluminum		0.1	3.7	3.6
Copper rolling and drawing		0.1	6.5	6.4
Fabricated metals	1.4			
Automotive stampings		1.0	4.6[2]	3.6
Machinery, except electrical	1.0			
Refrigeration and heating equipment		−1.3	2.1[2]	3.4
Electric and electronic equipment	1.6			
Radio and television sets		4.2	14.4[2]	10.2
Transportation equipment	1.6			
Motor vehicles and parts		0.8	6.2	5.3
Textile mill products	1.2			
Nonwool yarn mills		2.3	5.3	3.0
Rubber and misc. plastic products	0.8[1]			
Tires and inner tubes ·		1.1	7.3	6.3
Railroad transportation	3.1	1.5	8.6	7.1

[1]These ratios actually understate the extent of financial restructuring in the subindustries (tires and hydraulic cement) where M & A activity was concentrated.
[2]Productivity statistics are available through 1984.
Sources: Bureau of Labor Statistics, U.S. Department of Commerce; Morgan Stanley & Co.

petition. And industries such as mass transit, electric utilities, and some retailers have suffered outright declines in productivity in recent years, and have not undertaken much restructuring either.

Also notably absent from Table 1 are producers of capital equipment and some other high-tech items. The mediocre productivity performance in high-tech industries, despite considerable financial restructuring, is particularly worrisome. Until the early 1980s, the United States had enjoyed substantial trade surpluses in capital goods, reflecting comparative advantages in productive efficiency.

Over the past few years, however, those surpluses have dwindled steadily to the point where we actually were running a trade deficit in capital equipment in the second quarter of 1986. While the overvalued dollar undoubtedly contributed to that decline, lackluster productivity performance of late also has permitted foreign competitors to close the gap in productive efficiency, which has made the task of regaining lost market share more difficult.

WAGE CONCESSIONS

U.S. industry also has made progress in trimming wage costs. As recently as mid-1981, wage increases in manufacturing industries averaged 10 percent. By 1983, however, wage rate adjustments had plummeted on balance to about 3 percent and have remained around that subdued rate ever since. This deceleration in wages was far greater than would have been expected based on historical relationships with macroeconomic conditions alone—mainly unemployment and inflation. Indeed, from 1983 through 1986, wage inflation in manufacturing averaged an estimated one percentage point per year less than normal. A good deal of the abnormally abrupt easing in wages can be attributed to competitive pressures arising from extensive restructuring.

The unusually pronounced slowdown in wage inflation was concentrated in heavily unionized industries and coincided with an unprecedented outbreak of so-called "concessionary" settlements, which froze or even cut base wage rates over the life of multiyear agreements. In each of the past five years, with the sole exception of 1984, more than half of union workers reaching new labor contracts in manufacturing have accepted initial wage reductions or freezes. Likewise, wage "concessions" were pervasive in mining, construction, and the deregulated transportation industries—airlines and trucking.

Almost invariably, wage cuts and freezes have occurred at firms whose competitive positions deteriorated badly during the 1970s, either because wage premiums had risen substantially or because productivity performance had been dreadful. Moreover, by the 1980s, "new" competition from foreign producers or domestic nonunion firms emerged. Burdened with high costs and besieged by aggressive new competitors, many unionized firms were faced with a case of "do or die." In that light, the expense-cutting efforts of the past five years are an encouraging sign that U.S. industry is chipping away current cost disadvantages.

Table 2 gives some sense of how far we have come. In all of the industries listed, management and unions have negotiated concessionary settlements during the 1980s. As a result, wage premiums—as measured by the ratio of wage rates in the industry to the average for all nonfarm workers—have at least stabilized since 1981 and in some case have declined significantly. Nonetheless, as of 1986 all the ratios were still well above those that prevailed in the late 1960s. The combination of continued high premiums and the fact that the new low-cost competitors will not simply "go away" implies that pressures to reduce premiums further will persist for quite some time.

The bottom line is that the restructur-

Table 2

Ratio of Hourly Earnings in Selected Industries to Average for Private Nonfarm Production Workers

Industry	1969	1973	1977	1981	1983	1985	First half 1986
Trucking[1]	1.31	1.59	1.63	1.73	1.63	1.53	1.50
Autos[2]	1.39	1.45	1.57	1.70	1.70	1.73	1.72
Steel[3]	1.35	1.42	1.64	1.81	1.67	1.63	1.67
Rubber[4]	1.38	1.33	1.38	1.53	1.54	1.54	1.56
Mining	1.18	1.20	1.32	1.38	1.41	1.40	1.42
Machinery[5]	1.16	1.21	1.27	1.32	1.28	1.27	1.28
Primary metals	1.25	1.28	1.41	1.49	1.42	1.36	1.37

[1]Straight-time hourly wage rates are specified in Master Freight Agreements.
[2]SIC 3711, motor vehicles and car bodies.
[3]SIC 3312, blast furnaces and steel mills.
[4]SIC 301, tires and inner tubes.
[5]SIC 353, construction.

ing of U.S. industry during the 1980s has helped considerably to keep labor cost pressures at a minimum. As shown in Figure 1, over the past five years labor costs per unit of output in manufacturing literally have been flat. More significantly, the usual pattern of increasing cost pressures over the course of economic expansions has been decisively broken during the current business cycle. As we enter the fifth year of the upturn, unit labor costs in manufacturing still are showing no signs of a pickup.

THE TASK AHEAD

Much remains to be done before America's competitiveness problem disappears. The trade deficit, the most succinct measure of the severity of the difficulty and its principal symptom, is likely to shrink only marginally in 1987. Moreover, as noted earlier, many industries have made little progress as yet in improving productive efficiency.

The United States has three choices in confronting the problem. First, corporate restructuring can continue, raising productivity and lowering costs in the process. This constructive solution could eventually narrow the trade deficit, while

Figure 1

Growth of Unit Labor Costs in Manufacturing (in percentages)

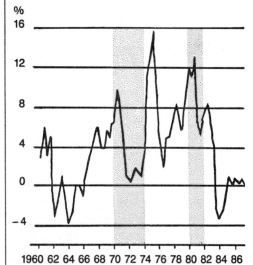

Shaded areas indicate recessionary periods as designated by the National Bureau of Economic Research.

enabling the nation to protect and enhance its high standard of living.

Second, the government could undertake monetary and fiscal-policies designed to lower the foreign exchange value of the dollar significantly. However, this alternative would make the nation poorer, since for a given endowment of human and fixed capital, the lower dollar merely raises the cost of foreign goods and services.

Third, the United States could erect meaningful protectionist barriers, turning this country into the world's premiere high-cost producer. In this event, even fewer foreigners would want to buy our high-priced products and services than currently do. In the end, even without foreign retaliation, which most likely would follow, protectionism would impoverish the nation just as lowering the dollar would.

We believe the United States will continue to restructure its economic base until America again becomes competitive in global markets. This implies further substantial downward pressures on costs and on inflation. In short, continued corporate restructuring represents not only the nation's best hope for resolving our current trade problems, but also will keep inflation remarkably quiescent for the foreseeable future.

POSTSCRIPT

Are There Too Many Hostile Takeovers?

Houseman asserts that the hands-off approach of the free marketeers within the Reagan administration provided the takeover artist with an unfair advantage in the stock market. Men such as Carl Icahn and Victor Posner have capitalized on these opportunities and in the process have accumulated millions of dollars of questionable gains. They play with the advantage of insider information. They force firms to pay greenmail, and if a takeover is actually consummated, it is more often than not heavily leveraged and underwritten by junk bonds. The end result of the exploits of these corporate raiders is a loss to the workers, stockholders, and the economy at large.

Paulus and Gay are unconcerned about the merger/acquisition wave of the 1980s. Indeed, they see direct and immediate benefits to this movement. These business practitioners see this activity as part of the process of corporate restructuring—a process that closes inefficient plants, modernizes others, sheds business with specialized management skills, bargains wage concessions and pares " 'fat' from bloated corporate bureaucracies." They argue that this is necessary if the United States is to remain competitive in the world market and avoid the ravages of inflation.

Many professional and popular publications contain articles on the most recent wave of hostile takeovers. Charles R. Knoeber's essay entitled "Golden Parachutes, Shark Repellents, and Hostile Tender Offers," which appeared in the March 1986 issue of the *American Economic Review,* presents the best summary currently available for the more technically minded. A number of other quasi-professional journals have also provided us with a number of essays about hostile takeovers, particularly after the Ivan Boesky insider trader scandal made the national headlines. For articles that are generally sympathetic toward mergers and acquisitions, see *Dunn's Business Month, Business Week, Forbes,* and *Fortune.* Another perspective is provided by Paul O. Gaddis in the July-August 1987 *Harvard Business Review.* In an essay entitled "Taken Over, Turned Out," Gaddis provides a first-hand account of what happens when a company is "taken over."

ISSUE 6

Should The Federal Government Deregulate American Business?

YES: Murray L. Weidenbaum, from "Weidenbaum Analyzes Benefit-Cost Analysis," *Across the Board* (February 1982)

NO: The Editors of *Dollars and Sense,* from "OSHA Hits Brown Lung Rules," *Dollars and Sense* (May/June 1982)

ISSUE SUMMARY

YES: Weidenbaum asserts that government decision makers should face the same economic constraints as business executives do in the private sector. They must insist that the benefits of their actions at least match the cost of their actions.

NO: The editors of *Dollars and Sense* contend that although benefit-cost analysis seems to have "a certain simple logic," it is neither simple nor objective. Rather, they believe benefit-cost analyses and the related cost-effectiveness approach are fatally flawed by an inherent social bias.

The key component of the free-market economists' attacks on government intervention is their campaign to eliminate, or at least reduce substantially, the regulation of private enterprise. These economists contend that this regulation results in higher consumer prices, reduced worker productivity, declining innovation and investment, rising unemployment rates, reversals in U.S. balance of payments position, increases in federal budget deficit, and just about every other problem that can be faced in the U.S. economic system. They are so alarmed about this issue because government intervention—particularly intervention that directly affects the productive process—is in direct violation of the precepts set down by Adam Smith and his fellow classical economists.

This has been a growing problem for the free-market economist because Congress markedly increased regulatory activity during the late 1960s and early 1970s. In order to offset this new wave of regulations, a counter-offensive was spearheaded by organizations such as the American Enterprise Institute, of which author Weidenbaum is a former president. Members of this group and other groups such as the Heritage Foundation, the Hoover Foundation, and the Foundation for Economic Education have testified before Congress, initiated their own journals (such as the *Journal of Regula-*

tion), written numerous popular and professional articles, elicited growing financial support from the business community, and established endowed professorships at a number of universities. Above all, they have directly influenced public opinion.

The free-market economists' impact has affected more than public opinion. The Democratic Congress that supported and sponsored many of the government regulations, despite the opposition of their conservative counterparts, is the same Congress that began to dismantle these regulations during the Reagan years. Legislation was passed that deregulated the airline industry, the trucking industry, and the natural gas industry. The Occupational Safety and Health Administration (OSHA), the Equal Employment Opportunity Commission (EEOC), and the Environmental Protection Agency (EPA) all felt the effects of substantial budget and staff reductions. The tide has apparently turned, and the free-market economists can rejoice in their triumphs under the Reagan administration.

Perhaps a bit late, the liberal community recognized the groundswell that was engulfing their programs. They reacted by engaging in their own rhetorical battles. But their emotional appeals to protect government regulation have, until late, been ineffective. The editors of *Dollars and Sense*, a radical magazine, have attempted to take the arguments about government regulation beyond rhetorical exchanges. Their essay represents a frontal attack upon Weidenbaum's benefit-cost analysis.

Thus, in the selections that follow, Weidenbaum outlines the basic arguments that have been used by the free-market economists to discredit and limit the extent of government regulation. The editors of *Dollars and Sense* present the liberal community's response to these arguments.

YES

Murray L. Weidenbaum

WEIDENBAUM ANALYZES
BENEFIT-COST ANALYSIS

Discussions of government regulation of product hazards, such as toxic substances, frequently conclude that decision-makers would be aided by the results of benefit-cost studies and related economic analyses. This article tries to explain the role of such quantitative analyses in the regulatory process.

The motive for incorporating benefit-cost analysis into public decision-making is to lead to a more efficient allocation of government resources by subjecting the public sector to the same type of quantitative constraints as those in the private sector. In making an investment decision, for example, business executives compare the costs to be incurred with the expected revenues. If the costs exceed the revenues, the investment usually is not considered worthwhile. If revenues exceed costs, further consideration is usually given the proposal, although capital constraints require another determination of the most financially attractive investments.

The government agency decision-maker does not face the same type of economic constraints. If the costs and other disadvantages to society of an agency action exceed the benefits and other advantages, that situation may not have an immediate adverse impact on the agency. However, such an action would have an immediate impact on a private business if one of its executives made an error. Such analytical information rarely exists in the public sector, so that, more often than not, the governmental decision-maker is not aware that he or she is approving a regulation that is economically inefficient. The aim of requiring agencies to perform benefit-cost analysis is to make the government's decision-making process more effective, and to eliminate regulatory actions that, on balance, generate more costs than benefits. This result is not assured by benefit-cost analysis, since political and other important, but subjective, considerations may dominate. This may result in actions that are not economically efficient, but are desired on grounds of equity or income distribution. Yet benefit-cost analysis may provide valuable information for government decision-makers.

It may be useful to consider the economic rationale for making benefit-cost analyses of government actions. Economists have long been interested in identifying policies that promote economic welfare, specifically by improving the efficiency with which a society uses its resources.

Benefits are measured in terms of the increased production of goods and services. Costs are computed in terms of the foregone benefits that would have been obtained by using those resources in some other activity. The underlying aim of benefit-cost analysis is to maximize the value of the social income, usually measured by the gross national product (GNP). For many years, certain Federal agencies (such as the Corps of Engineers and the Bureau of Reclamation) have used benefit-cost analysis to evaluate prospective projects.

[Typically,] initial regulatory effort—such as cleaning up the worst effects of pollution in a river—may well generate benefits greater than costs. But the resources required to achieve additional cleanup become disproportionately high, and at some point the added benefits may be substantially less than the added costs. For example, a study of the impact of environmental controls on the fruit and vegetable processing industry revealed that it cost less to eliminate the first 85 percent of the pollution than the next 10 percent. In beet sugar plants, it costs more than $1 a pound to reduce biological oxygen demand (BOD)—a measure of the oxygen required to decompose organic wastes—up to a level where 30 percent of pollution is eliminated. But it costs an additional $20 for a one-pound reduction at the 65 percent control level and an additional $60 for a one-pound reduction when over 95 percent control is achieved.

Another comparison is equally telling. The pulp and paper industry spent $3 billion between 1970 and 1978 complying with Federal clean-water standards, and achieved a 95 percent reduction in pollution. But to reach the new reduction goal proposed by the Environmental Protection Agency (EPA)—98 percent by 1984—would cost $4.8 billion more, a 160 percent increase in costs to achieve a 3 percent improvement in water quality. Thus, it is important to look beyond the relationship of the costs and the benefits of a proposed governmental undertaking to the additional (marginal) benefits and costs resulting from each extension of or addition to the governmental activities.

If regulatory activity goes unchecked, the result could be an excess of costs over benefits. Thus, benefit-cost analyses should be viewed as a tool for identifying the optimum amount of regulation, rather than as a means of debating the pros and cons of regulation in general. To an economist, "overregulation" is not an emotional term; it is merely shorthand for the regulatory activities in which the costs to the public are greater than the benefits. . . .

If a business decision in the private sector places an external burden on its neighbors, such as pollution, the firm does not include such a cost in its accounting, since it does not bear the burden. Public sector decision-makers, however, must, or at least ought to, consider all the effects of such a decision. Because their vantage point is the entire nation, government regulators—unlike their private sector counterparts—should attempt to include all costs and benefits, including those external to the government.

The agencies should do so because most regulatory actions have indirect effects on the economy. For example, requiring safety belts in automobiles has a direct impact on the cost of automobiles and on sales in the safety belt industry. It also influences the severity of auto accidents and has a ripple effect on the suppliers of the safety belt industry and their suppliers, and so on. If a regulatory decision is to be good, these indirect effects, as well as the direct impacts, must be taken into account.

The benefits and costs attributable to regulation are measured by the difference between the benefits and costs that occur in the presence of regulation and those that would prevail in its absence. Although the idea may seem straightforward, its application can be complex. Determining what would occur in the absence of regulation—which establishes a reference point for the calculations—may involve a considerable amount of judgment.

Table 1 shows how the incremental costs (the expenses that would not have been made in the absence of regulation) were computed in one study of water pollution control. Apparently the bulk of the costs would have been undertaken voluntarily.

Sometimes the indirect effects of regulation may be as important as the direct. Consider, for example, the question of mandatory standards to ensure the production of less hazardous consumer products. From time to time, suggestions have been made to require more protection in helmets and other recreational equipment used in playing football. Those using the safety helmets would be expected to receive the benefit of fewer or less severe injuries. However, such a safety standard could impose substantial costs on lower-income youngsters. Perhaps of greater concern, the standards might even contribute to more injuries since the price increases might result in more people playing football without any protective equipment at all. That example illustrates another basic thrust of benefit-cost analysis—to examine the proposed government action not only from the viewpoint of the impact on the business firm but also from the vantage point of the effects on the consumer.

A type of regulatory cost that is large, but difficult to measure, is a grouping that economists refer to as deadweight losses. Regulation often limits the range of permissible prices, practices, or processes. Those legal restrictions may inhibit the most productive use of resources. The loss of the higher output that would result in the absence of the regulatory activity—those deadweight losses—arises from an inefficient combination of factors. For example, the total efficiency of the economy is reduced when regulated transportation rates make it necessary for freight to be moved by rail rather than hauled at a lower cost by truck. That is so because more resources are used to achieve the same objective.

When political judgment suggests that it is not feasible to put a dollar sign on the benefits, a benefit-cost analysis still can be helpful by ranking the cost-effectiveness of alternatives. By using this method, which was originally developed for military programs, estimates are made of the costs of different ways to accomplish an objective. Cost-effectiveness analyses permit policy-makers to identify least-cost solutions. In this more limited approach, the analyst assumes that the objective is worth accomplishing. In the regulatory field, this approach may be particularly useful in dealing with programs to reduce personal hazards. Instead of dealing with such an imponderable question as the cost of a

Table 1

Calculation of Incremental Cost of Regulation

Steps	Example
Company identifies an action taken to comply with a specific regulation.	Installation of wastewater pretreatment system to remove 99 percent of pollutants in compliance with Title 40 of the *Code of Federal Regulations*, Chapter 1, Part 128.
Would action have been taken otherwise?	Pretreatment system without Title 40 would have been designed to remove 95 percent of pollutants.
What was the cost of the action?	$1,200,000 (from fixed-asset ledger data).
How much would the action that would have been taken in the absence of regulation have cost?	$800,000 (the cost of installing a 95-percent system).
What was the incremental cost?	$1,200,000 – $800,000 = $400,000.

human life, the emphasis shifts to identifying regulatory approaches that would maximize the number of lives saved after use of certain resources (such as people or capital), or minimize pain. Rather than a cold, systems approach, such attempts at objective analysis show true compassion for our fellow human beings by making the most effective use of the limited resources available to society.

A regulatory action has an impact not only in the present but also in the future. It is necessary, therefore, to place a lower value on future costs and benefits than on present costs and benefits. The basic notion here is that a given benefit is worth more today than tomorrow, and a given cost is less burdensome if borne tomorrow than today. (This is a restatement of the economic principle that a dollar received today is worth more than a dollar received tomorrow, because today's dollar could be invested and earn a return.) For this reason, future benefits and costs have less weight than today's benefits and costs.

This practice is important in evaluating regulatory actions. If the costs and benefits of two actions appear equal, and most of the benefits of one action occur after five years, while the benefits of the other action occur immediately, then the latter is the preferred alternative. Discounting of the future thus implies that the timing of any proposed action's costs and benefits is an important consideration in its evaluation.

Reliable measures of costs and benefits are not easily achieved or always possible. Should the loss of a forest be measured by the value of the timber eliminated? What of the beauty destroyed? What of the area's value as a wildlife habitat? In view of such questions, it is unlikely that agency decision-makers will be faced with simple choices.

However, the difficulties in estimating the benefits or costs of regulatory actions need not serve as a deterrent to pursuing the analysis. Merely identifying some of the important and often overlooked impacts may be useful in the decision-making process. Examples on the cost side include the beneficial drugs that are not available because of regulatory obstacles, the freight not carried because empty trucks are not permitted to carry backhauls, and the television stations that are not broadcasting because they were not licensed. On the benefit side, examples include a more productive work force that results from a lower rate of accidents on the job, savings in medical care because of safer products, and a healthier environment that results from compliance with governmental regulations.

At times the imperfections of benefit-cost analysis may seem substantial. Nevertheless, this analysis can add some objectivity to the government's decision-making process. While benefit-cost analysis is capable only of showing the effectiveness of an action, the subsequent decisions of elected officials and their appointees might be envisioned as representing society's evaluations of the equity effects of that action. Economists can provide benefit-cost analyses and studies of the distribution of those benefits and costs, leaving the final decision to society's representatives. Presumably, those individuals are better able to make political decisions on the impacts of the actions they contemplate. Despite its shortcomings, benefit-cost analysis is a neutral concept, giving equal weight to a dollar of benefits and to a dollar of costs.

Not all the criticism of benefit-cost may be valid. The idea of attempting to quantify the effects of regulation outrages some persons. They forget the objectives that economists have in developing such measurements. The goal is not to eliminate all regulation. As economists of all political persuasions have testified before a variety of Congressional committees, it is not a question of being for or against government regulation of business. A substantial degree of intervention in private activities is to be expected in a complex, modern society.

Critics who are offended by the notion of subjecting regulation to a benefit-cost test may unwittingly be exposing the weakness of their position: they must be convinced that some of their pet rules would flunk the test. After all, showing that a regulatory activity generates an excess of benefits is a strong justification for continuing it.

Despite talk of cold, systems approaches, economists are deeply concerned about people as well as dollar signs. The painful knowledge that resources available to safeguard human lives are limited causes economists to become concerned when they see wasteful use of those resources because of regulation.

General Motors, for example, calculates that society spends $700 million a year to reduce carbon monoxide auto emissions to 15 grams per mile, thus prolonging 30,000 lives an average of one year, at a cost of $23,000 for each life. To meet the 1981 standard of 3.4 grams per mile, the company estimates it will cost $100 million in addition, and prolong 20 lives by one year at an estimated cost of $25 million for each life. Human lives are precious, which is why it is so sad to note another use of that money. It has been estimated that the installation of special cardiac-care units in ambulances could prevent 24,000 premature deaths each year, at an average cost of approximately $200 for each year of life. Thus spending the $100 million for the special ambulances conceivably could save 500,000 lives a year.

Part of the problem in setting regulatory policy is that at times the benefits are more visible than the costs—not necessarily greater, but more evident. If the required scrubber for electric utilities results in cleaner air, we see the benefits. The costs are merely part of the higher electric bills we pay. Thus, the cost of regulation takes on the characteristics of a hidden sales tax that is paid by the consumer.

In the final analysis, the political factors in regulatory decision-making cannot be ignored. Many social regulations involve a transfer of economic resources from a large number of people to a small group of beneficiaries. The Occupational Safety and Health Act's coke-oven standard, for example, protects fewer than 30,000 workers, but is paid for by everyone who buys a product containing steel. So long as regulators avoid concentrating the costs on a small group that could organize political counterpressures, costly regulations can be promulgated easily.

Despite the limitations, there is a useful role for formal economic analyses of regulatory impacts in providing, at least, an ancillary guide to policymakers. As a Federal court stated in striking down [a proposed OSHA regulation]: "Although the agency does not have to conduct an elaborate cost-benefit analysis, . . . it does have to determine whether the benefits expected from the standards bear a reasonable relationship to the costs imposed by the standard." That court's common-sense approach might be the direction to which the public policy debates on regulation could profitably shift.

NO

The Editors of *Dollars and Sense*

THE COTTON INDUSTRY
PASSES THE BOLL

In 1970 the Department of Labor estimated that about 35,000 cotton workers were permanently disabled and over 100,000 (18% of the industry's workforce) were afflicted by byssinosis, commonly called "brown lung." Only a year earlier, a leading textile trade journal had scoffed, "We are particularly intrigued by the term 'byssinosis,' a thing thought up by venal doctors who attended last year's (International Labor Organization) meeting in Africa where inferior races are bound to be affected by new diseases more superior people defeated years ago."

Those superior people must be the bosses, because byssinosis has been diagnosed in workers of every color since it was first mentioned in medical literature in 1705. Almost three centuries later the manufacturers have finally had to face reality, coping with cotton dust exposure limits mandated by the federal Occupational Health and Safety Administration (OSHA) during the 1970s.

Unfortunately for textile workers, the manufacturers have found a new ally in current OSHA head Thorne Auchter, who is weaving a tangle of complex economic tales to justify severely weakening those cotton dust standards. Blatant racism is no longer used to discredit efforts to fight brown lung, but it has been replaced by a more subtle attempt to do the same thing through technical comparisons of "cost effectiveness."

CUTTING DOWN DUST

Byssinosis, a crippling respiratory disease affecting cotton mill workers, has been recognized in England since 1942 as an occupational illness for which workers deserve compensation. It causes shortness of breath, chest tightness, and coughing upon the employee's return to work on Mondays. Later these symptoms extend to other workdays, and the disease may eventually result in permanent disability or contribute to death.

The exact cause of the disease is not known, although it is accepted that high cotton dust levels accompany high incidence of the disease. Particularly troubling, it appears, is the dust that comes from "trash" (twigs and the bract that grows at the base of the cotton boll) mixed with the cotton.

Mechanical harvesters, now in common use, yield cotton with a much higher trash content than the old hand-picking method. The cotton is ginned on site, at the fields, to remove the seeds, and is then sold to the mills in huge bales. Unbaling, carding (combing into small strands), weaving, and other processing stages take place at the mills.

One way to reduce the risk of brown lung at all stages would be to improve the ginning process to remove more trash more safely. Ginning, however, is controlled by a different set of owners than milling. It is a seasonal, highly competitive, fluctuating, and low-profit business run by thousands of small operators. Ginners insist that the capital outlays needed for improved equipment would put them out of business.

OSHA proposed weak regulations on ginning in 1977, but the ginners' lobby prevented their adoption. Mill operators claim the high trash content of the cotton they must process is not *their* problem. In short, the ginners and mill owners pass the boll—but neither pays for the damaged health of the workers.

At the mills, however, cotton dust exposure regulations have been in effect since OSHA was created in 1970. The original standard was weak and often unenforced. Political pressure, lawsuits, and direct action by groups like the Brown Lung Association (a group of disabled workers and their supporters) and the Amalgamated Clothing and Textile Workers Union (ACTWU) resulted in stricter standards in 1976 and again in 1978.

These new standards specified that engineering controls (changes in the workplace, including ventilation and new machinery) had to be the primary long-range solution to the dust problem. Cheaper and less effective measures—such as wearing of respirators and removing workers who show signs of byssinosis—were recommended only as interim methods.

INSTANT POLICY—JUST ADD NUMBERS

The American Textile Manufacturers Institute challenged the 1978 standard on the grounds that OSHA had not justified it on a "cost-benefit" basis, nor proved its economic feasibility. This reasoning had frightening implications for potential regulation of thousands of other hazardous substances and suspected carcinogens. In effect, the companies proposed that a certain number of human lives had to be lost before OSHA could regulate a substance.

Cost-benefit analysis has a certain simple logic: Add up total costs to industry of a regulation and total benefits to workers from the regulation, and then compare. Instant social policy! All you have to do is look out there in the marketplace and see exactly what the regulation will cost, and what the improved health of the workers will be worth.

In fact, there is nothing simple or objective about the method. Any calculation about the size of costs or benefits involves political judgments that will be made differently by different observers. It is precisely because the economic system does not place a high enough value on workers' health (you can't sell it, after all) that regulations are needed in the first place.

On the practical side, how do you decide on a dollar value for a long healthy life, or retirement with dignity? How can you add up the benefits of regulation when the full health impact of brown lung—or asbestos or chemical poisoning—is not yet known? And where do you get reliable figures on the costs to industry?

One way to figure "benefits" to workers is to calculate how much more money a worker who dies or is forced to retire would have made if he or she had worked a normal lifetime. Depending on the prevailing wage, which for cotton mill workers is only 60% of the national average, that could be pretty low. For the 48% of the cotton workforce that is female, and the 20% that is black, expected earnings are particularly low. Does this mean their lives are worth less?

It doesn't take an economic whiz to realize that "benefits," as industry figures them, don't place much value on workers' lives. As a lawyer from the U.S. Chamber of Commerce put it, "Is a human life worth $10? Of course it is. But when you start going up the ladder, you have to start making some judgments, no matter how cold and callous it sounds."

As for costs to industry, the history of vinyl chloride regulation provides a clue to the abuse of cost-benefit techniques. When vinyl chloride standards were debated within OSHA in 1975, plastic manufacturers complained of compliance costs of $90 billion. Not only did that estimate turn out to be 300 times too high, but some manufacturers ended up making money from their efforts at compliance, because the new, safer, equipment also saved labor and materials.

The same may be true for cotton dust compliance. During the 1977 OSHA hear-ings, the manufacturers insisted that compliance with new standards would cost upwards of $2.3 billion. The figures supporting this estimate were left to the imagination. The companies refuse to release information they had about cost of new equipment that could meet OSHA's standards.

The Textile Workers Union was able to get some of that information from Czechoslovakia, where the more advanced technology is already in use. They also produced copies of requests cotton firms had made to the Treasury Department for rapid depreciation allowances on the old machinery that would have to be replaced. These requests included the industry's estimate of what the new machinery would cost: $450 million over a three-year-period, not $2.3 billion.

The union claimed the true cost would be even lower, because one factor overlooked by the cotton millers (and generally overlooked by manufacturers in any such cost-benefit analysis) was the improved productivity and durability of the new machines.

BACK TO THE DICTIONARY

The manufacturers' challenge to the '78 regulations went all the way to the Supreme Court, which finally didn't buy it. In June 1981, the Court ruled that "Congress has already defined the basic relationship of costs to benefits when it passed the Occupational Safety and Health Act of 1970." That relationship "places the benefit of worker health above all other considerations except the feasibility of achieving that benefit."

That decision sent industry racing back to the dictionary, but by this time they had a new ally—Reagan-appointed OSHA director Thorne Auchter. Less than a year after the Supreme Court decision, the cotton dust standard is again up for grabs, though this time the challenge has come in more subtle garb. Ostensibly because of "new health data," OSHA is now studying the "cost effectiveness of compliance (which) may result in reconsideration of the present standard."

In the new "cost-effectiveness" approach, unlike the cost-benefit analysis, benefits are not weighed against costs. Rather, different methods of complying with a given regulation are compared according to their costs. This makes sense only if the different methods can all reach the same standard, and if they don't compromise the goal of a healthy workplace. That is hardly what's going on, as OSHA's new management attempts to talk itself around the Supreme Court victory the agency's own lawyers won in 1981.

In the cotton dust case, the varying methods under consideration are engineering controls, respirators, and medical surveillance of workers. Only engineering controls—that is actual changes in the machinery used—decrease the dust levels associated with the disease.

Respirators are difficult to work with, and a study by the National Institute of Occupational Safety and Health has found that they are unreliable under real working conditions. Medical surveillance, therefore, has been a favorite of the industry. This involves monitoring of workers' health by the employer, and removal of any worker for whom byssinosis symptoms appear. It can help identify brown lung victims before the disease becomes chronic, but it is not foolproof and often comes too late.

In challenging the 1978 regulations at the time they were proposed, the textile firms argued that medical surveillance would be as effective as engineering controls. In the study that was supposed to back up this claim, however, anyone with a 60% or better breathing capacity was considered "normal" and unaffected by any work-related disease.

What's more, all the data in this study came from company doctors, to whom workers fear admitting brown lung symptoms because the result will be firing or rotation to lower-paying jobs. To top it off, the "study" had no control groups or standard statistical evidence, no clear methodology, no review by other scientists, and no authors willing to answer questions about it!

Yet strangely enough, when these same folks now submit a similar study, Auchter says "new health data" justify reviewing the standard. This time, the manufacturers' association claims that brown lung affects only 0.5% of cotton workers, not 18% as previously thought.

OSHA has not only bought this argument, but is going ahead with the companies' dirty work by commissioning its own "Regulatory Impact Analysis" study, once again relying on the medical and scientific data supplied by the industry. The union charges that four of the five guidelines for this analysis explicitly violate the 1981 Supreme Court decision.

The only way to conduct a meaningful cost-effectiveness study would be to have independent scientists do rigorous long-term studies of the two methods of preventing brown lung—engineering controls and medical surveillance—on two distinct test populations. Instead, it's likely that OSHA will "find" in the existing company health data enough justification to forget about engineering controls altogether, thereby saving millions for the employers.

A victory for the companies on this issue would set a precedent for "reevaluating" other current standards in other industries as well. The potential benefit to industry from avoiding government regulation and investment in a clean workplace is enormous—but the potential cost to workers' health is also.

POSTSCRIPT

Should the Federal Government Deregulate American Business?

It must be remembered that Weidenbaum does not oppose all government regulation. Rather, he pleads that proposed regulations should pass a simple test: Do the benefits associated with this regulation exceed the extra costs of imposing this regulation? He believes if the benefits do not exceed the costs, the regulation should not be introduced. Weidenbaum goes on to suggest that even when we can't "put a dollar sign on the benefits," we can use the potential benefits to rank the "cost effectiveness" of alternatives. That is, he maintains, the logic of cost-benefit analysis allows us to identify the least costly solutions.

The editors of *Dollars and Sense* challenge the validity of Weidenbaum's simple test. They assert that the application of the benefit-cost rule generally results in an overstatement of the costs and an understatement of the benefits. They also believe that benefit-cost analyses are biased in favor of the more affluent in society and penalize those of lesser means.

How you judge the validity of the above arguments depends in part on how you value the trade-off between equity and economic efficiency.

Professional and popular literature contain many articles on government regulation. The impact of the free-market economists is apparent in this literature. Nearly all of it is critical of government regulation. Murray L. Weidenbaum has contributed to this growing body of books, pamphlets, and articles. His work with Robert DeFina, *The Cost of Government Regulation of Economic Activity* (American Enterprise Institute, 1978) and his book *The Future of Business Regulation* (Anacorn Press, 1979) are excellent examples of the antiregulatory mood that has swept the country. Daniel Fusfeld responds to Weidenbaum in a short piece entitled "Some Notes on the Opposition to Regulation," *Journal of Post-Keynesian Economics* (Spring 1980), which details the types of unsafe products that would appear on the market if regulation did not exist, and Mark Green and Norman Waitzman provide a more sophisticated discussion of the social bias associated with benefit-cost analyses in their essay "Cost, Benefit, and Class," *Working Papers* (May/June 1980).

ISSUE 7

Do Firms Exploit Workers and Local Communities By Closing Profitable Plants?

YES: Barry Bluestone and Bennett Harrison, from "Why Corporations Close Profitable Plants," *Working Papers* (May/June 1980)

NO: Richard B. McKenzie, from "Frustrating Business Mobility," *Regulation* (May/June 1980)

ISSUE SUMMARY

YES: Professors Bluestone and Harrison assert that large modern corporations (particularly conglomerates) systematically milk profits from healthy firms, mismanage them, fail to maintain them, and then shut them down on the grounds that they are inefficient.
NO: Professor McKenzie argues that in a healthy market economy it is natural and necessary for some plants to move and others to close in order to achieve the benefits of economic efficiency.

No one denies that economic efficiency in a market economy is achieved by the application of the rule: "survival of the fittest." Inefficient firms are driven out of the marketplace by their efficient competitors. Thus, the ever-present threat of market failure makes each firm strive for the maximum degree of economic efficiency.

The fact that the market weeds out inefficient firms is one of the first lessons in an introductory economics course. It is this mechanism that determines the allocation of resources. That is, when an inefficient firm fails, the supply of factors of production that were previously employed by this inefficient firm are increased. The increase in the supply of factors of production causes factor prices to fall. The lower factor prices make the factors attractive for other, presumably efficient, firms. Thus, resources are "freed" from inefficient firms and "absorbed" by efficient firms.

The controversy over plant closings does not take exception to this notion of economic justice. Although some economists challenge the underlying assumptions of this allocation mechanism—such as the downward flexibility of wages, the ability to substitute a unit of labor in alternative occupations, or the mobility of labor—the current critics challenge the viability of this mechanism in today's concentrated industrial sector. They are concerned with two basic issues: the impact of large enterprises on local communities and the legitimacy of the allocation process when multiplant firms and multiproduct firms dominate the marketplace.

Critics such as Bluestone and Harrison stress the fact that the firms in today's marketplace are totally different from the firms of Adam Smith's day. If one of the modern-day firms closes its doors, large numbers of individuals are unemployed, and they flood the labor market of that region. Total income in that community falls. This sets off a multiplier effect that reduces business demand and the income of local businesses that provide goods and services to those workers who are now unemployed. Additionally, a plant closing impacts on the local tax base. Not only does the local community lose the property tax assessment of the closed plant (such facilities are rarely sold and renovated for alternative uses), but it loses property tax assessments on workers' homes when the supply of housing increases and home prices fall as workers leave the community. This decline in property tax collections, coupled with falling sales tax and income tax collections, can leave a community financially strapped just when increased demands are placed upon it by its high unemployment rate. Thus, closing a modern-day plant with its 500, one thousand, or five thousand employees is dramatically different than closing Adam Smith's pin factory with its six employees.

The second concern of critics is more fundamental. Multiplant firms and multiproduce conglomerates can work outside the realm of the traditionally conceived marketplace. That is, profits earned in one plant can be siphoned off for the benefit of a totally unrelated activity. This phenomenon forms the crux of this issue.

Professor McKenzie argues that the allocation of funds from one part of an enterprise to another part of the same enterprise is totally consistent with the classical economist's profit maximization rule. Professors Bluestone and Harrison argue that these transfers violate the internal logic of classical economics and that, in the process, these transfers impose immense hardships on the workers these firms employ and on the communities where they are located.

Whether public policy encourages or discourages plant relocations will depend upon the outcome of this debate. Should firms be granted tax concessions for investments in plant and equipment that replicate old plants in another part of the country? Should firms be relieved from retirement program obligations when these production facilities are no longer profitable? Should tax write-offs be allowed for firms that close down a marginally profitable plant? These and other policy questions can be resolved only when the debate between economists such as McKenzie and Bluestone/Harrison is settled.

YES

Barry Bluestone
and Bennett Harrison

WHY CORPORATIONS CLOSE
PROFITABLE PLANTS

Plant closings are becoming a grimly familiar story. The parent conglomerate, usually from a remote home office, announces one day that a well-established local factory is no longer competitive. Typically, the handwriting has been on the wall for years. The machinery is outmoded; the company's more modern factories are using newer equipment—and nothing foreshadows a shutdown like failure to reinvest. The workers have been told to hold down wages, or the plant will have to move; the town had been warned that property taxes must be abated or they will lose the plant altogether. Often these demands have been met.

But the dread day arrives anyway. Hundreds of jobs will be lost; the tax base will be devastated. The town elders wring their hands. Workers with seniority (those with roots in the community) are invited to pull up stakes and take lower wage jobs in company plants out of state.

A last ditch effort by workers to buy the plant fails; they can't raise the necessary capital. Although the factory is obsolete, oddly enough it is worth a king's ransom. Anyway, it must be a real lemon, or why would the company shut it down?

Why indeed?

The editorial pages of the *Wall Street Journal* suggest the reasons for plant relocation are obvious. Don't credit the Sunbelt's climate, says the *Journal*. The real cause of the sunbelt's economic growth is its superior attitude toward business. Labor costs (translation: wages) are lower; tax burdens (translation: public services) are lower. Plants must relocate, therefore, because in the high-cost Northeast and Midwest workers have greedily demanded decent wages, and communities have insisted on adequate school, police, fire, and sanitation services.

And anyway, plant closings, despite their human toll, mean that the system is performing the way it should. Capital mobility is an essential ingredient in our free-market economy. The profit-maximizing entrepreneur must be free to invest capital where it will return the highest possible yield.

From Barry Bluestone and Bennett Harrison, "Why Corporations Close Profitable Plants," *Working Papers*, vol. 7, no. 3 (May/June 1980). Copyright © 1980 by the Commonwealth Institute. Reprinted by permission.

Otherwise, we are sanctioning inefficiency: letting the economy as a whole operate below its optimum potential means allowing lower productivity and falling wages. And we surely don't want that.

Again and again, trade unions and state legislatures grappling with plant closings listen to business executives insist that plants close because they've ceased to be profitable: "If it could make money, do you really think we would shut it down?"

The contention seems plausible at first but, like so much in textbook economics, it simply fails to describe real life. Large modern corporations—and conglomerates in particular—will and frequently do close profitable branch plants or previously acquired businesses. They may do so for a variety of reasons that flow from the way conglomerates are organized. Centralized management and control produces pressure to meet corporate growth objectives and minimum annual profit targets; it also siphons off subsidiaries' profits to meet other corporate needs. Sometimes management by "remote control" actually creates the unprofitability of the subsidiary that eventually leads to shutdown—as when the home office is far removed from the production site or unfamiliar with the industry in which a subsidiary competes. Again, the textbook model of competition among entrepreneur-owned and managed businesses utterly fails to explain why plants relocate.

Modern industrial theory says large corporations are under constant pressure to grow, to expand their market share. Stability is often seen as a sign of decline, no matter how well run and steadily productive the plant. In a letter to an executive of the K mart discount department chain, Paul McCracken, former head of the President's Council of Economic Advisors, wrote: "History suggests that companies which decide to 'take their ease' are apt to be on the route to decay."

This pressure is reinforced by the corporation's need to offer growth stock in order to attract equity capital. Investors in growth stocks make their money from capital gains realized when they sell their stock rather than from steady dividends paid out by the firm. The purchase price of the stock is thus high in relation to the dividends it earns. However, only by growing can a company keep the price-to-earnings ratio high, and continue to attract investors to its stocks. In many situations it is easier for a corporation to boost its price-earnings ratio by acquiring efficient and profitable businesses—often in unrelated markets—than by developing new ventures or expanding existing operations. This option was particularly attractive during the mid-1960s and the late 1970s when the stock market tended to undervalue real assets. Then a corporation could acquire those assets at "bargain" prices.

Plants must also meet target rates of return. Many companies that are divisions or subsidiaries of parent corporations or conglomerates are now routinely required to meet minimum annual profit targets as a condition for receiving finance or executive "perks" from the home office. Many are ultimately shut down because they cannot achieve what the managers describe as the parent corporation's current "hurdle rate."

At Cornell University, studies of conglomerate destruction of viable businesses have found many cases in which conglomerates abandoned going concerns that did not meet the specified target rates of return. For example,

The Herkimer [New York] plant, producing library furniture, had been acquired by Sperry Rand in 1955. The plant had made a profit every year except one through the next two decades, and yet Sperry Rand decided to close the plant and sell the equipment [in part because it] was not yielding a 22 percent profit on invested capital. That was the standard used by this conglomerate/ management in determining an acceptable rate of return on its investments.

Another example is the experience of the Bates Manufacturing Company, a leading Maine textile operation. After several changes of ownership after World War II, all the mills except the one at Lewiston were sold to textile conglomerates. The Lewiston facility, along with a coal and energy business Bates had acquired, was then sold to two New York investors. At the time, Bates offered a steady but low return of 5 to 7 percent. The energy business, however, promised a 15 to 20 percent return. As one longtime manager at Bates put is, "These boys were not textile men, they were money men." And sure enough, they decided to close the textile plant in 1977, in order to put all their money into the energy business.

Again, in the lower Pioneer Valley of central Massachusetts, the Chicopee Manufacturing Company was generating an estimated 12 percent rate of return on its apparel products. The parent firm, Johnson & Johnson (whose principal line is pharmaceuticals), was dissatisfied with anything short of a 16 percent minimum, and announced that Chicopee would be shut down.

As times change, the hurdle rate may rise. In textiles and apparel, for example, Royal Little, the founder of Textron, told a Congressional investigative committee in 1948 that his conglomerate generally insisted that each of its subsidiaries earn 10 percent on total invested capital before taxes or risk being shut down. By the late 1970s, according to its own corporate reports, another clothing conglomerate, Genesco, was imposing a 25 percent hurdle rate on its various companies.

Whatever the target rate in a particular company at a particular time, the existence of the corporate hurdle rate means that in the era of monopoly capital, viable businesses can be closed even though they are making a profit—because it is not enough of a profit. Perhaps the most dramatic example of this phenomenon involved Uniroyal's closing of its eighty-seven-year-old inner tube factory in Indianapolis in 1978. The *Wall Street Journal* reported the story in the following way:

> The factory has long been the country's leading producer of inner tubes. Its $7 million to $8 million annual payroll sustains the families of nearly 600 employees.
>
> The company, in a formal statement, cited "high labor costs" and "steadily declining demand." Union and management officials who worked at the plant tell another story. They say that Uniroyal could have kept the plant operating profitably if it wanted to but that under pressure from the securities markets management decided to concentrate its energy on higher-growth chemical lines. Interviews with securities analysts support this theory. Richard Haydon, an analyst at Goldman, Sachs and Co., says: "You have one very large entity looking at a very small entity, but the small entity being very large to those people that work there. I think it's a truism that many companies have grown too big to look at the small market."

One consultant advises his corporate clients that, when the wage bill as a percent of sales rises, or when the rate of return on investment falls below some standard—he proposes the current money market interest rate—it is time to think about shutting down. "If capital does not work for you effectively, it should be invested elsewhere."

The case histories of Bates, Chicopee, and Uniroyal all have happy endings of one kind or another. Jobs at Bates were saved when the mill workers and some of the former managers chose to buy it. They were able to do so through an Employee Stock Ownership Plan arrangement, and in the first year after it was bought Bates earned a 17 percent after-tax profit. (See "Employee Ownership: How Well Is It Working?" by Daniel Zwerdling in *Working Papers* May/June 1979.) To keep Chicopee from closing, twenty-one savings banks in the Pioneer Valley created a fund for high-risk business development. This enabled Chicopee's management to buy the company. And Uniroyal factory workers saved their jobs with the help of the presidents of the Indianapolis City Council and the Rubber Workers Union. They persuaded local financiers to put up the capital to purchase the plant from Uniroyal. The profit forecast for the first year of operation predicts that $500,000 will be distributed among the workers, and another $500,000 invested in new machinery. At the moment, all three plants are operating in the black, reconfirming that the corporations had been about to shut down basically profitable enterprises.

Subsidiaries' profits are prey to corporate appropriation. Not only do many parent companies deny their branches and conglomerate subsidiaries the power to establish their own performance criteria, but the profits they *do* earn are generally repatriated to the parent firm, to be reallocated according to the latter's priorities. For example, in one subsidiary of a Fortune 500 corporation, the profits from its local specialty paper products operation are taken by the parent, which returns only enough capital to the mill to meet Environmental Protection Agency and basic maintenance requirements. "In fact, only 5 percent of capital expenditures over the past five years have gone for growth. In that period net assets have declined 26 percent and employment has declined 9 percent . . . "

A healthy subsidiary that generates excess capital is sometimes a "cash-cow." An example of this would be a regional industry that has run out of opportunities for local growth: the New England market for department store sales is thought by industry leaders to be more or less saturated. Therefore, "the local [New England] units of national holding companies and department store chains are made to serve as cash-cows for [stores in other] areas of the country."

The appropriation of a subsidiary's or a branch's surplus by the parent corporation introduces potentially severe structural imbalance into a plant's operations. During years when sales are good, the profits accrue to the parent. When times go bad, the operating company has been stripped of its revenues, and may be forced to go into the local capital markets for a loan. However, lack of control over its own future profit stream makes the servicing of this loan uncertain, and local banks or other leaders will deal with this uncertainty by charging a higher interest rate—and of course the parent firm may not even permit the branch or subsidiary to borrow on its own.

Thus, by becoming the banker to its various constituent plants or companies, the centralized corporation is able to enforce its own growth goals. At best, the subsidiaries are forced to compete directly with one another for access to their own profits. But in fact, conglomerates (and, since 1976, more and more large single-product corporations) have tended to place the capital so obtained into other, often totally unrelated, acquisitions instead of reinvesting in the sector—let alone the specific company—from which the surplus was redistributed.

The managers of K mart, for example, believe that their continuing operations will be throwing off far more cash than the department store business has traditionally been able profitably to absorb. As a result, industry sources estimate that by 1981 fully one-quarter K mart's available cash will have no place to go. One executive told *Fortune* magazine: "Time is running out and we are aware of it. K mart must search out new directions."

Yet at the same time—just to show the chaos and irrationality of the economic era in which we now live—Mobil Oil Corporation used a substantial part of its post-1973 inflated international oil profits not to expand domestic petroleum production, but to purchase Montgomery Ward, an established department store chain!

The diversification in the steel industry that led to the famous shutdown in 1977 of the Campbell plant of the Youngstown Sheet and Tube Company in Ohio began early in the decade. Between 1970 and 1976 the steel industry as a whole paid out 43 percent of after-tax profits in dividends. This rate was above average for all industry, yet the steel industry was simultaneously complaining that required pollution-control expenditures prevented them from upgrading their old plants and equipment. Some Wall Street an-

alysts have seen the high dividend rate as a strategy for holding on to investors while developing a plan for diversifying into new fields. In the late 1970s the industry has done just that—it has shifted capital into cement, petrochemicals, coal, natural gas, nuclear power plant components containers and packaging, and real estate.

According to U.S. Steel's annual reports, for example, the share of that corporation's annual plant and equipment investment going into actual production of steel fell from 69 percent in 1976 to just over half in 1979. For every dollar of old plant and equipment written off, only $1.40 in new investment was undertaken (in fact, the ratio of new capital spending to depreciation in the steel operations fell by 100 percent, from 2.9 to 1.4). But for every dollar of capital depreciation in its nonsteel operations, U.S. Steel spent nearly three dollars in new capital investment. By 1978, 44 percent of U.S. Steel's total worldwide assets were in nonsteel operations.

Youngstown Sheet and Tube Company was not owned by U.S. Steel, but by a New Orleans-based conglomerate, the Lykes Corporation. Lykes purchased it in 1969, when Sheet and Tube was the nation's eighth largest steel-making firm. The acquisition was financed mainly by a major loan package, which Lykes promised to pay off out of Sheet and Tube's very substantial cash flow. During the next eight years, Lykes used Sheet and Tube's cash to amortize that debt and to expand its nonsteel operations. . . . Before the merger, investment in plant and equipment averaged almost $10 million a year. After the acquisition by Lykes, the average fell to about $3 million per year, and would have had a *zero* trend if not for a few investment projects that were quickly abandoned during the 1975–76 recession. Clearly, Lykes was pursuing a pattern of planned disinvestment in its recent acquisition. This has led most financial analysts to agree that "Lykes must bear responsibility for a good deal of the failure at Youngstown Sheet and Tube." *Business Week* put it in its October 3, 1977, issue: "The conglomerators' steel acquisitions were seen as cash boxes for corporate growth in other areas." In a rather absurd postscript to the closing—which cost 4,100 Ohio workers their jobs—Lykes merged in 1978 with the owners of the Nation's *next* largest steel-maker, the conglomerate Ling-Temco-Vought. The argument used in court by Lykes and LTV to overcome antitrust objections to the merger was that their steel business was "failing," and could only be rescued by achieving financial scale economies through merger! The merger now makes Lykes-LTV the nation's third largest producer of steel. Thus does corporate profit appropriation encourage economic concentration.

This concentration in turn makes it possible for management to impose other costs by "remote control." Centralized control by a home office can impair the profitability of a newly acquired branch or subsidiary, and can even make the business actually unprofitable.

Sometimes the home office requires its new acquisition to carry additional management staff from headquarters, staff the subsidiary did without before and that are probably redundant. For example, in a recent issue of a New England trade magazine, a small manufacturer with 40 percent of the domestic hypodermic needle market was offered for sale by its conglomerate parent. The market analyst notes that "the parent corporation, a Fortune 500 company . . . has imposed an excess of staff and other requirements which add nonproductive costs to the operation. A *pro forma* [simulated balance sheet] eliminating this overlay of corporate expenses shows a much better picture." Recently freed from its former parent (the Esmark conglomerate), the Peabody tannery in Massachusetts projects a reduction in overhead and administrative support services of almost $500,000 during its first year.

In 1978, the New England Provision Company (NEPCO) of Dorchester, a Boston neighborhood, had its meat-packing operations shut down by the same LTV conglomerate that recently merged with the Lykes Corporation. The firm had been consistently profitable prior to its acquisition by LTV in the late 1960s. One factor turning profits into losses seems to have been LTV's insistence that NEPCO pay a fee to the parent for management services. This practice was also found to be present in the case of the Colonial Press in Clinton, Massachusetts, acquired in 1974 by Sheller-Globe, primarily a maker of auto parts, school buses, and ambulances, and closed three years later, in 1977. Colonial was charged an average of $900,000 a year in corporate overhead charges. Some months it was charged $200,000.

There was little justification for these charges. The Press was being forced to pay the costs of larger corporate activities from which it did not benefit. For example, Sheller-Globe maintained an entire department that was solely responsible for security. Given the conditions in the automotive industry there was some justification for these costs. However, Sheller-Globe's corporate policies meant that the security department applied the same systems to all divisions. The corporation built a link fence around three sides of the Colonial Press plant and hired twenty-two security guards. Upon exiting the plant, employees would often be searched for stolen goods. The level of theft at the Press could not possibly justify the cost of the fences and guards, yet Colonial Press was forced to bear part of these costs.

Sometimes the parent firm forces the subsidiary to purchase from particular distant providers, even if the subsidiary's managers could cut costs by purchasing locally. In the NEPCO case,

the firm was required to buy the meat it processed and packaged from [another LTV subsidiary, Wilson Foods and Sporting Goods] at inflated prices; and an inept marketing company was hired . . . , the result of a "sweetheart" contract arranged for the benefit of a former LTV executive vice president. . . .

Lykes imposed the same burden on Youngstown Sheet and Tube. According to the Senate hearings, YST ended up paying more for raw materials (coal and iron ore) from Lyke's mines after the merger than it would have paid on the open market. After the merger, YST began purchasing parts and equipment, which had previously been supplied locally, from a Lykes subsidiary at higher rates. This arrangement cost YST $60 million a year.

To tax the subsidiary in order to subsidize the operations of the headquarters (or its friends) is bad enough. But perhaps most serious of all are the cases where home office policy actually creates the unprofitability of the (previously profitable) subsidiary, through clumsy interference with the local managers who know the situation best. William F. Whyte's case study of the Library Bureau, a furniture

plant in Herkimer, N.Y., revealed just such a problem.

The plant had always had its own sales force and was not dependent upon Sperry Rand for its market. In fact, being part of the conglomerate imposed serious barriers in marketing. For example, it was a rule of Sperry Rand that the Library Bureau salesmen could not call on any customers served by Sperry Rand. While this left the Library Bureau its main markets with public and educational institution libraries, the rule barred the plant from selling to a large number of industrial and business firms that used library equipment. The [subsidiary] could only enter these markets through Sperry Rand salesmen who were unfamiliar with Library Bureau products and had more important things to sell. The handicaps were similar in the export field. . . . [According to the former] head of sales for Library Bureau . . . "We were not officially barred from exporting, but to sell anything outside of the country, we had to send our proposal to the international division, and it would just die there. We would never hear anything back."

Similarly, after its acquisition of the Colonial Press, Sheller-Globe immediately brought in outside management that, except for the newly installed president, had no experience in the publishing industry. Yet this outside group was given control over the most important decisions. In particular, Sheller-Globe wanted to change Colonial's orientation from sales to manufacturing. It wanted to emphasize producing books more efficiently rather than satisfying more clients. This decision impaired long-standing relations with the publishing companies that were Colonial's clients (these included Reader's Digest and Random House), since Sheller-Globe believed there was not a great deal of difference between "producing a steering wheel and producing a book."

Flexibility to accommodate customer's publication schedules was reduced. Colonial was no longer allowed to offer free warehouse space to publishers. The customer service and order departments were merged, resulting in misplaced orders and deteriorated customer relations. An expensive computerized management information system was installed, which so fouled up operations that "books were lost and there was often general confusion about what materials there were and where they were located." Publishers were no longer given itemized cost estimates, and in general, the management under Sheller-Globe mistreated its customers. As a result of all this, "the publishing industry become alienated and sales declined. . . . Decisions which were appropriate to the automotive industry proved disastrous in the book-printing industry."

This disaster has been somewhat mitigated by the reopening of the Press in 1979, as the Colonial Cooperative Press. With the help of the Massachusetts Community Development Finance Corporation and the Industrial Cooperative Association, the press was sold to the workers as a full-scale cooperative. However, it is a much smaller enterprise and it isn't clear whether or not it will succeed. The Colonial Press had over 1,000 workers. Colonial Cooperative Press has 75. Furthermore, in the two years it took to reorganize the plant, the Press lost many of its customers.

Whether or not it survives, this worker-purchase is another example of an ad hoc solution pulled together by the workers and their community as the conglomerate-owner abandoned them. There is no institution in the U.S. economy to which viable businesses can turn when they are sold out by a parent-corporation. Each plant must find its own solution within its particular local economy. Unlike the Chrysler Corporation they cannot turn to the federal government. But, also unlike the Chrysler Corporation, many of these conglomerate subsidiaries do not *need* to be bailed out, for they were not actually losing money to begin with. What they need is assistance in setting up autonomous, decentralized, locally owned operations.

The conventional wisdom about highly centralized management is that it makes possible a higher degree of efficiency in information and personnel management than ever before. But the evidence suggests that the managers of the giant corporations and conglomerates frequently "overmanage" their subsidiaries, milk them of their profits, subject them to strenuous or impossible performance standards, interfere with local decisions, and are quick to close them down when other, more profitable, opportunities appear. In 1975–76 Gulf and Western almost dumped the Brown Paper Company of Holyoke, Massachusetts, a leading producer of quality papers, and actually did sell off its most profitable product line to a Wisconsin competitor. By 1977 the plant's sales were up again to over $450 million.

Highly centralized organizations like Gulf and Western and Textron have positioned themselves so as to be able to make a profit either from a subsidiary's success or from failure that requires divestiture (since it can be treated as a tax loss and used to offset profits earned in other operations). From the point of view of capital asset management this may be the pinnacle of capitalist institutional creativity. But from the perspective of economic stability for working people and their communities, these clever capitalist giants are a disaster. The much-discussed trade-off between efficiency and equity turns out to mean capital management efficiency, but tremendous inefficiency at the level of actual production, to go along with the inequities imposed on workers and communities.

In short, modern monopoly capitalists will sell off or shut down profitable businesses if they think they can make even more money somewhere else. This strategy is not a recent one, nor have its harmful effects ever been unforeseeable. Here is Emil Rieve, president of the Textile Workers Union of America before a Congressional committee thirty years ago:

> Mr. Little is a capitalist, but in the field of finance rather than the field of production . . .
>
> I say this in the same sense that Hitler and Stalin are in the tradition of Napoleon and Alexander the Great. We have changed our attitude toward financial conquerors, just as we have changed our attitude toward military conquerors. Success is not the only yardstick.
>
> I do not know whether Mr. Little has broken any laws. But if he has not, our laws ought to be changed.

"Mr. Little" is Royal Little, founder of Textron, the Rhode Island conglomerate that first developed many of the strategies now in use. Textron was initially a textile company. This year the Securities and Exchange Commission has charged it with paying over $5 million in bribes to officials in eleven foreign countries in order to "stimulate" sales of its Bell Helicopters. Its chairman at the time was G. William Miller, the current Secretary of the Treasury.

Just as the law in other areas has gradually evolved over the years to recognize that property rights, though dominant, are not absolute, the law must be changed to temper arbitrary plant relocation. Fifty years ago, tenants had no rights arising from their occupancy of a building. Today, the law stipulates that a landlord must keep the building habitable, that he must provide heat and hot water, and that tenants may not be arbitrarily evicted. Some communities have authorized rent control and even rent strikes when the property is not kept in good repair.

Family law has undergone a similar evolution. A wife is no longer her husband's property, and a couple's tangible property is no longer assumed to be the fruits of the husband's labor. Even banking law has been amended to deny banks the right to shut down when the community would be denied essential banking services.

But laws dealing with plant relocation are back in the eighteenth century. Profitability is considered an absolute right, not a relative one; and the right of a plant to relocate in the name of greater profitability is still sacrosanct, even where management's judgment or motive is specious.

As Emil Rieve observed thirty years ago, laws that sanction promiscuous relocations must be changed. A handful of states are considering requiring a year's notice before companies may shut down plants. Legislation is also under discussion to require severance pay, as well as compensation to the community. Companies could be required to pay back all tax abatements; labor contracts could also demand that the parent company not shift the production to other plants; tax write-offs for shutdowns could be prohibited. The proposed legislation to require federal chartering of the largest corporations could also include a range of sanctions against arbitrary relocations.

Far from interfering with industry's "right" to use capital optimally, these sanctions could force parent companies that acquire independent firms to operate them efficiently. As things stand now, conglomerates are being rewarded for running their subsidiaries into the ground—and the employees along with them.

NO

Richard B. McKenzie

FRUSTRATING BUSINESS MOBILITY

Business mobility—the mirror image of the free play of economic forces—is a normal, indeed inevitable, feature of any dynamic and growing economy. Nonetheless, particular moves (plant closings, relocations, and the like) can and do evoke protests by the communities and workers left behind. They see themselves as somehow "wronged." And among the political remedies they seek are restraints on business mobility by government fiat.

Cities are worried about losing employers and tax revenues to the suburbs, the Snowbelt is worried about losing both of those and skilled workers as well to the Sunbelt, and politicians everywhere seem attracted to the notion that economic stability in their areas can be ensured by putting a check on management's freedom to pull up stakes. Two years ago when American Airlines announced its decision to move its headquarters from New York to Dallas, for example, New York Mayor Edward Koch termed it a betrayal, and a taxi union vowed to stop serving the airline's New York terminals. Fortunately for the airline and its passengers, as well as the cabbies, the threat was never made good. And American's headquarters was moved.

In recent years, bills that would seriously restrict business mobility have been introduced in the U.S. Congress and a number of state legislatures.* The scheme is also the centerpiece of Ralph Nader's current campaign to "democratize" corporate America, to make major corporations more responsive to the "general interest." (His vehicle is the Corporate Democracy Act of 1980, H.R. 7010.) If such a measure became federal law, it would substantially increase government intervention in business decision making, alter our national economic system in fundamental ways, and be, on balance, detrimental to the regional and local economies of the country in the bargain.

---

*At last count eleven, including the northeastern states of Connecticut, Maine, Massachusetts, New Jersey, New York, Pennsylvania, and Rhode Island, plus Illinois, Michigan, Ohio, and Oregon.—Eds.

From Richard B. McKenzie, "Frustrating Business Mobility," *Regulation* (May/June 1980). Copyright © 1980 by the American Enterprise Institute for Public Policy Research. Reprinted by permission.

THE "RUNAWAY PLANT PHENOMENON"

The general purpose of the restrictive legislation, which already has been enacted in Maine, is to remedy what has been called the "runaway plant phenomenon." Typically, the bills provide for a government agency to investigate business moves and rule on their appropriateness. For example, the National Employment Priorities Act, a 1977 proposal that was reintroduced in the House last August, by Representative William Ford (Democrat, Michigan) and sixty-one co-sponsors, would set up a National Employment Priorities Administration within the U.S. Department of Labor to investigate plant closings, to report its findings on the economic rationale for the decision and on employment losses and other impacts on the affected community, and to recommend ways of preventing or mitigating these harmful effects. (In the 1977 version, the investigation would determine whether "such closing or transfer" was "without [and presumably also "with"] adequate justification.") A bill pending since 1978 in the New Jersey General Assembly would vest similar responsibilities in a state agency called the Division of Business Relocation.

A second typical feature of bills designed to curb business mobility is the levying of penalties on firms that move. The Ohio bill, for instance, would require such firms to dole out to the employees left behind severance pay equal to one week's wage for each year of service and to pay the community an amount equal to 10 percent of the gross annual wages of the affected employees.

Under the Ford bill (H.R. 5040), a business that moved or closed would have to pay the workers left jobless 85 percent of their last two-years' average wage for a period of fifty-two weeks, less any outside income and government assistance. Besides, the firm would have to make a year's normal payments to any employee benefit plan and cover relocation expenses for employees who decided to move to any other company facility within the next three years. Workers over age fifty-four at the time of a move or closing would be entitled to full retirement benefits at age sixty-two instead of sixty-five or seventy. Failure to comply with the act would carry severe penalties—a combination of fines and the denial of tax benefits associated with a move. Finally, the local government would be owed an amount equal to 85 percent of the firm's average tax payments for the last three years. If the firm moved abroad and an "economically viable alternative" existed in the United States, the firm would have to pay "damages" equal to 300 percent of any tax revenue lost to the U.S. Treasury. Any payment required under the act, not met by the firm, and paid by the federal government would become a debt owed by the firm to the federal government.

Third, the kind of legislation under consideration here generally provides for government assistance to the people and entities adversely affected. Under the Ford bill, for instance, the U.S. secretary of labor, with the advice of a relocation advisory council, would be empowered to provide financial and technical assistance to employees who lost their jobs, to the communities affected by plant relocations, and even to businesses themselves—those that might decide *not* to relocate if government assistance were available. Assistance to employees would take the from of training programs, job placement services, job search and relocation expenses, in addition to such existing welfare benefits as food stamps, unemployment compensation, and housing allowances. Federal grants for additional social services and public works projects would go directly to the community. Assistance to businesses would be given as technical advice, loans and loan guarantees, interest subsidies, and the assumption of outstanding debt, but only if the Secretary of Labor were to determine that the aid would "substantially contribute to the economic viability of the establishment." The New Jersey and Ohio proposals provide for similar community and employee aid.

Fourth, under the various bills, firms are required to give advance notice of their plans to move or close—up to two years' notice in the Ohio bill and in the proposed Corporate Democracy Act of 1980. The prenotification requirement in the Ford bill varies with the size of the anticipated loss in jobs: two years for firms expecting the loss to be greater than 500, one year for 100 to 500, and six months for less than 100. The legislation proposed in New Jersey requires only a one-year notice. Exceptions could be made, of course, but generally only if the firms can show that meeting the requirement would be unreasonable.

Fifth, the various bills usually require that businesses offer their employees, to the extent possible, comparable employment and pay at the new location. And finally, each of the bills contains some minimum-size cutoff point. The proposed National Employment Priorities Act, for example, would apply only to firms with more than $250,000 in annual sales. But it should be noted that many McDonald's restaurants do that much business in a year. The bills' reach, typically, is both wide and deep.

DRAWING THE BATTLE LINES

In describing the changing regional structure of the U.S. economy, *Business Week* magazine observed: "The second war between the states will take the form of political and economic maneuver. But the conflict can nonetheless be bitter and divisive because it will be a struggle for income, jobs, people and capital" (May 17, 1976). And so it promises to be. When he introduced the original National Employment Priorities Act in 1977, Representative Ford gave us a preview of the economic rationale of the political battle lines and some flavor of the ensuing debate:

> The legislation is based on the premise that such closings and transfers may cause irreparable harm—both economic and social—to workers, communities, and the Nation. . . . My own congressional district suffered the effects of the runaway plant in 1972 when the Garwood plant in Wayne moved and left 600 unemployed workers behind. . . . [T]he reason these firms are moving away is not economic necessity but economic greed. For instance, the Federal Mogul Company in Detroit signed a contract in 1971 with the United Auto Workers and 6 months later announced it would be moving to Alabama. A spokesman for the company was quoted as saying that they were moving "not because we are not making money in Detroit, but because we can make more money in Alabama."

Two years later, in introducing his significantly revised 1979 bill, Representative Ford stressed that business movements from the Northeast during the last decade had resulted in a million lost jobs in manufacturing and pointed to studies showing the suicide rate among workers displaced from their jobs by plant closings at thirty times the national average. He also noted,

> It is well established that the affected workers suffer a far higher incidence of heart disease and hypertension, diabetes, peptic ulcers, gout, and joint swelling than the general population. They also incur serious psychological problems, including extreme depression, insecurity, anxiety, and the loss of self-esteem.

A veritable chamber of horribles!

So it should come as no surprise that the campaign for government restrictions on business mobility adopts the rhetoric of war. Phrases like "second war between the states," "counter-attacks," and "fierce and ruinous state warfare" fill popular accounts of regional shifts. The economic conflict at the heart of attempts to control business relocations is viewed as "us" against "them"—North versus South, the Snowbelt versus the Sunbelt.

Such rhetoric may serve transient political purposes. But it distorts public perception of economic conditions in different parts of the country and hides nonsensical arguments behind the veil of "urgency" as to government action. Thus, it is instructive to examine the major arguments made to support restrictive legislation.

CHANGES IN POPULATION

The contention is made that southward business movements have increased the rates of population growth in the South and Southwest. The corollary is that the North is actually losing people, especially highly educated workers, and that the population shifts that have been occurring are larger than can be accommodated by existing political institutions.

Table 1

Population Growth Rates, by Region, 1950–1977

Region	1950–1960	1960–1970	1970–1977
Northeast	13.2	9.8	0.4
New England	12.8	12.7	3.3
Middle Atlantic	13.3	8.9	– 0.4
North Central	16.1	9.6	2.3
East North Central	19.2	11.2	2.0
West North Central	9.5	6.1	3.4
South	16.4	14.3	11.2
South Atlantic	22.6	18.1	11.8
East South Central	5.0	6.3	8.0
West South Central	16.6	14.0	12.3
West	38.9	24.2	12.7
Mountain	35.1	20.9	21.0
Pacific	40.2	25.2	10.1
U.S. Total	18.5	13.4	6.4

Source: Adapted from Richard B. McKenzie, *Restrictions on Business Mobility* (Washington, D.C.: American Enterprise Institute), Table 1.

What do the data actually show? First, as is evident in Table 1, the population growth rates of the Northeast and North Central regions have indeed declined significantly since the 1950s, but so have the population growth rates of *all* regions, including the South and West. (Only the Middle Atlantic states experienced a net decline in the 1970–1977 period, and that decline was very modest.) Further, and here Table 2 is in point, these changes in population growth rates have been caused as much or more by "natural" factors—changes in family life styles, the costs of rearing children, the widespread use of contraception, and the legality of abortions—as by net outmigration.

Second, aggregate data on population shifts blur the complex picture of who moves and for what reasons. Many of the people who moved south in the 1970s are the same people who moved north in the 1950s and 1960s. Others (for example, retirees) have moved south for reasons

Table 2

Average Annual Growth Rates in Population by Region and Cause, 1960–1970 and 1970–1976

Region	Population		Natural Increase		Net Migration	
	1970–1976	1960–1970	1970–1976	1960–1970	1970–1976	1960–1970
Northeast	0.1	0.9	0.4	0.9	– 0.3	0.1
North Central	0.3	0.9	0.6	1.0	– 0.3	– 0.1
South	1.5	1.3	0.8	1.2	0.7	0.2
West	1.6	2.2	0.8	1.3	0.8	1.0
U.S. Total	0.9	1.3	0.7	1.1	0.2	0.2

Source: McKenzie, *Restrictions on Business Mobility,* Table 2.

wholly unrelated to business location. Still others have moved because of new and expanding industries in the South, not because of relocations from elsewhere. It is also interesting to note that a major source of the above average population growth of the South Atlantic states (11.8 percent in the 1970–1977 period) has been the extraordinary growth of a single state, Florida (over 25 percent).

Third, a favorite argument in support of restrictions on business mobility is that the South and West are gaining a disproportionate share of highly educated and highly skilled workers, leaving the North and Midwest with a preponderance of uneducated, unskilled, and thus low-income workers. Now the new wave of outmigration from the North of course includes many highly educated and skilled people; but the proponents of restrictive legislation greatly exaggerate the quite undramatic facts. For instance, in the 1975–1977 period substantially more unemployed male workers moved from the Northeast to the South, (23,000) than from the South to the Northeast (14,000), and virtually the same pattern held for unemployed female workers. (The Northeast also exported more un-

employed workers to the West than it imported from the West.)

Other considerations are equally revealing. Far more people below the poverty line migrated from the Northeast to the South (133,000) than vice versa (39,000) in the 1975–1977 period. (Much the same point can be made about the migration of low-income people between the Northeast and West.) In addition, while more people with one or more years of college migrated from the Northeast to the South (151,000) than from the South to the Northeast (102,000), those with *some* college education were a significantly greater proportion of the southern migrants to the North (56.3 percent) than the other way around (40.3 percent). (The same cannot be said about the migration of college-educated people between the Northeast and the West.) In short, it simply is not clear that the South or the West is receiving from the North a disproportionate number of highly trained, high-income people. Some—but no tidal wave.

Finally, most people move within a region, not among regions—and mostly they stay within the same state. Indeed, of the people who moved to a different house in the 1975–1977 period, approximately 60 percent stayed in the same county! Hence, if business relocation rules are seen as a means of restraining migration, and *insofar as migration results from business relocations at all*, these rules will in fact restrain migration *within* regions and states more than *among* regions. And insofar as such rules are designed to retard the economic development of the South and West by restricting the migration of people and jobs, it follows in all likelihood that they also will restrict the economic development of *all* regions, the North along with the rest.

CHANGES IN INCOME

Edward Kelley, in a position paper of the Ohio Public Interests Campaign, claims that business movements are reducing individual incomes and the tax collections of the governments in the North: "As the manufacturing base of the [northern] economy declines, so does the tax base. There are fewer taxable industrial locations and fewer people paying taxes" (*Industrial Exodus: Public Strategies for Control of Runaway Plants*, 1977). Yet in fact individual incomes in the North have been rising over the years. It is also true that individual incomes have been growing faster in the Southeast, Southwest, and West. What is happening, as the accompanying figure clearly shows, is that the relative incomes of the regions

are converging. Personal income in the North has decreased relatively (while increasing absolutely), but it still averages 25 percent higher than personal income in the South. In short, if business movements owe something to the disparity in regional incomes and if regional incomes are converging, it would seem that Representative Ford and Mr. Nader have proposed a solution to a problem that is being solved anyway, and predictably so, by normal market forces. In fact, because of the convergence of regional incomes, business mobility is likely to be less dramatic in the future than it was in the past.

The movement of businesses to the South does not necessarily mean that the North is made worse off, absolutely, or that improvement in living standards

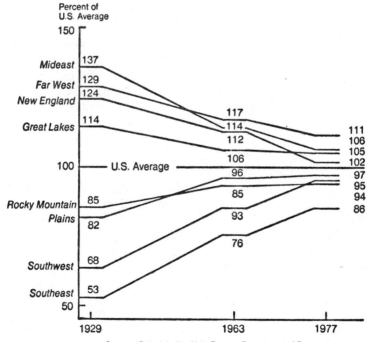

INDEX OF REGIONAL PER CAPITA
DISPOSABLE INCOME

Source: Calculated by Yale Brozen, Department of Economics, University of Chicago.

there has been retarded. Indeed, the converse may be reasonably argued—namely, that the movement of people and industry south has contributed to an improved standard of living in the North. By moving south where production costs are lower, businesses are able—at least in the long run—to provide goods to northern markets at lower prices than if they had stayed in the North. And they can expand production at lower cost. In not too many years, this increases both national income and, because the prices of goods are lower, the purchasing power of *all* workers' incomes, including those in the North.

THE DECLINE IN NORTHERN MANUFACTURING JOBS

The claim that the North has lost a million or so manufacturing jobs in the last ten years suggests an economic problem serious enough to justify severe restrictions on entrepreneurial freedom. In fact, however, the claim misinterprets the actual state of employment opportunities in the North. The narrow focus on *manufacturing* employment hides the very important fact that *total* employment in the North has risen continually and significantly during the last several decades.

As Table 3 shows, manufacturing employment in the Northeast and East North Central regions did indeed decline by about 1 million jobs between 1969 and 1979; but in the same period total nonagricultural employment grew substantially, by 4.5 million jobs, reflecting the strong upward trend in service and government employment during the period. Moreover, since 1975 even manufacturing employment in the North has begun to move up again. If business relocation rules are designed to thwart the move-

Table 3

Nonagricultural Employment in the Northeast and East North Central Regions, 1965–1979
(in thousands)

Year (monthly average)	Total Employment	Manufacturing Employment
1979 (Dec.)	38,100	10,172
1978	36,331	10,153
1977	35,408	9,886
1976	34,288	9,601
1975	33,376	9,396
1974	34,826	10,423
1973	34,506	10,533
1972	33,358	10,093
1971	32,803	10,027
1970	33,249	10,936
1969	33,358	11,201
1968	32,384	11,055
1967	31,589	11,007
1966	30,867	11,034
1965	29,464	10,472

Note: The Northeast and East North Central regions include Maine, Vermont, New Hampshire, Connecticut, Rhode Island, Massachusetts, New York, Pennsylvania, New Jersey, Ohio, Indiana, Illinois, Michigan, and Wisconsin.
Source: *Statistical Abstract of the United States, 1965–1977,* and *Employment and Earnings,* 1978 and 1979.

ment of manufacturing jobs generally, they may well have the ironic effect of choking off this recent reversal of the long-term downward trend in northern manufacturing jobs.

Finally, it must be stressed that only a very small percentage of the 1 million lost manufacturing jobs in the North can be attributed to business migration in any case. A study by Peter Allaman and David Birch of the Massachusetts Institute of Technology shows that just 1.5 percent of the North's job losses in the 1969–1972 period stemmed from the outmigration of firms, while a recent extension of that study by James Miller of the Department of Agriculture puts the figure at 1.6 percent for the 1969–1975 period. In other words, as Miller concluded, the impact of firm migration on the reallocation of manufacturing employment among regions "was trivial compared to the net effect of starts, closures and stationary firms."

An added inducement to this alleged movement south, it is often argued, is the "wage-attraction" of the South. However, it is more illuminating to assess the impact of "wage-push" in the North. From the wage-attraction perspective, it may appear that low-paid workers in the South are stealing business from and causing economic harm to the North. But the wage-push perspective suggests that wages in the North are higher and on the rise for such classical economic reasons as competition for workers from the developing service sector in the North. In other words, manufacturers are forced to pay higher wages or risk losing their labor force to more rapidly expanding sectors of the economy. Firms that move south are "pushed" south, having been outbid for labor resources in the North. From this perspective, industrial movements to the South are a consequence of gains made by many workers in the North—and the "runaway plant phenomenon" is a positive force in the dynamic and growth economy, South *and* North.

Even if northern manufacturing firms were to be restricted from moving south by legislation, the movement of manufacturing jobs to the South, though impeded, would not be stopped. Firms move because costs of production in the new location are lower—and anticipated profits higher. Restrictions on business mobility would cause new firms to spring up in southern locations and existing southern firms to expand by more than they otherwise would. Because of cost disadvantages, firms in the old northern locations would be induced by natural market forces—*which relocation rules at-*

tempt to override—to contract their operations or to go out of business.

COMPARATIVE COST ADVANTAGES

And this of course is the key, this ill-conceived attempt to improve on "nature" by those who urge regulation to restrict business mobility. Even at the risk of accentuating the obvious, it is helpful to return to a first principle or two. People in different parts of the country trade with one another because differences in their costs of production make it to their mutual advantage to do so. Specialization in trade leads to maximum output from the resources available to the community as a whole. And, because the conditions of production—the availability of resources, technology, consumer preferences for work and for goods—continually change, so do the comparative costs from region to region. What once was relatively advantageous to produce in the North may, for any number of reasons, become less costly to produce in some other region. This constantly shifting calculus of costs can be altered by changes in the relative scarcity of resources, worker education levels, or regional preferences for services. Whatever the reason, the cost of producing any particular good in one region can go up and, as a consequence, the production of that good moves elsewhere—all, to repeat, very "naturally."

Pinning down the precise reasons for changes in regional economic structures is difficult in the best of circumstances. In recent decades, however, the comparative advantages of the North have indeed changed, and for two principal reasons. First, the demand for services in the North has increased rapidly, more so than in other parts of the country; and this in turn has increased the cost of resources, including labor, for all other sectors of the northern economy. Also, environmental legislation has placed more severe restrictions on industrial production in the congested North than in many other parts of the country and has increased the relative costs of manufacturing there. The unavailability of "pollution rights" in the North has caused many firms to look to locations with less present pollution and less stringent immediate pollution-control standards—to the South and West, for example.

Undeniably, these changes in regional production costs, and the economic adjustments that result from them, can and do cause hardship for some. But restricting business mobility is a cure worse than the disease. Such restrictions would force employers to lock labor and other resources into comparatively inefficient uses—resources that could and should be moving into expanding sectors of various regional economies. Thus, governmental rules that impede the movement of manufacturing industry out of the North would not only retard the development of industry in the South (or elsewhere) but, by the same token, would retard the development of the service sector in the North. The overall result would be increased nationwide production costs and reduced national production and income.

THE WORST OF WORLDS

States and communities that are mulling over business mobility restrictions may believe they would be protecting their economies by protecting their industrial bases, but in fact they would be hurting them—and themselves. What company would want to move into an area that had substantial economic penalties for moving out? What entrepreneur would want to start a business in a community or state that had penalties for changing locations? Companies interested in profits will always try to settle in those areas that leave them free to make the basic decisions on when to shift among products, when to close, and when to move. States or communities that do not impose restrictions will obviously have a competitive advantage over those that do—which makes it equally obvious why Representative Ford and others, who want restrictions in their own areas, are seeking through federal legislation to have *all* areas of the country abide by the same rules. And this simply tightens the squeeze on U.S. industry in world markets and provides yet another marginal inducement for U.S. firms to locate their production facilities in foreign countries where such restrictions are not in place.

Indeed, viewed from whatever perspective, restrictions on business mobility constitute an idea whose time one hopes will never come. Predictably, restrictions would tend to reduce the efficiency of resource allocation; reduce national and regional income levels; and reduce the ability of the economy to respond to changes in people's tastes and to changes in technology, in the availability of resources, and in the mix of demand for particular goods and particular services. In short, they represent a bad bargain all around—for the communities and workers affected (in spite of the appearance of near-term relief), for Representative Ford's constituents as much as everyone else, for the U.S. economy generally, for entrepreneur and taxpayer alike.

POSTSCRIPT

Do Firms Exploit Workers and Local Communities By Closing Profitable Plants?

Professors Bluestone and Harrison find that there are several common factors in plant closings undertaken by a number of large conglomerates: Excess funds are milked from one enterprise and transferred to a totally unrelated enterprise—often resulting in disinvestment in the "cash cow" and the eventual reduction in its profitability; the parent corporation may assign an unwarranted share of the conglomerate's common costs to one enterprise—thereby reducing its profitability; and management may force the firm to purchase its supplies from other subsidiaries of the conglomerate—even if these supplies are more costly than those from other sources. According to Bluestone and Harrison, the end result is that a potentially profitable plant may be run "into the ground—and their employees along with them."

Professor McKenzie argues that the movement of industry from the Northeast and North Central states to the Sunbelt is a natural economic phenomenon that should be encouraged rather than discouraged. He maintains that plant closings in the North and the movement South and West are caused by differentials in factor costs and that as long as these differentials exist, the migration will continue. Second, McKenzie argues that the labor freed from the industrial plants that are closed in the North can now enter the growing service sector in the North. Prior to the Sunbelt migration, he explains, the North's service sector competed with its industrial sector for labor; this drove the price of labor up and pushed industrial firms out of the North. Third, he believes the North's consumers are benefited by the migration of firms to the South and West. Since production costs are lower, these firms can sell their output at lower prices.

Professor McKenzie's arguments are fully articulated in his book *Restriction on Business Mobility: A Study in Political Rhetoric and Economic Reality* (American Enterprise Institute, 1979). An interesting complementary piece to McKenzie that discusses the weaknesses of worker-owner takeovers of closed plants is "Youngstown Sheet and Tube—A Classic Takeover Case," *The Center Magazine* (November/December 1979). Arthur Shostak examines the private costs of displaced workers in his article "The Human Costs of Plant Closings," *Federationist* (August 1980). Lastly, many of the problems articulated by Bluestone and Harrison are contained in the United States Senate, Committee on the Judiciary, *Hearings on Mergers and Industrial Concentration, 95th Congress* (Government Printing Office, 1979).

ISSUE 8

Should Congress Guarantee U.S. Workers the Right to Parental Leave?

YES: U.S. House of Representatives—Committee on Education and Labor, from "Background and Need for Legislation," *Parental and Medical Leave Act of 1986* (July 21, 1986)

NO: Steve Bartlett, Thomas Tauke et al., from "Separate Dissenting Views on H.R. 4300," *Parental and Medical Leave Act of 1986* (July 21, 1986)

ISSUE SUMMARY

Yes: The supporters of H.R. 4300 maintain that there is a "growing conflict between work and family" that can be corrected by guaranteeing workers the "right to unpaid family leave."

No: Congressmen Bartlett, Tauke, Armey, Fawell, and Henry, dissenting members of the House Committee on Education and Labor, argue that H.R. 4300 may be "well-intentioned" but that it is also "rigid and inflexible," "anti-small business," and the first attempt by Congress to legislate national standards for major employee leave and health benefits—a step Congress has avoided in the past.

The American workplace has changed dramatically in recent years as more and more women of all ages have joined the workforce. A few statistics brings this into sharp focus: (1) currently 44 percent of the workforce is female, and if current trends prevail, more than 50 percent of the workforce will be female by the end of the century; (2) from the 1950s to the 1980s the percentage of mothers who worked more than tripled; indeed, by 1981 mothers with preschool children were more likely to be in the workforce than married women with no children; (3) in the early 1970s, less than 30 percent of married women with a child under the age of two were in the workforce; 15 years later one out of two mothers with children under two years of age worked; and (4) the "Ozzie and Harriet family," in which the husband goes to work and the wife stays home to raise the children, now represents only 7 percent of American households; female-headed households represent 16 percent of all households.

As fewer parents, either by choice or by necessity, stay home to raise their children, the clash between work responsibilities and home responsibilities becomes more apparent. Parents struggle to find ways to accommodate their work schedules to the ever-present and ever-changing demands of their children. Women need medical leave for childbirth. Both men and women need time for early child rearing so that "bonding" can occur. One parent also needs the ability to leave the workplace to care for a seriously ill or injured child. But if there are no parental rights guaranteed in the workplace, a mother or father who attempts to fulfill her or his responsibility may jeopardize her or his job. That is, employers may simply terminate the worker or withhold promotions and/or wage increases in retaliation for absences from the workplace.

Given this real or imagined threat to the economic well-being of a growing number of American families, Congress began to consider the need for some intervention as early as 1968. In that year President Johnson's Advisory Council on the Status of Women suggested that female workers should be safeguarded against the temporary loss of their wages due to pregnancy. Two years later this same Council proposed that pregnancies should be treated in the same manner as any other medical condition. That is, a pregnant women should be entitled to sick leave, disability, and other medical benefits.

Since Congress did not immediately move to enact legislation that would explicitly protect the rights of pregnant workers, attempts were made in the early 1970s to protect the rights of pregnant workers by bringing discrimination cases to the courts under Title VII of the Civil Rights Act of 1964 and the equal protection clause in the U.S. Constitution. These pleas were denied by the Supreme Court and consequently Congress enacted the Pregnancy Discrimination Act of 1978 as an amendment to Title VII. This legislation in large part eliminated the worst abuses that were suffered by pregnant workers. It allowed women to work until childbirth unless medical complications prevented this; it assured women the right to return to their jobs; it provided them with the same benefits given to other temporarily disabled workers, such as paid sick leave, personal leave, disability benefits, hospitalization and medical insurance.

In brief, this legislation was antidiscriminatory in language and intent. It obligated employers to provide the same benefits for workers who were temporarily disabled because of pregnancy as for other temporarily disabled workers. However, if an employer provided no worker with any disability benefits, it was in compliance with the law. In this case, the employer did not "discriminate" against the pregnant worker when the firm did not provide maternity leave.

Although the Pregnancy Discrimination Act has gone a long way toward protecting the rights of millions of working women, it still leaves the rights of many other women and men unprotected. It is in this context that H.R. 4300 was introduced on March 4, 1986, by Congressman William Clay (D-Mo.). This legislation was assigned to the Committee on Education and Labor and the Committee on Post Office and Civil Service. The Committee on Post Office and Civil Services by a vote of 18–0 ordered H.R. 4300 to be favorably reported to the full House. Although the Committee on Education and Labor favorably reported H.R. 4300, there were dissenting views. The following excerpts are representative of the debate that surrounded the introduction of H.R. 4300.

YES

BACKGROUND AND NEED FOR LEGISLATION

The tensions between employment and family life, two of the vital concerns of most Americans, have always existed. Recent economic and social changes have significantly exacerbated the tensions. Private sector practices and government policies have failed to keep pace with and respond to these new realities, imposing a heavy burden on families, employees, employers and society as a whole. This bill provides a sensible response to the growing conflict between work and family by establishing a right to unpaid family leave and temporary medical leave for all workers.

THE NEED FOR FAMILY LEAVE

The United States has experienced what can only be characterized as a demographic revolution with profound consequences for the lives of working men and women and their families. Today, ninety-six percent of fathers work and more than sixty percent of mothers also work. Female participation in the labor force has risen from 19 percent in 1900 to more than 52 percent today; 44 percent of the U.S. labor force is now female. Between 1950 and 1981, the labor force participation rate of mothers tripled. By 1981, a larger percentage of mothers of preschool aged children participated in the labor force than did the percentage of married women with no minor children in 1950 and all women in 1900. The fastest growing segment of this group is comprised of women with children under the age of three. Nearly 50 percent of all mothers with children under one year of age are now working outside of the home. And half of all children in two-parent families have both parents in the workforce.

Equally dramatic is the unprecedented divorce rate of fifty percent and the increase in out-of-wedlock births, which has left millions of women to struggle as heads of households, supporting themselves and their children in an era of high living costs. Women represent the sole parent in 16 percent of

From "Background and Need for Legislation," *Parental and Medical Leave Act of 1986*, U.S. House of Representatives.

all families. At the same time, a majority of women workers remain in female intensive, relatively low paid jobs and are less likely than men to have adequate job protections and fringe benefits. Each of these phenomena, which affect women of all races, are most pronounced for black and other minority women. Single women heads of households, who work full-time in the labor force, often cannot keep their families above the poverty line.

Another demographic change relevant to the leave needs of all employees involves the growing number of elderly in our society. Currently, more than 2.2 million family members provide unpaid help to ailing relatives. In the case of the elderly, the most common caregiver is a child or spouse. About 38 percent of those caring for elderly relatives are children, and 35 percent are spouses. The average age of persons caring for elderly family members is 57 years.

Similarly, the percentage of adults in the care of their working children or parents due to physical and mental disabilities is growing. There is a trend away from institutionalization, which has been shown to be cost ineffective and often detrimental to the health and well-being of persons with mental and physical disabilities. Though independent living situations are often preferable, deinstitutionalization can result in increased care responsibilities for family members, many of whom are also of necessity wage earners. This trend toward home care is laudable because of the strong benefits it provides to the health and well-being of families; however, it can also add to the tension between work demands and family needs.

The significance of these demographic changes is apparent. Where men and women alike are wage earners, the crucial unpaid caretaking services traditionally performed by wives—care of young children, ill family members, aging parents— has become increasingly difficult for families to fulfill. Yet these functions— physical caretaking and emotional support, are performed best by families. Indeed, in many instances, only families can perform them adequately. Society has long depended on the family to meet these needs and being able to provide such care has supported and strengthened families. Depriving families of their ability to meet such needs seriously undermines the stability of families and the well-being of individuals, with both economic and social costs. Yet today, at a magnitude significantly greater than ever before, American business requires the services of women and men alike. Modern families have made painful sacrifices to adapt to the needs of business and to the demands of wage earning. Business must make some modest accommodations to the needs of working families, in order to preserve the most essential of the traditional functions of the family.

The testimony of individual working people before the Committee demonstrated the difficulties faced by today's working families. Lorraime Poole, an employee of a larger municipality, testified to her heartbreak when she could not accept a long-awaited adoptive baby that had become available to her. Her employer had told her that she would lose her job if she took time off from work to receive the child and the adoption agency would not place the child unless assured that she would take some time off to be with the child. Ms. Poole was left with no choice but decline the placement. Stephen F. Webber, a coal miner and member of the executive board of the United

Mine Workers of America, after describing his union's efforts to negotiate for family leaves, stated:

Caring for a seriously ill child presents special problems to working miners. Treatment centers for serious illnesses such as cancer are often located in urban centers, forcing families in rural communities to travel great distances. I think in particular, of one coal miner I know, whose child has cancer, and who must travel nearly 400 miles round trip each month from his rural home to take his child for treatment at a medical center in Morgantown, West Virginia.

His testimony included other compelling examples, including that of a miner whose five-year-old son became comatose after choking on a piece of food and required twenty-four-hour-a-day care, care that the miner, a single parent and sole wage earner, had to provide or arrange. A working mother, Iris Elliot, described to the Committee the difficulties she faced as a full-time worker with a pre-school-aged son and a seriously ill infant. Her employer, a national corporation, had no family leave policy. Ms. Elliot was offered a 90-day personal leave, without pay or job protection, but she could not risk losing her position or health benefits as the sole medical insurance carrier for her family. She concluded her testimony by saying "No parent should ever have to be torn between nurturing their seriously ill child and reporting to work like I did."

Experts who testified before the Committee confirmed the importance of family leaves. Dr. T. Berry Braselton, associate professor of pediatrics at Harvard, and Dr. Eleanor S. Szanton, executive director of the National Center for Clinical Infant Programs, provided support for a leave to care for infants, explaining, in the words of Dr. Szanton,

While children require careful nurturing throughout their development, the formation of loving attachments in the earliest months and years of life creates an emotional "root system" for future growth and development. How are these attachments formed? Through the daily feeding, bathing, diapering, comforting and "baby talk" that are all communications of utmost importance in beginning to give the child the sense that life is ordered, expectable and benevolent. . . . In short, these factors affect the baby's cognitive, emotional, social and physical development. . . . Once parents and babies do establish a solid attachment to each other, the transition to work and child care is likely to be easier for parents and for the child. Parents who have cared for their infant for several months are likely to understand a good deal about their child's unique personality and the kind of caregiver or setting which will be most appropriate. Babies, for their part, who have already begun the process of learning to love and trust their parents are better able to form—and to use—trusting, warm relationships with other adults.

Meryl Frank, director of the Infant Care Leave Project of the Yale Bush Center in Child Development and Social Policy, reported on the conclusions and recommendations of the Project's Advisory Committee on Infant Care Leave. The Advisory Committee echoed the views of Dr. Brazelton and Dr. Szanton, and concluded that the "infant care leave problem in the United States is of a magnitude and urgency to require immediate national action." The Advisory Committee, whose members include academics and professionals in child development, health and business, recommended a 6-month minimum leave, with partial income replacement for the first 3 months and benefit continuation and job protection for the entire leave period.

The Committee was also provided the recommendations of the Economic Policy Council of the United Nations Association of the United States of America (EPC). During 1984, the EPC, which is comprised of corporate executives, union presidents and academics, studied the economic and demographic trends transforming the family and labor force and issued a report in December of 1985 of its findings, entitled *Work and Family in the United States: A Policy Initiative*. The EPC recommended a 6–8 week job protected maternity leave, with partial income replacement; a 6-month unpaid, but job protected, parental leave; job protected disability leave for all workers; the provision of temporary disability insurance to all workers; and the establishment of a national commission on contemporary work and family patterns.

THE EXTENT OF EXISTING FAMILY AND RELATED MEDICAL LEAVE POLICIES

Many of the various aspects of family and related medical leaves, particularly with regard to pregnancy and parenting, have been extensively studied. However, currently, there is still no comprehensive study of the range of family leaves provided by American businesses. Many employers provide "personal leave" which is often available for family crises such as the serious illness or death of a child or parent. Such leave is almost universally unpaid and highly discretionary. Employees sometimes are able to take their vacation leaves (a benefit that is usually paid) at times of such crises. Only a small percentage of employers have policies providing a leave specifically for purposes of caring for ill family members.

Considerable study and attention has been paid to the aspects of family and medical leave relating to pregnancy, maternity and less frequently, paternity. Such leave has been the subject of litigation since the early 1960's, based upon the Equal Protection Clause of the U.S. Constitution and Title VII of the Civil Rights Act of 1964, as women workers sought equal treatment in the work place. The amendment of Title VII in 1978, by the Pregnancy Discrimination Act (PDA), has especially had a significant impact on the perception of women as wage earners and on the availability and nature of both parental and medical leave. Under the PDA, an employer is prohibited from discriminating on the basis of pregnancy, childbirth and related medical conditions. The PDA further provides that "women affected by pregnancy, childbirth, or related medical conditions shall be treated the same for all employment-related purposes, including receipt of benefits under fringe benefit programs, as other persons not so affected but similar in their ability or inability to work." 42 U.S.C. sec. 2000e-k.

This language requires that employers adhere to two basic principles. First, they must permit physically fit pregnant employees to continue to work just as any other physically fit employee would be permitted to work (traditionally, women were terminated or placed on mandatory unpaid leave early in pregnancy). Second, when they become physically unable to work because of a complication of pregnancy or due to childbirth and the recovery period following childbirth, they are entitled to any sick leave, disability, health insurance or other benefit extended to other employees who, because of a physical condition, are unable to work.

The result has been that employers, to comply with the law, permit pregnant women to work unless or until they are unable to work and then provide whatever compensation or leaves they provide to other employees temporarily unable to work for medical reasons. As a practical matter, this means that many pregnant employees work until they give birth and then are on medical leave (paid if the employer compensates other disabled workers) for the physical recovery period following childbirth (typically 6–8 weeks). Some employers provide an additional unpaid leave period following disability to allow a parent to stay home with a new baby. This additional "parental leave," if given, must, under Title VII, be available to parents of either sex.

In response to litigation and the influence of the PDA, thousands of companies have reevaluated their personnel policies and implemented policies responsive to the needs of their changed workforces. In addition, four of the five states which provide temporary wage replacement under a state disability insurance program (California, New Jersey, New York and Rhode Island) extended their coverage to pregnancy and childbirth related work disabilities. (The fifth state, Hawaii, included such coverage from the inception of its state disability insurance program in 1969.) These long-standing state programs have proven to be both successful and cost-effective wage replacement systems for workers who are unable to perform their jobs due to non-work related illnesses, injuries or other medical reasons.

Several of the recent studies on parental leaves were described to the Committee in hearings held in October 1985 and April 1986. Catalyst, a national non-profit research organization, conducted a survey of the policies of Fortune 1500 companies and issued its *Report on a National Study of Parental Leaves* in 1986. Catalyst reported that 95% of the survey's respondents offered short-term disability leave during a worker's (including a pregnant worker's) period of inability to work; 38.9% with full pay and 57.3% with partial pay. Of this 95%, 90.2% continued full fringe benefits during disability leave. Moreover, 51.8% of the responding companies offered some unpaid leave to women for a parenting leave (as distinct from the disability leave) and guaranteed their right to return; 40% to the same job, nearly 50% to a comparable job. One third of these employers offered four to six months and 7.2% offers over six months of family leave. Only 37% of these companies extended the parental leave right to fathers and often on a different (and less extended) basis than to mothers. Additionally, only 27.5% of the respondents offered benefits to workers who adopt children.

The Catalyst Survey found that approximately 75% of the companies granting both kinds of leaves rerouted the work of employees on leave and a large percentage of the companies hired temporaries to supplement their rerouting strategy or to fully take over the absent employee's work. Significantly, 86.4% of the respondents stated that setting up a leave period and arranging to continue benefits was relatively easy. As part of its report to corporations, Catalyst recommended that companies provide disability leave, with full or partial pay, and unpaid parental leave for up to 3 months, with reinstatement to the same or comparable position after any leave.

The employers who do provide these crucial leaves recognize the significant benefits that flow to employers from doing so. As Ms. Jeanne F. Kardos, director of employee benefits at Southern New England Telephone, explained in her testimony in support of this bill:

There are several factors which caused us to develop our benefit philosophy with regard to maternity and parental care. Along with many leading companies in the country, we recognize that women with children are in the work force to stay. Whether they are single parents or not, they have special needs involving pregnancy and child-rearing at some point after birth or adoption. The special needs of these parents and more than that, the benefits which accrue to them and their children from this early participation in child-rearing, cannot be ignored any more than the widely accepted need for medical or pension benefits.

In addition, one of the most important concerns we share with our employees is an interest in their careers. It is clear that forcing them to choose between the children and their jobs, or to compromise on either, produces at least one loser—maybe two. Adequate disability and parental leave can solve these problems. The employee returns to the company when he or she is prepared to do so, and the company retains an important asset.

Lastly, we want our benefit plans to be recognized as progressive and competitive. We know that it will help in attracting talented individuals and if they are happy with their benefits, they'll want to stay with us.

The Catalyst Survey, because it focused on Fortune 1500 companies, overstates the protections offered to new parents by employers generally. A survey of 1,000 small and medium sized firms, conducted in 1981 by Sheila Kamerman and Alfred Kahn of the Columbia University School of Social Work, provides an important companion to the Catalyst Study. According to Kamerman and Kahn, less than 40% of all working women received paid disability leave for the six to eight week recovery period after childbirth. This figure, which is far lower than the Fortune 1500 figures reported by Catalyst, probably reflects the fact that small and medium size employers are less likely to provide disability benefits to any worker. (These findings may also reflect the earlier survey date of the Columbia Study, which was undertaken much closer in time to the April 1979 effective date of the PDA than was the Catalyst Survey; smaller employers may not yet have adjusted their policies at the time of the first survey.) Eighty-eight percent of the companies provided "maternity" leave, but only 72% formally guaranteed the same or comparable job and retention of seniority. Thirty-three percent of the respondents provided leaves of 2 months or less, 28 percent provided 3 months of leave, 19 percent provided 4–6 months and 8 percent provided over 6 months. Twelve percent granted leave but on a discretionary basis. Only 25 percent of the respondent firms said that they permitted men to take parental leave, and many of those companies did so only for a few days at the time of childbirth.

The Catalyst and Kamerman and Kahn studies, taken together, indicate that employees of large companies are far more likely to be provided with paid disability leave following childbirth than are employees of small and medium sized firms. The small and medium size firms respond to new parent employees by providing unpaid "maternity leaves," a full third of which extend only for the period of the mother's physical inability to work. It is likely that many of those firms providing leave for that period of time also grant unpaid leave to other disabled employees and thus provide the same benefit for both pregnancy and non-pregnancy-related disability. A significant percentage of both Fortune 1500 companies and the small and medium companies studied by Kamerman and Kahn treat fathers seeking parental leave less favorably than mothers, in clear violation of Title VII.

These studies, more fundamentally, indicate the wide variation among employers, large and small, in the provision of parental, as distinguished from disability, leaves, and the inadequacy of many leave policies.

The inadequacy of existing leave policies is perhaps most clearly seen when the family and related medical leave policies of the United States are compared to those of the rest of the world. With the exception of the United States, virtually every industrialized country as well as many Third World countries have national policies which require employers to provide some form of maternity or parental leave. One hundred and thirty-five countries provide maternity benefits, 125 with some wage replacement. These policies are well established, with France, Great Britain and Italy having had laws requiring maternity benefits since before World War I, which are now part of more general paid sick leave laws providing benefits for all workers unable to work for medical reasons. Among the more industrialized countries, the average minimum paid leave is twelve to fourteen weeks with many also providing the right to unpaid, job-protected leaves for at least one year. Leave is provided either through a national paid sick leave system or as part of a national family policy designed to enhance and support families. The long-established practices of these countries stand in marked contrast to the complete lack in this country of a standard minimum policy for family leave.

NO

Steve Bartlett,
Thomas Tauke, Richard Armey,
Harris Fawell, and Paul Henry

SEPARATE DISSENTING VIEWS ON
H.R. 4300, THE FAMILY
AND MEDICAL LEAVE ACT OF 1986

The Family and Medical leave Act of 1986, H.R. 4300, addresses important issues regarding employee leave-taking to care for the sick and newborn. While well-intentioned, it nevertheless decides what type of leave programs are best for virtually all American employers and employees instead of letting those decisions be worked out on an individual basis. The trend in employee benefits for the past several years has been to establish flexible benefit programs permitting individual employees to choose the benefit package best suited to their needs. H.R. 4300 mandates rigid and inflexible requirements that must be a part of all employer benefit plans, regardless of whether the employees want it or will ever be able to use it.

There is no disagreement that funds available for benefits are limited. H.R. 4300 could place businesses around the country in a position of having to cut back on current benefits in order to pay for those mandated by the legislation. H.R. 4300 is anti-small business. It takes the leave policies of some of the nation's biggest businesses and imposes them on the nation's smallest, without regard to whether they are in a financial position to provide the liberal benefits required.

Further, H.R. 4300 represents the first time that serious consideration has been given to legislating national standards for major employee leave and health benefits. Yet, the Committee on Education and Labor is reporting H.R. 4300 after conducting limited hearings that failed to show that such broad Federal legislation is necessary. It has spent an inadequate amount of time studying this far-reaching proposal which would, upon passage, reshape the current benefit plans of virtually every business in the country.

At first blush, this legislation's flaws are not readily apparent. We urge our colleagues to read the following eight points carefully. In our opinion, H.R.

From "Separate Dissenting Views on H.R. 4300, The Family and Medical Leave Act of 1986," *Parental and Medical Leave Act of 1986*, U.S. House of Representatives.

4300 could work to the detriment of many workers because of a number of reasons, including the reduction of other important benefits.

1. *H.R. 4300 represents the first time that comprehensive national standards for major employee leave and health benefits have been given serious consideration in Congress.*

H.R. 4300 presents something of a test to us as lawmakers. It poses a significant question—how deeply does Congress want to become involved in employee benefit issues? H.R. 4300 can legitimately be characterized as a Pandora's Box. For example, proponents of the bill have intimated that H.R. 4300, which calls for unpaid leave, will be followed in future years by legislation mandating paid leave. Congress has not yet legislated whether and to what extent health care coverage should be provided, the number of dollars that should be placed in employee pension plans or the amount of life insurance that should be carried for each employee. Mandating the kind of rigid and inflexible leave requirements proposed by H.R. 4300, however, would place Congress in the midst of discussions that, until now, have wisely been left to negotiations between employees and employers.

Having crossed the Rubicon on developing private sector benefit policies with enactment of H.R. 4300, Congress will have great difficulty resisting future demands for more expansive employee benefits.

2. *Requiring businesses to provide one particular benefit, in this case a leave benefit, will force many to cut back on other benefits in order to absorb the cost of those imposed by H.R. 4300.*

The trend in employee benefit programs for the past decade has been away from providing a single benefit program to which all employees must subscribe, and towards serving up benefits "cafeteria style." Recognizing that a business can only allocate a certain dollar amount per employee for benefits, cafeteria plans offer a broad range of choices permitting each employee to select those that meet his or her individual needs.

Previously, two-income families may have carried conventional plans that largely duplicated one another. With cafeteria plans, each wage earner can select a different plan which, when combined, give their family far broader protections that would otherwise be possible. At Procter & Gamble, for example, one of the choices available for employees is buying more vacation time or putting the benefit money away from child care.

The sharp contrast to prevailing practice, H.R. 4300 would legislate against the trend toward flexible benefits. It would require that each employee's benefit "budget" be spent on a benefit that the employee may not need nor want. We would urge our colleagues to ask single employees and married employees with no children whether they want to be legally required to have their benefit dollars used to purchase a parental leave benefit, when they may never be in a position to take advantage of it. Our colleagues may also wish to ask employees who have no dependent parents whether they would have any objection to a law requiring them to carry dependent care coverage. At a time when employees are demanding flexible benefit plans, H.R. 4300 would force less flexibility.

It should also be added that employers are not required to provide health benefits, and that H.R. 4300 only requires that those who currently do so to maintain those benefits while the employee is on leave. Enactment of H.R. 4300, therefore, could force a marginal business to reduce benefit costs by discontinuing them altogether.

3. *The Committee of Education and Labor has not given this legislation adequate consideration.*

This legislation is being brought to the floor of the House of Representatives on the basis of limited consideration by the Education and Labor Committee. Considering the immense impact that it will have on every form of business in the country, our failure to further explore the impact of this legislation is of great concern.

It would seem that a prerequisite to the Congress accepting a labor law proposed by the House Education and Labor Committee is a comprehensive hearing record containing testimony clearly establishing that institutional abuse or inequity exists requiring a Federal legislative remedy. That has not happened with H.R. 4300.

All members of Congress are painfully aware of how many small businesses have failed recently, and how fragile many business situations—both large and small—are around the country. All of us know of companies in our districts which are barely surviving. It is ironic and telling that the Committee has spent far less time on hearings leading up to this Federally imposed leave policy than a benefits manager would spend designing one for his or her company.

Evidence of the superficial consideration given to the drafting of H.R. 4300 can be found in its numerous flaws. For example, H.R. 4300 confounds the application of Section 504 of the Rehabilitation Act of 1973 which protects persons with disabilities from discrimination in Federally assisted or conducted programs. Despite the fact that H.R. 4300's reemployment guarantees will require increased hiring and discharge of temporary employees, the bill fails to address the distortion that these discharges will create in employer experience ratings in unemployment compensation (UC) programs (experience ratings govern UC taxes; the less terminations, the lower the tax). Further, the legislation requires employers to continue health benefits for leave-taking employees, but does not address H.R. 4300's relationship with similar provisions contained in the COBRA legislation enacted earlier this year. Clearly, legislation as comprehensive as H.R. 4300 should not be rushed forward without its sponsors having first remedied conflicts with other laws.

4. *A leave policy drafted in Washington, and applicable to hundreds of thousands of unique employer, employee, business situations around the country could result in a severe economic hardship to a number of businesses, particularly small ones.*

In recent days the call from the House floor has been to improve the competitiveness of American industry. The notion of a Federally mandated leave policy stands in direct conflict to our recent deliberations.

One of the principal arguments used in support of this legislation is that other countries, particularly the European industrialized nations, have already enacted some form of parental leave laws. Those same nations, however, are no longer able to generate a significant number of new jobs for their citizens. The combined effect of the liberal European labor laws is such that few companies are willing any more to risk the investment capital in Europe.

Many U.S. businesses are responding to the needs of working parents. A major study of the leave policies of 384 large

U.S. corporations prepared by Catalyst, Inc., for example, demonstrated that 95% already provide short-term disability leave and over half give unpaid leave for maternity purposes, the bulk of which lasts three months or longer, with a reinstatement guarantee at the conclusion of the leave period.

Studies such as the one prepared by Catalyst demonstrate that benefit programs are not uniform, but are designed to take into consideration the individual circumstances of each company. No such discretion is available under H.R. 4300's rigid requirements. As explained in more detail in the majority's report, H.R. 4300 takes the employee relations policies of the IMB's of this country and imposes them by law on small typewriter repair companies. It infers that a small office products company in a suburban mall has the same financial and staffing resources as a Fortune 500 corporation doing business world-wide. Small business enterprises employ 49% of the labor force. Last year, 65,000 small business failed. Should it be enacted, H.R. 4300 is likely to contribute to increased failures in future years, in every part of the country.

5. H.R. 4300 will force a number of marginal businesses to restructure their hiring practices in such a way as to avoid, to the extent possible, hiring women of childbearing age and persons with past histories of serious health conditions and disabilities.

In order to meet the staffing obligations that would result from H.R. 4300's job guarantee provisions, employers may covertly discriminate in their hiring practices against those who seem likely to utilize the leave benefits. For example, if two equally qualified women were applying for a particular position, and one is of childbearing age while the other is not, H.R. 4300 would encourage the employer to hire the latter person. Similarly, if an individual with a history of serious illness or disability applies for a job, the liberal leave requirements of H.R. 4300 may result in the employer being hesitant to offer the individual a position, knowing that the law permits the individual to take six months leave during each twelve month period.

6. In a time of limited resources and an explosion of litigation in Federal courts, H.R. 4300 would create a new Federal bureaucracy to enforce the comprehensive requirements of this legislation and a new enforcement scheme involving the Department of Labor.

A Federally mandated program generates disputes over interpretation of eligibility criteria and the nature of the benefit provided. H.R. 4300, imposed by Congress on an unwilling business community, will result in a rash of disputes. In addition, yet another unwilling partner, the Department of Labor, would be given the responsibility for reviewing all settlements and ensuring enforcement of all decisions. Considering the superficial consideration given the issue and the lack of definition of key terms, passage of H.R. 4300 will yield numerous court cases and administrative disputes.

7. It is simply inappropriate for the Congress to be mandating parental and medical leave policies for thousands of employers around the country when it is unwilling to accept those policies for itself.

The Committee would saddle American employers with mandatory leave and benefit requirements, but is unwilling to accept those same requirements for itself. H.R. 4300 would cover nearly all types of American business—private sector employees, Federal government employees, and employees of state, county and local governments. Conspicuously absent from this list are the employees of the United States Congress.

8. H.R. 4300 is not a "no-cost" bill.

The majority report states that the technical changes made during the markup process "further assure the bill will result in long term savings for employers." This statement is highly questionable and defies business practice. One of the fundamental premises of this legislation is that employers should be required to continue the employee's health, disability and life insurance benefits while on leave and then restore the returning employee to the same or similar position at the conclusion of the leave. Employers will be required to hire temporary replacements at full pay and benefits, and then discharge them if another position cannot be found within the company. Because many of these replacement workers can only be promised a temporary position, employers may have to pay premium wage rates to get the quality of help that is needed. In many circumstances, the use of temporary help for long periods of time to replace key regular personnel results in reduced productivity and the remaining employees having to work greater overtime.

In conclusion, we would stress that formulation of employee leave and benefit policies is best left to individual employers and their employees who are in a better position to identify the needs of all concerned. Despite its good intentions, and because of its numerous flaws, H.R. 4300 does not merit support.

POSTSCRIPT

Should Congress Guarantee U.S. Workers the Right to Parental Leave?

In this debate, supporters of H.R. 4300 contend that the presence of growing numbers of working mothers in the marketplace creates a conflict between work and family responsibilities. That is, when the head of a single parent family works, or when both parents in a traditional family works, one or both of the parents can be "torn between nurturing their seriously ill child and reporting to work." Similarly, pregnant workers who are employed by firms who do not provide leaves of absence for those who are temporarily disabled are unprotected by the Pregnancy Discrimination Act of 1978. These workers must "choose between the children and their jobs" or they must "compromise" on one or both. This produces at least one loser—maybe two.

The dissenters in this debate argue that H.R. 4300 is inflexible and out of step with the modern day trend of allowing individual workers to choose a benefit package from a menu of alternative fringe benefits. They go on to list eight objections: three political objections and five economic objections. Their economic concerns are: (1) since there is a firm that has a finite budget for fringe benefits, the opportunity costs of this legislation would be to force the firm to "cut back on other benefits"; (2) this legislation would be particularly troublesome for small businesses and it might conflict with attempts to improve the "competitiveness of American industry"; (3) "marginal business" will have an incentive to avoid "hiring women of childbearing age"; (4) "a new federal bureaucracy" will have to be created to "enforce the comprehensive requirements of this legislation and by definition this will lead to increased costs and inefficiencies"; and (5) firms will have to "pay premium wage rates" and, because they will be forced to "use temporary help for long periods of time," they will experience "reduced productivity."

The debate over this bill did not end in 1986. In the U.S. Senate, Christopher Dodd (D-Conn.) introduced S. 52278 on April 9, 1986. Senator Dodd's bill, also called the Parental and Medical Leave Act of 1986, was referred to the Committee on Labor and Human Resources. In October 1987, this committee began hearings on the S. 52278 bill. A copy of these hearings, including a comprehensive cost study conducted by the General Accounting Office (GAO), should be available in your library. A most comprehensive review of the proposed legislation appeared in the Summer 1987 issue of *Notre Dame Journal of Law, Ethics and Public Policy.* An essay in that issue by James Carr, "Bringing Up Baby: The Case for a Federal Parental Leave Act," discusses the need and feasibility of implementing H.R. 4300. For more background information see Dana E. Friedman's essay in *Across the Board* (March 1987); Nadine Taub's article in *The Nation* (May 31, 1986); David Blakenhorn's opinion in the *New York Times* (April 7, 1987); or the comments found in the *Employee Benefit Plan Review* (June 1986).

The debate over parental leave has yet to be resolved by Congress. Senator Dodd's bill ultimately died in committee and didn't make it to the Senate floor for a vote. However, Senator Dodd reintroduced a similar piece of legislation, now called the Family and Medical Leave Act, in the 101st Congress. The bill has made it out of committee but, as of this writing (January 1990), it has not yet been scheduled for a vote on the Senate floor, which is the next step in the process of enacting legislation into law.

ISSUE 9

Was It a Mistake to Increase the Minimum Wage?

YES: The Editors of *Nation's Business,* from "Minimum Wage Myths," *Nation's Business* (June 1987)

NO: Teresa Ghilarducci, from "Women's Jobs and the Minimum Wage," *Testimony Prepared for the Pennsylvania House of Representatives* (August 26–27, 1987)

ISSUE SUMMARY

YES: The editors of the *Nation's Business* insist that support for the minimum wage is based on eight myths that ignore the fact that a higher minimum wage "hurts the very employees it is intended to help."
NO: Economist Ghilarducci maintains that both "advocates and detractors of the minimum wage" have ignored the impact it has had on the economic well-being of "women workers."

In the midst of the Great Depression, Congress passed the Fair Labor Standards Act (FLSA) of 1938. In one bold stroke, it established a minimum wage rate of $0.25 an hour, it placed controls on the use of child labor, it defined the normal workweek to be 44 hours a week, and it mandated that time and a half be paid to anyone working longer than the normal work-week. Fifty years later the debate concerning child labor, the workweek, and overtime pay have long subsided, but the debate over the minimum wage rages on.

The immediate and continued concern over the minimum wage compo-nent of the FLSA should surprise few. Although $0.25 an hour seems to be a paltry sum compared to today's wage rates, in 1938 it was a princely reward for work. It must be remembered that jobs were hard to come by and unemployment rates at times reached as high as 25 percent of the workforce. When work was found, any wage seemed acceptable to those who roamed the streets with no "safety-net" to protect them or their families. Indeed, consider the fact that $0.25 an hour was 40.3 percent of the average manufacturing wage rate for 1938, while in 1987 the minimum wage rate of $3.35 an hour was only 34.2 percent of the average manufacturing wage rate.

Little wonder then that the business community in the 1930s was up in arms. They argued that if wages went up, two things would happen and they were both bad. Prices would rise and this would choke off the little demand for goods and services that existed in the marketplace, and the demand for workers would have to fall. The end result would be a worsening of the economic depression then underway, and little or no hope of employment for the very people who should benefit from the Fair Labor Standards Act.

In the face of these dire projections, Congress chose to move forward. It was intent upon creating a wage floor that would ensure a standard of living for the working poor that was minimally acceptable to society at large. Over the years this floor has been regularly modified and adjusted. As Table 1 in Ghilarducci's essay indicates, the minimum wage rose from its 1938 level of $0.25 per hour to $3.35 in 1981. It is important to note that there was no increase from 1981 until the fall of 1989. This period represents the longest elapsed time between the establishment of new floors. Prior to this, the 1939–1945 World War II period and the 1968–1974 Vietnam years represented the longest periods without a minimum wage increase. Both of these periods were characterized by rising real wages. Unlike the previous two periods, the 1981–89 period was one of falling real wages. Indeed, prices rose by more than 30 percent in this period.

The erosion of the minimum wage actually can be traced back to 1978. Even though the minimum wage rate was increased in 1979, 1980, and again in 1981, these increases did not keep pace with the rate of inflation. Thus for all practical purposes, the minimum wage remained unchanged for more than a decade.

Democrats in Congress, led by Senator Edward M. Kennedy (D-Mass.) and Representative Augustus F. Hawkins (D-Calif.) have long fought for an increase in the minimum wage. Their efforts finally bore fruit in the fall of 1989. President Bush, after vetoing an earlier version of the bill, signed into law legislation that triggers a 45 cent-per-hour increase in the minimum wage beginning April 1, 1990. This $3.80 wage rate will jump to $4.25 in April 1991. The compromise reached between President Bush and the Democratic congressional leadership hinged upon the introduction of a subminimum "training wage," which the president wanted and the Democrats fought. The new "training wage," which is pegged at 85 percent of the prevailing minimum wage, targets teenagers with little work experience. These 16–19-year-old workers can be paid this lower wage for three months, or up to six months in special cases.

The wisdom of minimum wage legislation is the subject of lively debates in the U.S. Congress, in state legislatures, in the media, and among economists. The U.S. Chamber of Commerce's position is well argued by the editors of the *Nation's Business*, who maintain that such a bill will not improve the well-being of low-income families. Indeed, they argue that the very people this bill is intended to help will be very seriously hurt by this legislation. Teresa Ghilarducci, on the other hand, believes that we have all ignored the impact of this legislation on the increasingly large number of women who live in poverty.

YES

The Editors of
The Nation's Business

MINIMUM WAGE MYTHS

The public will pay for an increase in the federal minimum wage through higher prices and fewer jobs.

That is overwhelmingly the view of an organization of employers from a cross section of American business. And business legislative strategists are trying to convey that view to Congress as part of a campaign to head off a strong drive to raise the wage floor by nearly 40 percent over three years.

The minimum wage is now $3.35 an hour. Legislation pending in Congress would bring it to $4.65 by 1990 and would provide for automatic increases thereafter by setting the wage at 50 percent of the average nonsupervisory, private-industry wage.

At the recent annual meeting of the U.S. Chamber of Commerce, delegates representing grass-roots businesses predicted massive impact on their companies if the wage-increase-and-escalator plan goes through. Three quarters said they would raise prices, cut their existing work forces, defer new hiring or reduce the number of hours that present employees worked.

Others said they would respond to a mandated increase with such steps as cutting profit margins, reducing services or accelerating labor-saving methods. Fifty-five percent of the employers polled said they would have to raise wages of workers who now earn above the minimum to preserve existing differentials.

The principal congressional sponsors of the minimum wage legislation are Sen. Edward M. Kennedy (D-Mass.), chairman of the Senate Committee on Labor and Human Resources, and Rep. Augustus Hawkins (D-Calif.), chairman of the House Committee on Education and Labor. They argue that inflation has drastically eroded the purchasing power of the $3.35 minimum wage since it took effect in 1981 and that many entry-level workers will be condemned to poverty unless that figure is raised substantially.

Leading the opposition are Sen. Orrin Hatch (R-Utah), senior Republican on Kennedy's committee, and Rep. Steve Bartlett (R-Tex.), a member of Hawkins' committee. They spotlight the impact of a wage increase in terms of higher unemployment and higher prices. They argue that a higher wage would actually hurt the very people that proponents say would be helped.

At the same time, Hatch and Bartlett say that business people are going to have to become more active in making their views known to Congress if the Kennedy-Hawkins bill is to be stopped.

The congressional push for a substantial increase in the minimum wage is part of an overall campaign by organized labor on several fronts to capitalize on Democratic control of both houses of Congress. The AFL-CIO and other labor organizations played major roles in the 1986 election campaign, where Democrats gained control of the Senate for the first time since President Reagan's first victory in 1980.

While the Democrats retained control of the House throughout the Reagan years, GOP control of the Senate remained a formidable and usually impenetrable obstacle to legislation backed by organized labor and its congressional allies.

Now, says Hatch, "all the labor stuff the unions are trying to put on business is going to be overwhelming." As senior Republican on the Labor Committee, he remains at the head of opposition to labor initiatives he views as detrimental to the economy.

And, in a strong counterattack on the minimum-wage push, Hatch plans to press for a youth minimum wage, which would permit employers to pay younger workers at a rate less than the federal minimum during the summer vacation period. That approach, he says, would encourage employers to hire and train youths they could not afford to hire if required to pay the full minimum.

Meanwhile, the fight over the proposed increase in the current $3.35 wage floor continues. The Minimum Wage Coalition to Save Jobs, the lead (sic) business organization fighting the wage increase, is rallying opposition to the bill because of its potentially adverse impact on the economy. A statement from the coalition says:

"A new minimum wage increase will aversely affect employment opportunities for the low-skilled, especially among our youth. . . . Economic studies show that raising the minimum wage results in massive unemployment and disemployment (which occurs when new jobs are not created because of high labor costs). In other words, the increase hurts the very employees it is intended to help.

"How else can business cope? Raising prices in response to wage increases will only renew the inflation spiral we have finally brought under control. More often, employers are forced to eliminate jobs or reduce employee hours. And the entry-level, low-skilled positions primarily held by young people are the first to go."

Goals of the Washington-based coalition, which represents business and trade associations as well as individual companies, include the closing of "the information gap" on the hidden costs of raising the minimum wage.

"The public does not understand the full economic impact of this increase proposal, which, on the surface, appears well-intentioned," the coalition says.

A key to achieving that understanding, the group adds, is dispelling the myths that surround the wage issue. The coalition makes these comparisons:

Myth: The typical minimum wage earner is a head of a household supporting a family.

Reality: The typical minimum wage employee is young, single, resides at home and works part time.

Myth: Raising the minimum wage is a way to reduce poverty.

Reality: A study by the Congressional Budget Office shows that over 80 percent of minimum wage workers do not fit the profile of the working poor. Seventy percent of minimum wage workers live in a family where at least one other member holds a job.

Myth: Raising the minimum wage has no negative impact on employment.

Reality: The federal Minimum Wage Study Commission reports that each 10 percent of increase in the wage results in a loss of 80,000 to 240,000 jobs for teenagers. In addition, some studies indicate that, although the percentage job loss of teenagers is greater, the absolute number of jobs lost by adults is greater. One study for the commission indicates a 10 percent increase in the minimum wage could wipe out 2.7 million jobs for adults.

Myth: A minimum wage increase is essential to welfare reform.

Reality: Only 16 percent of household heads below the poverty income level work at a full-time job year-round. Raising the required wage payment for low-skilled persons decreases the likelihood of alternative employment opportunities for these people, resulting in more pressure on the welfare system, not less. While tax reform has resulted in removing the disincentives that poor people faced in getting jobs (by eliminating taxes for the working poor), minimum wage increases destroy many entry-level jobs.

Myth: Raising the minimum wage will encourage the low-skilled and unemployed to seek jobs.

Reality: Increasing the minimum wage does not guarantee either a job or a wage increase to the least skilled. The low-skilled are the first to lose their jobs when the minimum wage is raised. Entry-level jobs are not created when labor costs go up. Where are the plentiful gas station attendants and department store clerks of 10 years ago? Their jobs fell victim to the last minimum wage increase.

Myth: Raising the wage floor will affect only those employees currently earning minimum wage.

Reality: An increase in the minimum will "ripple" through the job market and increase wages for skilled and experienced employees earning more than the minimum without corresponding increases in productivity. The Minimum Wage Study Commission reported that wage increases to those already earning more than minimum wage will be more costly to employers than the legislated increase of the minimum wage. The result will be wage-driven inflationary pressure on the economy.

Myth: Businesses can offset higher labor costs through price increases to consumers.

Reality: Some increased labor costs can be offset by higher prices. However, higher prices spark consumer resistance. The result is lessened demand for services, thus fewer workers and firms in service industries. To the extent that higher wages are offset by higher prices, the net result of the minimum wage increase is that employees are back where they started. The only way wages can be increased in real terms is for workers to acquire additional skills through training and education, not for Congress to pass laws that mandate higher wages.

Myth: A rise in the minimum wage has no impact on competitiveness with foreign businesses.

Reality: There are some low-wage manufacturing industries where minimum wage increases will further hurt their abilities to compete. These industries—shoes, textiles, apparel—are already struggling. As these and other industries are forced to raise their basic labor rates, entire wage structures ratchet upward. The effect on international competition is harmful.

Coalition strategists say their initial challenge is to generate as much grass-roots support as possible for their plan to show members of Congress the difference between those myths and realities. Their ammunition includes a series of studies and analyses conducted over the past several years.

Some of those studies did not work out as the initiators intended. For example, the Minimum Wage Study Commission cited by the coalition was appointed by President Carter with a mandate to determine, among other things, "the beneficial effects of the minimum wage, including its effect in ameliorating poverty among working citizens."

Commission research, the coalition says, "confirmed the conclusions of all prior empirical evidence—that the minimum wage causes disemployment in teens and has no effect on low-wage incomes." The coalition adds:

"Nevertheless, the commission ignored its own findings and recommended that the level of the minimum wage be raised periodically by indexing it to the average wage paid in the economy and that the coverage of the minimum wage be extended by eliminating from current law various exempt categories of work. These incongruous recommendations are really not surprising in view of the ideological purposes of the commission."

A hard-hitting minority report asserted: "The evidence against the minimum wage is so overwhelming that the only way the commission's majority was able to recommend that it be retained was to ask us not to base any decisions on facts."

Another insight into the issue is provided by the Economic Policy Division of the U.S. Chamber of Commerce, which has documented the inflationary/unemployment impact of a higher minimum wage. Graciela Testa-Ortiz, director of the Chamber's Forecasting Section, comments on the figures: "The evidence is incontrovertible. Nevertheless, the myths persist, and every few years legislators propose yet another increase in the minimum wage. In the process, they congratulate themselves for such a clear expression of their superior morality and compassion. Yet, this exercise in easy ethics only leads to greater hardship for all Americans."

Why, then, does the issue keep recurring? Because, says Testa-Ortiz, "some groups do reap benefits from regulations whose overall impacts on the economy are negative."

She cites various studies showing that the existence of a minimum wage allows a higher union wage structure than would otherwise be possible. Testa-Ortiz further cites a study showing that, as a result of one minimum wage increase, 85 percent of members of labor unions were expected to see higher pay, compared with only 44 percent of nonunion workers.

She comments further: "To young, inexperienced workers, minimum wage jobs are an extension of schooling, since those jobs offer them the training and the work experience to move on to higher paying jobs. The minimum wage deprives the youth of America not only of the opportunity to get a job, but also of needed experience and on-the-job training, while it does nothing to alleviate poverty."

Amid mounting evidence that continuing increases in the minimum wage are hurting those they are supposed to benefit, the basic philosophy of the wage floor is being re-examined.

Richard B. Berman, a Dallas business executive and chairman of the minimum wage coalition, says the concept of a minimum wage has become archaic. The policy of a federally mandated wage level was introduced in 1938, he says, to cover Depression-era conditions that no longer exist.

"A better alternative," Berman says, would be to "let free market forces of supply and demand naturally set the wage floor in a given market, taking into account regional differences in cost of living and unemployment."

NO

Teresa Ghilarducci

WOMEN'S JOBS AND
THE MINIMUM WAGE

The following is based on testimony for the Pennsylvania House of Representatives, August 26–27, 1987.

In 1987, working full time in America can make you poor—poorer than collecting welfare. Someone working full time must earn $4.30 per hour to keep a family of 3 out of poverty. Unfortunately, the federal minimum wage requires that employers pay only $3.35 per hour. This means the income for 5 percent of all U.S. workers who earn the minimum wage or less is at the poverty level. Approximately another 5 percent, who earn slightly more than the minimum wage, are not much better off.

One rationale for the minimum-wage law, first established in 1938, was that a minimum wage prevented wages from falling so low that workers could not provide for their own subsistence; the minimum wage was to supply a ballast for our social principles, as well as for the earnings of workers. Since 1938, working full time at the minimum wage yielded a subsistence income (sometimes more) for a family of 3. In 1987, however, the minimum wage is just 78 percent of the poverty wage. This is the lowest percentage of the poverty wage that has existed in the United States since 1950—12 years before the War on Poverty was declared!

The minimum wage does not just establish absolute standards. It also establishes the position of workers relative to one another, in that it influences the size of the gap between the lowest-paid worker in society and the typical manufacturing worker. In 1950, minimum-wage workers earned approximately half of what manufacturing workers earned. In 1987, the minimum wage is 34 percent of the average manufacturing wage. Thus, the wage ratio between the lowest-paid worker and the factory worker went from 1:2 in 1950 to only 1:3 in 1987. The relationship among the minimum wage, the average manufacturing wage, and the poverty wage for selected years from 1938 to 1987 is presented in Table 1.

The minimum wage is due for an increase if it is to achieve its historical purpose. However, a substantial increase in the minimum wage in the late

From Teresa Ghilarducci, "Woman's Jobs and the Minimum Wage." *Testimony Prepared for the Pennsylvania House of Representatives.*

Table 1

**The Relationship Among the Minimum Wage,
Average Manufacturing Wage, and Poverty Wage, 1938–1987**

Year	Minimum Wage	Minumum Wage as a Percentage of Average Manufacturing Wage	Minimum Wage as a Percentage of Poverty Wage
1938	$0.25	40.3%	46.0%
1939	0.30	47.6	46.0
1945	0.40	39.2	57.1
1950	0.75	52.1	79.8
1956	1.00	51.3	94.3
1961	1.15	49.6	98.3
1963	1.25	50.8	104.4
1967	1.40	49.6	107.2
1968	1.60	53.2	117.5
1974	2.00	45.3	103.8
1975	2.10	43.5	100.0
1976	2.30	44.1	103.1
1978	2.65	43.0	103.9
1979	2.90	43.3	102.5
1980	3.10	42.6	96.3
1981	3.35	41.6	95.7
1987	3.35	34.2	78.0

Sources: *The Wall Street Journal,* September 1987; *US Statistical Abstract.*
The poverty level in 1967 was adjusted for inflation to obtain the poverty wage for each year.
Full-time work is 2,040 hours per year.

1980s would produce unprecedented effects because the labor market has undergone significant structural changes since 1938. Women have entered the labor market to stay. In a few years, 50 percent of the full-time labor force will be women. Sexism exists as a backdrop to this dramatic change and helps to explain the persistent concentration of women in the lowest-paid occupations and why women are paid less than men are in almost every occupation.

Another factor to be considered in the role of the minimum wage in contemporary society is that an increasing number of working women are becoming heads of households. Thus, the feminization of poverty, the massive entrance of women into the workforce, and the existence of labor-market discrimination against women all suggest a new protective role for the minimum wage. This is the role that the advocates of the minimum wage have failed to emphasize; it may be the most important reason why a minimum-wage increase would enhance social welfare. That is, the minimum wage and female earnings are inextricably linked.

Raising the minimum wage leads the list of labor issues facing the 1987–1988 U.S. Congress. The business community's fierce opposition relies on a 49-year-old case against the minimum wage. The business community's basic argument is that firms should not be forced into bankruptcy because they are required to meet an increase in the minimum wage, as this would diminish the jobs available to the marginal workers. The Chamber of Commerce, small-business organizations, and other employer groups claim this would hurt the people who have the fewest skills and need the work experience the most. A lobbyist for the restaurant industry stated that the minimum wage "is less a business issue than a jobs issue." Moreover, a *ripple effect* is feared: a minimum-wage increase would bump up wages farther along the pay scale and cause price increases and unemployment. These consequences depend on specific economic relationships and on the specific magnitudes of these relationships, which have been debated by economists since the minimum wage was introduced.

WAGES AND EMPLOYMENT

The debate surrounding the minimum wage focuses on the relationship between wages and labor demand. The Minimum Wage Commission in 1981 reported that the effect of the minimum wage on employment is negative, but small. The negligible effect is due to the fact that the demand for labor depends on two factors: the marginal productivity of labor and the overall demand for the product. The commission concluded that if employment demand grows over time, a minimum-wage increase could easily be accompanied by an *increase* in employment, since the negative employment effect might well be smaller than the positive growth effect of the demand for labor. Indeed, if wages do not increase at the same time that the demand for labor increases, then profits grow at the expense of wages.

The importance that small business has attached to defeating a minimum-wage increase is understandable. Since 1981, small businesses have endured a record number of bankruptcies, suffered severe competition from large firms (which in turn have been challenged by international competition), witnessed vanishing support from the Small Business Administration, and watched with alarm the passage of a pro-big-business 1986 tax reform. It is not surprising, therefore, that small businesses vehemently oppose an increase in the minimum wage. The passage of a higher minimum wage would further weaken small businesses' competitive position, while its defeat would give them a victory.

Although small businesses may have good reasons to be interested in defeating a minimum-wage increase, a low minimum wage may not be in their own best interest. It is a collective-action problem: what may be harmful for an individual firm, such as an increase in labor costs, may, in fact, be beneficial for all firms. A higher minimum wage means that firms can retain productive workers without losing their competitive position and will not incur the community's wrath, since they will be seen to be raising wage standards within the community.

In a typical American city experiencing deindustrialization, the major benefit from an increase in the minimum wage is to the growing sectors of trade and services, in which pay is traditionally at or near the minimum level and in which the newest entrants to the labor force are women. The minimum wage would establish a wage floor for these individuals. This would force firms to compete on the basis of efficiency and product quality, rather than on the basis of labor costs. This is especially important in emerging industries and in growing industries.

A survey of the economic studies concerning the minimum wage reveals five generalized conclusions. First, a 10-percent increase in the minimum wage would yield a 1-percent drop in employment, but this drop would likely be accompanied by an increase in schooling among teenagers. Second, the effect on adult employment would be negligible. Third, the ripple effect, the effect of the minimum wage on wages above the minimum, ends at wage rates that are 150 percent of the minimum wage. The ripple effect is smaller when the gap between the minimum wage and the average manufacturing wage is large. Fourth, management productivity and labor productivity would increase. Management would become more efficient in its attempts to make up the increase in costs, and workers would be more committed to the workplace at higher pay levels. Fifth, there is no clear-cut evidence that the cost of a minimum wage would be passed on in the form of increased prices.

Despite the evidence presented in these high-quality studies on the minimum wage, any forecasts based on these studies are subject to serious biases. Conclusions must be based on evidence gathered in a period of time when the majority of minimum-wage workers were not women and permanently in the labor force. This labor-market change will affect significantly the impact of the minimum wage in the next decade. For instance, low-wage workers, most of whom are women (approximately 66 percent), would, theoretically, demand certain products and services if wages were increased. Since the demand for services increases when women work (and women dominate the low-paying jobs in the service, clerical, and sales occupations), we can expect that an increase in the minimum-wage rate would increase the demand for the services produced by minimum-wage workers. This in turn would increase the demand for minimum-wage workers.

THE MINIMUM WAGE AND WORKING WOMEN

In the United States between the years 1970 and 1980, women filled 60 percent of the new jobs created. They also tended to enter the lowest-paying occupations in retail trade, the services, and clerical work. In a city such as South Bend, Indiana, a community that has experienced economic dislocations due to manufacturing-plant shutdowns, the impact of women's entry into the labor force has been profound. Computer simulations for the South Bend Standard Metropolitan Statistical Area (SMSA) revealed that if the minimum wage were raised to $4.65 per hour, women workers' total income would increase by $22 million and overall wage income would increase by $33 million, which would represent only a 5-percent increase in total income within the SMSA.

Several reasons explain why women would receive two-thirds of the benefits arising from an increase in the minimum wage in South Bend (and presumably across the nation). First, the nation has experienced a transition from a manufacturing-dominated economic base to a services-and-trade economic base. Women are entering the labor market at the same time that low-paying industries and occupations are growing and high-paying industries are in decline.

A second reason is that part-time jobs are 6 times more likely to pay minimum wages than full-time jobs, and women are twice as likely to hold part-time jobs than men are (relatively more women than men report involuntary part-time work—they work part time only because full-time work is unavailable). A low minimum wage creates a large gap between the wages of a part-time job and the wages of a full-time job. Firms tend to develop a two-tiered labor force. One tier is comprised of workers who earn high wages, are trained on the job, and have many fringe benefits. The second tier consists of part-time, temporary workers who do not have fringe benefits. A higher minimum wage would reduce the gap between the tiers and may reduce a firm's incentive to substitute part-time jobs for full-time jobs. This would particularly aid women workers.

A frequently cited 1982 study concerning the effects of the minimum wage on adult workers reported that in 1975, relative to men, women received larger pay increases due to a minimum-wage boost in 1974. However, the female layoff rate was much larger in the 1974 recession. Peter Linneman, the author of the study, concluded that this was due to the fact that the 10¢-per-hour minimum-wage increase in 1974 brought the cost of female workers past the point of their marginal productivity. In essence, Linneman presumed that females were less-skilled workers because they earned less than their male counterparts. A subsequent review of the literature dismissed Linneman's study for making stronger-than-warranted inferences about the minimum wage and suggested that women may have been laid off first during the recession for other reasons, such as sex discrimination.

A third reason for why women would benefit more from a minimum-wage increase is that an increase may help reduce poverty rates among children. The relationship between poverty and the minimum wage is not straightforward. Working full time at minimum wage yields less than the poverty-level income for families of 2 or more persons. But most people who make the minimum wage do not live in poor families, although low earners tend to live with other low earners. This fact explains why there is a weak correlation between poverty and the minimum wage but that the probability of being poor is 4 times higher for minimum-wage workers than for other workers. This suggests that the young workers (age 24 years or younger), who constitute 60 percent of those workers who earn less than $4.35 per hour, are supplementing their families' low incomes.

This generalization has one important exception: approximately 35 percent of working women who were heads of households earned less than $159 per week in 1984 (an hourly wage of less than $4.00 per hour). This compares to the fact that fewer than 19 percent of male heads of households earned less than $159 per week. (A related fact to be considered is that male heads of households, unlike female heads of households, often have spouses who provide a second income.)

Finally, women are less likely to be unionized than men; 12 percent of women workers are unionized as compared to 25 percent of working men. This results in women having less bargaining power relative to their employers. In the absence of a union, a minimum-wage law provides an important wage floor.

A minimum-wage increase would restructure the wage distribution at the bottom. Currently, most new jobs created in retail and wholesale trade and in the service sector pay approximately $8,000 per year. One reason why these jobs pay less is because they are nonunion. Nationally, 23 percent of minimum-wage workers are in technical, clerical, and sales occupations, and 52 percent are in service occupations. The fact that these jobs are being created at the same time that adult women are dramatically increasing their labor-force participation means that, in the absence of unionization, a minimum-wage increase would permanently change the wage structure of women's jobs. This could be accomplished without much risk of reducing employment in these expanding occupations and industries. In South Bend, for instance, the service industry provides 26 percent of all jobs but only 23 percent of all income; the retail industry provides 19 percent of all jobs but only 9 percent of total income. Women make up 55 percent of all full-time workers in retail (mostly nonmanagerial jobs) and more than 60 percent in service jobs.

MINIMUM WAGE AND THE LOW-PAID LABOR MARKET

A low-paid labor market can be insulated from other jobs because of the racial, ethnic, and/or gender composition of the workforce, the special features of the industry, and/or certain geographical barriers. If these sources of insulation exist, then some institutional or administered change, whether it be in the form of union activity or in the form of a minimum wage, is needed to shore up wages. In the jargon of economists, this is the process in which monopsonistic exploitation is reduced. Economists posit a formal model for this situation: a segmented labor market. This is a market in which discrimination and other social forces decrease the amount of competition between men and women for all available jobs. This in turn means that competition does not work to achieve an efficient allocation of resources. One piece of evidence that points to a segmented labor market is the distribution of pay by sex and educational level. A college-educated woman earns about the same pay as a male who has dropped out of high school (respectively, $19,885 and $18,575). See Table 2.

Table 2

Average Earnings and Educational Attainment by Sex in 1984

Educational Level	Earnings	
	Women	Men
Some HS	$11,808	$18,575
HS Grad	14,076	22,312
Some College	16,241	24,737
College	19,885	33,086

Source: Barbara Bergmann, *The Economic Emergence of Women* (New York: Basic Books, 1987), p. 67.

Economic theory presumes that in competitive markets, wages are set when equally empowered agents haggle and dicker in a free marketplace until all workers receive the highest wage available for their skills. However, the data in Table 2 do not support this view. In noncompetitive markets wages can only be protected from downward pressures by huge increases in demand, by government regulation, or by other measures like collective-bargaining agreements. In the 1930s, when the minimum wage was established, it was high unemployment that kept wages below subsistence levels; in the 1980s, the entry into the workforce of new workers who would accept low wages—women—caused a downward pressure on wages.

In conclusion, the most common argument leveled against a minimum-wage increase is that raising the minimum wage would cause firms to reduce employment. Yet the facts do not support this argument. An advantage of raising the minimum wage at this time is that service and retail industries depend on domestic, geographically based demand (thus, they cannot easily relocate or be replaced by cheap foreign competition). Also, prices in the service and trade sectors are relatively low, and employers enjoy high profits. All of these factors indicate a situation in which employers have the ability to pay higher wages.

It is not likely that hospitals, fast-food restaurants, and department stores will go out of business if they must pay their lowest-paid workers another $1.40 per hour. Even when the percentage increase in wages is large, a large percentage of a small wage is still small; consequently, an increased minimum wage would increase total costs only slightly. Adult employment is not reduced by an increase in the minimum wage, because firms' hiring decisions depend on many factors, including demand for the goods or services and lack of substitutes for the labor inputs. The major factor determining how much firms will pay is what everyone else pays for similar jobs. Therefore, a minimum-wage increase would raise the pay of the lowest earners, increase total industry costs by a small amount, and redistribute income from the economy in general and the employer in particular to the worker. And, as is evident in the 1980s, these workers are mainly women.

Neither advocates for nor detractors of the minimum wage have sufficiently addressed the effect of the minimum wage on women workers. What is new in the minimum-wage debate in the 1980s is that the statutory minimum wage is becoming the major floor beneath women's earnings and, increasingly, it is the standard used by the fastest-growing and most profitable industries in the United States to decide what to pay their employees.

POSTSCRIPT

Was It a Mistake to Increase the Minimum Wage?

The editors of the *Nation's Business* take a dim view of minimum wage legislation. In short, they argue that the "public will pay" for this legislation in the form of "higher prices and fewer jobs." Their assertions are founded on a number of public and private studies of the minimum wage. Most notably, they turn to President Carter's Minimum Wage Study Commission, the Minimum Wage Coalition to Save Jobs, which is a report issued by a group of business organizations, and analyses conducted by the U.S. Chamber of Commerce. Based on these studies, *Nation's Business* concludes that support for the minimum wage is grounded on eight fundamental myths that demonstrate that the advocates of the legislation simply don't understand basic economic principles.

Ghilarducci defends the new minimum wage floor by admitting that the minimum wage may have a negative effect on employment. But she believes this will have a small effect and will be more than offset by the positive value of the new wage floor. In defense of this position, she argues that if over time the demand for the goods and services produced by labor increases, this will in turn increase the demand for labor and "easily" offset a "minimum wage increase." Indeed, under these conditions she speculates that in the absence of a new wage floor, "profits grow at the expense of wages." She goes on to note that the new floor has a benefit that is often overlooked by even its advocates. In particular, she maintains that a higher minimum wage will help redress the wage differential between men and women. In her words, this will provide a "floor beneath women's earnings."

There is much written about the pros and cons of the minimum wage. One excellent review of the history of this legislation and the arguments that have raged back and forth over its legitimacy these last 50 years is found in Howard Wachtel's book, *Labor and the Economy* (Academic Press, 1984). If you care to receive information from the business community, you might write the Minimum Wage Coalition to Save Jobs: P.O. Box 28261, Washington, D.C. 20038. If, on the other hand, you would care for organized labor's view of this issue, write the AFL-CIO headquarters: 815 Sixteenth St., N.W., Washington, D.C. 20006. To review the congressional hearings on the Minimum Wage Restoration Act of 1987, you will find this in the Senate as S. 837 and in the House of Representatives as H.R. 1834 in the government documents section of your library.

PART 2

Macroeconomic Issues

Government policy and economics are tightly intertwined. Fiscal policy and monetary policy have dramatic impact on the economy as a whole, and the state of the economy can often determine policy goals. Decisions regarding welfare payments or tax rates must be made in the context of broad macroeconomic goals, and the debates on these issues are more than theoretical discussions. Each has a significant impact on our economic lives.

Has American Government Become Too Big?

Should the Government Take Action to Increase the Savings Rate?

Should the Capital Gains Tax Be Lowered?

Is Workfare a Good Substitute for Welfare?

Do Federal Budget Deficits Matter?

Is the Financial Institutions Reform, Recovery, and Enforcement Act of 1989 the Solution to the Savings and Loan Crisis?

ISSUE 10

Has American Government Become Too Big?

YES: William Simon, from *A Time for Truth* (McGraw-Hill, 1978)

NO: John Kenneth Galbraith, from "The Social Consensus and the Conservative Onslaught," *Millenium Journal of International Studies* (Spring 1982)

ISSUE SUMMARY

YES: Former treasury secretary Simon argues that government has gone too far in its efforts to provide "cradle-to-grave security." According to Simon, wealth can only be created through the free operation of markets, and it is imperative that productivity and the growth of productivity be given the highest economic priority.

NO: Harvard economist Galbraith believes that the services provided by government contribute as much to the well-being of society as those provided by the private sector. Although taxes may reduce the freedom of those who are taxed, the freedom of those who benefit from the tax-financed programs is enhanced.

Even in a free enterprise, capitalistic, market economy like that of the United States, government has certain legitimate functions to perform. One such function is to provide for national defense. Another is to establish and maintain the code of laws that represents the ground rules for social and business relationships and activities. A third function is to take care of those who, through no fault of their own, are unable to take care of themselves. A fourth is to establish monetary and fiscal policies to promote price stability, employment, and economic growth. Finally, the government must make adjustments if the price a firm charges for its product does not include the costs imposed upon society by the production of that item.

Both liberals and conservatives accept these activities as legitimate governmental functions. The disagreement is over the amount of government action that is necessary and the specific action that should be taken. Conservatives demand that government's role be limited and that, when government must intercede, it should do so in a manner that preserves as much private initiative as possible. Liberals see a need for greater government involvement, with government choosing the quickest and most effective path to its goal.

In their arguments in favor of limited government, conservatives cite the intrinsic value of individual freedom: Individual freedom is an end in itself and is of the utmost importance. But more than this, individual freedom works to the benefit of the larger society: Society benefits because individual freedom promotes the efficient use of scarce resources. As evidence of this relationship, conservatives point to the great wealth of the United States and the high standard of living enjoyed by the average American, as compared to conditions in countries where government involvement is much more extensive. They also believe that political freedom cannot be maintained without economic freedom. Finally, they contend that any increase in the role of government means an equal reduction in individual freedom and individual incentives.

Liberals do not deny the importance of individual freedom, but they are less willing to accept the notion that economic efficiency is significantly impaired when the government tempers the workings of the market in order to promote equity. They argue that some persons can be taxed with only a minor loss of economic freedom so that the lot of others may be improved. To the question, "Does absolute political freedom demand complete economic freedom for each individual?" liberals respond with a resounding "no!" Indeed, they maintain that restricting the economic freedom of some does not necessarily reduce their political freedom and may, at the same time, enhance the economic freedom of others.

Conservatives give greater emphasis to national defense than do liberals. With respect to social welfare programs, the conservative effort is to ensure that only the "truly needy" receive benefits and that benefits should not be such so as to reduce individual initiative or incentive to work. To promote price stability, employment, and growth, conservatives promote slow and steady growth in the money supply, coupled with low rates of taxation and a balance between government taxes and revenues. As for the final function of government, conservatives believe that the difference between private costs and public costs is not as large as the liberals suggest. Accordingly, safety and environmental regulations are not promoted by conservatives, whereas they are by liberals.

The debate between Simon and Galbraith is not a debate between a conservative and a liberal over some specific issue or program. Rather, it is a debate on philosophical grounds—on the relationship between the size of government and the extent of individual freedom, and between individual freedom and economic performance. It is also a debate regarding the appropriate stance one should take regarding the nature of government. Should individuals take Simon's position that "state intervention in the private and productive lives of the citizenry must be presumed to be a negative, uncreative, and dangerous act"? Or should individuals support Galbraith's view that government programs to promote "good education, health care, and law enforcement do not impair liberty or foretell authoritarianism"?

YES
William Simon

THE ROAD TO LIBERTY

Normally in life, if one finds oneself in a situation where *all* known courses of action are destructive, one reassesses the premises which led to that situation. The premise to be questioned here is the degree of government intervention itself—the very competence of the state to function as a significant economic ruler. But to question that premise is to hurl oneself intellectually into a free market universe. And that the social democratic leaders will not do. A few may actually understand—as did the brilliant Chancellor Erhard in postwar Germany—that the solution to shortages, recession and unemployment, and an ominous decline in technological innovation is to dispense with most intervention and regulation and allow men to produce competitively in freedom. But they know that if they proposed this, they would be destroyed by the political intellectuals of their countries. . . .

What we need today in America is adherence to a set of broad guiding principles, not a thousand more technocratic adjustments. [I] shall not waste my time or yours with a set of legislative proposals. Instead, I will suggest a few of the most important general principles which I would like to see placed on the public agenda. They are actually the conclusions I have reached in the course of working on this book.

• The overriding principle to be revived in American political life is that which sets individual liberty as the highest political value—that value to which all other values are subordinate and that which, at all times, is to be given the highest "priority" in policy discussions.

• By the same token, there must be a conscious philosophical prejudice against any intervention by the state into our lives, for by definition such intervention abridges liberty. Whatever form it may take, state intervention in the private and productive lives of the citizenry must be presumed to be a negative, uncreative, and dangerous act, to be adopted only when its proponents provide overwhelming and incontrovertible evidence that the benefits to society of such intervention far outweigh the costs.

From William Simon, *A Time for Truth*, (McGraw-Hill, 1978). Copyright © 1978 by McGraw-Hill Publishing Company. Reprinted by permission.

• The principle of "no taxation without representation" must again become a rallying cry of Americans. Only Congress represents American voters, and the process of transferring regulatory powers—which are a hidden power to tax—to unelected, uncontrollable, and unfireable bureaucrats must stop. The American voters, who pay the bills, must be in a position to know what is being economically inflicted on them and in a position to vote men out of office who assault their interests, as *the voters* define those interests. Which means that Congress should not pass bills creating programs that it cannot effectively oversee. The drive to demand scrupulous legislative oversight of our policing agencies, such as the CIA, is valid; it should be extended to *all* agencies of the government which are also, directly or indirectly, exercising police power.

• A critical principle which must be communicated forcefully to the American public is the inexorable interdependence of economic wealth and political liberty. Our citizens must learn that what keeps them prosperous is production and technological innovation. Their wealth emerges, not from government offices or politician's edicts, but only from that portion of the marketplace which is *free*. They must also be taught to understand the relationship among collectivism, centralized planning, and poverty so that every new generation of Americans need not naively receive the Marxist revelations afresh.

• Bureaucracies themselves should be assumed to be noxious, authoritarian parasites on society, with a tendency to augment their own size and power and to cultivate a parasitical clientele in all classes of society. Area after area of American life should be set free from their blind power drive. We commonly hear people call for a rollback of prices, often unaware that they are actually calling for the destruction of marginal businesses and the jobs they furnish. People must be taught to start calling for a rollback of the bureaucracy, where nothing will be lost but strangling regulation and where the gains will always take the form of liberty, productivity, and jobs.

• Productivity and the growth of productivity must be the *first* economic consideration at all times, not the last. That is the source of technological innovation, jobs and wealth. This means that profits needed for investment must be respected as a great social blessing, not as a social evil, and that the envy of the "rich" cannot be allowed to destroy a powerful economic system.

• The concept that "wealth is theft" must be repudiated. It now lurks, implicitly, in most of the political statements we hear. Wealth can indeed be stolen, but only *after* it has been produced, and the difference between stolen wealth and produced wealth is critical. If a man obtains money by fraud or by force, he is simply a criminal to be handled by the police and the courts. But if he has earned his income honorably, by the voluntary exchange of goods and services, he is not a criminal or a second-class citizen and should not be treated as such. A society taught to perceive producers as criminals will end up by destroying its productive processes.

• Conversely, the concept that the absence of money implies some sort of virtue should be repudiated. Poverty may result from honest misfortune, but it also may result from sloth, incompetence, and dishonesty. Again the distinction between deserving and undeserving poor is important. It is a virtue to assist those who are in acute need through no fault of their own, but it is folly to glamorize men simply because they are penniless. The crude linkage between wealth and evil, poverty and virtue is false, stupid, and of value only to demagogues, parasites, and criminals—indeed, the three groups that alone have profited from the linkage.

• Similarly, the view that government is virtuous and producers are evil is a piece of folly, and a nation which allows itself to be tacitly guided by these illusions must lose both its liberty and its wealth. Government has its proper functions, and consequently, there can be both good and bad governments. Producers as well can be honest and dishonest. Our political discourse can be rendered rational only when people are taught to make such discriminations.

• The "ethics" of egalitarianism must be repudiated. Achievers must not be penalized or parasites rewarded if we aspire to a healthy, productive, and ethical society. Able-bodied citizens must work to sustain their lives, and in a healthy economic system they should be enabled and encouraged to save for their old age. Clearly, so long as the government's irrational fiscal policies make this impossible, present commitments to pensions and Social Security must be maintained at all cost, for the bulk of the population has no other recourse. But as soon as is politically feasible—meaning, as soon as *production* becomes the nation's highest economic value—the con-

tributions of able-bodied citizens to their own future pensions should be invested by them in far safer commercial institutions, where the sums can earn high interest without being squandered by politicians and bureaucrats. American citizens must be taught to wrest their life savings from the politicians if they are to know the comfort of genuine security.

• The American citizen must be made aware that today a relatively small group of people is proclaiming its purposes to be the will of the People. That elitist approach to government must be repudiated. There is no such thing as the People; it is a collectivist myth. There are only individual citizens with individual wills and individual purposes. There is only one social system that reflects this sovereignty of the individual: the free market, or capitalist, system, which means the sovereignty of the individual "vote" in the marketplace and the sovereignty of the individual vote in the political realm. That individual sovereignty is being destroyed in this country by our current political trends, and it is scarcely astonishing that individuals now feel "alienated" from their government. They are not just alienated from it; they have virtually been expelled from the governmental process, where only organized mobs prevail.

• The growing cynicism about democracy must be combated by explaining why it has become corrupted. People have been taught that if they can get together big enough gangs, they have the legal power to hijack other citizens' wealth, which means the power to hijack other people's efforts, energies, and lives. No decent society can function when men are given such power. A state does need funds, but a clear cutoff line must be established beyond which no political group or institution can confiscate a citizen's honorably earned property. The notion that one can differentiate between "property rights." and "human rights" is ignoble. One need merely see the appalling condition of "human rights" in nations where there are no "property rights" to understand why. This is just a manifestation of the socialist myth which imagines that one can keep men's minds free while enslaving their bodies.

These are some of the broad conclusions I have reached after four years in office. Essentially they are a set of guiding principles. America is foundering for the lack of principles; it is now guided by the belief that *unprincipled* action—for which the respectable name is "pragmatism"— is somehow superior. Such principles as I have listed do not represent dogma. There is, as I said, nothing arbitrary or dogmatic about the interlocking relationship between political and economic liberty. The history of every nation on earth demonstrates that relationship, and no economist known to me, including the theoreticians of interventionism and totalitarianism, denies this. If liberty is to be our highest political value, this set of broad principles follows consistently. . . .

It is often said by people who receive warnings about declining freedom in America that such a charge is preposterous, that there is no freer society on earth. That is true in one sense, but it is immensely deceptive. There has never been such freedom before in America to speak freely, indeed, to wag one's tongue in the hearing of an entire nation; to publish anything and everything, including the most scurrilous gossip; to take drugs and to prate to children about their alleged pleasures; to propagandize for bizarre sexual practices; to watch bloody and obscene entertainment. Conversely, compulsion rules the world of work. There has never been so little freedom before in America to plan, to save, to invest, to build, to produce, to invent, to hire, to fire, to resist coercive unionization, to exchange goods and services, to risk, to profit, to grow.

The strange fact is that Americans are constitutionally free today to do almost everything that our cultural tradition has previously held to be immoral and obscene, while the police powers of the state are being invoked against almost every aspect of the productive process. Even more precisely, Americans today are left free by the state to engage in activities that could, for the most part, be carried on just as readily in prisons, insane asylums, and zoos. They are not left free by the state to pursue those activities which will give them *independence*.

That is not a coincidence. It is characteristic, in fact, of the contemporary collectivist, in both America and Europe, to clamor that freedom pertains exclusively to the verbal and emotional realms. It allows the egalitarian socialist the illusion that he is not trying to weave a noose for the throats of free men, and it renders him all the more dangerous to the credulous. It is difficult, indeed, to identify as a potential tyrant someone who is raising a righteous uproar over your right to fornicate in the streets. But in this as well, our contemporary "liberators" are not original. I transmit to you a warning by Professor Nisbet, professor of humanities at Columbia University, included in his essay "The New Despotism." He says something I consider vital for the contemporary citizen to know because it is the final reason for the invisibility surrounding the destruction of some of our most crucial liberties:

> [M]ore often than not in history, license has been the prelude to exercises of extreme political coercion, which shortly reach all areas of a culture. . . . [V]ery commonly in ages when civil rights of one kind are in evidence—those pertaining to freedom of speech and thought in, say, theater, press and forum, with obscenity and libel laws correspondingly loosened—very real constrictions of individual liberty take place in other, more vital areas; political organization, voluntary association, property and the right to hold jobs, for example. . . .
>
> There are, after all, certain freedoms that are like circuses. Their very existence, so long as they are individual and enjoyed chiefly individually as by spectators, diverts men's minds from the loss of other, more fundamental social and economic and political rights.
>
> A century ago, the liberties that now exist routinely on stage and screen, on printed page and canvas would have been unthinkable in America—and elsewhere in the West, for that matter, save in the most clandestine and limited of settings. But so would the limitations upon economic, professional, education and local liberties, to which we have by now become accustomed, have seemed equally unthinkable half a century ago. We enjoy the feeling of great freedom, of protection of our civil liberties, when we attend the theater, watch television, buy paperbacks. But all the while, we find ourselves living in circumstances of a spread of military, police and bureaucratic power that cannot help but have, that manifestly does have, profoundly erosive effect upon those economic, local and associative liberties that are by far the most vital to any free society.
>
> From the point of view of any contemporary strategist or tactician of political power indulgence in the one kind of

liberties must seem a very requisite to dimunition of the other kind. We know it seemed that way to the Caesars and Napoleons of history. Such indulgence is but one more way of softening the impact of political power and of creating the illusion of individual freedom in a society grown steadily more centralized, collectivized and destructive of the diversity of allegiance, the autonomy of enterprise in all spheres and the spirit of spontaneous association that any genuinely free civilization requires.

I cite this for another reason. Like others whom I have quoted at length at several points in this book, Mr. Nisbet stands as a living illustration of what I mean by a counterintellectual. It is only the scholar with a profound understanding of the nature of liberty and the institutions on which it rests who can stand ultimate guard over American cultural life. It is only he who can offer the American citizen the authentic and profound choices that our political system and our press no longer offer him.

I do not mean to imply here that it is only on a lofty, scholarly level that the fight can be conducted, although it unquestionably must begin at that level. At any time and on any social level the individual can and should take action. I have done so in my realm, and you, too, can work for your liberty, immediately and with impact. . . .

Stop asking the government for "free" goods and services, however desirable and necessary they may seem to be. They are not free. They are simply extracted from the hide of your neighbors—and can be extracted only by force. If you would not confront your neighbor and demand his money at the point of a gun to solve every new problem that may appear in your life, you should not allow the government to do it for you. Be prepared to identify any politician who simultaneously demands your "sacrifices" and offers you "free services" for exactly what he is: an egalitarian demagogue. This one insight understood, this one discipline acted upon and taught by millions of Americans to others could do more to further freedom in American life than any other.

There is, of course, a minimum of government intervention needed to protect a society, particularly from all forms of physical aggression and from economic fraud and, more generally, to protect the citizen's liberty and constitutional rights. What that precise minimum is in terms of a percentage of the GNP I am not prepared to say, but I do know this: that a clear cutoff line, beyond which the government may not confiscate our property, must be sought and established if the government is not to invade every nook and cranny of our lives and if we are to be free and productive. It is with *our* money that the state destroys our freedom. It is not too soon to start the process of tightening the leash on the state on the individual level, above all, by refusing to be a parasite. In the lowest-income groups in our nation there are men and women too proud, too independent to accept welfare, even though it is higher than the wages they can earn. Surely such pride can be stimulated on the more affluent levels of our society. . . .

It is with a certain weariness that I anticipate the charge that I am one of those "unrealistic" conservatives who wishes to "turn back the clock." There is a good deal less to this criticism than meets the eye. History is not a determinist carpet rolling inexorably in the direction of collectivism, although an extraordinary number of people believe this to be the case. The truth is that it has unrolled gloriously in the opposite direction many times. Above all, the United States was born. There is nothing "historically inevitable" about the situation we are in. There is also nothing "realistic" in counseling people to adjust to that situation. That is equivalent to counseling them to adjust to financial collapse and the loss of freedom. Realism, in fact, requires the capacity to see beyond the tip of one's nose, to face intolerably unpleasant problems and to take the necessary steps to dominate future trends, not to be crushed passively beneath them.

The time plainly has come to act. And I would advise the socially nervous that if our contemporary "New Despots" prefer to conceive of themselves as "progressive" and denounce those of us who would fight for liberty as "reactionary," let them. Words do not determine reality. Indeed, if language and history are to be taken seriously, coercion is clearly reactionary, and liberty clearly progressive. In a world where 80 percent of all human beings still live under harrowing tyranny, a tyranny always rationalized in terms of the alleged benefits to a collectivist construct called the People, the American who chooses to fight for the sanctity of the individual has nothing for which to apologize.

One of the clearest measures of the disastrous change that has taken place in this country is the fact that today one must intellectually justify a passion for individual liberty and for limited government, as though it were some bizarre new idea. Yet angry as I get when I reflect on this, I know there is a reason for it. Seen in the full context of human history, individual liberty *is* a bizarre new idea. And an even more bizarre new idea is the free market—the discovery that allowing millions upon millions of individuals to pursue their material interests as they choose, with a minimum of interference by the state, will unleash an incredible and orderly outpouring of inventiveness and wealth. These twin ideas appeared, like a dizzying flare of light in the long night of tyranny that has been the history of the human race. That light has begun to fade because the short span of 200 years has not been long enough for most of our citizens to understand the extraordinary nature of freedom. I say this with genuine humility. I came to understand this late in life myself, inspired by a very special perspective: I was flying high over the land of one of the bloodiest tyrants on earth. But having understood it, I cannot let that light die out without a battle.

NO
John Kenneth Galbraith

THE SOCIAL CONSENSUS AND THE CONSERVATIVE ONSLAUGHT

THE ECONOMIC AND SOCIAL CONSENSUS

In economic and social affairs we value controversy and take it for granted; it is both the essence of politics and its principal attraction as a modern spectator sport. This emphasis on controversy regularly keeps us from seeing how substantial, on occasion, can be the agreement on the broad framework of ideas and policies within which the political debate proceeds.

This has been the case with economic and social policy in the industrial countries since the Second World War. There has been a broad consensus which has extended to most Republicans and most Democrats in the United States, to both Christian Democrats and Social Democrats in Germany and Austria, to the Labour and Tory Parties in Britain, and to Liberals and Progressive Conservatives in Canada. In France, Italy, Switzerland and Scandinavia also, policies have generally been based on a consensus. Although the rhetoric in all countries has been diverse, the practical action has been broadly similar.

All governments in all of the industrial countries, although differing in individual emphasis, have agreed on three essential points. First, there must be macroeconomic management of the economy to minimise unemployment and inflation. This, particularly in the English-speaking countries, was the legacy of Keynes. Second, there must be action by governments to provide those services which, by their nature, are not available from the private sector, or on which, like moderate-cost housing, health care and urban transportation, the private economy defaults. Finally, there must be measures—unemployment insurance, old age pensions, medical insurance, environmental protection, job-safety and produce-safety regulation, and special welfare payments—to protect the individual from circumstances with which he or she, as an individual, cannot contend, and which may be seen as a smoothing and softening of the harsh edges of capitalism.

There is no accepted term for the consensus which these policies compromise. 'Keynesian' policy refers too narrowly to macroeconomic action;

From John Kenneth Galbraith, "The Social Consensus and the Conservative Onslaught," *Millennium Journal of International Studies* (Spring 1982). Copyright © 1982 by John Kenneth Galbraith. Reprinted by permission of the author.

'liberal' or 'social democratic' policy has too strong a political connotation for what has been embraced in practice by Dwight E. Eisenhower, Gerald Ford, Charles de Gaulle, Konrad Adenauer, Winston Churchill and Edward Heath. I will not try to devise a new term; instead I will refer to the broad macroeconomic, public-service and social welfare commitment as the economic and social consensus, or just 'the consensus.' It is the present attack on this consensus—notably in Mrs. Thatcher's government in Britain and by Ronald Reagan's government in the United States—that I wish to examine.

THE CONSERVATIVE CHALLENGE TO THE CONSENSUS

The ideas supporting the economic and social consensus have never been without challenge. Keynesian macroeconomic management of the economy, the first pillar of the consensus, was powerfully conservative in intent. It sought only to correct the most self-destructive feature of capitalism (the one Marx thought decisive), namely its tendency to produce recurrent and progressively more severe crisis or depression, while leaving the role of the market, the current distribution of income and all property rights unchallenged. Despite this, numerous conservatives, especially in the United States, for a long time equated Keynesian economics with subversion. There was discomfort among conservatives when, thirty years after Keynes's *General Theory*[1] was published and the policy it prescribed was tending visibly towards obsolescence, Richard Nixon, in an aberrant moment, was led to say that all Americans, including Republicans, were Keynesians now. A reference to the welfare policies of the consensus—'the welfare state'—

has always encountered a slightly disapproving mood; something expensive or debilitating, it was felt, was being done for George Bernard Shaw's undeserving poor. The need to compensate for the failures of capitalism through the provision of lower-cost housing, lower-income health care and mass transportation has been accepted in all countries; but, in the United States at least, not many have wanted to admit that this is an unavoidable form of socialism. In contrast, in all countries at all times there has been much mention of the cost of government, the level of taxes, the constraints of business regulation and the effect of these on economic incentives.

There has always been a likelihood, moreover, that an attack on the economic and social consensus would be taken to reflect the views of a larger section of the population than was actually the case, because a large share of all public comment comes from people of relatively high income, while the consensus is of greatest importance to those of lowest income. High social business and academic position gives access to television, radio, and the press, and those who are professionally engaged in the media are, themselves, relatively well off. It follows that the voice of economic advantage, being louder, regularly gets mistaken for the voice of the masses. Furthermore, since it is so interpreted by politicians, it has much the same effect on legislatures and legislation as a genuine shift of opinion.

In the last thirty-five years we have had many such shifts of opinion—all drastically to the right. Professor Friedrich Hayek with his *Road to Serfdom;*[2] Senator Goldwater in 1964; the unpoor, non-black, distinctly unradical Dayton, Ohio housewife, the supposed archetype discovered by two American scholars; Vice President Spiro Agnew; George Wallace; and Enoch Powell in Britain—they were all, in their turn, seen to represent a growing new conservative mood, before being, each in his turn, rejected.

However, even if proper allowance is made for the dismal success, in the past, of conservative revival, it seems certain that there is now not only in the United States but in other industrial countries as well, an attack on the economic and social consensus that has a deeper substance. Mrs. Thatcher and Mr. Reagan have both won elections. Of course, much, if not most, of Mr. Reagan's success in 1980 must be attributed to President Carter's economists—to the macroeconomic management that combined a severe recession with severe inflation with a drastic slump in the housing industry with particular economic distress in the traditional Democratic industrial states, and all these in the year of the election. (Economists do some things with precision.) But *effective* macroeconomic management was one part of the consensus and, obviously, there is nothing wrong with the way it now functions.

THE CONSERVATIVE ONSLAUGHT

There is, indeed, substance to the conservative attack on the economic and social consensus, especially in Britain and the United States. It strikes at genuine points of vulnerability. This, however, is not true of all of the attack; some of it is merely a rejection of reality—or of compassion. The conservative onslaught we now witness needs careful dissection and differentiation. . . .

THE SIMPLISTIC ATTACK

The *simplistic* attack, which is currently powerful in the United States, consists in a generalised assault on all the civilian services of modern government. Education, urban services and other conventional functions of government; government help to the unemployed, unemployable or otherwise economically incapable; public housing and health care; and the regulatory functions of government are all in the line of fire. People, in a now famous phrase, must be left free to choose.

In its elementary form this attack on the consensus holds that the services of government are the peculiar malignity of those who perform them; they are a burden foisted on the unwilling taxpayer by bureaucrats. One eloquent American spokesman for this view, Mr. William Simon, the former Secretary of the Treasury, has said that,

> Bureaucrats should be assumed to be noxious, authoritarian parasites on society, with a tendency to augment their own size and power and to cultivate a parasitical clientele in all classes of society.[3]

There must, he has urged, 'be a conscious, philosophical prejudice against any intervention by the state into our lives.'[4] If public services are a foisted malignancy—if they are unrelated to need or function—it follows that they can be reduced more or less without limit and without significant social cost or suffering. This is implicit, even explicit, in the simplistic attack.

Other participants in this line of attack are, superficially at least, more sophisticated. Professor Arthur Laffer of the University of Southern California has supported the case with his now famous curve, which shows that when no taxes are levied, no revenue is raised, and that when taxes absorb all income, their yield, not surprisingly, is also zero. Taxes that are too high, as shown by a curve connecting these two points, have at some point a reduced aggregate yield. The Laffer Curve—which in its operative ranges is of purely freehand origin—has become, in turn, a general case against all taxes. Let there be large horizontal reductions, it is argued, and the resulting expansion of private output and income—for those who will believe anything—can be great enough to sustain public revenues at more or less the previous level. For the less gullible, the Laffer Curve still argues for a large reduction in the cost and role of the government.[5]

Another stronger attack on the public services comes from Professor Milton Friedman and his disciples. It holds that these services are relentlessly in conflict with liberty: the market accords to the individual the sovereignty of choice; the state, as it enlarges its services, curtails or impairs that choice—a cumulative and apocalyptic process. By its acceptance of a large service and protective role for the state, democracy commits itself to an irreversible descent into totalitarianism and to Communism. Professor Friedman is firm as to the prospect. He argues that,

> If we continue our present trend, and our free society is replaced by a collectivist society, the intellectuals who have done so much to drive us down this path will not be the ones who run the society; the prison, insane asylum, or the graveyard would be their fate.[6]

Against this trend he asks,

> shall we have the wisdom and the courage to change our course, to learn from experience, and to benefit from a 'rebirth of freedom'?[7]

I have called this attack on the social consensus simplistic: it could also be called rhetorical and, by the untactful, vacuous, because it depends almost wholly on passionate assertion and emotional response. No one, after reflection, can conclude that publicly rendered services are less urgently a part of the living standard than privately purchased ones—that clean water from the public sector is less needed than clean houses from the private sector, that good schools for the young are less important than good television sets. In most countries public services are not rendered with high efficiency, a point worthy of real concern. But no way has ever been found for seriously reducing outlays for either efficiently or inefficiently rendered services without affecting performance. Public bureaucracy has a dynamic of its own, but so does private bureaucracy. As road builders promote public highways and public educators promote public education, so private weapons firms promote weapons and other corporate bureaucracies promote tobacco, alcohol, toothpaste and cosmetics. This is the common tendency of organisation, as we have known since Max Weber. Good education, health care and law enforcement do not impair liberty or foretell authoritarianism. On the contrary, the entire experience of civilised societies is that these services are consistent with liberty and enlarge it. Professor Friedman's belief that liberty is measured, as currently in New York City, by the depth of the uncollected garbage is, as I have previously observed, deeply questionable.

Taxes on the affluent do reduce the freedom of those so taxed to spend their own money. 'An essential part of economic freedom is freedom to choose how to use our income.'[8] But, unemployment compensation, old-age pensions and other welfare payments serve even more specifically to increase the liberty of their recipients. That is because the difference for liberty between considerable income and a little less income can be slight; in contrast, the effect on liberty of the difference between *no* income and *some* income is always very, very great. It is the unfortunate habit of those who speak of the effect of government on freedom that they confine their concern to the loss of freedom for the affluent. All but invariably they omit to consider the way income creates freedom for the indigent.

The differential effect of taxes and public services on people of different income is something we must not disguise. Taxes in industrial countries are intended to be moderately progressive; in any case, they are paid in greatest absolute amount by people of middle income and above. Public services, in contrast, are most used by the poor. The affluent have access to private schools, while the poor must rely on public education. The rich have private golf courses and swimming pools; the poor depend on public parks and public recreation. Public transportation is most important for the least affluent, as are public hospitals, public libraries and public housing, the services of the police and other municipal services. Unemployment and welfare benefits are important for those who have no other income, while they have no similar urgency for those who are otherwise provided.

We sometimes hesitate in these careful days to suggest an apposition of interest between the rich and the poor. One should not, it is felt, stir the embers of the class struggle. To encourage envy is uncouth, possibly even un-American or un-British. However, any general assault on the public services must be understood for what it is; it is an attack on the living standard of the poor.

NOTES

1. John Maynard Keynes, *The General Theory of Employment Interest and Money* (London: Macmillan, 1936).

2. Fredrich von Hayek, *Road to Serfdom* (London: Routledge and Kegan Paul, 1944).

3. William Simon, *A Time for Truth* (New York: McGraw-Hill, 1978), p. 219.

4. *Ibid.*, p. 218.

5. Professor Laffer's inspired use of purely fortuitous hypotheses, it is only fair to note, has been a source of some discomfort to some of his more scrupulous academic colleagues.

6. Professor Friedman's foreword in William Simon, *op. cit.*, p. xiii.

7. Milton and Rose Friedman, *Free to Choose* (New York: Harcourt Brace Jovanovich, 1979), p. 7.

8. *Ibid.*, p. 65.

POSTSCRIPT

Has American Government Become Too Big?

Simon offers a series of conclusions drawn from his analysis of the appropriate size and role of government. First, he contends that individual liberty is the highest political value. Second, he believes "there must be a conscious philosophic prejudice against any intervention by the state into our lives, for by definition such intervention abridges liberty." Simon's third conclusion is that there is an "inexorable interdependence of economic wealth and political liberty." Simon also believes that bureaucracies should be viewed as forces of evil, which reduce liberty, productivity, and jobs; that productivity and its growth must be given the highest priority at all times; that wealth is not theft and poverty is not virtue; and that property rights are an essential part of human rights. Simon stresses the essential conservative position that individual liberty and the free market will continue to "unleash an incredible and orderly outpouring of inventiveness and wealth."

In defending the liberal view of the legitimacy of government and the usefulness of its activities, Galbraith begins by citing a broad consensus regarding social policy in industrial countries. This consensus involves three points: government must take action to minimize unemployment and inflation; government must provide those things "which, by their nature, are not available from the private sector"; and government must act "to protect the individual from circumstances with which he or she cannot contend." He goes on to argue that conservative attacks, like those of Simon, are simplistic because it is clear that the services provided by government contribute as much to society's well-being as do those produced by private business firms and that these government-provided "services are consistent with liberty and enlarge it." Indeed, he admits that taxes may reduce the freedom of those who are taxed but maintains that those who benefit from the tax-financed programs experience an increase in freedom.

For a more complete discussion of these issues, see *A Time for Truth*, by William E. Simon (McGraw-Hill, 1978); *Economics and the Public Purpose*, by John Kenneth Galbraith (Houghton Mifflin, 1973); *The Denigration of Capitalism: Six Points of View*, edited by Michael Novak (American Enterprise Institute, 1979); "Reflections on Social Democracy," by Alfred S. Eichner, in *Challenge* (March/April 1982); and *Capitalism and Freedom*, by Milton Friedman (University of Chicago Press, 1962).

ISSUE 11

Should the Government Take Action to Increase the Savings Rate?

YES: Lou Ferleger and Jay R. Mandle, from "The Saving Shortfall," *Challenge* (March-April, 1989)

NO: Milton Friedman, from "What is the 'Right' Amount of Saving?" *National Review* (June 16, 1989)

ISSUE SUMMARY

YES: Economists Ferleger and Mandle believe that the savings rate is too low and this has forced the monetary authority to keep interest rates high so as to attract foreign saving. The high interest rates have restricted U.S. economic growth. In order to increase saving, Ferleger and Mandle recommend the imposition of a tax on consumption, but the tax should be "aggressively progressive" and should only be imposed when the economy is strong.
NO: Free-market economist Friedman maintains that there is no particular number that represents the "right" amount of saving. Rather, the right amount of saving is that which people freely choose to save. He maintains that it is not the proper function of government to determine the level of saving: "government has no business meddling in our family planning: whether about how many heirs we have or how much wealth we choose to leave them."

When Ben Franklin said "A penny saved is a penny earned," he was extolling the virtues of individual thrift. To spend less than is earned, to save, means that a person can have funds available for future spending. If the savings can be lent to someone and interest earned on the amount lent, then future consumption could increase by even more than the amount saved. However, to extol the benefits of savings is not to declare how much should be saved.

When the discussion shifts from the individual perspective to the national economy, much the same argument can be made concerning the benefits of saving. In the case of the national economy, saving translates into investment, and investment means that the nation's capital stock is increasing. This, in turn, means that the nation's ability to produce goods and services is increasing. Thus, more future production and consumption is possible. This does not mean that more saving is always preferred to less. Because all saving is not automatically translated into investment, it is possible that increased saving may decrease total spending in the economy, and the reduction in total spending or aggregate demand may mean a decrease in current production and an increase in unemployment. So it is possible that saving may be either too little (impeding future production and consumption) or too much (generating a current recession).

In taking a national perspective, it is important to recognize that saving is an activity undertaken by various sectors of the economy. First, there is personal saving, undertaken by individuals, which can be defined, in terms of the national income accounts, as the difference between disposable personal income and personal outlays. In 1987 personal saving totaled $104.2 billion. Second, there is saving by the business sector of the economy. A simple definition of business saving is the amount firms have set aside for depreciation plus the amount of profits that firms have left after paying taxes to the government and dividends to stockholders. In 1987 business saving totaled $561.1 billion. Third, government can save by spending less than it collects in taxes. In 1987 the federal government had a deficit, spending $157.8 billion more than it collected in taxes. However, on a combined basis, state and local units of government saved $52.9 billion. Combining federal, state, and local units of government, this sector of the economy had a deficit in the amount of $104.9 billion. If you combine the personal, business, and government sector savings, that yields a total gross figure of $560.4 billion ($104.2 + $561.1 − $104.9).

If the United States were a closed economy, this last figure would be the amount of funds available for investment. But when firms borrow money for investment, they actually have four choices. Besides borrowing from personal savings, other business firms, or various units of government, business firms can also borrow from abroad. In 1987 Gross Private Domestic Investment in the United States was $712.9 billion. The difference between Gross Private Domestic Investment and the amount of saving available from the three domestic sources represents borrowing from abroad. In effect, the United States was using foreign saving to compensate for a shortfall in domestic saving.

It is figures like these that make economists like Ferleger and Mandle believe that the United States is saving too little. They believe that government needs to take action to stimulate domestic saving. In this argument, Ferleger and Mandle represent the liberal view, identifying a problem and suggesting government action to redress the problem. While some conservative economists may agree with the analysis and recommendations offered by Ferleger and Mandle, Friedman speaks as a true conservative, taking what he calls the "classical liberal position." He argues that government has no business trying to decide for persons how much they should save.

YES

Lou Ferleger and Jay R. Mandle

THE SAVING SHORTFALL

At least two hypotheses underlie the view that the saving rate in the United States should be increased. One of these hypotheses is that an inadequate saving rate is responsible for poor productivity in the American economy in recent years. The argument is that insufficient saving is responsible for a relatively low level of investment and this, in turn, is the reason that labor productivity has not been as dynamic as it should be.

Another is that because domestic saving is low, the country has become increasingly dependent upon the supply of saving from abroad. Monetary authorities in the United States, according to this view, must set the interest rate at a level higher than would be the case if domestic saving was adequate and they did not have to be concerned with attracting funds from abroad. The problem however, is that such high interest rates act as a brake on economic growth by reducing both new investment and discouraging consumption. Ultimately, according to this second hypothesis, that brake is attributable to low savings rates within the country.

The following will give you the basic U.S. data on saving, investment, and productivity growth by which to evaluate these arguments. Saving and investment are reported as a percentage of the national income in order to show their movements relative to the size of the economy as a whole. The sources of savings also are provided. Domestic saving has its origins in private households, the business sector, and government. A fourth source, net foreign saving, is also reported. This variable is treated as a residual between domestic saving and investment. The data are grouped according to cycles of economic growth and contraction. By doing so it is possible to compare different periods while holding constant the cyclical movements in the economy.

Table 1 provides information on the relationship between the rate of investment and the growth rate in labor productivity. During periods of economic expansion, the years on the left-hand side of the table, the growth

From Lou Ferleger and Jay R. Mandle, "The Saving Shortfall," *Challenge* (March/April 1989). Reprinted with permission of publisher, M.E. Sharpe, Inc., 80 Business Park Drive, Armonk, NY 10504.

in productivity fell from 2.9 percent in the 1960s to about 1.8 percent in the 1970s and 1980s. Similarly the productivity performance worsened during the periods of slow growth or decline.

At the end of the 1960s productivity increased even when the economy was in recession. In contrast, during the recessions of both 1974–75 and 1979–82, productivity actually declined. Clearly, coming out of the 1974–75 recession, if not earlier, America's productivity performance experienced a substantial worsening.

This table, however, also makes it clear that the deterioration in productivity was not associated with decreasing investment rates. The 1974–75 and 1976–78 periods—those in which the decline in productivity first became obvious—are actually ones in which investment stood at relatively high levels.

Furthermore, the subsequent years do not show much of a dropoff in this measure. The investment rate for the years 1983–87, during which productivity growth was poor, stood at a level above that for the period 1961–68, during which productivity growth was quite high. Declining investment rates, in short, are not responsible for the decrease in productivity growth increases.

Tables 2 and 3 show the level and sources of domestic saving and the relationship between domestic saving and private investment in the United States. It is clear that the availability of domestic saving relative to private investment has declined. In the current period of expansion, domestic saving constituted only 16.6 percent of national income compared to levels of about 20 percent in earlier years.

These negative trends coincided with the years of the Reagan tax cuts. What seems to have occurred is that the tax changes were responsible for both the decreased personal saving and increased government borrowing which were only partially offset by an increase in the saving rate by the business sector.

TAPPING FOREIGN FUNDS

The decrease in domestic saving in conjunction with a constant rate of investment has necessitated tapping foreign sources of funds. This dependence on overseas financing was greater in 1983–87 than in any other period since 1961. In those years recourse to overseas saving required a flow that came to more than 3 percent of national income, greater than twice the highest previous level of dependence experienced since 1961.

The data support only one of the two hypotheses under consideration. They do not support the first hypothesis that decreasing saving, and therefore investment, are responsible for the declining trend in productivity growth. On the contrary, the investment rate has not declined, and so insufficient saving, acting to constrain investment, cannot be the source of the productivity problem in the United States.

But at the same time, the reason that it has been possible to maintain stable investment rates is that the United States has increasingly found abroad its sources of finance for its investment. This finding is consistent with the hypothesis that there has been an undesirable increase in dependency on overseas saving. If either domestic saving were higher or the government deficit were smaller, there would be less need to attract saving from other countries, with the likely result being lower interest rates in the United States.

Table 1

Investment Rate and Rate of Growth of Labor Productivity, 1961–1987
(% of total national income and % annual productivity growth)

PROS	INV	PROD	REC	INV	PROD
1961–68	18.8	2.9	1969–71	18.8	0.9
1972–73	20.8	2.5	1974–75	18.5	−0.2
1976–78	21.1	1.7	1979–82	20.2	−0.4
1983–87	19.9	1.8			

PROS = Years of rapid growth; REC = Years of negative or slow growth; INV = Investment;
PROD = Rate of labor productivity growth.
Source: Economic Report of the President, February 1988.

Table 2

Sources of Domestic Saving
(% of total national income)

PROS	PS	+	BS	+	GS	=	DS	REC	PS	+	BS	+	GS	=	DS
1961–68	5.8		14.6		−0.4		20.0	1969–71	6.5		13.3		−0.8		19.0
1972–73	7.1		14.1		0.2		21.4	1974–75	8.1		14.3		−2.7		19.7
1976–78	6.1		16.1		−1.3		20.9	1979–82	6.2		16.0		−1.7		20.5
1983–87	4.2		16.3		−3.9		16.6								

PROS = Years of rapid growth; REC = Years of negative or slow growth; PS = Personal saving;
BS = Business saving; GS = Government saving; DS = Domestic saving.
Source: Economic Report of the President, February 1988.

Table 3

Estimate of Net Foreign Saving Requirement
(% of total national income)

PROS	DS	−	INV	=	NFS	REC	DS	−	INV	=	NFS
1961–68	20.0		18.8		1.2	1969–71	19.0		18.8		0.2
1972–73	21.4		20.8		0.6	1974–75	19.7		18.5		1.2
1976–78	20.9		21.1		−0.2	1979–82	20.2		21.0		−0.8
1983–87	16.6		19.9		−3.3						

PROS = Years of rapid growth; REC = Years of negative or slow growth; DS = Domestic saving;
INV = Private investment.
Source: Economic Report of the President, February 1988.

This analysis suggests, therefore, that it would be desirable to raise the level of domestic saving. Doing so would reduce our saving dependency, although it would not do much with regard to our productivity difficulties.

One way to increase saving would be to introduce a new consumption tax, which would raise the cost of commodities, discourage consumption and, in the process, raise the personal saving rate. It would also, by increasing government revenues, reduce public sector borrowing requirements. As a result, an increased fraction of private investment could be financed with internally generated funds, rather than requiring money made available from foreign sources.

In considering the desirability of such a tax, however, at least three additional considerations must be addressed. The first is that, as we have noted above, such a tax will have little impact on American productivity. This means that its potential beneficial results should not be overstated. A consumption tax will not seriously improve the economy's long-term competitiveness and its ability to generate good paying jobs.

Second, the fairness of a consumption tax must also be considered. An indiscriminate sales tax can be seriously regressive, taxing a lower proportion of the income of the rich than that of the rest of the population. In fact, however, any new taxes introduced should be aggressively progressive, if only to reverse the trends in tax policy implemented by the Reagan Administration.

A consumption tax can be progressive, but only if it is applied exclusively to those discretionary purchases made by the wealthy. No tax at all should be attached to the basic goods and services essential to the well-being of low and moderate income households and persons.

TIMING IS IMPORTANT

Finally, care must be taken concerning the timing of such a tax. In the wrong context an increase in taxes can produce a recession and rising unemployment. Since the threat of recession increases the longer growth is sustained, the present period probably is not a good time to introduce a new tax. The current cycle of economic growth is quite long by historical standards, and there is a real threat that it will soon slip into recession. By reducing consumption, a sales tax might produce just enough downward pressure to result in layoffs and mounting unemployment.

Such an outcome would mean that once again the burden of economic adjustment would be placed on those who are the least powerful in the economy— those threatened with unemployment. A new consumption tax, progressive in its effect, and with the desirable intent of raising domestic saving, must await a period of renewed growth when its implementation would not threaten rising unemployment. At the moment, increased foreign indebtedness is preferable to an economic downturn caused by new taxes.

The data suggest that Reagan supply-side economics, while doing nothing for the long-term productivity problem in the United States, produced distinctly perverse results with respect to the country's international indebtedness. The additional income received as a result of the Reagan tax cuts was spent and not saved and the government's loss of revenue increased its need to borrow money. Reagan tax policy, in short, was the principal reason that overseas credit became essential to America's continued economic expansion.

The upshot of this dependency will be, in the future, as it has been in the recent past, twofold. First is an increased loss of income by the people of the United States in the form of interest paid to those abroad from whom we borrow.

The second is a decreased ability to use monetary policy in response to domestic conditions because of our continuing need to attract overseas savings to come to this country. Obviously a tax increase, in one form or another, correcting the damage done by Reaganomics, is needed. However, a reconstruction of the tax structure, gutted by the Reagan Administration, probably should await a future when it would be less likely to create rising unemployment.

In the meantime, problems of productivity and competition persist. These difficulties will not be solved by making more savings available because they are not and never were rooted in an insufficiency of investment. Here, as we have argued, a solution rests on enhancing the population's productive capacity. Rapid growth, improved education and a restructured work environment would go a long way in this regard. These are the foundations of a real supply-side economics, rather than the debt inducing fraud which the Reagan program represented.

NO

Milton Friedman

WHAT IS THE 'RIGHT' AMOUNT OF SAVING?

"The U.S. is saving too little." That has become the battle cry of the doom-and-gloomers of all shades of opinion—left, right, and center. Low saving, we are told, condemns the U.S. to becoming a second-rate nation, or even a banana republic. It threatens our future standard of living, and imposes unjustified burdens on future generations.

How fashions change! By chance, I recently came across notes of a course on business cycles that I taught nearly half a century ago (in 1940). Glancing through the notes, I was struck by how much attention I paid to what was then the favorite battle cry: We're saving too much. Class period after class period was devoted to describing and criticizing the now nearly forgotten under-consumption theories of the business cycle.

Then as now, the concern was with maintaining economic growth. However, the perceived threat was not too little saving to finance investment, but too little consumption to provide an incentive to invest. Unless consumers spent more lavishly, we were doomed—or so we were told—to secular stagnation. The railroad revolution had come and gone, the automobile and electric-power revolutions had come and gone, and no comparable new industries were in sight to absorb the potential savings of a fully employed economy—so spake the prophets, Alvin Hansen and John Maynard Keynes. Only a sharp rise in the propensity to consume or large doses of government deficit spending could fill the gap left by the exhaustion of investment opportunities.

In fact, the alleged "oversaving" of the 1930s did not condemn us to "secular stagnation" and permanent high levels of unemployment. No more will the alleged "undersaving" of the 1980s condemn us to low growth and a declining standard of living. That may be our fate but, if so, for very different reasons.

A "shortage of investment opportunities," if it had existed, would have produced a market reaction in the form of lower interest rates, which would have encouraged investment in lower-yielding projects—including investment abroad—and discouraged savings. Similarly, the currently much deplored reduction in the propensity to save, if it exists, combined with ample investment opportunities, is working its own cure by keeping interest rates high enough to moderate any reduction in saving, to attract capital from abroad, and to discourage investment in low-yielding projects. These and related market reactions are adequate to avoid the dire consequences that are the stock in trade of the doom-and-gloomers who are always in our midst.

AS PRESCRIPTIONS FOR POLICY, BOTH THE earlier and the current battle cries rest on an unstated, and I believe fallacious, assumption: that it is a proper function of government to determine the level of saving. The proponents of this view seldom attempt to justify it except by citing the dire consequences that are alleged to follow from failure to achieve the "right" level of saving. And they never specify what they regard as the "right" level of saving—just calling for less and less, or more and more—nor do they even discuss the criteria that can be used to decide what the "right" level is.

Currently, net saving in the United States is about 1.5 per cent of the national income. This is the excess of private net saving of 3.5 per cent of the national income over government dissaving of about 2 per cent. (These figures are all rough estimates and, in my view, seriously understate the actual value of the addition to the nation's physical wealth

correctly measured, but that is not relevant to my present purpose so I shall here regard these figures as correct.*) If 1.5 per cent is too low, what is the right level? Is it the roughly 15 per cent reported as saved by the Japanese? Or the roughly 10 per cent reported as saved by the West Germans? Or the roughly 4 per cent reported as saved by the British? How are we to judge?

As a classical liberal, my answer is straightforward. The right level—at least to a first approximation—is the level that would emerge if all the separate households were free to divide their income between current and future consumption in accordance with their own values, provided only that the terms on which they could do so were not distorted and did not impose uncompensated costs or benefits on other households—in economic jargon, if there were no external effects.

Suppose, to take an extreme case for the sake of argument, the end result was zero saving: that is, given the rate of return on capital, the members of the community on the average did not regard the reward from saving as sufficient to justify sacrificing current consumption in order that they or their progeny could have still higher consumption in the future. Some households might be spending on consumption more than they were currently earning, for example, those composed of older persons or of young persons with young children;

*The published estimate is the difference between two large, independently estimated aggregates—income and consumption—which explains why it is "rough." The major biases leading to understatement are two: first, the treatment of spending on automobiles and other durable goods as current consumption; second, the exclusion from income and hence from saving of any capital gains, whether nominal or real.

other households might be spending on consumption less than they were currently earning, for example, those composed of persons at their peak earnings with few dependents. But dissaving and saving would just offset one another. Would there be anything wrong with that outcome?

The critics will say, But that would mean no growth. Perhaps so, but what is wrong with that? If the members of the community are satisfied on the average with their present level of living and do not wish to economize in order that they or their progeny can have a still higher level tomorrow, whom are they harming? Not themselves, since any household that disagrees with the consensus is free to save and to provide a higher future level of living for itself or its heirs. But, we shall be told, that means other nations may catch up to our current high level of living and indeed may surpass us. Again, on individualistic grounds, what of it? If keeping up with the Joneses is less than admirable for individuals, why is it different for nations?

A rational answer must call on external effects: unintended results of the separate individual actions. And indeed there are some that may need to be considered. The most obvious is national security. If we fall behind other nations, and those nations are our enemies, we may be unable to finance a large enough defense effort. In principle, this is a valid argument. However, in current circumstances, there are two obvious answers. First, as it happens, our leading competitors—Japan and the Common Market countries—are our allies, not our enemies. If they get richer, that benefits us through the widening range of international trade, and enables us to improve our defenses, while at the same time it enhances the defensive capacities of these allies as well. Second, we now spend only about 6 per cent of our income on defense. Surely, if necessary, we could increase that substantially out of our current level of income.

Other effects of this kind are vaguer, and I find myself hard put to identify any for which I can readily make a persuasive case. For what other purpose are some of us justified in forcing others of us to save?

And that is especially true if we shift from the extreme case that I posed to the real world. In that world, households are not free to choose between current and future consumption on terms that are technically possible. The terms are distorted, and distorted in such a way as to discourage savings. Out of every dollar of income earned in the United States, a substantial fraction goes to finance government spending. The households that have earned the income cannot use that fraction for either current or future consumption. Further, the taxes imposed are not neutral but tend to be biased against saving. Nonetheless, net saving in the United States has been consistently positive for the past two centuries, except only during deep depressions, and is positive today, though lower than it has generally been in the past. That is a remarkable phenomenon, attributable, I believe, to the high rate of return on capital that a free private-market economy—even one hobbled as ours has been by unwise government spending and intervention—can generate.

The policy implications of the classical liberal viewpoint are clear. We jointly decide to transfer part of our income to government to spend on our behalf. Whether that decision be made wisely or not, it is desirable that government finance its spending in such a way as to minimize the distortion in the incentive for us to save the rest of our income or spend it on consumption. It is not easy to specify precisely the method of taxation that would have that effect, but the objective is clear: to avoid interfering with our freedom to choose how much we want to save out of the income that is left to us after financing government spending so long as we do not interfere with the ability of our fellows to do likewise.

The government has no business meddling in our family planning: whether about how many heirs we have or how much wealth we choose to leave them.

POSTSCRIPT

Should the Government Take Action to Increase the Savings Rate?

Economists Ferleger and Mandle state that there are two arguments for increasing the savings rate. The first argument is that a low savings rate means low investment, which lowers the growth rate of productivity. They find no evidence to support the last part of this argument; the slowdown in productivity growth is not associated with lower rates of investment. The second argument is that the shortfall in domestic saving requires the monetary authority to keep interest rates high in order to attract funds from abroad, and this reduces economic growth. They find evidence to support this argument and conclude that something must be done to increase the savings rate.

Economist Friedman begins by stating that concern over the savings rate is not new. What is new is the nature of the concern: Fifty years ago economists were concerned that the rate was too high, while today the concern is that the rate is too low. Friedman believes that both the old and the new concerns rest on a "fallacious assumption: that it is the proper function of government to determine the level of savings." He believes that the market automatically worked to correct any imbalances that existed fifty years ago and will work to correct any imbalances that exist today. He then addresses the question of what is the right amount of saving. He offers the classical liberal answer: "the level that would emerge if all the separate households were free to divide their income between current and future consumption in accordance with their own values, provided the terms on which they could do so were not distorted and did not impose uncompensated costs or benefits on other households."

Conservative and liberal commentary on the arguments presented by Friedman is provided by Herbert Stein, Robert M. Solow, Evan G. Galbraith, Peter G. Peterson, Antonio Martino, Benjamin M. Friedman, and James M. Buchanan in the *National Review* (June 16, 1989). Additional readings on this issue include "What's Wrong with a Declining National Saving Rate?" by William D. Nordhaus, *Challenge* (July-August 1989); "There's No Simple Explanation for the Collapse in Saving," by Barry P. Bosworth, *Challenge* (July-August 1989); "U.S. Net Foreign Saving Has also Plunged," by Peter Hooper, *Challenge* (July-August 1989); "The Saving Shortfall Reconsidered," by Robert Guttmann, *Challenge* (September-October 1989); and *Tax Policy and National Savings in the United States*, by A. Lans Boneberg (International Monetary Fund, 1988). For a set of readings regarding the consumption tax, see *The Consumption Tax*, edited by Charles E. Walker and Mark A. Bloomfield (Ballinger Publishing Company, 1987).

ISSUE 12

Should the Capital Gains Tax Be Lowered?

YES: Robert W. Kasten, Jr., from "Lower Capital Gains Rate Will Gain Revenue," *Congressional Record-Senate* (February 7, 1989)

NO: John Miller, from "Helping the Rich Help Themselves," *Dollars and Sense* (June 1989)

ISSUE SUMMARY

YES: Senator Kasten wants to reduce the tax rate on capital gains because such a reduction will increase government revenues, stimulate the economy and the job market, and bring the U.S. economy more in line with "our European and Asian competitors."

NO: Professor of economics John Miller is against a cut in the tax rate on capital gains because he believes that the benefits will primarily go to the rich and that it will not stimulate investment. Instead, he proposes an increase in the tax rate on short-term capital gains.

To finance any of its activities, the federal government has to raise revenue, and one method at its disposal is taxation. But controversy over taxes is ceaseless, for a variety of reasons. There are disagreements over the reasons why government needs revenue and disagreements over the types of taxes that are used to raise revenue. And there are disagreements over the effects of taxes on the allocation of resources and the distribution of income and what constitutes a "good" tax as opposed to a "bad" tax. What one perceives as a good tax, another may view as confiscation. So every year it seems that some part of the tax code is the target of reformers who argue that change is necessary in order to make taxes fairer, to make taxes simpler, to raise more revenue, to stimulate investment, to stimulate savings, or to make the economy more competitive internationally. A look at the changes to the federal tax code during the 1980s provides an appropriate illustration of how the controversy over taxes has been played out most recently.

In 1981 Congress passed and President Reagan signed into law the Economy Recovery Tax Act. This was a major revision to the federal tax code, which substantially reduced personal tax rates. Every year after this legislation was passed, there were additional changes, and 1986 saw a major overhaul in the federal tax code with the passage and signing of the Tax Reform Act of 1986. Designed to make the tax system fairer and simpler, this legislation brought about another substantial reduction in tax rates. One additional feature of the 1986 Tax Reform Act was that it treated capital gains, long-term as well as short-term, as ordinary income. Given the history of tax controversy, it should not be surprising that various interest groups began seeking modification of the 1986 tax law almost immediately. The debate in this issue addresses one of the newer proposals for modifying the 1986 tax law—the proposal to again give special tax treatment to long-term capital gains.

To understand capital gains taxation it is necessary to understand capital gains. Capital gains can be simply defined as the profit earned when a person sells an asset at a price higher than the price at which it was purchased. Until 1986, tax laws usually distinguished between long-term and short-term capital gains. Short-term capital gains were profits realized within one year; that is, less than one year had elapsed between the purchase of an asset and its sale. Long-term capital gains were profits realized over a year or more. Short-term capital gains were taxed as ordinary income while long-term capital gains were taxed at a lower rate. Why this differential treatment in capital gains tax rates? The logic was that short-term capital gains were the result of speculative activity while long-term capital gains were good for the economy—something to be encouraged by preferential tax treatment.

This distinction ended with the Tax Reform Act of 1986. Almost immediately arguments were raised to reinstitute the preferential treatment of long-term capital gains. During 1989 several different proposals for lowering the tax rate on long-term capital gains were introduced in Congress. President Bush offered his own proposal for a capital gains tax cut. As of this writing (January 1990), the debate over a reduction in the tax rate on long-term capital gains continues.

Should the tax rate on long-term capital gains be reduced? Senator Kasten of Wisconsin supports such a change and introduced legislation to this end. He believes the reduction in this tax rate would benefit the economy. Economist Miller strongly disagrees; in fact, not only does he oppose a reduction in the tax on long-term capital gains, he proposes an increase in the tax rate on short-term capital gains.

YES

Robert W. Kasten, Jr.

LOWER CAPITAL GAINS RATE WILL GAIN REVENUE

President Bush's proposal to reduce the capital gains tax will—once again—spark the debate over capital gains and tax revenues. This debate is becoming as predictable as the annual return of the seasons. We have been through the same debate year in, year out—and some people continue to refuse to learn from American economic history. One year ago, 2 years ago, and even as far back as 1978, we have heard the very same argument against reducing the capital gains tax: That it would somehow lose precious tax revenues for the Federal Government.

Skeptics said about the 1978 capital gains tax cut that it would do little for investment and do much to erode tax revenues. I remember then-Treasury Secretary Michael Blumenthal asserting that the proposed capital gains rate reduction from 50 to 28 percent would cost the Treasury over $2 billion in revenue. He said, "The measure would do little for capital formation and would waste revenues."

Secretary Blumenthal objected. But in Congress, cooler economic heads prevailed—and the House and Senate agreed with my distinguished Wisconsin colleague, the late Congressman Bill Steiger, that it was time to cut the capital gains tax.

That was a cut in the tax on capital gains. Well, what happened? Did revenues go down? We've been through this time, and time, and time again—and you can go through the facts on this until everyone is blue in the face, but people just don't listen.

The fact is, taxes paid on capital gains increased from $9.1 billion in 1978 to $11.7 billion in 1979, and to $12.5 billion in 1980. In 1981, we cut the top rate on

From Robert W. Kasten, Jr., "Lower Capital Gains Rate Will Gain Revenue," *Congressional Record*, vol. 135, no. 12 (February 1989).

capital gains even further to 20 percent, and capital gains tax revenues rose to $12.7 billion in 1981, $12.9 billion in 1982, $18.5 billion in 1983, $21.5 billion in 1984 and $24.5 billion in 1985. Tax revenues to the Treasury were 184 percent higher in 1985 than in 1978.

These are all IRS figures. Nobody denies them. But a lot of people insist on ignoring them—and persist in making statements about revenues that are contrary to facts.

[A]llow me to quote from last week's Washington Post editorial on capital gains: " . . . revenues would certainly drop. Taken all together, over a period of several years, the effect on revenues would be zero at best and possibly a substantial loss." Does this sound familiar? It should—it's the same old discredited nonsense we've been hearing year in, year out since 1978.

[T]his blithe disregard for the facts—a disregard which is no doubt ideologically motivated—does nothing to expand public understanding of this issue. I would like to take this opportunity to explain to my colleagues once again why lower capital gains rates lead to higher tax revenues.

I

This revenue windfall will come from three sources. First, because the tax cost of selling equities will be cut in half, lower capital gains rates will lead to greater realizations by stockholders. These greater realizations will lead to permanently higher receipts from the capital gains tax.

As the historical record shows, capital gains taxes paid continued to climb several years after the tax rate cuts of 1978 and 1981. Many econometric studies of capital gains rates and revenues have quantified this potential realization effect. Harvard Prof. Lawrence Lindsey estimates that a flat 15-percent capital gains rate would increase capital gains taxes paid by $31 billion over 3 years.

II

Second, a lower capital gains tax rate increases the value of stocks. Taxing capital gains at a high rate reduces the potential return on investment—and this future return translates into a lower price for the stock today. Conversely, a lower capital gains rate will increase stock prices, giving the Government more gains to tax.

III

Third, and most important, a lower capital gains rate will raise GNP. Even the Congressional Budget Office admits that "lower rates on gains could increase savings and capital formation and channel more resources into venture capital." What CBO failed to recognize, however, is that this increased capital formations means that the entire tax base will grow even faster—resulting in an even greater increase in overall revenues to the Federal Government.

Most studies and available statistics on the revenue impact of the 1978 and 1981 tax cuts have focused solely on the realization effect and the subsequent increase in capital gains taxes paid. In doing so, they have neglected other important sources of revenue growth—and have, therefore, underestimated the potential revenue gains.

This week, President Bush will propose a cut in the capital gains tax as part of this fiscal 1990 budget plan. The administration will estimate that this proposal will have no revenue effect, or would raise revenue. The opponents of the proposal will once again charge that the tax rate cut will lose billions in tax revenue over the long run.

I am today calling upon the administration to clear the air—to tell the truth, the whole truth on this issue. The President's budget message must make it clear that revenues will rise as a result of this proposal. These revenues will result from increased realizations, and also from the increase in the value of current assets, and the increase in the rate of GNP growth. If Treasury cannot provide a complete, dynamic estimate now, they should promise that one will be furnished in the near future. More than anything else, the resolution of the revenue question will provide a major spark to the capital gains reform movement.

I believe that we can achieve a bipartisan consensus on capital gains this year—just as we did in 1978 and in 1981. Last week, I introduced a capital gains reform bill, S. 171, which would provide a capital gains tax cut for the sale of corporate stock. My bill would also partially index all capital assets for inflation.

In my discussions with administration officials, I have found all concerned to be receptive to my new approach on capital gains. In the 7th year of our recovery, when the odds of continued growth appear to be against us, it is more essential than ever that we do what we can to promote continued economic expansion.

That means we have to come up with a bipartisan, progrowth, projobs, capital gains reform bill. My bill is an olive branch to all sides of this debate—and a call to unity on the goals of American jobs, competitiveness and productivity.

[N]ow more than ever, we must focus on these economic goals. Because of the high capital gains rate, individuals have no incentive to assume the extra risk associated with investment in growth stocks.

As a result, entrepreneurs are finding it more difficult to secure investment funds from private sources. This shortage of startup capital today threatens to rob our economy of innovations, productivity gains, and job opportunities in the future.

Without start-up capital, many of today's dynamic, young companies—such as Apple Computers, Federal Express, and Cray Research, which is an important employer in my State of Wisconsin—never would have made it from the blackboard to the marketplace.

Other countries recognize the benefits of encouraging long-term investment—in fact, many do not tax capital gains at all. Their commitment to long-term investment has created new technologies and new innovations—and better products. We buy their products. They take our money. And U.S. jobs move overseas.

I ask unanimous consent that a table comparing the taxation of capital gains in the United States with our European and Asian competitors be printed in the RECORD.

There being no objection, the material was ordered to be printed in the RECORD, as follows: *(Please turn to tables on next page)*

Table 1

**Capital Gains Rates and The
Associated Revenue**
(In billions of dollars)

Year	Revenue	Tax rate (percent)
1968	$ 5.9	26.9
1969	5.3	27.5
1970	3.2	32.2
1971	4.4	34.4
1972	5.7	45.5
1973	5.4	45.5
1974	4.3	45.5
1975	4.5	45.5
1976	6.6	49.125
1977	8.1	49.125
1978	9.1	49.125
1979	11.7	28
1980	12.5	28
1981	12.7	28
1982	12.9	20
1983	18.5	20
1984	21.5	20
1985	24.5	20
1986	46.4	20

Source: Research Paper No. 8801, U.S. Treasury
Department.

Table 2

**Comparison of U.S. Taxation of
Capital Gains with Some of Our
European and Asian Competitors**

Country	Percent[2]
United Kingdom	40
United States	33
Sweden	18
Canada	17.51
France	16
West Germany	0
Belgium	0
Italy	0
Netherlands	0
Hong Kong	0
Singapore	0
South Korea	0
Taiwan	0
Malaysia	0
Japan	([1])

[1]No capital gains tax until Mar. 3, 1989 (except
for substantial trading or substantial shareholders). After Mar. 3, 1989 shareholder has a
choice of a 20 percent national and a 6 percent
local tax on net gain at the time of filing, or 1
percent of sales proceeds withheld at source (this
option is available only on shares listed for at least
1 year).

[2]Maximum long-term capital gains tax rates.
Source: Arthur Anderson and Co., April 1987.

NO

John Miller

HELPING THE RICH HELP THEMSELVES

Only in a supply-side world would a President propose a tax cut in order to increase government revenues. And only in trickle-down America would this President herald the cut as "tax reform" when 64% of the benefits are targeted to the richest 0.7% of taxpayers, while the bottom 60% of taxpayers would receive less than 3% of the largess. Yet this is precisely what George Bush is proposing with his capital-gains tax cut plan.

A capital gain is income from the sale of a personally owned asset—be it stocks, bonds, real estate, gold, or old paintings—that has gone up in value. Under current laws, effective since the Tax Reform Act of 1986, capital gains are taxed at the same rate as other income. But the Bush administration wants to exempt almost half of some categories of capital gains from taxation, claiming this will spur trading in financial assets, which in turn will lead to growth in tax revenues. Not only that, the Bush team argues that the tax break will trigger more long-term investment, helping to revitalize the economy.

There are a few things wrong here. Most evidence indicates that reducing taxes on capital gains will decrease tax receipts, not boost them. In addition, the tax cut is unlikely to have much effect on long-term investment—and particularly on the productive investments needed to rebuild the U.S. economy. That leaves one reason for the tax cut: to give the rich a bonus. A capital-gains tax break would so overwhelmingly benefit the wealthy that it would make the Reagan tax cuts of the early 1980s seem progressive by comparison.

The Bush administration is right that the capital-gains tax needs reform. But true reform would go in the opposite direction—closing old loopholes, not opening new ones.

THE UNKINDEST CUT OF ALL

Here's how the Bush proposal works. The proposal effectively cuts the capital-gains tax rate from 28% to 15%. Forty-five percent of profits from the sale of most assets held for three years or longer would be excluded from taxation. This means that a wealthy tax-payer with capital gains would pay a 28% tax on only the remaining 55% of the income from their long-term capital gains, or the equivalent of a 15.4% tax rate. Actually, the rate would be "capped" at 15%—the same rate currently charged on the taxable income of the poorest families. In a feeble gesture toward curbing speculation, the tax break would not exempt capital gains on real estate and art objects, nor gains on assets held for less than three years.

Setting a lower effective tax rate for capital gains than for other income is not a new idea: capital gains were taxed at bargain rates continuously from 1921 to 1986. But the 1986 Tax Reform Act marked a significant departure. In return for dramatically lower personal income tax rates, the Reagan administration agreed to tax capital gains as ordinary income. As Vice President, Bush promised Congress that broadening the tax base to include all capital-gains income would provide the necessary revenues to offset the revenues lost from lowering tax rates on the wealthy.

Now, as President, Bush wants to keep the new lower personal income taxes for the rich and to reinstitute the preferential treatment of capital gains. The combination of the two would leave the tax on capital gains at its lowest level since 1942. At the same time, Bush asks us to believe that he can now increase revenues by reversing the very measures he argued earlier were necessary to maintain tax revenues.

SUPPLY-SIDE MAGIC

The supply-side rationale behind Bush's revenue claim is simple, if fanciful. The supply-siders claim that if capital-gains taxes are cut, property-owners will suddenly begin to sell previously hoarded assets. The point out that, currently, there is only one way to beat the capital-gains tax: hold onto your assets until you die. When inheritors sell the property, they only pay taxes on capital gains that accrue after the date of inheritance. So, the argument goes, with gains taxes so high, substantial numbers of wealthy individuals have decided to hold onto their property for life—or at least until the tax rate drops. If the capital-gains tax was lowered, many of them would sell the property to realize the capital gains.

In theory, property owners' increased willingness to cash in on capital gains could boost the total amount of taxable capital gains enough to offset the decreased tax rate. Bush administration projections hold that Treasury revenues would rise by nearly $5 billion in the next year (as capital gains increase 120%) and continue to grow for the following two fiscal years.

But in 1980, when presidential candidate Ronald Reagan made similar claims about the effects of cutting income taxes, George Bush denounced them as "voo-doo economics." And today, almost no one outside the Oval Office agrees with the Bush administration's projections. If asset owners don't sell more, the annual loss to the Treasury from the tax cut would be $17 billion—increasing the projected deficit by almost one-fifth—and few tax experts believe that they'll sell enough to wipe out this loss.

For instance, two major non-partisan institutions of Congress examined the effects of the proposed changes in the capital-gains tax. The Congressional Budget Office estimated that the Bush scheme could lose from $4 billion to $8 billion a year. The Joint Congressional Committee on Taxation projected that while the proposal would raise revenues the first year, it would lose $13.3 billion over the next five years.

The history of capital-gains taxation offers confirmation that asset-owners' responsiveness to tax changes is not strong enough to justify Bush's optimistic revenue claims. After Jimmy Carter and a Democratic Congress lowered capital-gains taxes in 1978, stock sales rose in 1979, only to decline in 1980. And since 1986, when capital-gains taxes rose from 20% to 28%, capital gains have not decreased, but rather increased by more than 15% in nominal terms.

REVIVING INVESTMENT?

The Bush administration asserts that in addition to enhancing government revenues, a tax break on capital gains would revive long-term investment in the 1990s—this time by affecting how the wealthy act as buyers. Lower taxes on capital gains would increase investors' rate of return, encouraging more investment and contributing to higher growth rates in the decade ahead. Because the tax cut applies only to gains on property held for three years or more, it allegedly would lengthen the planning horizon of investors. And with lower capital-gains taxes, owners of stocks supposedly would become more active traders, supplying capital to new, more productive uses.

But many in the business world find these arguments almost as far-fetched as the supply-side revenue claim—and progressives have even less reason to accept them. Business Week editorialized, "The issue is how to guide [the money of large institutional investors] into long-term investment. . . . It won't be easy, but tinkering with the capital-gains rate is like pouring buckets of water on a burning house." Other business interests have expressed alarm that cutting the capital-gains tax rate would lead to investment guided by tax avoidance, rather than by market conditions.

Instead of taxing capital gains at a lower rate than ordinary income, Business Week, the Los Angeles Times, and others have argued that investment can better be stimulated by adjusting capital gains for inflation before taxing them. They contend that inflation has discouraged long-term investment by forcing investors to pay taxes not only on profits but also on capital gains generated by inflation. With inflation indexing, investors could pay taxes only on their "real" capital gains, not on inflation.

From a progressive viewpoint, both the Bush plan and the inflation-indexing alternative fall short as ways of encouraging productive investment. For one thing, both proposals overstate the influence of capital-gains taxation on new investment. These tax-cutting proposals seek to spark new investment by making new stock issues more attractive to investors. But the vast majority of stock sales affected by capital-gains taxes are not new issues but resales of existing stock, which generate no new investment. Furthermore, stock issues finance only a small fraction of new investment. In the 1970s and 1980s less than 10% of the money corporations raised from outside sources has come from selling stock (see "Beyond the Boom," D&S, June 1986). Even Business Week concludes that "the real problem in venture capital" is not that potential investors are deterred by the high tax rate on gains, but rather that there is "too much money chasing too few opportunities."

Since tax changes have limited effects on the volume of investment, the important question is whether they help to redirect the investment. Cutting capital-gains taxes across the board does nothing to direct capital to productive uses—such as plant, equipment, infrastructure, or education. But cutting capital-gains taxes selectively could affect the character of investment. By denying the capital-gains exemption to income from the sale of non-productive property, the capital-gains tax could discourage financial speculation and direct investment toward more productive uses.

BONANZA FOR THE WEALTHY

While cutting capital-gains taxes is unlikely to increase government revenues or do much for investment, it will certainly succeed in redistributing income—to the rich. Capital gains go almost entirely to the wealthy. The wealthiest 5% of all taxpayers receive 85% of capital gains; the richest .7% of taxpayers receive 70% of capital gains. Five of every six taxpayers with incomes of more than $1 million a year have capital-gains income, but fewer than one in every 20 taxpayers earning $10,000 or less have it.

Thus, cutting capital gain taxes amounts to what Robert McIntyre, Director of Citizens for Tax Justice (CTJ), calls a "bonanza for the wealthy." CTJ estimates that about two-thirds of the benefits of the Bush cut would go to the richest 685,000 people in the nation, or less than 1% of taxpayers. These taxpayers, all with incomes over $200,000, would receive an average tax cut of about $25,000. For the 80% of families earning less than $60,000 a year the average tax savings from the Bush plan would be only $20.

The one-sided distributional effect of cutting capital-gains tax is reinforced in the Bush proposal by the fact it does not apply to the sale of homes, which qualified for the capital-gains exemption prior to 1986. As a sop for the less fortunate, the Bush proposal would allow families with taxable income of less than $20,000 to sell their homes tax free.

FAIR TAXES INSTEAD

A more progressive tax policy would stiffen taxes on capital gains, not cut them. On the national level, Jesse Jackson's "Budget Plan for Jobs, Peace, and Justice" included measures along these lines. Besides proposing to restore personal income taxes on the wealthy to their pre-1986 levels, the Jackson budget favored closing the loophole that allows the rich to avoid capital-gains taxation at death. This makes a lot more sense—and is far more likely to raise revenue—than countering the loophole by lowering gains taxes on the rich as Bush proposes. The Jackson plan also would have imposed a "securities-transfer excise tax" of 0.5% on the sale of certain kinds of financial assets, a tax that would reduce short-term speculative merger and acquisition activity.

Even some investors and economic theorists support such policies. Fifty years ago, John Maynard Keynes, the economist whose theories underpin much of modern economic policy, favored "a substantial securities transfer tax" to mitigate "the predominance of speculation over enterprise in the United States." On Wall Street today, Warren Buffet, the head of Berkshire Hathaway and arguably the most successful securities investor in America, favors "a confiscatory

100% tax on short-term capital gains"—taxing away all short-term gains to remove the incentive for speculation.

Increasing short-term capital-gains taxes has also found support in state and local governments. Since 1973, Vermont has imposed a short-term capital-gains tax on land sales in an attempt to slow the pace of development. Rhode Island also recently considered taxing short-term capital gains on real estate in order to curb housing speculation.

Both the Rhode Island bill, defeated by fierce opposition from the real-estate lobby, and the Vermont law contain several features that could be adopted in a progressive national capital-gains tax:

• To favor long-term investment, impose higher taxes on short-term capital gains, not lower taxes on long-term gains as Bush proposes.

• Define the short term in several different gradations subject to different tax rates, including near-confiscatory rates for the shortest term and most likely speculative investment. The Rhode Island tax proposal defined the short term to be 5 years and imposed tax rates ranging from 80% for six-month investments to 15% for investments held the full five years. The Vermont law has a similar feature and also mandates a tax rate that increases with the amount of profit, similar to the income tax.

• Specify the type of investment subject to the short-term capital-gains tax, directing the flow of investment away from speculative activity. The Rhode Island bill applied only to non-owner-occupied housing, exempting owner-occupied residences from the short-term gains tax.

• Use the revenues from the short-term capital-gains tax to fund domestic spending or non-speculative public investment. In the Rhode Island bill, tax revenues were to go to a neighborhood preservation fund.

Unlike the Bush proposal, these progressive alternatives would promote equality, raise revenues, and strengthen the economy. The burden of a beefed-up capital-gains tax would fall chiefly on those with incomes above $200,000, the same people who benefited most from the Reagan tax cuts. Furthermore, such a tax could be the first step toward a more explicit and progressive industrial policy, cooling speculation and directing investment into needed areas. Selective tax rates could guide resources into more socially worthwhile investments, such as education. Finally, the revenues raised from the capital-gains tax would provide funds to restore the cuts in domestic spending, or to reduce the budget deficit, or even to fund investment in publicly-owned industry. Instead of Bush's thinly disguised giveaway to the wealthy, we could have a capital-gains tax policy that would actually do us all some good.

NOTES

SOURCES: Robert McIntyre, "Tax Americana," *The New Republic*, March 27, 1989; Congressional Budget Office, "How Capital Gains Tax Rates Affect Revenues," 1989; Jesse Jackson, "Paying for Our Dreams: A Budget Plan for Jobs, Peace, and Justice," 1988; and various materials from Citizens for Tax Justice, 1311 L St. NW, Washington, DC 20005.

POSTSCRIPT

Should the Capital Gains Tax Be Lowered?

Senator Kasten begins his case for a reduction in the tax rate on capital gains by arguing that a rate reduction will not reduce tax revenues of the federal government. To support his argument, he reviews what happened when the capital gains tax rate was cut in 1978 and in 1981: In spite of these cuts, "tax revenues to the Treasury were 184 percent higher in 1985 than in 1978." He offers three reasons why a cut in the tax rate can be expected to increase governmental revenues: (1) a lower rate will stimulate the sale of assets whose price has increased; (2) a lower rate will increase the value or price at which stocks can be sold; and (3) a lower rate will stimulate the economy and thus increase revenues from other tax sources. Kasten also supports a reduction in the tax rate on capital gains because it is "pro-growth and pro-jobs." The final reason why Kasten supports a reduction in the capital gains tax rate involves international considerations. He compares the rate of capital gains taxation in the United States with those imposed by European and Asian competitors. In this comparison only one country, the United Kingdom, has a higher rate, and many countries do not tax capital gains at all. The implication is that if the United States is to remain competitive internationally, it must reduce the tax rate on capital gains.

Economist Miller believes that the tax rate on long-term capital gains should not be reduced. Such a reduction, at least in the form proposed by President Bush, would benefit mainly the rich: "65% of the benefits are targeted to the richest 0.7% of taxpayers." In addition, Miller believes that a cut in the capital gains tax rate will reduce governmental revenues. Here he uses estimates provided by the Congressional Budget Office and the Joint Congressional Committee on Taxation, as well as what happened after 1986 when the tax was raised. Miller also denies that the tax cut would stimulate productive investment. Here he asserts that capital gains taxation has little effect on productive investment.

Senator Kasten has written several articles that further develop his views: "Capital Gains: The Right Cuts," *Washington Post* (February 7, 1989) and "The Kindest Cut of All—Reducing Capital Gains Tax," *Chicago Tribune* (February 22, 1989). For another strong endorsement of a cut in the capital gains tax, see the testimony before the Senate Finance Committee on Capital Gains Taxation by Paul Craig Roberts (March 14, 1989). For a more balanced perspective, see "Tax Options for 1989: Revising Capital Gains Rates," by Elizabeth Wehr, *Congressional Quarterly* (December 10, 1989). For arguments against a reduction in the capital gains tax, see "Capital Pains," by Laura Sanders *Forbes* (July 19, 1989); "Tax Deform," by Robert S. McIntyre, *The New Republic* (August 21, 1989).

ISSUE 13

Is Workfare a Good Substitute for Welfare?

YES: Lawrence M. Mead, from "Prepared Statement of Lawrence M. Mead, 'Workfare versus Welfare,' " *Hearings Before the Subcommittee on Trade, Productivity, and Economic Growth of the Joint Economic Committee, U.S. Congress* (April 23, 1986)

NO: Morton H. Sklar, from "Prepared Statement of Morton H. Sklar, 'Workfare versus Welfare,' " *Hearings Before the Subcommittee on Trade, Productivity, and Economic Growth of the Joint Economic Committee, U.S. Congress* (April 23, 1986)

ISSUE SUMMARY

YES: Political scientist Mead is an advocate of the work ethic. He urges Congress to make work a fundamental condition of receiving welfare assistance.

NO: Attorney Sklar rejects Mead's contention that work must be a key ingredient in any welfare system. His experience suggests that a work requirement is inappropriate for many welfare recipients and not cost-effective for those who would be asked to work.

Given American society's traditional commitment to a market system and its fundamental belief in self-determination, Americans are not much at ease in enacting social welfare legislation that appears to give someone "something for nothing," even if that individual is clearly in need. Thus, when we trace the roots of the existing U.S. social welfare system back to its origins in the New Deal legislation of President Roosevelt, created during the Great Depression of the 1930s, we see that many of the earliest programs linked jobs to public assistance. One exception to these early programs was Aid to Families with Dependent Children (AFDC), which is one of the oldest public assistance programs and was established as part of the 1935 Social Security Act. This program provides money to families in which there are children but no breadwinner. In 1935, and for many years thereafter, this program was not particularly controversial because the number of beneficiaries was relatively small and the popular image of an AFDC family was that of a white woman with several young children who had lost her husband as a result of a mining accident, an industrial mishap, or perhaps World War I.

In the early 1960s, as the U.S. economy prospered, poverty and what to do about it captured the attention of the nation. The Kennedy and Johnson administrations focused their social welfare programs on poor individuals—a minority of the population, especially, but not exclusively, a black minority, left behind as the general economy grew and set new record highs. Their policies were designed to address the needs of those who were trapped in "pockets of poverty," a description popularized in the early 1960s in the writings of Michael Harrington (1929–1989), a political theorist and prominent socialist. Between 1964 and 1969 the number of AFDC recipients increased by more than sixty percent and the costs of the program more than doubled. The number of AFDC families continued to grow throughout the 1970s, and the program became increasingly controversial.

In part, the controversy grew because of the increase in recipients and the increase in costs and in part because the program became increasingly identified in the public mind as a black or ethnic minority program. A welfare mother was now perceived as a woman in a big-city public housing project whose children had been deserted by their father. This change in perceptions, which corresponded only partially with changes in reality, made "welfare" a controversial issue. It has now become, perhaps, the most controversial of all the many government programs that provide public assistance.

In the 1980s, direct attacks began to be made on AFDC by social critics such as Charles Murray. Murray charged AFDC with encouraging welfare dependency, teenage pregnancies, the dissolution of the traditional family, and, of course, an erosion of the basic American work ethic. These criticisms set the stage for the first major reforms in AFDC in twenty-five years. The 1987 legislation proposed in Congress required absent parents to make child-support payments, mandated many recipients to accept jobs, and insisted that those who lacked a high school education complete their education. The 1987 legislation laid the foundation for the debate that we will join in the following readings. What conditions should be imposed upon those who receive welfare checks? Should recipients be asked to work? Is this the most cost-effective means of eliminating poverty? These and other questions are addressed in the readings that follow.

YES

Lawrence M. Mead

PREPARED STATEMENT OF LAWRENCE M. MEAD

My name is Lawrence M. Mead. I am an Associate Professor of Politics at New York University. I have been researching federal welfare and employment programs for about ten years. Much of what I will say is drawn from my recent book, *Beyond Entitlement*[1]

I. THE WORK PROBLEM

While most people who rely on Aid to Families with Dependent Children (AFDC) leave the rolls in under two years, 38% remain on for five years or more.[2] Nonwork is a serious problem on AFDC. Only 15% of welfare mothers work at a given time, according to government surveys, and the rate is still lower among the long-term cases.[3] Nonwork is one of the keys to solving poverty and dependency in the United States. If more of the poor worked, many fewer would need support. There would be more political support for a generous antipoverty policy. Most important, chances for integration would improve.

The traditional explanations for nonwork are no longer persuasive. Most of the long-term poor and dependent are nonwhite,[4] and it could claimed until recently that they were simply kept out of the job market by discrimination. But in recent decades, a black middle class has appeared, and a number of nonwhite groups—West Indians, Asians—have done conspicuously well economically. Nor can the dysfunctions of today's underclass—crime and illegitimacy as well as nonwork—be seen as "rational" responses to discrimination, since the poor themselves are the main victims.

Some cite other social barriers. Allegedly, the economy does not provide enough employment for the poor. Particularly, the decline of manufacturing has reduced the number of jobs available to the uneducated. Or the poor are kept from working by child care responsibilities or lack of skills. Thus, to raise welfare work levels would take massive new government programs to provide jobs, child care, and training.[5]

From U.S. Congress. Subcommittee on Trade, Productivity, and Economic Growth of the Joint Economic Committee. *Workfare Versus Welfare*. 99th Cong., 2d sess., 23 April 1986. 40-49.

However, job creation in the service sector has been prodigious in recent decades. The "high tech" economy seems to create nearly as many low- as high-skilled jobs. Many of these positions require little more initially than an ability to read, get to work on time, and take orders. The presence of 5 to 10 million illegal aliens in the country certifies that at least low-skilled work is widely available. There is little evidence that relatively low-placed groups such as blacks, teenagers, and women are confined in unattractive jobs for reasons beyond low skills. Most of their unemployment is due to turnover in jobs rather than lack of jobs. The main reason the long-term poor do not work steadily today is problems of work discipline peculiar to them, not the limitations of the labor market.[6]

Government services are much less critical to work than is often claimed. Training programs have little impact on skills, but in any event mothers with low skills seem to escape welfare through work as often as the better-prepared. And while many working mothers could use child care programs, most arrange, and prefer, informal care through friends and relatives. Mothers with children under 6 are just as likely to work their way off welfare as those with children in school.[7]

Another approach says that nonwork results from the disincentives in welfare. Allegedly, AFDC breaks up families because eligibility is usually limited to single parents with children, and it discourages work because most of what recipients earn is deducted from their welfare grants. Using this reasoning, conservatives demand cuts in welfare for the employable while liberals recommend stronger work incentives—i.e., allowing recipients to keep more of their wages as an inducement to work. More broadly, conservatives blame the generous social programming of the 1960s and 1970s for the increasing behavioral problems among the underclass.[8]

Experience has shown that these proposals are impolitic. The Reagan Administration has achieved only marginal cuts 8 in welfare benefits, while proposals by Presidents Nixon and Carter to reform welfare on work incentive lines were rejected by Congress. More significant, research and experience have not shown that welfare incentives have much affect on work effort either way. Stronger work incentives were added to AFDC in 1967, then largely withdrawn in 1981, without affecting work levels palpably. And if dysfunction among the poor rose when social spending boomed, it has not yet declined even though welfare benefits have fallen by a third, allowing for inflation, in the last 15 years.[9]

A better explanation for nonwork is simply that the dependent poor have seldom been expected to work. Welfare and the other programs that give them income and services have been permissive. They have seldom required their clients to work or otherwise function in return for support. This reflects the liberal social analysis of the Great Society period, which attributed all problems of the poor to social forces and refused to hold them accountable even for personal conduct. The onus lay entirely on government to make work happen by providing new benefits to the poor, including cash, education, training, and child support.

Unfortunately, the poor are irresolute about achieving work, and a permissive policy cannot change this. Studies show that they accept mainstream values such as employment, contribution to families, and obedience to the law, but that they less often observe them than the better-off. They feel that difficult circumstances prevent them living by norms that, in principle, they accept. Without setting standards, federal programs could not close this gap between intention and behavior. Instead, they strengthened the "welfare mentality" of the poor—their tendency to see all solutions, like all problems, coming from outside themselves.[10]

II. THE NEED FOR OBLIGATION

The evidence is that work requirements might raise work levels on welfare significantly, though they have not done so yet. The work tests first added to AFDC in 1967 were ineffective mainly because they lacked sufficient authority. In practice, too few of the employable recipients were subject to the Work Incentive (WIN) program, the first work program in AFDC. In 1971, Congress mandated that all employable recipients to WIN, and job entries jumped sharply.[11]

But WIN required at most that employable recipients look for work, on pain of reductions in their welfare grants. In 1981, Congress allowed states to toughen the requirements further. They might now for the first time institute workfare, that is require clients actually to work in return for benefits. About half the states have since instituted more demanding AFDC work programs of some kind. Typically, they mandate that employable recipients, or at least new applicants for AFDC, participate in varying combinations of job search, training, and work in government agencies. According to studies by the Manpower Demonstration Research Corporation (MDRC), programs in San Diego and West Virginia have raised the share of the employable engaged in these activities to over 60%.[12]

According to my own studies of WIN, the participation rate is the key to welfare work, and participation hinges on obligation. To raise participation, an office must provide clients with necessary services (especially child care) and then require them to join in job search or some kind of training or subsidized job program. The higher the proportion of clients so obligated, the higher the proportion that goes to work. Economic factors—the availability of jobs, the employability of clients, the number of staff available to serve them—matter too, but less so than the degree of work obligation. Apparently, nothing improves clients' employment fortunes so much as simply expecting them to work.

Most WIN staff interviewed for these studies had come to similar conclusions. Few believed that the barriers often cited to welfare work were decisive. Few said that jobs were literally unavailable—even in depressed areas of New York City. "Good" jobs were scarce, but low-paid jobs were commonplace. While most supported training for those who could get "better" jobs, many said that WIN had sometimes used training as a substitute for work. Few believed that government child care was essential for mothers to work. Typically, mothers who demanded care from the program were seeking to avoid participation; those who wanted to work arranged care themselves. Staff complained most bitterly, not about the job market or their own resources, but about their limited *legal* ability to penalize, through welfare reductions, the few clients who resisted work.[13]

III. AN ASSESSMENT OF WORKFARE

The MDRC studies permit a preliminary assessment of these new requirements, though experience is still limited. I will use "workfare" here broadly to include any definite requirement to participate in job search, training, or public sector employment in return for welfare benefits.

The traditional question asked by liberals about welfare work is whether the recipients benefit, by conservatives whether the welfare rolls and costs to government are reduced. In these terms, the new programs appear to yield definite but limited gains. Compared to recipients not subject to the new requirements, clients who have been in workfare more often work and earn somewhat more. Lower proportions remain on welfare, and their welfare grants are smaller. Notably, the employment and earnings gains were highest in programs involving required work, not just job search.

Budgetary savings are less clear. Workfare costs more at the outset than plain income maintenance because of the required child care, training, and government jobs. These costs are recouped later in reduced welfare costs as more recipients to go work, either reducing their grants or lifting them off welfare entirely. Of the three programs for which MDRC has compete data, two saved money. All three were worthwhile if other benefits, to society and the recipients, are included.[14] No doubt, testimony from MDRC will explicate these findings.

However, these economic questions are not the most important ones to ask about workfare. They reflect the traditional, "New Deal" preoccupation of American politics with the scale of government. Liberals want larger government to serve the individual, while conservatives want to reduce public burdens on the private sector. Implicitly, both assume that social programs must be benefit-oriented. Liberals tend to regard work or training as another benefit for the recipients alongside case assistance. Conservatives realize this approach is permissive, but their usual response is simply to cut back such programs and let the marketplace impose work discipline.

Neither stance easily appreciates the real point of workfare—to change the *character* of government rather than its scale. Properly understood, work is not another benefit for the recipient but an *obligation* balancing the benefits they are already receiving from society. Neither is it a way to cut back welfare, at least at the outset. The point, rather, is to avoid exempting recipients from normal social obligations, to require that they function *even if* they are dependent.

Viewed politically, the potential of workfare to raise participation levels outweighs all the economic results. Unlike politicians, the public is much more concerned with the character than the extent of welfare. Polls reveal little sentiment either to expand or contract welfare, but intense disquiet at the "abuses" associated with welfare—fraud and abuse, nonpayment of child support by absent fathers, and above all nonwork. The public is humanitarian but *not* permissive. It wants welfare to help the needy but also to uphold social standards. The traditional liberal and conservative positions on welfare violate one side or the other of this public mind. Potentially, workfare could satisfy both. It helps the needy, but in a *demanding* way.

To the public, the moral issues in welfare dwarf the economic ones. The social dysfunction linked to dependency is much more distressing than the cost of welfare. Americans wish they could view AFDC recipients as "deserving" in the same manner as beneficiaries of Social Security and other social insurance programs. More than anything else, higher work levels would make welfare more "respectable." Polls indicate that if assistance could be given by way of work, voters would want to spend *more* on the poor rather than less. Thus, workfare deserves the support of those who seek a generous social policy.[15]

The other critical political fact about workfare is that the recipients themselves accept it. Compared to plain welfare, workfare may not make the recipients much better off economically, but it responds directly to the difficulty they have in living up to the norms they profess. Conservatives tend to say that recipients who fail to work are ripping off the public, while liberals say they have made a "rational" decision not to work in view of the constraints. But these characterizations project on the dependent the self-reliant psychology of the better-off. In fact, the dependent are usually depressed, not cynical, about nonwork. They fail to work, not out of calculation, but because they feel overwhelmed by the logistics of work, as well as by ordinary domestic crises.

By mandating work, workfare helps change employment from an aspiration into a reality. It provides necessary support services, but it also requires that mothers get out of the house in the morning, a spur they need. In my studies, WIN staff said that recipients very seldom contested the work obligation in principle. Nearly always, they accepted it, and they saw participation in WIN as positive. In the MDRC studies, the great majority of workfare clients viewed the participation requirement as fair. They also felt their jobs were meaningful, not "makework." At most, many of those in public positions where they "worked off" their grants would have preferred regular, paid employment.[16]

How do we reconcile these findings with the common view that workfare is "punitive"? One explanation is that critics often see work requirements as invidious in the same way as the restraints on sexual activity that welfare agencies have sometimes tried to impose on recipients. Allegedly, to require work is demeaning in the same manner as raiding a welfare family in the middle of the night to see if there is a man in the house. But the evidence is that recipients view work demands quite differently from intrusions into their personal lives. The latter are private, but work is a public matter about which the agency may inquire, since it affects the size of the welfare grant and the cost to society.[17]

Also, workfare was first used in local general assistance programs intended for groups not eligible for federal welfare, usually two-parent families and single men. In these programs, many more of the employable recipients were men, and many more of them resisted work, than in AFDC. Inevitably, efforts to make them work took on a harsh tone. And when workfare appeared in AFDC, in experimental programs before 1981, the impetus usually came from conservative state officials interested in "program integrity." They saw workfare mainly as a way to deter the employable poor from seeking welfare or to drive them off the rolls, thus limiting assistance to the unemployable or "truly needy."[18] In contrast, the recent AFDC work programs have not been punitive.[19] Their purpose is much more to raise work levels *on* welfare than to limit assistance.

A final explanation is that those who say workfare is punitive are usually quite different from the recipients. That sentiment comes from the leaders of welfare advocacy groups, but typically they are working, not on welfare. Maybe they once were on welfare, but they are now upwardly mobile. Like other self-reliant Americans, they are able to live out the work ethic without either assistance or obligation from government. They would resent being told to work, and so they should. But they err in generalizing from their own experience to that of recipients generally. Most welfare recipients do not resent work demands. Many know they need the structure of workfare programs, with their combination of supports and requirements, actually to achieve work.

The main shortcoming of workfare may be that initially it reaches mainly welfare mothers, not the men who father their children and should normally be supporting them. For constitutional reasons, government cannot force people to work except as a condition attached to benefits it gives them. Since it is usually mothers who receive AFDC, they are the easiest to obligate. There is no comparable benefit for men. While they receive some welfare and training services, they seldom rely on it to live as the women do. Most of their income comes from a combination of erratic work, informal subsidy from the mothers, and "hustling" in the underground economy.

A work policy for men would have to orchestrate a number of lesser obligations, not all of them federal. Some men are on AFDC (either teenagers not in school or unemployed fathers, in states covering them); they can be, and are, required to work in the same way as mothers. Child support enforcement can be strengthened. Work in available jobs can be made an eligibility requirement for federal training programs. Standards in the schools can be raised, to ensure that youths leaving school can read. Perhaps most important, police measures

are needed to constrict the underground economy. These steps together might gradually do for men what workfare does for women—cause them to accept available jobs in the legal labor market.

On balance, workfare is certainly worthwhile. The long-term poor are notably unresponsive to the opportunities around them. They have not taken advantage of existing employment, as recent immigrant groups have, nor have benefit-oriented social programs done much to help them. Workfare has drawn a stronger response from this group than anything yet tried. That alone makes it the most promising development in social policy since the Great Society.

IV. IMPLEMENTATION

However, workfare raises substantial implementation questions. The most fundamental of these are political. As mentioned above, federal politicians prefer benefit-oriented programs, or reductions in such programs, to the combination of benefits and requirements represented by workfare. Congress has allowed workfare in AFDC, but it has not yet mandated it, as the Reagan Administration wants. Proposals to do so will arouse continuing resistance, not withstanding the strong evidence for them. Liberals will say they are punitive, and conservatives will say they perpetuate big government.

A lesser, but substantial issue is cost. As mentioned, for a given caseload, workfare usually costs more than plain welfare, at least at the outset. The states that currently impose workfare have financed it fairly easily with a combination of welfare, WIN, and other training monies. But most of these programs cover only the employable among new applicants for AFDC and usually not all of them. The added cost would be greater if all employable applicants and recipients were covered. How much greater is difficult to say, since it is uncertain how recipients would react. If they all waited to be obligated, did nothing for themselves, and were placed in government jobs, a vast public employment structure would be needed. If they all took private sector jobs, costs might even be lower than now, because of welfare savings from earnings. An outcome in the middle is likely. One plausible estimate, by the Ways and Means Committee, is that a serious work program covering the whole caseload would cost $2 billion.[20]

While that is much less than CETA, the major public employment program of the 1970s, it clearly raises an issue in the current fiscal climate. There is danger that even existing training funds, on which workfare has relied, will be eliminated due to budget balancing under Gramm-Rudman-Hollings.

Another major challenge is administrative.[21] To implement serious work requirements would be a strenuous test for existing work and welfare programs at the local level. Handling the increased caseload is only one aspect. Such a policy would have to overcome the considerable resistance, both political and bureaucratic, that these agencies have shown to past work requirements, helping to explain their poor record. While the political climate in welfare is more conservative than a decade or so ago, the priority in welfare administration is still to avoid errors in grants payment rather than to use work to divert people from welfare. Employment programs have not generally given a high priority to mandatory welfare clients, preferring to serve jobseekers who come to them volun-

tarily. To overcome these impediments from the federal level is difficult, given the frictions inherent in the intergovernmental system.

To overcome the inertia will require a sustained effort at administrative development, not something American government is good at. Washington has to make clear a will to enforce work, and local officials must be made to carry it out. One mechanism here must be stronger fiscal sanctions to force local programs to work actively with more of their caseloads; under WIN, they have to serve no more than 15% of the employable clients. Another need is a number of legal changes to make it easier to obligate the recipients to participate.[22]

The key to successful implementation is voluntary compliance. Once the work mandate is clear to staff and clients alike, they are more likely to conform without pressure, cutting both costs and administrative problems. Voluntary compliance is what makes the income tax system so much more efficient than welfare work. Many of the same poor people who fail to work regularly and face no pressure to do so pay their taxes honestly without prompting, because the obligation is accepted and enforced. While the IRS faces rising tax evasion, it still has to monitor many fewer cases to achieve compliance than work programs would at the outset.

Achieving voluntary compliance is a complex process requiring both political leadership from the top and strong administrative sanctions over a considerable time. It is no accident that the new work programs that have achieved the highest participation are in localities— San Diego and West Virginia—with a long commitment to welfare employment. Work by the dependent will become usual only when it is seen as an inviolable adjunct of welfare—as inevitable as "death and taxes."

In view of the challenges, a political commitment to workfare should be combined with administrative caution. The AFDC law should be changed to mandate active participation in work or training for all employable recipients, but the implementation should be phased in. Raise the share of the employable that work programs must obligate to participate from 15% to perhaps 30%, with gradual increases after that to 50% or more, alongside appropriate funding increases. To obligate half the employable to work or train is probably feasible, and it would establish work rather than nonwork as the norm on welfare, the threshold needed to promote voluntary compliance over the longer term.

In contrast, the Administration has proposed to cut funding for WIN, yet to raise the participation rate required of states to 75%. In the short term at least, it is contradictory to seek more welfare work and expect funding to fall, and 75% participation is impracticable.

To mandate work is a new venture in American social policy. Many politicians and administrators find it distinctly uncongenial. It violates our traditional conception of government as the servant and not the master of the individual. But for the long-term poor, such requirements seem essential to functioning and, thus, to social integration. Welfare work will be enforced when our leaders accept, as the public already seems to, that it is essential to greater equality in American life.

NOTES

1. Lawrence M. Mead, *Beyond Entitlement: The Social Obligations of Citizenship* (New York: Free Press, 1986).

2. Mary Jo Bane and David T. Ellwood, "The Dynamics of Dependence, The Routes to Self-Sufficiency," study prepared for the Department of Health and Human Services (Cambridge, Mass: Urban Systems Research and Engineering, June 1983), ch. 2.

3. *Beyond Entitlement*, pp. 74–5. The proportion of welfare mothers working anytime in the year is higher, perhaps a third or more. And many welfare women work without reporting the income to welfare. These facts indicate a capacity to work, but they do not solve the welfare work problem, since the effort is seldom sustained and working "off-the-books" involves cheating on welfare. See Mildred Rein, *Dilemmas of Welfare Policy: Why Work Strategies Haven't Worked* (New York: Praeger, 1982), chs. 5–6.

4. Greg J. Duncan et al., *Years of Poverty, Years of Plenty, The Changing Economic Fortunes of American Workers and Families* (Ann Arbor: Institute for Social Research, University of Michigan, 1984), tables 2.2, 3.2.

5. William Julius Wilson, *The Declining Significance of Race: Blacks and Changing American Institutions*, 2nd Ed. (Chicago: University of Chicago Press, 1980); Leonard Goodwin, *Causes and Cures of Welfare: New Evidence on the Social Psychology of the Poor* (Lexington, Mass.: D. C. Heath, 1983), ch. 7.

6. *Beyond Entitlement*, chs. 2, 4.

7. Bane and Ellwood, "Dynamics of Dependence," ch. 3; Suzanne H. Woolsey, "Pied-Piper Politics and the Child-Care Debate," *Daedalus*, vol. 106, no. 2 (Spring 1977), pp. 127–45.

8. For the conservative view, see Charles Murray, *Losing Ground: American Social Policy, 1950–1980* (New York: Basic Books, 1984). For the liberal view, see Henry J. Aaron, *Why Is Welfare So Hard to Reform?* (Washington, D.C.: Brookings, 1973).

9. *Beyond Entitlement*, ch. 4.

10. *Beyond Entitlement*, ch. 3; Ken Auletta, *The Underclass* (New York: Random House, 1982), chs. 3–15.

11. *Beyond Entitlement*, pp. 121–4.

12. Judith M. Gueron, *Work Initiatives for Welfare Recipients: Lessons from a Multi-State Experiment* (New York: Manpower Demonstration Research Corporation, March 1986), pp. 10–11.

13. Lawrence M. Mead, "Expectations and Welfare Work: WIN in New York City," *Policy Studies Review*; vol. 2, no. 4 (May 1983), pp. 648–62, and "Expectations and Welfare Work: WIN in New York State," *Polity*, vol. 18, no. 2 (Winter 1985), pp. 224–52. The latter study is summarized in *Beyond Entitlement*, ch. 7. Preliminary results from a study now underway show similar results for WIN nationwide.

14. Gueron, *Work Initiatives for Welfare Recipients*, pp. 14–19.

15. *Beyond Entitlement*, chs. 9–10.

16. Gueron, *Work Initiatives for Welfare Recipients*, pp. 13–14.

17. Joel Handler and Ellen Jane Hollingsworth, *The "Deserving Poor": A Study of Welfare Administration* (New York: Academic Press, 1973), p. 84.

18. Judith M. Gueron and Barbara Goldman, "The U.S. Experience in Work Relief," (New York: Manpower Demonstration Research Corporation, March 1983), pp. 1–33. For a sophisticated statement of the "program integrity" approach, see Blanche Bernstein, *The Politics of Welfare: The New York City Experience* (Cambridge, Mass.: Abt Books, 1982).

19. Gueron, *Work Initiatives for Welfare Recipients*, p. 13.

20. Rein, *Dilemmas of Welfare Policy*, p. 81.

21. The following discussion summarizes *Beyond Entitlement*, pp. 135–47, 182–6.

22. For details, see *Beyond Entitlement*, pp. 144–6.

NO

Morton H. Sklar

PREPARED STATEMENT OF
MORTON H. SKLAR

Members of the Committee:

My name is Morton Sklar. Since 1978 I have served as Legal Counsel, and Director, of Jobs Watch, a public interest project providing information, clearinghouse, and support services on a variety of issues related to unemployment, with a special emphasis on job training and welfare to work activities. While at Jobs Watch I prepared and published in 1983 the first national survey examining how extensively and in what form the states and localities were attaching workfare requirements to the receipt of welfare benefits. I served as legal counsel on two major lawsuits involving workfare, one of which, the *Milwaukee County* case, produced a finding by the U.S. Seventh Circuit of Appeals that a workfare program had unlawfully displaced regular civil service workers, and had failed to provide workfare participants with a fair and reasonable wage for the work they were required to perform.

Since Jobs Watch lost its funding in August of 1985, I have been continuing to work, on an independent basis, directly with a number of communities involved with the adoption and/or implementation of workfare programs, including California, where the statewide Greater Avenues for Independence (GAIN) program was recently adopted, and New York, where a statewide workfare requirement has been proposed and is now before the legislature. I also have been conducting a statewide evaluation of job training programs generally in the state of Virginia, with the final report due out in June.

Because of the recommendations that I am about to make in this testimony, it is important to stress that the analytical and on-site field work that forms the basis for my assessment is not restricted to workfare. It has covered a broad variety of program policies and initiatives designed to assist welfare recipients and others dealing with longer-term joblessness become gainfully employed.

With this broader perspective in mind, one of the most important suggestions that I can make, and the one overriding thought that I would hope this

From U.S. Congress. Subcommittee on Trade, Productivity, and Economic Growth of the Joint Economic Committee. *Workfare Versus Welfare*. 99th Cong., 2d sess., 23 April 1986. 8-23.

testimony leaves you with, is that *the debate over federal welfare-to-work policy should not be put in terms of "Workfare Versus Welfare,"* as these hearings have (inappropriately, I think) been titled. I would hope, when the Congress completes its examination of recent experiences with workfare, and has had a chance to review several other welfare to work policy options that have proven far more effective, that they will see that the choice does not boil down to workfare on one hand, or welfare dependency on the other. There are several viable policy and program alternatives that are far more effectively geared to improving the job holding potential of welfare recipients than workfare.

It would be self-defeating, unduly expensive and contradictory to the lessons we have learned about job training in the past few years for Congress to in any way encourage or facilitate the adoption of workfare by states and localities. The goal of Congressional policy and action on the welfare to work issue would be more profitably directed towards encouraging job training approaches that experience has shown to be more effectively directed towards reducing welfare dependency and improving the job holding ability of recipients.

1. What Workfare Is and Isn't

To understand why my principal recommendation is to support policy options other than workfare it is important to see what workfare is (and seeks to do), and what its virtues and deficiencies are in comparison with alternative approaches.

In essence, workfare is similar to the public service jobs type of approach that Congress became disenchanted with in the old Comprehensive Employment and Training Act (CETA) program, and de-

leted under the current Job Training Partnership Act (JTPA) system. But workfare is far less than CETA's public service employment (PSE) effort, since PSE represented paid, full-time (though temporary) jobs with all of the status and benefits of regular civil service employment. Workfare assignments tend to be in lesser skilled positions, and more sporadic in nature than PSE, since the tasks and hours assigned vary for each participant. How can it be that the more legitimate type of work and on-the-job training experiences of PSE are seen as totally discredited by Congress on the one hand, while the much less substantial public service assignments of workfare are now being considered a viable training approach for welfare recipients?

The other aspect of what workfare is and is not that must be borne in mind is that it is not a training program. With an expenditure of less than $600 on average per participant, it is not really intended to deal, nor can it deal, with any of the job skill or academic deficiencies that force people to be on welfare instead of in the labor market. To that extent, workfare seems primarily designed to serve as a penalty or discouragement to the receipt of assistance benefits rather than a way to promote eligibility.

Much has been made of the fact that a goodly proportion of workfare participants report (in the recent Manpower Demonstration Research Corp. survey and elsewhere) a generally positive feeling about their experience. This has more to do with the strong motivation for, and interest in work that the vast majority of welfare recipients already have, than the ability of workfare to stimulate a work ethic.

The assumption that the only thing that keeps welfare recipients on the rolls is a lack of motivation to work is a gross misconception. Half of recipients (and an even higher proportion of the employable recipients that workfare would apply to) find jobs and leave welfare in their own right after a relatively brief stay in the program. The remainder of employable recipients, who make up only approximately 7% of all those receiving welfare, remain in the program for longer than two year stints. But this is the group that is least likely to benefit from workfare, or be motivated by experience, since they face the types of more serious academic and skill deficiencies that are not affected or improved by short-term work assignments.

2. Workfare Does Not Save Money

Another misconception about what workfare is and is not that needs to be addressed is the widespread assumption that the program saves money. Recent experiences with workfare in state after state prove the contrary—that in fact the program costs substantially more than it saves through reduced welfare payments.

State agency audits found:

• in Georgia, that "savings from non-participation and employment" were exceeded by nearly 5 to 1.

• in Florida, that "from the government/taxpayer's perspective, for every dollar spent, only 16 cents was returned, a net loss of 84 cents."

• in Connecticut, that "the program produced direct costs to the state of $6,884,625 . . . and a savings of $1,871,216" for a greater than 3 to 1 cost over savings ratio.

These findings are typical of the independent and government sponsored evaluations of workfare. The promise that proponents of workfare hold out for easy savings through reduced welfare rolls does not generally pan out in practice. This is partly because of the relatively high costs of administering the program, and in part because workfare does not result in long-lasting job placements—only temporary benefit terminations, or the revolving door of welfare to dead-end job and back to welfare again.

The one study that seems to hold more of a promise for some beneficial effects from workfare is the evaluation conducted by the Manpower Demonstration Research Corporation (MDRC), some of whose initial results were recently summarized in a report written by MDRC's vice-president Judith Gueron. MDRC took an in-depth look at demonstration welfare to work programs in several states, including Arkansas, California, Maryland, Virginia, and West Virginia.

MDRC reported employment gains among participants in two of the more effective programs (San Diego and Baltimore) of from 3 to 8 percentage points relative to other welfare recipients, and a favorable benefits over costs result of from $100 to $2,000 per participant over a five year period. These results seem at variance with my earlier conclusion of workfare being a costly and ineffective program. But MDRC pointed to some important provisos in making their findings. One was that the Baltimore and San Diego programs in particular were not straight workfare. In Baltimore's program, especially, a wide mix of remediation and training activities was added to the workfare component. So it would not be fair to characterize MDRC's favorable findings as applying to workfare in general.

Along the same lines, the MDRC demonstrations were of limited scope in terms of the number of participants. They cautioned readers that it would be unfair and inaccurate to assume that every jurisdiction that attempted a workfare program for larger segments of the welfare population would obtain similar results. MDRC warned that their findings "should not be used to draw conclusions about the quality of programs—or the reactions of welfare recipients—if workfare-type requirements are implemented on a larger scale, are differently designed, or are of longer duration."

Further evidence of the desirability of treating MDRC's findings with caution is the fact that in the program that MDRC viewed as producing the most effective results—San Diego's—earlier findings suggested that cost benefits and employment gains were attributable mostly to other aspects of the San Diego program than workfare.

In sum, it is unlikely that the positive gains that MDRC identified in its best demonstration programs can be duplicated on much larger scale operations, especially when implemented by jurisdictions that do not offer the additional funding and program support elements that were featured in its model experiments. More telling in the debate over the value of straight workfare programs are the preponderantly negative results achieved by every other state where the approach was attempted and evaluated.

3. Workfare Threatens Existing Civil Service Jobs

One of the aspects of the workfare debate that has always irritated, and amused me at the same time, is the claim of supporters of the program that it does not feature make-work assignments, but rather provides valuable work experiences that benefit participant and society alike. What is troubling about this claim is that if it is true then almost by definition we are talking about workfare recipients performing—for the equivalent of the minimum wage—the very same tasks that would otherwise be performed by civil service employees at higher wage rates. What this means is that we would be replacing salaried workers with unsalaried workfare recipients.

This perhaps would produce some savings to the government, but it would strike at the heart of the notion that workfare is designed to promote employment and the work ethic. Instead, to the extent that this type of worker displacement occurs, workfare would cause or promote continued unemployment, and undercut the principle of pay being commensurate with the work performed and prevailing wage rates.

And in fact, we have very concrete evidence that this is exactly what is occurring under workfare. Last August, the U.S. Seventh Circuit Court of Appeals, in the *Milwaukee County* case, issued the nation's first court finding that a workfare program was illegally displacing civil service personnel, and had failed to pay workfare participants the full and fair value of their work by not meeting prevailing wage requirements. In Lackawana, New York, a similar case has been filed because several city sanitation workers were laid off, and then found themselves assigned to do the very same work as workfare participants, at a lower rate of pay.

Proponents of workfare are fond of claiming that the displacement of workers really is not a problem because there is language in most workfare program statutes prohibiting this result. But the existence of statutory standards does not mean that the prohibited conduct is not taking place, especially when the burden of monitoring the problem and bringing the complicated litigation falls to welfare recipients, and when the temptation for governments to cut corners and costs by using a cheaper workforce is so great. As the attorney who handled the successful *Milwaukee County* case, I can tell you first-hand that even when there is an obvious situation of illegal displacement taking place, it is a difficult matter to prove because the government will always claim that budgetary limits rather than the easy availability of workfare labor was the reason for layoffs in civil service personnel.

The statutory prohibition against displacement, however well drafted, is a difficult tool to use. The only real protection against the practice is to deny the use of, or strictly limit the amount of workfare, because displacement, or the refusal to rehire previously laid off personnel, is almost an inevitable consequence of making a low paid alternative workforce available to government agencies.

If you take a look at a recent report issued by the American Federation of State, County and Municipal Employees Union in New York State (attached), you will see why displacement is almost an inevitable companion of workfare. Their survey of workfare assignments in the state found participants performing virtually the same tasks as regular employees, with exactly the same job titles, except that the word "assistant" was added. The *Milwaukee County* and *Lackawana* cases are not aberrations.

4. Recent Lessons From Experience

It is because of the problems and limits of workfare that states and local jurisdictions have begun to move away from the straight workfare model, and to favor a wider and more effective mix of program approaches. California, Massachusetts and New York are probably the best cases in point. This summer the California legislature rejected their governor's proposed workfare package, substituting what they call GAIN, the Greater Avenues for Independence program. GAIN includes workfare assignments (called pre-employment preparation) as part of a much broader system of more legitimate training activities, but the California Department of Social Services estimated in their legislative material that no more than 15% of participants in GAIN would be assigned to workfare. Instead, recognizing that the underlying problem relates to academic and job skill deficiencies, they *guaranteed* academic remediation as the very first activity for *every participant* that has literacy deficiencies (estimated at 50% of recipients), allowed recipients to enter and complete education and training programs, and made available more effective training components, such as supported work.

The Massachusetts CHOICES program follows the same pattern. An early effort to adopt a statewide workfare program was rejected and replaced with a comprehensive system of training and supportive services. Participants play a major role in determining the most suitable component to fit their needs in order to foster their own commitment to make the program work effectively.

Just this past month, the New York State legislature also rejected Governor Cuomo's proposal to make a straight workfare program a part of the fiscal 1987 budget package, and are likely to adopt a more comprehensive training system along the lines of GAIN later this spring.

The two critical common elements in these experiences is that in all three states:

• a straight workfare proposal was rejected, and

• each state made a commitment to a more effective investment in the employment potential of welfare recipients by stressing more legitimate remediation and training efforts, and by backing up this choice with *additional state funding* to make the remediation activities and necessary supportive services more meaningful.

Let us hope that their message reaches Congress and federal level decisionmakers. To phrase the policy debate as a choice between welfare and workfare is to ignore the benefits of what we have learned about the deficiencies of workfare, and to fly in the face of the clear direction that states are moving towards by their own choice.

5. What Are the Alternatives—What Can Congress and the Federal Government Do?

Given the strong popular sentiment against welfare costs, and the strict budgetary constraints we are facing, it is not enough for a federal welfare to work policy to be based on a rejection of the workfare approach. What direction should be taken?

The two models that have shown themselves to be most effective are the supported work program, and the comprehensive training and services approach of the type embodied in the California GAIN and Massachusetts CHOICES programs.

The Supported Work approach was applied on a demonstration basis by MDRC in 1975–1978 in 15 sites. The program was found to be "most effective in preparing for employment a substantial number of women who have been on welfare (AFDC) for many years." Recipients had to have been on welfare for at least 30 of the previous 36 months in order to participate. Their average stay on welfare was 8.5 years. This was clearly the most difficult category of recipients to assist.

After an average of 9.5 months of comprehensive remediation and training assistance, costing approximately $7,000 per participant, the program produced substantial employment and income gains for these long-term welfare mothers. Most important, these results produced long-term net savings to the government of between $3 and $10 thousand per participant.

In other words, if one of the principal purposes of welfare reform is to cut welfare costs, the best way to do it, and the most lasting, is to make a more substantial investment in terms of both time and money. These investments will far more than pay for themselves.

In essence, that is also the principle underlying the GAIN and CHOICE programs. California added $137 million to provide for effective child care services for participants. Massachusetts added $5.8 million earmarked for supported work program assignments, and $18 million more for other training options. California mandated remedial education for every participant needing it, and Massachusetts allocated $2.7 million for a similar purpose.

All these are evidence of the growing recognition that an investment in time and funding is the proper and more effective approach to the employment promotion aspects of welfare reform.

It would be a great shame to see a federal policy that discourages this approach and looks instead to shortcut methods for cutting the welfare rolls, such as workfare. What federal policy should do is to:

1. encourage the type of state discretion that produced the GAIN and CHOICES programs, without imposing mandatory workfare requirements;

2. provide financial support and incentives for states that can show above average employment gains for welfare recipients (and especially for long-term recipients); and

3. encourage the use of the most effective program approaches such as supported work and remedial education.

Of course, the most appropriate question, and one that is close to the top of Congress' concerns, is where the funding for this policy of encouraging longer-term remediation is going to come from. I would suggest two sources.

One, which will probably be viewed as somewhat surprising is the Job Partnership Training Act. What we are learning about JTPA from independent assessments such as the Grinker-Walker study is that, contrary to Reagan Administration claims, the program is not working effectively. At current funding levels, only 3% of eligible unemployed people can participate in JTPA. That fact, plus the strong pressures of the program to produce fast placements at very low cost and in very brief periods of time, have led to creaming—the provision of assistance to those who need service least, and who are already in the best position to find work. This result is a direct contradiction of the stated goal of the program to serve those most in need of employment assistance.

Contractor after contractor, service delivery area official after service delivery area official, private industry council member after private industry council member in Virginia (where I have been working most closely) and elsewhere, all convey the same message—the makeup of the current JTPA program discourages service to the more long-term unemployed, and forces us to concentrate relatively short-term and low-cost efforts on those who are largely job-ready in their own right.

It's true that JTPA produces good participation statistics and good placement rates. But these figures belie the true contribution (or lack of contribution) of the program. Its fast-in and fast-out high volume approach cannot hope to deal with job training needs in a realistic and meaningful way.

I would suggest taking JTPA's funding and remodeling the program to target exclusively on the harder to employ, such as long-term welfare recipients. This would mean reversing JTPA's present orientation by keying the indicators of the program's performance to successful placements of those needing more substantial forms of assistance, rather than those needing only fast-in and fast-out service.

A second funding source that deserves exploration is a revised version of the Unemployment Insurance (UI) program. Roger Vaughn, former assistant director of New York State's employment and training office, was one of the first to suggest using UI as a basis for self-supported, guaranteed training (or retraining) for dislocated workers and others needing this assistance. The virtue of this approach is that it would make training part of a self-insurance system financed primarily by employers and employees themselves, rather than a governmental benefit program that might attach the stigma of a grant-in-aid to the receipt of benefits. There is a great deal of logic in linking training to a system designed to provide for the temporary needs of the unemployed.

What makes Vaughn's proposal different from similar ones that would add training insurance to UI is his suggestion that long-term, unemployed people such as welfare recipients, including those that have been unable to contribute to the training fund because they have been jobless, would also be able to draw on these resources for training purposes. This makes sense because once employed, these recipients would then become paying participants in the UI training fund.

There is one other funding source that also should be mentioned. Employed welfare recipients become taxpayers instead of tax users. Our initial investment in improving their employment potential will be returned several fold through tax payments they will make.

Summary

Summarizing my recommendations to you:

1. The debate over federal welfare-to-work policy should not be put in terms of "Workfare Versus Welfare." Congress should be supporting and seeking to encourage the adoption of policies and programs that are far more effective than workfare in helping welfare recipients become employed on a long-term basis. Workfare is the least effective and probably the most costly (measured in terms of long-term effects) approach.

2. There is not one program or policy approach that is best suited to assist every welfare recipient find work. The fifty percent of welfare recipients who currently find work and leave the program in a short time need little more than job search and referral assistance. Recipients who are long-term unemployed need the type of academic and skill training designed to deal with the barriers that keep them from being considered employable. Few in either category receive any benefits from the type of unpaid public service work experience that workfare represents.

3. What you put in, you get out. You can't expect to produce positive change in the hard-core unemployed with quick, low-investment approaches such as workfare. A person with literacy problems can't be made employable with a 6 to 8 week stint in workfare, or in a low-cost job training program costing $600 per participant. The long-term cost of doing little or nothing to change recipients' basic employability profiles is far greater than making an initial investment in human capital that is designed to improve employability on a more lasting basis. Proven programs such as Supported Work and others that deal with the core issues of academic and job skill deficiencies that keep welfare recipients from becoming employed deserve to be the focus of national welfare-to-work policies.

4. Among the sources of funding that should be considered to support a more effective federal training effort for welfare recipients are:

• a revamped Job Training Partnership Act program that focuses assistance more carefully on the hardest to employ, and encourages (rather than discourages as is presently the case) the type of longer-term remediation that makes the most effective difference in the employability of welfare recipients; and

• an expanded Unemployment Insurance (UI) program that adds a training support component, and makes it available (through UI's joint employer/employee contribution system) to all long-term unemployed or dislocated workers.

I appreciate being given this opportunity to participate in Congress' consideration of welfare reform policy needs, and would be pleased to continue to work with you in any way that you would find useful.

POSTSCRIPT

Is Workfare a Good Substitute for Welfare?

Mead argues that the fundamental problem with AFDC is that "welfare mothers" are not obligated to work. Since few of these recipients of welfare aid have experienced the discipline of the workplace, they become disinterested and discouraged with all that happens around them. They give up the right of self-determination. They let others take over their lives. They slip out of the American mainstream and get caught in the brackish, backwater eddies of "welfare dependency."

Sklar does not reject the importance that Mead attaches to work experience. Rather, he argues that blaming all the problems of welfare on a lack of a work obligation is a "gross misconception." He finds that the problems of those who are welfare dependent are far more complex. Those who seem trapped are those who are least able to compete in the marketplace. They are poorly educated. They have low skill levels. In short, they are the least likely to benefit in a fundamental sense from short-term work experience.

What we find in this discussion are two views of the poor. In some fundamental sense, Mead argues that the poor are poor because they are lazy. If they would just go out and get work, they would no longer need assistance. Sklar attributes idleness to a lack of job skills, not laziness. For him, it is a matter of eliminating the barriers to employment. This is not an inexpensive project.

Addressing the problems of those in need is well documented in the literature. Certainly one place to begin is to read the testimony of the other expert witnesses that appeared before the Subcommittee on Trade, Productivity, and Economic Growth in April 1986. Then turn to those who contributed to two turning points in welfare policy—one to the left and one to the right: Michael Harrington, *The Other America* (Macmillan, 1962), and Charles Murray, *Losing Ground: American Social Policy 1950–1980* (Basic Books, 1984). Next turn to the changes in the law concerning work requirements for welfare recipients. For example, in the Omnibus Budget-Reconciliation Act of 1981, states were allowed to establish mandatory Community Work Experience Programs (CWEP), where adults could be "mandated" to participate in CWEP training or jobs as a condition of receiving public assistance. These legislative changes and others are nicely summarized in U.S. House of Representatives, Committee on Ways and Means, *Background Material and Data on Ways and Means* (Washington, D.C.: U.S. Government Printing Office, 1987). Finally, look at Mead's detailed argument in his book *Beyond Entitlements: The Social Obligations of Citizenship* (The Free Press, 1985).

ISSUE 14

Do Budget Deficits Matter?

YES: Alan Greenspan, from "Deficits Do Matter," *Challenge* (January-February 1989)

NO: Charles R. Morris, from "Deficit Figuring Doesn't Add Up," *New York Times Magazine* (February 12, 1989)

ISSUE SUMMARY

YES: Federal Reserve Chairman Greenspan believes that federal government budget deficits, in the long run, hurt the economy. The deficits crowd out or reduce net private domestic investment. This means a reduction in the rate of growth in the nation's capital stock. This, in turn, means less capital per worker and a reduction in labor productivity. If workers are less productive, then the output of goods and services is smaller, and standards of living decline.

NO: Morris, a writer who covers national affairs, argues that there is little empirical evidence to support the arguments that federal government deficits hurt the economy. That is, there is no real basis for linking budget deficits to higher rates of inflation, higher interest rates, lower savings rates, less net private investment, and trade deficits. He believes that there is no budget deficit crisis—"except for the inevitable crisis of credibility if we lean too long on the button for the siren marked 'false alarm.' "

The Full Employment and Balanced Growth Act of 1978 lists a number of employment goals for the federal government. Besides the familiar objectives of full employment, price stability, and increased real income, the act specifically mentions the goal of a balanced federal budget. This means that the government is to collect taxes in an amount equal to its expenditures. Despite this legislative call to action, the federal government has failed to balance its budget, and recent deficits have been of record proportions. For example, between the years 1940 and 1975, there were only two instances when the deficit was in excess of $50 billion: 1944 and 1975. For the years 1980 through 1988, the federal government deficit has averaged about $140 billion, reaching a record high of more than $200 billion in 1986.

When the federal government runs a deficit it sells securities: treasury bills, notes, and bonds. In this respect, the government is just like a business firm that sells securities to raise funds. The total of outstanding government securities is called the public or national debt. Thus, when the federal government runs a deficit, the public debt increases by the amount of the deficit, and the public debt at any point in time is a summary of all prior deficits (offset by the retirement of securities if the government chooses to repurchase its securities when it has a budget surplus). By the end of 1989 the total public debt was approximately $2.5 trillion. The debt is owned by (been purchased by) different groups including individuals, commercial banks, pension funds, life insurance companies, federal government agencies, state and local governments, and corporations. Some securities are also sold to foreign individuals, businesses, and governments.

There are two major questions to be considered regarding federal government budget deficits. The first question concerns the causes of the deficit. One possibility is that the government spends more than it collects in revenues because it does not exercise fiscal restraint. That is, it is easy for politicians to spend money but difficult for them to increase taxes to fund the increased spending. Every elected official wants to point to the benefits of increased spending—new roads or increased Social Security payments—and no politician wants to be attacked in a bid for re-election as someone who increased taxes. But the budget position of the government is also influenced by the state of the economy. The deficit is likely to increase if the economy enters a recession. A downturn in economic activity will decrease tax revenues (lower incomes mean less income tax revenues) and will increase government spending (more expenditures for such programs as unemployment compensation). Because a deficit can arise for different reasons, it is important to understand exactly what forces create a deficit.

The second major question about deficits, the one addressed in this issue, concerns the economic consequences of deficits. Some economists perceive the deficits as harmful. With a deficit, the government borrows funds that would otherwise be available to business firms, who in turn could have built new factories and purchased new machinery, etc., with the borrowed funds. This is referred to as "crowding out," since government borrowing to finance deficits reduces private investment. The reduction in investment slows the growth of productivity, and this means that the ability of the economy to produce goods and services is also reduced. Greenspan argues in this fashion. Others believe that deficits are not really harmful to the economy. They argue that events during the 1980s support their position: in spite of record deficits, the economy has shown remarkable progress with relatively low inflation rates and falling unemployment. Morris uses such evidence in making his claim that much of the clamor about the deficits has little or no factual basis.

In their opposing views on the issue of budget deficits, Greenspan takes what might be called the traditional conservative position, while Morris supports the conventional liberal perspective. But not all conservatives agree with Greenspan and some liberals disagree with Morris.

YES

Alan Greenspan

DEFICITS DO MATTER

There is a significant view being expressed lately, fortunately to date a minority opinion, that federal government deficits do not matter much. Or in any event, there is no urgency in coming to grips with them. In fact, deficits do matter. Over the long term, they have a corrosive effect on the economy, and it is from this perspective that the case for bringing down the deficit is compelling. More important, the long run is rapidly turning into the short run. If we do not act promptly, the imbalances in the economy are such that the effects of the deficit will be increasingly felt and with some immediacy.

It is beguiling to contemplate the strong economy of recent years in the context of very large deficits and to conclude that the concerns about the adverse effects of the deficit on the economy have been misplaced. But this argument is fanciful. The deficit already had begun to eat away at the foundations of our economic strength. And the need to deal with it is becoming ever more urgent. To the extent that some of the negative effects of deficits have not as yet been felt, they have been merely postponed, not avoided. Moreover, the scope for further such avoidance is shrinking.

To some degree, the effects of the federal budget deficits over the past several years have been muted by two circumstances, both of which are currently changing rapidly. One was the rather large degree of slack in the economy in the early years of the current expansion. This slack meant that the economy could accommodate growing demands from both the private and public sectors. In addition, to the extent that these demands could not be accommodated from U.S. resources, we went abroad and imported them. This can be seen in our large trade and current-account deficits.

By now, however, the slack in the U.S. economy has contracted substantially. And, it has become increasingly clear that reliance on foreign sources of funds is not possible or desirable over extended periods. As these sources are reduced along with our trade deficit, other sources must be found, or demands for saving curtailed. The choices are limited; as will become clear, the best option for the American people is a further reduction in the federal budget deficit, and the need for such reduction is becoming more pressing.

From Alan Greenspan, "Deficits Do Matter," *Challenge* (January/February 1989). Reprinted with permission of publisher, M.E. Sharpe, Inc., 80 Business Park Drive, Armonk, NY 10504.

Owing to significant efforts by the administration and the Congress, coupled with strong economic growth, the deficit has shrunk from 5 to 6 percent of gross national product a few years ago to about 3 percent of GNP today. Such a deficit, nevertheless, is still very large by historical standards. Since World War II, the actual budget deficit has exceeded 3 percent of GNP only in the 1975 recession period and in the recent deficit experience beginning in 1982. On a cyclically adjusted or structural basis, the deficit has exceeded 3 percent of potential GNP only in the period since 1983.

THE SAVING FACTOR

Government deficits, however, place pressure on resources and credit markets, only if they are not offset by saving elsewhere in the economy. If the pool of private saving is small, federal deficits and private investment will be in keen competition for funds, and private investment will lose.

The U.S. deficits of recent years are threatening precisely because they have been occurring in the context of private saving that is low by both historical and international standards. Historically, net personal plus business saving in the United States in the 1980s is about 3 percentage points lower relative to GNP than its average in the preceding three decades.

Internationally, government deficits have been quite common among the major industrial countries in the 1980s, but private saving rates in most of these countries have exceeded the deficits by very comfortable margins. In Japan, for example, less than 20 percent of private saving has been absorbed by government deficits, even though the Japanese

general government has been borrowing almost 3 percent of its gross domestic product in the 1980s. In contrast, over half of private U.S. saving in the 1980s has been absorbed by the combined deficits of the federal and state and local sectors.

Under these circumstances, such large and persistent deficits are slowly but inexorably damaging the economy. The damage occurs because deficits tend to pull resources away from net private investment. And a reduction in net investment has reduced the rate of growth of the nation's capital stock. This in turn has meant less capital per worker than would otherwise have been the case, and this will surely engender a shortfall in labor productivity growth and, with it, a shortfall in growth of the standard of living.

POWER OF GOVERNMENT

The process by which government deficits divert resources from net private investment is part of the broader process of redirecting the allocation of real resources that inevitably accompanies the activities of the federal government. The federal government can preempt resources from the private sector or direct their usage by a number of different means. The most important are: 1) deficit spending, on- or off-budget; 2) tax-financed spending; 3) regulation mandating private activities such as pollution control or safety equipment installation, which are financed by industry through the issuance of debt instruments; and 4) government guarantees of private borrowing.

What deficit spending and regulatory measures have in common is that the extent to which resources are preempted by government actions, directly or indirectly, is not sensitive to the rate of interest. The federal government, for example, will finance its budget deficit in full, irrespective of the interest rate it must pay to raise the funds. Similarly, a government-mandated private activity will almost always be financed irrespective of the interest rate that exists. Borrowing with government-guaranteed debt may be only partly interest-sensitive, but the guarantees have the effect of preempting resources from those without access to riskless credit. Government spending fully financed by taxation does, of course, preempt real resources from the private sector, but the process works through channels other than real interest rates.

Purely private activities, on the other hand, are, to a greater or lesser extent, responsive to interest rates. The demand for mortgages, for example, falls off dramatically as mortgage interest rates rise. Inventory demand is clearly a function of short-term interest rates, and the level of interest rates, as they are reflected in the cost of capital, is a key element in the decision on whether to expand or modernize productive capacity. Hence, to the extent that there are more resources demanded in an economy than are available to be financed, interest rates will rise until sufficient excess demand is finally crowded out.

The crowded-out demand cannot, of course, be that of the federal government, directly or indirectly, since government demand does not respond to rising interest rates. Rather, real interest rates will rise to the point that private borrowing is reduced sufficiently to allow the entire requirements of the federal on- and off-budget deficit, and all its collateral guarantees and mandated activities, to be met.

A FISCAL FACT

In real terms, there is no alternative to a diversion of real resources from the private to the public sector. In the short run, interest rates can be held down if the Federal Reserve accommodates the excess demand for funds through a more expansionary monetary policy. But this will only engender an acceleration of inflation and, ultimately, will have little if any effect on the allocation of real resources between the private and public sectors.

The Treasury has been a large and growing customer in financial markets in recent years. It has acquired, on average, roughly 25 percent of the total funds borrowed in domestic credit markets over the last four years, up from less than 15 percent in the 1970s. For the Treasury to raise its share of total credit flows in this fashion, it must push other borrowers aside.

The more interest-responsive are the total demands of these other, private borrowers, the less will the equilibrium interest rate be pushed up by the increase in Treasury borrowing. That is, the greater the decline in the quantity of funds demanded, and the associated spending to be financed, for a given rise in interest rates, the lower will be the rate. In contrast, if private borrowing and spending are resistant, interest rates will have to rise more before enough private spending gives way. In either case, private investment is crowded out by higher real interest rates.

Even if private investment were not as interest-elastic as it appears to be, crowding out of private spending by the budget deficit would occur dollar-for-dollar if the total supply of saving were fixed. To the extent that the supply of saving is induced to increase, both the equilibrium rise in interest rates and the amount of crowding out will be less. However, even if more saving can be induced in the short run, it will be permanently lowered in the long run to the extent that real income growth is curtailed by reduced capital formation.

SHORT-TERM MENTALITY

But aggregate investment is only part of the process through which the structure of production is affected by high real interest rates. Higher real interest rates also induce both consumers and business to concentrate their purchases disproportionately on immediately consumable goods and, of course, services. When real interest rates are high, purchasers and producers of long-lived assets, such as real estate and capital equipment, pull back. They cannot afford the debt-carrying costs at high interest rates, or if financed with available cash, the forgone interest income resulting from this expenditure of the cash. Under such conditions, one would expect the GNP to be disproportionately composed of shorter-lived goods, such as food, clothing, services, etc.

Indeed, statistical analysis demonstrates such a relationship—that is, a recent decline in the average service life of all consumption and investment goods and a systematic tendency for this average to move inversely with real rates of interest. In other words, the higher real interest rates, the heavier the concentration on short-lived assets. Parenthetically, the resulting shift toward shorter-lived investment goods means that more *gross* investment is required to provide for replacement of the existing capital stock, as well as for the *net* investment necessary

to raise tomorrow's living standards. Thus, the current relatively high ratio of gross investment to GNP in this country is a deceptive indicator of the additions to our capital stock.

Not surprisingly, we have already experienced a disturbing decline in the level of net investment as a share of GNP. Net investment has fallen to 4.7 percent of GNP in the 1980s from an average level of 6.7 percent in the 1970s, and even higher in the 1960s. Moreover, it is low, not only by our own historical standards, but by international standards as well.

International comparisons of net investment should be viewed with some caution because of differences in the measurement of depreciation and in other technical details. Nevertheless, the existing data do indicate that total net private and public investment, as a share of gross domestic product over the period between 1980 and 1986, was lower in the United States than in any of the other major industrial countries except the United Kingdom.

TEMPORARY REPRIEVES

It is important to recognize, as I indicated earlier, that the negative effects of federal deficits on growth in the capital stock may be attenuated for a while by several forces in the private sector. One is a significant period of output growth in excess of potential GNP growth—such as occurred over much of the past six years—which undoubtedly boosts sales and profit expectations and, hence, business investment. Such rates of output growth, of course, cannot persist, making this factor inherently temporary in nature.

Another factor tending to limit the decline in investment spending would be any tendency for saving to respond positively to the higher interest rates that deficits would bring. The supply of domestic private saving has some interest elasticity, as people put off spending when borrowing costs are high and returns from their financial assets are favorable. But most analysts find that this elasticity is not sufficiently large to matter much.

Finally, net inflows of foreign saving can be, as recent years have demonstrated, an important addition to saving. In the 1980s, foreign saving has kept the decline in the gross investment-GNP ratio, on average, to only moderate dimensions (slightly more than one-half percentage point) compared with the 1970s, while the federal deficit rose by about 2 1/2 percentage points relative to GNP. Net inflows of foreign saving have amounted, on average, to almost 2 percent of GNP, an unprecedented level.

Opinions differ about the relative importance of high U.S. interest rates, changes in the after-tax return to investment in the United States, and changes in perception of the relative risks of investment in various countries and currencies in bringing about the foreign capital inflow. Whatever its source, had we not experienced this addition to our saving, our interest rates would have been even higher and domestic investment lower. Indeed, since 1985, when the appetite of private investors for dollar assets seems to have waned, the downtrend in real long-term rates has become erratic, tending to stall with the level still historically high.

Looking ahead, the continuation of foreign saving at current levels is questionable. Evidence for the United States and for most other major industrial nations over the last 100 years indicates that such sizable foreign net capital inflows have not persisted and, hence, may not be a reliable substitute for domestic saving on a long-term basis. In other words, domestic investment tends to be supported by domestic saving alone in the long run.

Clearly, the presumption that the deficit is benign is false. It is partly responsible for the decline in the net investment ratio in the 1980s to a sub-optimal level. Allowing the deficit to persist courts a dangerous corrosion of our economy. Fortunately, we have it in our power to reverse this process, thereby avoiding potentially significant reductions in our standard of living.

NO

Charles R. Morris

DEFICIT FIGURING DOESN'T ADD UP

In the few months since George Bush's election, there has been a remarkable swing of sentiment on the Federal budget deficit. In November, a sharp drop in the financial markets was regarded by some as signaling a deficit "crisis." Former and present Federal Reserve Chairmen Paul A. Volcker and Alan Greenspan, former Presidents Gerald R. Ford and Jimmy Carter and economists of every political allegiance took up the cry: without very fast action to cut the deficit right away, we were facing an American recession, a world economic crisis, or worse.

With the sudden blooming of President Bush's unexpected honeymoon with Congress and the news media, the deficit issue is rapidly fading from view. Most economists, bankers, stockbrokers, editorial writers and Congressmen still believe that Federal budget deficits cause high inflation and high interest rates, sap savings and investment, are at the root of our trade deficit and have converted America into "the world's largest net debtor." But they are being reassured that, though all these bad consequences *do* follow deficits, they work so slowly as to be imperceptible. In other words, instead of a crisis, we have a mini-recession forever.

Without doubt, a major quiver in the financial markets will send the deficit flags flying again. But for once, the deficit Pollyannas may have the stronger argument, if for different reasons than usually stated. Remarkably, there has never been strong evidence for the malevolent consequences of a Federal budget deficit: virtually all of the arguments in favor of urgent action on the current deficit are supported only by the most tenuous connections between theory and evidence, or are not supported at all, or are misleading or actually false. As David Hale, chief economist of Kemper Financial Services, who believes the deficit is important, freely concedes, the fundamental relations are "very murky . . . either very difficult to quantify or you can't quantify them at all."

The gap between the prevailing wisdom and the economic evidence is partly a matter of politics and partly just honest confusion. But more fundamentally, it points up basic flaws in our conventional understanding of how a modern economy works.

The standard model of a modern economy runs roughly as follows: A country's total output (its gross national product, or G.N.P.) is the sum of private consumption and investment and government spending. When the government increases its own spending beyond what it takes in as taxes—creating a budget deficit—it is putting more money into private hands. So total spending—and the G.N.P.—rise.

But the temporary stimulus to the G.N.P. comes at a cost. The increased borrowing by the government to pay its deficit will cause interest rates to rise, because the government action will have heightened competition among borrowers bidding for the available pool of capital. Alternatively, if the Federal Reserve increases the supply of money to accommodate the borrowing, the additional spending power will cause inflation to rise. Things get more complicated when international effects are taken into account, but, in general, the spur to consumption in the deficit country should cause a temporary spurt in imports, such as VCR's and autos, causing a deficit in trade.

How well does this conventional picture comport with reality? Do government deficits actually increase inflation and interest rates and reduce savings and investment? And what is the impact of deficits on America's trade balance and international financial standing? More fundamentally, how do we measure a deficit in the first place?

DEFINING THE DEFICIT

The importance of a budget deficit depends crucially on the size of the economy. A $100 billion deficit will have five times the impact on a $1 trillion economy as on a $5 trillion economy, the current size of our own. Charting changes in budget deficits without reference to changes in the size of the economy is a gross misrepresentation; and the present deficits, in fact, become much less frightening when they are expressed as a percentage of the G.N.P.

The current policy debate also confuses Federal deficits with overall government deficits. State and local surpluses reduce private spending and retire debt just as Federal surpluses do. In recent years, in fact, state and local surpluses have been quite large, the recent problems in Massachusetts and New York notwithstanding.

. . . [T]he annual overall government deficits in the 1980's, expressed as a percentage of the G.N.P., have never reached the record level set in 1975, and the present deficit level is in a range seen rather frequently in the past, even in the conservative Eisenhower years. (Just as pacifistic Democrats make wars, fiscally upright Republicans have always run up the biggest deficits.)

Even more important is the changing nature of Federal spending. President Dwight D. Eisenhower's big deficits came from buying things, like tanks or roads. But only about a third of the modern Federal budget actually is used to purchase goods and services. The remaining two-thirds are transfer payments of one form or another—including interest payments—and make no direct contribution to the G.N.P. Money is merely shuffled from one set of potential spenders to another.

The largest transfer payments are those paid through the Social Security trust fund (about $223 billion in 1988), although there are many others, including Federal and military pensions and welfare payments. There is no satisfactory way to measure their impact on the economy.

The government raises money, mostly from taxes, but some from borrowing, and gives it to transfer recipients. The standard rhetoric that the government borrows from savings to support consumption is not accurate. Some portion of that money raised would have otherwise been used for consumption and some portion for investment and savings. Moving the money from one set of owners to another undoubtedly changes those proportions, but there is no way to know by how much, or even in what direction—although there are economists with strong views on all sides of the issue. (The only sure thing, as conservatives point out, is that to manage it all, the size of government increases.)

The impact of Federal interest payments—about $150 billion in 1988, roughly equal to the entire deficit—is even more ambiguous. Pension funds, banks and other financial institutions hold the lion's share of Federal debt, in the form of Treasury notes and bonds. To pay interest, the Government sells Treasury paper to those institutions and then pays the proceeds back to them. (About $25 billion is paid to foreigners, who own about 15 percent of the Federal debt, but that is a tiny amount in a $5 trillion economy.) Whatever the economic impact of the interest-payment churning process, it is far too small even to be measured.

Interest payments overstate the deficit in other ways: currently, the Federal Government is paying approximately 9 percent interest on its money. About half of that is just covering the loss of purchasing power due to inflation, and constitutes no change in wealth one way or the other. After all, a borrower who pays 5 percent interest during a time of 5 percent inflation is not giving anything extra back to his lenders.

If the inflation premium is considered in the figuring of Federal interest payments, as Robert Eisner of Northwestern University has suggested, and state and local surpluses are taken into account, the total government deficit dwindles to near the vanishing point. The question, in short, is not whether the glass is half full or half empty, but whether there is a glass on the table at all.

INFLATION AND INTEREST RATES

Assuming away the problem of how big the deficit really is, do budget deficits increase inflation and interest rates? The experience of the last 10 years provides an unequivocally negative answer. Interest rates and inflation fell as sharply as the Federal deficit rose; the mild uptick in inflation and interest rates in the last year or so, conversely, comes at a time when the deficit is finally falling.

In fact, there is no evidence that over the last 40 years budget deficits have been associated with higher interest rates or inflation—if anything, the correlation runs in the opposite direction. Economists, like Paul Evans of Ohio State University, have conducted elaborate statistical analyses—controlling for lag effects, inflation, the experience in different countries—without finding any consistent effects from government deficits.

The United States Treasury Department conducted an exhaustive survey of the economic literature in 1984, and found "no systematic relationship between government budget deficits and interest rates. . . ." Some studies, to be sure, claimed to find some such effects; but there was always another drawing the opposite conclusion from the same data.

The budget deficit is frequently blamed for making American interest rates higher than in other countries—in the 1980's, interest rates in this country have been higher than in, say, Japan or Germany. But American rates began to shoot up in the late 70's, before the deficit rose, in reaction to the high, and extremely volatile, American inflation in the 70's, a time when German and Japanese prices were much more stable.

Tracking changes in American, Japanese and German rates shows no consistent pattern. For example, the gap between American and Japanese government bond rates more than doubled between 1980 and 1981, when the American budget deficit was actually falling. The gap then narrowed as the deficit peaked, and began to rise last year as the deficit dropped. In all seven major industrial countries (including Canada, England, France and Italy) in the 1980's, in fact, inflation-adjusted interest rates almost always dropped as budget deficits rose, and vice versa. As Rudolph G. Penner, former director of the Congressional Budget Office, recently phrased it: "One would expect a positive relationship between the deficit and real interest rates. This relationship has been devilishly difficult to document statistically."

SAVINGS AND INVESTMENT

It is taken as a truism that government budget deficits reduce savings and investment: the spur to spending increases consumption, the logic goes, at the same time as government borrowing reduces total savings. The result is lower investment and, over the long term, a less productive economy. The experience of the 1980's in the United States is consistent with that picture: both savings and net business investment have dropped as the deficits rose.

But it is reasonable to ask whether it is generally true that budget deficits reduce total national savings. The surprising answer is that it is not. Robert J. Barro of Harvard University has tracked the interplay of savings and deficits in a number of countries, and the results are frequently—usually, Barro argues—the opposite of what one would expect. Canada and Italy have run very large budget deficits for the last decade, and both have seen very strong increases in private savings. In Israel, England and Denmark, private savings rose sharply to offset big government deficits in the early 1980's, then dropped sharply as their budgets moved into surplus, keeping overall national savings rates roughly constant.

The most one can conclude is that the relationship between budget deficits and savings is practically random. Indeed, the comparative youthfulness of American adults probably has much more influence on savings patterns in this country.

According to the World Bank, 26 percent of the American population is between the ages of 20 and 34, compared to only 21 percent in Japan and 23 percent in West Germany. By contrast, 30 percent of Japanese and 28 percent of West Germans are between the ages of 35 and 54, compared to only 23 percent in the United States.

In demographic terms, these are massive differences; and it should be no surprise that younger people save less. (Projected figures show how rapidly the American population will age in coming decades; one would expect a substantial reversal of savings patterns, quite independently of Federal budget practices.)

The much-lamented decline in American business investment similarly merits a closer look. In the first place, during the 1980's, gross business investment ran at an average 10.9 percent of the G.N.P., actually higher than the last 40 years' average of 10.2 percent. The figure that causes concern, however, is the decline in net business investment—that is, gross investment less depreciation allowances—which has dropped sharply, from a postwar average of 3 percent and a 1979 peak of 3.9 percent to an average of only 2.3 percent in the 1980's.

But the net investment data are suspiciously inconsistent with the strong increase in American manufacturing productivity in the 1980's; at about 4 percent a year since 1982, it is one of the fastest rises on record. Logically enough, Prof. Allan H. Meltzer of Carnegie Mellon University decided to look at the Commerce Department's depreciation schedules to see if they explain part of the mystery. He found that the schedules are based on a set of 1935 guidelines called "Winfrey's rules," which generally assume different investment lives than obtain in a modern business. When Meltzer applies new schedules—developed within the Commerce Department—he says "much, but not all, of the drop in net investment simply disappears."

INTERNATIONAL DEBT AND TRADE DEFICITS

If measurement problems bedevil analyses of investment trends, they almost preclude sensible discussion of America's international financial position. To begin with, that staple of editorial jeremiads, that America has become the "world's largest net debtor," with more than $500 billion in net foreign debt, is flatly untrue.

The "largest net debtor" rhetoric stems from a misuse of the Commerce Department's international balance-sheet accounts. The accounts list all foreign assets owned by Americans—by the Federal Government, private corporations and individuals—and compare the total to all assets in the United States owned by foreigners. All of the hotels in Honolulu that are owned by Japanese hotel chains, for example, are included in the "international debt" totals, although they hardly constitute "debt" in any meaningful sense of the word. The totals show that the value of foreign assets in America has been increasing rapidly and now exceeds American assets abroad by more than $500 billion.

But, oddly enough, through most of the 1980's, Americans earned about $20 billion a year more on their foreign assets than foreigners did on their American assets; and at present, the inflow and outflow of earnings is precisely equal. How does the earnings record square with the "largest net debtor" rhetoric?

The answer, again, lies with accounting conventions. The Commerce Department generally values assets at their purchase price. The big American overseas investment drive came in the 1950's and 60's, so American overseas assets tend to have a much lower book value than the assets purchased by foreigners in the 80's. Monetary gold, an "asset," is valued at $42.22 an ounce, one-tenth its actual value. Asset-pricing conventions, that is, make the balance-sheet accounts utterly meaningless as a measure of American "indebtedness." The more directly relevant earnings figures, on the other hand, imply that America has been a creditor nation throughout the 1980's, and is now roughly in balance with the rest of the world.

The recent shift from a strong American surplus position to a rough balance, however, is clearly related to the trade deficit. The trade deficit is frequently confused with the budget deficit because they are both roughly the same size; and it is assumed that budget deficits cause trade deficits. But the 1980's are the first time in American postwar history that trade deficits and budget deficits have consistently moved in the same direction. And in the rest of the world, there is no such correlation. England, for example, had a sharply rising trade deficit and a sharply rising budget *surplus*—over the same period.

There are also much better available explanations for the trade deficit. By the beginning of the decade, East Asia and, to a lesser extent, West Germany, had built an enormous store of productive capacity and needed to expand their overseas markets. To do so, they drastically cut prices by bidding up the value of the dollar against their own currencies. At the very same time, the United States abruptly stopped sending between $75 billion and $100 billion to Latin America each year in the form of bank loans. (Ironically, our accounting rules made us look richer as we piled up Brazilian and Mexican i.o.u.'s—they are "assets"—while the inflow of high-quality cars, television sets and machine tools somehow make us poorer.)

One way or another, a major readjustment of trade and capital flows was inevitable, with or without a Federal budget deficit. Doubtless, international capital realignments, American savings trends and Federal fiscal policies all interacted in some subtle way, but it defies logic and history to contend that Federal budget policy "caused" such a seismic shift.

Trade performance is, in any case, a poor measuring rod for American industrial might. American companies have long since spread across the globe in pursuit of local markets, a much more efficient strategy than shipping goods across oceans. Foreign branches of American companies sold $640 billion worth of goods overseas in 1986, almost five times that year's trade deficit. Imports from those branches, in fact, made up more than 15 percent of total American imports, or more than half the total trade deficit.

Twenty-five years ago, Europeans met the American overseas investment drive with the same complaints about selling off national "patrimonies" that are heard in this country today, and they were just as ill-founded. American companies consistently reinvest half to two-thirds of their overseas earnings in their host countries; apart from the loss of the long French lunch hour, Europe has clearly gained as a result. Significantly, the Japanese company that purchased Firestone Tire recently announced a billion-dollar investment program in its North American operations.

There is, in short, no evidence of a trade or debt "crisis," and the link between the trade and budget deficits is indirect and elusive at most. The world's industrial powers are much more evenly matched than a decade or so ago, but in that there are benefits as well as challenges for America—hardly the best of all possible worlds, perhaps, but hardly cause for ringing the fire bells.

WHY THE CLAMOR?

The obvious question, then, is why all the clamor? There are a number of bad reasons and one or two good ones.

Partisan political considerations, of course, rank high on the list; or as Carnegie Mellon's Professor Meltzer puts it: "Read my lips, eat my words." The deficit has been the major blot on the Republican economic record, and clearly puts President Bush on the defensive on his "no new taxes" pledge.

Irving Kristol, the editor of The Public Interest, points to the media bandwagon effect: "The media has been accustomed to organizing coverage around crises, and the deficit is about the only one on hand."

The deficits are also a powerful curb on the "Iron Triangle" of Washington special interests that resist spending cuts and create new spending needs:

• Congressmen, who don't score points with constituents by cutting spending. Without the deficit clamor, how could Congress sit still for $1 billion worth of military-base closings? The deficit provides the political air cover for a tax increase to ease the budget-cutting pressures.

• The financial community, which wants action on the deficit because markets more on gusts of emotion. If enough authorities insist there is a crisis, investors, in turn, may behave cautiously, as if there really was one.

• The economics profession, which is, as a whole, in an awkward position if there is no deficit crisis. It is one more confirmation of the deficiencies of the conventional wisdom, but there is no obvious new theory to replace the old one. Educating the political and journalistic elite in fundamental principles has been a long and painstaking process; jettisoning well-established rules is dangerous without new canons of equal clarity to take their place.

The deficit has also become a kind of lightning rod, attracting all the pent-up frustrations of the public at the inability of a divided national executive and legislature to accomplish *anything* in the modern era of special-interest politics. A sensible farm policy, defense policy, entitlements policy, may all be beyond us, but surely the deficit is a problem of sufficient simplicity and starkness to deal with.

There is, finally, at least one good reason to worry about budget deficits: they are a form of moral hazard. The false crisis over the budget deficit prevents the nation from dealing with the real, deep-seated problems it faces, issues of resource allocation and intergenerational equity. What is the proper role of government in a modern mixed economy? What about the looming problem of caring for our aged? The Social Security trust fund is now running a surplus in the $100 billion range, accounting for much of the recent reduction in the Federal deficit. (Taxes are taxes, and one tax dollar closes a deficit as effectively as any other, regardless of its ultimate purpose.) The long-term question, however, is whether there will be enough of a surplus when the baby-boom generation turns 65.

It is unreasonable to expect fundamental problems such as these to be sensibly addressed in the present cloud of exaggeration and confusion. And they are far too complicated for decision-making during a crisis. But there is, after all, no crisis—except for the inevitable crisis of credibility if we lean too long on the button for the siren marked "false alarm."

POSTSCRIPT

Do Budget Deficits Matter?

Federal Reserve chairman Greenspan begins by examining the argument that recent budget deficits have been associated with a strong economy and, therefore, can be ignored. He terms this argument "fanciful," for the harmful effects of recent deficits have been "muted" by two special circumstances that cannot be expected to continue: economic slack and large trade and current account deficits. The fundamental problem with current deficits is that they have not been "offset by saving elsewhere in the economy," and this has led to higher real interest rates. As a consequence, net investment as a percentage of Gross National Product has been falling, from 6.7 percent during the 1970s to 4.7 percent during the 1980s. This decline in investment means that workers will have less capital to work with and productivity will increase less rapidly. The long-term implication is that the ability of the economy to produce goods and services will be reduced and the American standard of living will be less than it could have been: "Allowing the deficit to persist courts a dangerous corrosion of our economy."

Morris begins with a statement of the conventional arguments against budget deficits: they cause inflation, increase interest rates, reduce saving and investment, and contribute to the U.S. trade deficit. Some economists also argue that recent deficits have helped convert the United States into the world's largest net debtor. But, he asserts, there is little evidence to support these arguments. He cites several studies that indicate that there is little or no relationship between budget deficits and interest rates. Morris admits that the savings rate is now less than it has been, but he attributes this to demographics and not to the budget deficits. He also admits that the rate of investment has declined, but then he explains that the data may be biased because of the procedures used by the Commerce Department in calculating net investment. The net debtor status of the United States may also be affected by the procedures used by the Commerce Department, and, therefore, the situation may not be as bad as it looks. As for the trade deficit, Morris states that the budget deficit is not the primary factor; the trade deficit is more the result of other developments, including economic growth in other countries, variations in exchange rates, and the growth of U.S. multinational firms. Given the lack of evidence for the harmful effects of budget deficits, Morris states that the "clamor" over the budget deficits has arisen for sever "bad" reasons, including "partisan political consideration," "the media bandwagon effect," and the fact that efforts to reduce budget deficits are a way to limit the power of Washington's special interest groups. Thus, the controversy over the budget deficit is misleading and distracts us from confronting our real problems: "The false crisis over the budget deficit prevents the nation from dealing with the real, deep-seated problems it faces, issues of resource allocation and intergenerational equity."

There are any number of readings regarding the budget deficit. One might begin with a look at the federal budget as contained in an annual series entitled *The Guide to the Federal Budget,* by Stanley E. Collender (The Urban Institute Press). For a discussion of the problems of measuring the deficit, see *How Real Is the Deficit?* by Robert Eisner (Free Press, 1986). Other interesting books include *The Deficit Dilemma,* by Gregory B. Mills and John Palmer (The Urban Institute, 1983); *Federal Budget Deficits,* by Paul N. Courant and Edward M. Gramlich (Prentice Hall, 1986); and *The Debt and the Deficit,* by Robert Heilbroner and Peter Berstein (Norton, 1989). For contrasting views on the need for a constitutional amendment to balance the budget, see "Less Red Ink," by Milton Friedman (*The Atlantic,* February 1983) and "You Can't Balance the Budget by Amendment," by Gardner Ackley (*Challenge,* November-December 1982). Other interesting articles include "Is the Deficit Really So Bad?" by Jonathan Rauch (*Atlantic Monthly,* February 1989); "The Social Security Surplus: A Solution to the Federal Budget Deficit?" by C. Alan Garner (*Economic Review,* Federal Reserve Bank of Kansas City, May 1989); and "The Macroeconomic Effects of Deficit Spending," by K. Alec Chrystak and Daniel L. Thornton (*Review,* Federal Reserve Bank of St. Louis, November/December 1988).

ISSUE 15

Is the Financial Institutions Reform, Recovery, and Enforcement Act of 1989 the Solution to the Savings and Loan Crisis?

YES: Donald W. Riegle, Jr., from "An address on the floor of the U.S. Senate" *Congressional Digest* (June-July 1989)

NO: Kent Conrad, from "An address on the floor the U.S. Senate," *Congressional Digest* (June-July 1989)

ISSUE SUMMARY

YES: Michigan senator Riegle believes legislation is urgently needed to address the savings and loan crisis. While not perfect, the proposed legislation (FIRREA) accomplishes three critical objectives that will work to preserve government deposit insurance and promote depositor confidence: (1) it separates the various functions of the Federal Home Loan Bank Board; (2) it curtails excessive risk taking by savings and loan associations; and (3) it "clarifies and renews the Federal Government commitment to maintaining a vital and competitive thrift industry as an integral part of the Nation's housing finance system."

NO: North Dakota senator Conrad recognizes the need for government action to resolve the savings and loan crises. Although the legislation has a number of desirable features, he opposes it because it will be too costly to taxpayers. It is too costly because necessary borrowing is done off budget, the assumptions used in initial cost estimates are unrealistic, and prior resolutions by the Federal Savings and Loan Insurance Corporation (FSLIC) are open-ended.

Up until the mid-1970s, the savings and loan industry thrived. S & Ls offered time and savings deposits at interest rates higher than those available at commercial banks and, as deposits grew, funds were readily available to lend. These funds were invested in mortgage loans—the thrift industry was the primary financier of the housing industry. In its heyday, the industry was described as a 3-6-3 industry: borrow at 3 percent, lend at 6 percent, and be on the golf course by 3 in the afternoon!

But during the 1970s, faced with new competition for the savings of depositors and interest rate instability, savings and loan associations began to experience difficulties. In an effort to breathe new life into the industry, Congress passed two pieces of legislation: the Depository Institutions Deregulation and Monetary Control Act of 1980 and the Garn-St. Germain Depository Institutions Act of 1982. Essentially, savings and loans were given new powers to attract deposits and new powers to lend for purposes other than home mortgages. For a time it appeared that the condition of the industry was improving. However, new problems arose during the recession of 1982 and some thrift owners began to abuse the new powers of the thrifts brought about by deregulation. The number of insolvent institutions began to increase and the resources of the FSLIC (which provides government insurance on deposits at S & Ls) were insufficient to pay off depositors.

Upon assuming office in January 1989, the Bush administration submitted to Congress its solution to the crises: The Financial Institutions Reform, Recovery, and Enforcement Act of 1989 (FIRREA). The first part of the proposed legislation focuses on reform. Essentially, it separates regulatory functions from insurance functions. Insuring deposits of both commercial banks and savings and loans is now to be handled by the FDIC (Federal Deposit Insurance Corporation), while the regulation of savings and loans now falls to the Treasury Department. The second part of the legislation involves the financing necessary to make good on savings-and-loan insolvencies. To help the industry recover, some $150 billion is needed. These funds are to come from three sources: $50 billion from new borrowing, the remainder from the savings and loan industry itself (through higher deposit insurance premiums and special assessments on the regional Federal Home Loan banks) and from the U.S. taxpayer. The third part of the legislation is keyed to enforcement—actions to prevent future fraud and insider abuse and to bring to justice those who had engaged in illegal activity.

As FIRREA made its way through Congress, controversy erupted on a number of points. One particular issue was whether the $50 billion of new borrowing should be done off budget, as proposed by President Bush, or on budget. The former would involve a higher interest cost but satisfy the letter of the Gramm-Rudman-Hollings law, which sets limits on federal government budget deficits. On budget financing would lower the interest cost but require either an exemption from Gramm-Rudman-Hollings, new taxes, or a reduction in government spending in other areas. Another issue was the distribution of the total cost of the package: If too much of the cost was placed on currently solvent institutions, they themselves might become insolvent. Another issue was the complexity of FIRREA: Did anyone really understand this very complex piece of legislation? Even the total cost of FIRREA was uncertain; the cost of this bailout depends on future conditions, including interest rates and deposit growth at surviving thrift institutions.

The two readings represent the views of two Democratic senators. Senators Riegle and Conrad agree that something should be done. The question is, is this particular piece of legislation the best that could be accomplished? Riegle believes it is while Conrad does not.

YES
Donald W. Riegle, Jr.

THE SAVINGS AND LOAN CONTROVERSY

I rise on the savings and loan package that is before the Senate. The new Administration has made deposit insurance its top domestic priority and rightly so. The thrift industry is in a crisis situation. The Federal Savings and Loan Insurance Corporation is presently insolvent and it has to be restored to financial solvency.

It is not surprising that American investors, both large and small investors, are justifiably concerned about the soundness of the Federal deposit insurance system. The situation demands action and we bring a package of action to the floor.

The act itself accomplishes three critical objectives in combination. These objectives will work to preserve a system of Federal deposit insurance in which all depositors can justifiably have confidence.

First, the act breaks the unfortunately close relationship between the thrift industry and its regulators. The act does this by separating the insurance, regulatory, credit and promotional functions of the Federal Home Loan Bank Board from one another. The act places the insurance functions under the FDIC, the regulatory functions under the Treasury Department, and the promotion and chartering functions under a new, independent, Federal Home Loan Bank Agency.

Second, the act curtails excessive risk-taking by federally insured thrifts. It imposes new capital requirements on thrifts. It places tight controls on the investment activities of State-chartered thrifts and their subsidiaries. These State-chartered thrifts are responsible for the lion's share of thrift losses. The act also strengthens the qualified thrift lender test to ensure that the benefits of Federal thrift charters do not flow to entities whose activities undermine the soundness of the industry. And the act places stronger controls on the commercial real estate lending authority of federally chartered thrifts.

Finally, the act clarifies and renews the Federal Government commitment to maintaining a vital and competitive thrift industry as an integral part of the Nation's housing finance system.

Many people ask how important the savings and loan industry is today in meeting the housing needs of our country. I should note that last year over

From Donald W. Riegle, Jr., "An address on the floor of the U.S. Senate," *Congressional Digest* (June/July 1989, Savings and Loan Controversy, Pro and Con), pp. 172, 174, 176, 178, 180.

half of all the mortgage origination activity done in the United States, individual mortgages and for families, were made by savings and loans.

So, while there are other competitors in that business, if suddenly we were to see the savings and loan industry across the 50 States vanish from the picture we would have an enormous disruption in mortgage lending and home ownership which is tough enough now for people to achieve and would just be that much more difficult for people to achieve.

This is a vital industry. It needs to be preserved to meet that central public purpose and that is also, I might say, the view of the Bush Administration stated both by the President and by the Secretary of the Treasury.

There was a problem over the last several years in the area of fraud and insider abuse. Now, there is in this legislation $50 million set aside for the Justice Department to go out after those individuals who defrauded the system and who looted the system, to track them down and bring them to justice and recover everything we can financially.

We had, in addition to those two major causes of this difficulty, a regional recession that was generally concentrated in the Southwest. Since the mid-1980s, the economy of that part of the country has taken a real beating. Among the eight regions of the country, the Southwest and Rocky Mountain regions ranked lowest in personal income growth, between 1982 and 1988.

Inevitably, a weak economy harms even strong conservative lenders and for weak, speculative lenders a weak economy can be devastating. Loans secured by overvalued property became large losses when property values fell very sharply. Real estate development loans turn sour when buyers or tenants fail to materialize. That is a major part of what capsized the system coming into the late eighties.

Then there was a response of the regulators. As the thrift industry continued to deteriorate, the regulators generally downplayed the problems and, by and large, when actions were taken, usually moved to loosen the required standards. As balance sheets eroded, the regulators lowered the capital standard and allowed almost anything to count as capital.

Thrift failures have cost the FSLIC an estimated $78 billion so far this decade. Nobody knows for sure how much more money it will take to resolve the problem once and for all. Responsible estimates range from $50 billion, on the one hand, to over $150 billion on the other. This is clearly a problem of unprecedented scale for us to have to face and solve.

This bill and legislation can properly be called emergency legislation intended primarily to provide funds to resolve current and expected failures of federally insured thrifts and to restore the value of insured deposits. By using every means available to us, this legislation also aims to prevent a recurrence of this massive systemic failure of the industry and its regulators.

Given the severe time constraints and the extraordinary complexity of the problem, I am satisfied that this is the best bill we could produce under the circumstances. But I also want to say at this point that if someone were to ask if this package, as well-crafted as I think it is under the circumstances, within the limitations that we find confining us, is this package absolutely a fail-safe package that will get the job done in the future and are we certain we can have that kind of an outcome. I would have to say that we cannot give that kind of a guarantee.

We can say that it provides the best and the most prudent option for the S&L industry to restore itself over a period of time. But there is no certain guarantee that this plan or any plan will work exactly the way we would like to. Future events could occur that would require further adjustments to this legislation as we go down the line.

In general, S. 774 responds to the crisis in the thrift industry in three ways. First, the act provides an administrative and financial vehicle for raising and disbursing funds needed to resolve thrifts that have failed already or are expected to fail in the near future. Second, the act creates new regulatory structures to preserve the soundness of the Federal deposit insurance system and Federal thrift regulation. Third, the act places new limits on the abilities of both State and federally chartered thrifts to engage in excessively risky activities that pose substantial risk to the Federal Deposit Insurance System. In addition, I am proud to report that this bill strengthens the Administration's proposal in several important respects:

It provides stronger restrictions on the activities of State thrift institutions. It strengthens the qualified thrift lender test. It refines the Federal thrift charter. It limits loans to one borrower and adopts new loan to value ratios. It reforms thrift industry regulation to separate the credit and regulatory functions of the Federal Home Loan Banks. And it provides the FDIC with new procedures for suspending the deposit insurance of any institution that has no tangible capital.

Having said that, I think we can, in fact, say that within the bounds of the situation that we find ourselves, this package is the soundest and toughest package that we can put together, particularly in the time limits available to us.

I want to indicate, in terms of the structural inadequacies of the existing regulatory system, that we have moved in every way to change and substantially overhaul the structure of the system. By the nature of the legislation, the bill does not, as it cannot, legislate the judgment of the future regulators, nor does it try to micromanage their actions. There are things they must do in their capacity that we cannot undertake to direct them to do or do for them.

Inadequacies in the existing system of thrift regulation have contributed significantly to the crisis in the industry. Many of these inadequacies are structural in nature. This bill radically reforms the existing regulatory structure in an effort to create a more vigorous and successful regulatory scheme.

To summarize, the problems of the thrift industry cannot wait. The estimates are that losses today in savings and loans that need to be dealt with by a replenished insurance fund are running somewhere between $500 million and $1 billion a month. That is every 30 days. So there is a lot of money at stake here in the future, in terms of future losses that can be prevented and should be prevented.

That is one of the reasons why it is essential that we act quickly and put these reforms in place that can deal with this problem.

We worked very hard to find a way to shave down the costs. We feel we did find such a way. It involves how we handle the accounting recognition of the losses that have taken place, but if we do it in a direct, on-budget fashion, we can actually then finance directly through the Treasury to borrow the money that has to be raised and we can do it at a lower interest cost and save the American people $4.5 billion over the 30 years of this program, or roughly $150 million a year.

To me that is a lot of money. I know around this town we deal in large amounts and after a while, if we are talking about a problem that is in excess of $150 billion, there is a question as to how much that amount of savings on the margin really amounts to. I think it amounts to enough that it was really worth fighting to try to save it.

However, the Administration feels very strongly on this issue and has threatened to veto over that issue. They have threatened an extended debate here on the Senate floor that would delay action if we were to pursue that course.

I do not propose to rehash in any great detail that particular issue, except to say I felt strongly about it and feel strongly about it now. I felt we had made a good effort to find a way to get the costs down. Let us not forget, we have wrung every dime we know how to wring out of the savings and loan industry, in the condition they find themselves in. So any additional costs have to be carried by the taxpayer, and that means any additional cost that we can prevent saves the taxpayer. So that was our purpose and that is why we developed it as we did.

I repeat again, there are no guarantees on this. We have done the best job we know how to do in terms of putting this package together within the constraints and the realities that are out there. There are a lot of savings and loans today that are struggling. We think we have provided the kind of rational and prudent stairsteps for them to climb over a period of time up to a stronger position. Not all will make it. We tried to do it in a way that protects the solvency of the system and will allow as many as possible to make it. Those that do not make it or if

the system is altered in a way that causes more thrifts in the future to slide backward and slide into insolvency, then those just increase the costs to our Government and increase the cost to taxpayers.

So we have been very sensitive to try to balance the job of crafting a national thrift charter that can be profitable, that can meet the public interests, that can attract capital, but do it in a safe and sound, prudent manner that can protect the solvency of the insurance fund in the future.

We think this bill structures this balance as well as it is possible to do, given the facts that we face.

NO

Kent Conrad

THE CRISIS IN THE THRIFT INDUSTRY

I rise today to inform my colleagues that I intend to vote against the FSLIC bill.

But first I want to make it clear that I do not want my vote in any way to diminish the hard work members of the Banking Committee have put into this bill. They faced a truly awesome task: resolving a crisis that has been estimated at anywhere from $50 to $150 billion. And they had to move quickly because the crisis is growing at an alarming rate, they had to address extremely complex questions of regulation, supervision, and enforcement to ensure that the crisis does not recur and they sought to minimize the cost to taxpayers. They are to be commended for the time, thought and effort that went into producing this legislation.

I also want to make it clear that I fully understand the need for legislation to address the savings and loan crisis. While I share the outrage of my constituents—and of taxpayers across the country—that a combination of economic factors, fraud, mismanagement and lax supervision has created this enormous problem, we cannot allow blameless depositors to lose their life savings. These deposits were made with the clear understanding that they were insured and we cannot break our commitment to depositors. At the same time, we must reform the structure of the savings and loan industry to eliminate the causes of today's crisis and ensure that the taxpayers of this country never again are forced to fund a bailout of this magnitude.

The committee bill that we are discussing today makes significant steps in that direction. I wish to point out just a few of the problems it corrects. The close relationship between the industry and its regulators and supervisors entailed a conflict of interest that encouraged overseers of the industry to overlook problems—ultimately magnifying the problem. The bill restructures oversight by separating the agency charged with regulating the industry from that charged with promoting it. Much of the problem was caused by high-flying thrifts that took advantage of loose regulation and that made risky loans. The bill strictly limits the activities of thrifts and enacts tough new standards for thrifts. Abusive real estate appraisal practices contributed

From Kent Conrad, "An address on the floor of the U.S. Senate," *Congressional Digest* (June/ July 1989, Savings and Loan Controversy, Pro and Con), pp. 185, 187, 189.

billions of dollars to the FSLIC problem. The bill establishes new guidelines for real estate appraisal.

Despite these admirable provisions, however, I have decided to vote against the bill because I believe it fails one crucial test: it will not minimize the cost to the taxpayer of resolving the FSLIC problem. We cannot in good faith continue to tell the American taxpayer that there is not enough money for housing, for the war on drugs, for education, for health care, for essential air service, or for any of dozens of other programs that provide tangible goods and services to them while at the same time passing a bill which could cost billions of dollars unnecessarily—and which will provide those taxpayers with nothing in return.

There are several reasons I believe this bill will cost taxpayers too much. First, the financing mechanism adds several billions of dollars for the sake of an accounting trick. Off-budget financing is simply a gimmick to make it look like the Government is not borrowing money when it really is. And it is an expensive gimmick: the Senate Banking Committee estimates that off-budget financing will result in higher interest rates that will end up costing the taxpayers an additional $4.5 billion when compared with his on-budget plan. Thus, I strongly believe that the bailout should be financed on-budget.

While proponents of off-budget financing argue that we cannot finance this scheme on-budget because of the Gramm-Rudman-Hollings law, their argument simply does not hold up. Ignoring the fact that the off-budget financing plan itself clearly violates the spirit of the law, the Gramm-Rudman deficit targets were set because it was hoped that cutting the deficit would have a favorable effect on a number of economic factors. Government borrowing to finance additional Government spending, it was argued, has a detrimental effect on the economy.

However, in this case the money has already been spent; the economic effects have already been experienced. By financing the bailout on-budget the Federal Government merely would be substituting an explicit debt for the implicit debt it has already incurred. Borrowing the money honestly—on-budget—will not have a negative impact on the economy. The chairman of the Federal Reserve Board, the Congressional Budget Office [CBO] and the General Accounting Office all agree that the FSLIC bailout should not be included in the Gramm-Rudman-Hollings calculation. I don't believe the financial markets or the American people are going to be fooled by the off-budget gimmick. Instead, I think they are going to be angered by its additional cost.

Borrowing the money honestly also could allow the Government to shut down and liquidate insolvent thrifts more quickly. These insolvent thrifts are costing the taxpayers tens of millions of dollars a day; the sooner we can shut them down the lower the cost to the taxpayer. Allowing the U.S. Treasury to borrow the money as needed to shut these thrifts down would avoid these unnecessary costs.

A second reason I believe this legislation will cost too much is that it relies heavily on Administration assumptions that are unrealistic, and any shortfalls between optimistic assumptions and reality will be financed by the taxpayers. For example, the Administration assumes that the cost of resolving institutions that will fall into difficulty in the future will be only $50 billion, but numerous experts believe the problem will be much bigger.

The Administration estimates that savings and loans deposits will grow at a record rate and that this deposit growth will generate significant increases in insurance premiums—which will, in turn, be used for the bailout. However, S&Ls are now experiencing net withdrawals, and the interest rates offered by S&Ls are expected to decline. Consequently, it is not surprising that the CBO estimates that deposit growth will be much slower and will result in $5.5 billion less in insurance premiums than the Administration projects. These mistaken assumptions could end up costing the taxpayers over $100 billion more than the Administration admits.

Finally, there appears to be no limit to the costs of some of the agreements into which the FSLIC entered last December. These deals provided the new operators of bankrupt S&Ls guaranteed returns on assets, they guaranteed the book value of assets regardless of actual market value, they waived many regulations, and they granted many tax benefits. The documentation of these deals is incomplete, and the open-ended nature of the guarantees means that no one is sure how much these deals will cost. Further, these newly created thrifts have no incentive to be managed carefully, and the regulatory breaks give them an unfair advantage over thrifts that were responsibly managed and did not go bankrupt. This combination could result in further significant drains on the thrift industry insurance fund and increase the cost of the bailout. While the bill touches on this issue, it does not go as far as I would like toward restructuring these deals and saving money for taxpayers.

In conclusion, I strongly support the stricter standards in the bill. I applaud the tougher enforcement standards to punish fraud and other abuses. I believe the restructuring of the regulatory arrangement is necessary to prevent the recurrence of this crisis. And I appreciate the need to move quickly to resolve this crisis.

However, if we are to ask the American taxpayers to pay hundreds of billions of dollars for the mistakes and problems of the savings and loan industry, the least we can do is to make sure that none of those dollars are spent needlessly. While I accept the arguments for acting quickly, we cannot allow the pressure to act quickly to force us to act poorly. This is an exceedingly complex piece of legislation; the Banking Committee has held dozens of meetings and heard from over 50 witnesses in its efforts to deal with the intricacies of the issue. But I believe it is unreasonable to expect Senators who, like me, are not on the committee to fully understand, debate and vote on this complex, 564-page bill only days after it became available. The next generation of taxpayers—the generation that will be paying for our mistakes—will not accept the excuse that we did the best under the circumstances. The best under the circumstances is simply not good enough if it costs the taxpayers tens of billions of dollars needlessly.

Because I believe legislation to address the FSLIC crisis is urgently needed, because this legislation is the only legislation available to address the crisis, and because this legislation contains many important and necessary reforms, it is only with reluctance that I have decided to vote against it. I hope that my objections will be cleared up as this bill moves through the legislative process. However, I firmly believe that in its present form S. 774 will cost the taxpayers of this country much more than it should, and consequently I cannot support it.

POSTSCRIPT

Is the Financial Institutions Reform, Recovery, and Enforcement Act of 1989 the Solution to the Savings and Loan Crisis?

Riegle recognizes the need for quick action to resolve the savings and loan crisis: without quick action, depositors of solvent savings and loans might lose confidence and create an even worse crisis. He believes that the Financial Institutions Reform, Recovery, and Enforcement Act (FIRREA) is an appropriate solution because it creates a new regulatory structure, which separates the thrift industry from its regulators; it imposes new capital requirements, which will reduce the risky lending activities of the thrift industry; and it demonstrates that the federal government is ready to honor its deposit insurance commitments and to assure proper financing of the housing industry.

Conrad recognizes the crisis in the thrift industry and the need to take corrective action. However, in reviewing the good and bad points of FIRREA, he believes the negatives outweigh the positives and, therefore, he must vote against this particular rescue effort. As for the good points, Conrad mentions two. FIRREA imposes a new regulatory structure that exposes "a conflict of interest that encouraged overseers of the industry to overlook problems—ultimately magnifying the problem." FIRREA also contains new restrictions and standards that would curb excessively risky lending by savings and loan associations. Outweighing these positives is the fact that FIRREA fails to "minimize the cost to the taxpayer." So in spite of the need for action, the excessive cost forces Conrad to oppose FIRREA.

FIRREA became law in August 1989. In its final form, the $50 billion borrowing was split between on budget ($20 billion) and off budget ($30 billion). But the debate over thrift insolvencies continues. As of January 1990, new estimates indicate that it's likely to cost $24 billion *more* than the government previously allocated to make good on savings-and-loan insolvencies. For very useful background information on FIRREA, the savings and loan crises, the evaluation of banking legislation, a description of federal agencies regulating financial institutions, as well as the views of other senators on FIRREA, see the June-July 1989 issues of *Congressional Digest*. For a critique of the initial Bush administration's version of FIRREA, see "Too Little, Too Late," by William Niskanen and Catherine England, *National Review* (May 19, 1989), and "Bush's Bail-Out Bonanza," by Vince Valvano, *Dollars & Sense* (May 1989). For an alternative to FIRREA, see "How to Solve the S & L Mess," by L. William Seidman, *Challenge* (January-February 1989). Other interesting articles are: "Savings Industry's Costly Fraud," by Thomas C. Hayes, *New York Times* (January 10, 1989) and "S & L Busts: It Wasn't Just the Crooks," by Byron Harris, *Wall Street Journal* (March 2, 1989).

PART 3

International Trade

For many years America held a position of dominance in international trade. That position has been changed by time, events, and the emergence of other economic powers in the world. Decisions that are made in the international arena will, with increasing frequency, influence our lives. Protectionist measures are being discussed in Congress, and the jobs of many Americans may depend on the outcome of those discussions. The willingness and ability of Third World nations to devote resources to paying their debts will directly affect the U.S. domestic banking system. And the impact that multinational corporations have on host countries—South Africa is a case in particular—has ramifications in the United States as well.

Should the United States Protect Domestic Industries from Foreign Competition?

Can the Third World Pay Its Debt Without U.S. Help?

Can Strict Economic Sanctions Help End Apartheid in South Africa?

ISSUE 16

Should the United States Protect Domestic Industries from Foreign Competition?

YES: Bob Kuttner, from "The Free Trade Fallacy," *The New Republic* (March 28, 1983)

NO: Michael Kinsley, from "Keep Free Trade Free," *The New Republic* (April 11, 1983)

ISSUE SUMMARY

YES: Columnist Bob Kuttner alleges that David Ricardo's eighteenth-century view of the world does not "describe the global economy as it actually works" in the twentieth century. He says that, today, "comparative advantage" is determined by exploitative wage rates and government action; it is not determined by free markets.

NO: Social critic Kinsley replies that we do not decrease American living standards when we import the products made by cheap foreign labor. He claims protectionism today, just as it did in the eighteenth century, weakens our economy and only "helps to put off the day of reckoning."

The basic logic of international trade does not differ from the basic logic of domestic trade. The fundamental questions of "what?" "how?" and "for whom?" must be answered. The difference is that, in this case, the questions are posed in an international arena. This arena is filled with producers and consumers who speak many different languages, use different currencies, and are often suspicious of the actions and/or reactions of foreigners.

However, if markets work the way they are expected to work, free trade simply increases the extent of the market and, therefore, increases the advantages of specialization. Market participants should be able to buy and consume a greater variety of inexpensive goods and services after the establishment of free trade than they could before free trade. You might ask: Why, then, do some wish to close our borders and deny our citizenry the benefits of free trade? The answer to this question is straightforward: These benefits do not come without a cost.

There are two sets of winners and two sets of losers in this game of free trade. The most obvious winners are the consumers of the "cheap" imported goods. These consumers get to buy the low-priced color TV sets, automobiles, or steel that is made abroad. Another set of winners are the producers of the exported goods. All the factors in the export industry, as well as in those industries that supply the export industry, experience an increase in their market demand. Therefore, their income increases. In the United States, agriculture is one such export industry. As new foreign markets are opened, farmers' incomes increase, as do the incomes of those who supply the farmers with fertilizer, farm equipment, gasoline, and other basic inputs.

On the other side of this coin there are losers. The obvious losers are those who control the factors that are employed in the import-competing industries. These factors include the land, labor, and capital that are devoted to the production of United States-made color TV sets, United States-made automobiles, and United States-made steel. "Cheap" foreign imports displace the demand for these products. The consumers of exported goods are also losers. For example, as United States farmers sell more of their products abroad, less of them are available domestically. As a result, the domestic price of these farm products rises.

The bottom line is that there is nothing "free" in a market system. Competition—whether it is domestic or foreign—creates winners and losers. Historically, we have sympathized with the losers when they suffer at the hands of foreign competitors. However, we have not let our sympathies seriously curtail free trade. Kuttner argues that we can no longer afford this policy. He maintains that United States workers face "unfair foreign competition." He asserts that the international rules of the game have changed. Michael Kinsley replies that this is "pure, unadorned protectionism." He goes on to conclude that "each job 'saved' will cost other American workers far more than it will bring the lucky beneficiary."

YES   Bob Kuttner

THE FREE TRADE FALLACY

In the firmament of American ideological convictions, no star burns brighter than the bipartisan devotion to free trade. The President's 1983 Economic Report, to no one's surprise, sternly admonished would-be protectionists. An editorial in *The New York Times*, midway through an otherwise sensibly Keynesian argument, paused to add ritually, "Protectionism might mean a few jobs for American auto workers, but it would depress the living standards of hundreds of millions of consumers and workers, here and abroad."

The Rising Tide of Protectionism has become an irresistible topic for a light news day. Before me is a thick sheaf of nearly interchangeable clips warning of impending trade war. With rare unanimity, the press has excoriated the United Auto Workers for its local content legislation. *The Wall Street Journal's* editorial ("Loco Content") and the *Times's* ("The Made-in-America Trap") were, if anything, a shade more charitable than Cockburn and Ridgeway in *The Village Voice* ("Jobs and Racism"). And when former Vice President Mondale began telling labor audiences that America should hold Japan to a single standard in trade, it signaled a chorus of shame-on-Fritz stories.

The standard trade war story goes like this: recession has prompted a spate of jingoistic and self-defeating demands to fence out superior foreign goods. These demands typically emanate from overpaid workers, loser industries, and their political toadies. Protectionism will breed stagnation, retaliation, and worldwide depression. Remember Smoot-Hawley!

Perhaps it is just the unnerving experience of seeing *The Wall Street Journal* and *The Village Voice* on the same side, but one is moved to further inquiry. Recall for a moment the classic theory of comparative advantage. As the English economist David Ricardo explained it in 1817, if you are more efficient at making wine and I am better at weaving cloth, then it would be silly for each of us to produce both goods. Far better to do what each does best, and to trade the excess. Obviously then, barriers to trade defeat potential efficiency gains. Add some algebra, and that is how trade theory continues to be taught today.

To bring Ricardo's homely illustration up to date, the economically sound way to deal with the Japanese menace is simply to buy their entire cornu-

From Bob Kuttner, "The Free Trade Fallacy," *The New Republic*, vol. 188, no. 12 (March 1983). Copyright © 1983 by The New Republic, Inc. Reprinted by permission of *The New Republic*.

copia—the cheaper the better. If they are superior at making autos, TVs, tape recorders, cameras, steel, machine tools, baseballs, semiconductors, computers, and other peculiarly Oriental products, it is irrational to shelter our own benighted industries. Far more sensible to buy their goods, let the bracing tonic of competition shake America from its torpor, and wait for the market to reveal our niche in the international division of labor.

But this formulation fails to describe the global economy as it actually works. The classical theory of free trade was based on what economists call "factor endowments"—a nation's natural advantages in climate, minerals, arable land, or plentiful labor. The theory doesn't fit a world of learning curves, economies of scale, and floating exchange rates. And it certainly doesn't deal with the fact that much "comparative advantage" today is created not by markets but by government action. If Boeing got a head start on the 707 from multibillion-dollar military contracts, is that a sin against free trade? Well, sort of. If the European Airbus responds with subsidized loans, is that worse? If only Western Electric (a U.S. supplier) can produce for Bell, is that protection? If Japan uses public capital, research subsidies, and market-sharing cartels to launch a highly competitive semiconductor industry, is *that* protection? Maybe so, maybe not.

Just fifty years ago, Keynes, having dissented from the nineteenth-century theory of free markets, began wondering about free trade as well. In a 1933 essay in the *Yale Review* called "National Self-Sufficiency," he noted that "most modern processes of mass production can be performed in most countries and climates with almost equal efficiency." He wondered whether the putative efficien-

cies of trade necessarily justified the loss of national autonomy. Today nearly half of world trade is conducted between units of multinational corporations. As Keynes predicted, most basic products (such as steel, plastics, microprocessors, textiles, and machine tools) can be manufactured almost anywhere, but by labor forces with vastly differing prevailing wages.

With dozens of countries trying to emulate Japan, the trend is toward worldwide excess capacity, shortened useful life of capital equipment, and downward pressure on wages. For in a world where technology is highly mobile and interchangeable, there is a real risk that comparative advantage comes to be defined as whose work force will work for the lowest wage.

In such a world, it is possible for industries to grow nominally more productive while the national economy grows poorer. How can that be? The factor left out of the simple Ricardo equation is idle capacity. If America's autos (or steel tubes, or machine tools) are manufactured more productively than a decade ago but less productively than in Japan (or Korea, or Brazil), and if we practice what we preach about open trade, then an immense share of U.S. purchasing power will go to provide jobs overseas. A growing segment of our productive resources will lie idle. American manufacturers, detecting soft markets and falling profits, will decline to invest. Steelmakers will buy oil companies. Consumer access to superior foreign products will not necessarily compensate for the decline in real income and the idle resources. Nor is there any guarantee that the new industrial countries will use their burgeoning income from American sales to buy American capital equipment (or computers, or even coal), for they are all striving to develop their own advanced, diversified economies.

Against this background of tidal change in the global economy, the conventional reverence for "free trade" is just not helpful. As an economic paradigm, it denies us a realistic appraisal of second bests. As a political principle, it leads liberals into a disastrous logic in which the main obstacle to a strong American economy is decent living standards for the American work force. Worst of all, a simple-minded devotion to textbook free trade in a world of mercantilism assures that the form of protection we inevitably get will be purely defensive, and will not lead to constructive change in the protected industry.

The seductive fallacy that pervades the hand-wringing about protectionism is the premise that free trade is the norm and that successful foreign exporters must be playing by the rules. Even so canny a critic of political economy as Michael Kinsley wrote in these pages that "Very few American workers have lost their jobs because of unfair foreign trade practices, and it is demagogic for Mondale and company to suggest otherwise." But what is an unfair trade practice? The Common Market just filed a complaint alleging that the entire Japanese industrial system is one great unfair trade practice!

To the extent that the rules of liberal trade are codified, they repose in the General Agreement on Tariffs and Trade (stay awake, this will be brief). The GATT is one of those multilateral institutions created in the American image just after World War II, a splendid historical moment when we could commend free trade to our allies the way the biggest kid on the block calls for a fair fight.

The basic GATT treaty, ratified in 1947, requires that all member nations get the same tariff treatment (the "most favored nation" doctrine), and that tariffs, in theory at least, are the only permissible form of barrier. Governments are supposed to treat foreign goods exactly the same as domestic ones: no subsidies, tax preferences, cheap loans to home industries, no quotas, preferential procurement, or inspection gimmicks to exclude foreign ones. Nor can producers sell below cost (dumping) in foreign markets. . . .

In classical free trade theory, the only permissible candidate for temporary protection is the "infant industry." But Japan and its imitators, not unreasonably, treat every emerging technology as an infant industry. Japan uses a highly sheltered domestic market as a laboratory, and as a shield behind which to launch one export winner after another. Seemingly, Japan should be paying a heavy price for its protectionism as its industry stagnates. Poor Japan! This is not the place for a detailed recapitulation of Japan, Inc., but keep in mind some essentials.

The Japanese government, in close collaboration with industry, targets sectors for development. It doesn't try to pick winners blindfolded; it creates them. It offers special equity loans, which need be repaid only if the venture turns a profit. It lends public capital through the Japan Development Bank, which signals private bankers to let funds flow. Where our government offers tax deductions to all businesses as an entitlement, Japan taxes ordinary business profits at stiff rates and saves its tax subsidies for targeted ventures. The government sometimes buys back outdated capital equipment to create markets for newer capital.

The famed Ministry of International Trade and Industry has pursued this essential strategy for better than twenty years, keeping foreign borrowers out of cheap Japanese capital markets, letting in foreign investors only on very restricted terms, moving Japan up the product ladder from cheap labor intensive goods in the 1950s to autos and steel in the 1960s, consumer electronics in the early 1970s, and computers, semiconductors, optical fibers, and just about everything else by 1980. The Japanese government also waives antimonopoly laws for development cartels, and organizes recession cartels when overcapacity is a problem. And far from defying the discipline of the market, MITI encourages fierce domestic competition before winnowing the field down to a few export champions. . . .

The Japanese not only sin against the rules of market economics. They convert sin into productive virtue. By our own highest standards, they must be doing something right. The evident success of the Japanese model and the worldwide rush to emulate it create both a diplomatic crisis for American trade negotiators and a deeper ideological crisis for the free trade regime. As Berkeley professors John Zysman and Steven Cohen observed in a careful study for the Congressional Joint Economic Committee last December, America, as the main defender of the GATT philosophy, now faces an acute policy dilemma: "how to sustain the open trade system and promote the competitive position of American industry" at the same time.

Unfortunately, the dilemma is compounded by our ideological blinders. Americans believe so fervently in free markets, especially in trade, that we shun interventionist measures until an industry is in deep trouble. Then we build it half a bridge.

There is no better example of the lethal combination of protectionism plus market-capitalism-as-usual than the steel industry. Steel has enjoyed some import limitation since the late 1950s, initially through informal quotas. The industry is oligopolistic; it was very slow to modernize. By the mid-1970s, world demand for steel was leveling off just as aggressive new producers such as Japan, Korea, and Brazil were flooding world markets with cheap, state-of-the-art steel.

As the Carter Administration took office, the American steel industry was pursuing antidumping suits against foreign producers—an avenue that creates problems for American diplomacy. The new Administration had a better idea, more consistent with open markets and neighborly economic relations. It devised a "trigger price mechanism," a kind of floor price for foreign steel entering American markets. This was supposed to limit import penetration. The steelmakers withdrew their suits. Imports continued to increase.

So the Carter Administration moved with characteristic caution toward a minimalist industrial policy. Officials invented a kind of near-beer called the Steel Tripartite. Together, industry, labor, and government would devise a strategy for a competitive American steel industry. The eventual steel policy accepted the industry's own agenda: more protection, a softening of pollution control requirements, wage restraint, new tax incentives, and a gentlemen's agreement to phase out excess capacity. What the policy did not include was either an enforceable commitment or adequate capital to modernize the industry. By market standards, massive retooling was not a rational course, because the return on steel investment was well below prevailing yields on other investments. Moreover, government officials had neither the ideological mandate nor adequate information to tell the steel industry how to invest. "We would sit around and talk about rods versus plate versus specialty steel, and none of us in government had any knowledge of how the steel industry actually operates," confesses C. Fred Bergsten, who served as Treasury's top trade official under Carter. "There has never been a government study of what size and shape steel industry the country needs. If we're going to go down this road, we should do it right, rather than simply preserving the status quo." . . .

The argument that we should let "the market" ease us out of old-fashioned heavy industry in which newly industrialized countries have a comparative advantage quickly melts away once you realize that precisely the same non-market pressures are squeezing us out of the highest-tech industries as well. And the argument that blames the problem on overpaid American labor collapses when one understands that semiskilled labor overseas in several Asian nations is producing advanced products for the U.S. market at less than a dollar an hour. Who really thinks that we should lower American wages to that level in order to compete?

In theory, other nations' willingness to exploit their work forces in order to provide Americans with good, cheap products offers a deal we shouldn't refuse. But the fallacy in that logic is to measure the costs and benefits of a trade transaction only in terms of that transaction itself. Classical free-trade theory assumes full employment. When foreign, state-led competition drives us out of industry after industry, the costs to the economy as a whole can easily outweigh the bene-

fits. As Wolfgang Hager, a consultant to the Common Market, has written, "The cheap [imported] shirt is paid for several times: once at the counter, then again in unemployment benefits. Secondary losses involve input industries . . . machinery, fibers, chemicals for dyeing and finishing products."

As it happens, Hager's metaphor, the textile industry, is a fairly successful example of managed trade, which combines a dose of protection with a dose of modernization. Essentially, textiles have been removed from the free-trade regime by an international market-sharing agreement. In the late 1950s, the American textile industry began suffering insurmountable competition from cheap imports. The United States first imposed quotas on imports of cotton fibers, then on synthetics, and eventually on most textiles and apparel as well. A so-called Multi-Fiber Arrangement eventually was negotiated with other nations, which shelters the textile industries of Europe and the United States from wholesale import penetration. Under M.F.A., import growth in textiles was limited to an average of 6 percent per year.

The consequences of this, in theory, should have been stagnation. But the result has been exactly the opposite. The degree of protection, and a climate of cooperation with the two major labor unions, encouraged the American textile industry to invest heavily in modernization. During the 1960s and 1970s, the average annual productivity growth in textiles has been about twice the U.S. industrial average, second only to electronics. According to a study done for the Common Market, productivity in the most efficient American weaving operations is 130,000 stitches per worker per hour—twice as high as France and three times as high as Britain. Textiles, surprisingly enough, have remained an export winner for the United States, with net exports regularly exceeding imports. (In 1982, a depressed year that saw renewed competition from China, Hong Kong, Korea, and Taiwan, exports just about equaled imports.)

But surely the American consumer pays the bill when the domestic market is sheltered from open foreign competition. Wrong again. Textile prices have risen at only about half the average rate of the producer price index, both before and after the introduction of the Multi-Fiber Arrangement.

Now, it is possible to perform some algebraic manipulations and show how much lower textile prices would have been without any protection. One such computation places the cost of each protected textile job at several hundred thousand dollars. But these static calculations are essentially useless as practical policy guides, for they leave out the value over time of maintaining a textile industry in the United States. The benefits include not only jobs, but contributions to G.N.P., to the balance of payments, and the fact that investing in this generation's technology is the ticket of admission to the next.

Why didn't the textile industry stagnate? Why didn't protectionism lead to higher prices? Largely because the textile industry is quite competitive domestically. The top five manufacturers have less than 20 percent of the market. The industry still operates under a 1968 Federal Trade Commission consent order prohibiting any company with sales of more than $100 million from acquiring one with sales exceeding $10 million. If an industry competes vigorously domestically, it can innovate and keep prices low, despite being sheltered from ultra-low-wage foreign competition—or rather, thanks to the shelter. In fact, students of the nature of modern managed capitalism should hardly be surprised that market stability and new investment go hand in hand.

The textile case also suggests that the sunrise industry/sunset industry distinction is so much nonsense. Most of America's major industries can be winners *or* losers, depending on whether they get sufficient capital investment. And it turns out that many U.S. industries such as textiles and shoes, which conventionally seem destined for lower-wage countries, can survive and modernize given a reasonable degree of, well, protection.

What, then, is to be done? First, we should acknowledge the realities of international trade. Our competitors, increasingly, are not free marketeers in our own mold. It is absurd to let foreign mercantilist enterprise overrun U.S. industry in the name of free trade. The alternative is not jingoist protectionism. It is managed trade, on the model of the Multi-Fiber Arrangement. If domestic industries are assured some limits to import growth, then it becomes rational for them to keep retooling and modernizing.

It is not necessary to protect every industry, nor do we want an American MITI. But surely it is reasonable to fashion plans for particular key sectors like steel, autos, machine tools, and semiconductors. The idea is not to close U.S. markets, but to limit the rate of import growth in key industries. In exchange, the domestic industry must invest heavily in modernization. And as part of the bargain, workers deserve a degree of job security and job retraining opportunities.

Far from being just another euphemism for beggar-thy-neighbor, a more stable trade system generally can be in the interest of producing countries. Universal excess capacity does no country much of a favor. When rapid penetration of the U.S. color TV market by Korean suppliers became intolerable, we slammed shut an open door. Overnight, Korean color TV production shrank to 20 percent of capacity. Predictable, if more gradual, growth in sales would have been preferable for us and for the Koreans.

Second, we should understand the interrelationship of managed trade, industrial policies, and economic recovery. Without a degree of industrial planning, limiting imports leads indeed to stagnation. Without restored world economic growth, managed trade becomes a nasty battle over shares of a shrinking pie, instead of allocation of a growing one. And without some limitation on imports, the Keynesian pump leaks. One reason big deficits fail to ignite recoveries is that so much of the growth in demand goes to purchase imported goods.

Third, we should train more economists to study industries in the particular. Most economists dwell in the best of all possible worlds, where markets equilibrate, firms optimize, the idle resources re-employ themselves. "Microeconomics" is seldom the study of actual industries; it is most often a branch of arcane mathematics. The issue of *whether* governments can sometimes improve on markets is not a fit subject for empirical inquiry, for the paradigm begins with the assumption that they cannot. The highly practical question of *when* a little protection is justified is ruled out *ex ante*, since neoclassical economics assumes that less protection is always better than more.

Because applied industrial economics is not a mainstream concern of the economics profession, the people who study it tend to come from the fields of management, industrial and labor relations, planning, and law. They are not invited to professional gatherings of economists, who thus continue to avoid the most pressing practical questions. One economist whom I otherwise admire told me he found it "seedy" that high-wage autoworkers would ask consumers to subsidize their pay. Surely it is seedier for an $800-a-week tenured economist to lecture a $400-a-week autoworker on job security; if the Japanese have a genuine comparative advantage in anything, it is in applied economics.

Fourth, we should stop viewing high wages as a liability. After World War II, Western Europe and North America evolved a social contract unique in the history of industrial capitalism. Unionism was encouraged, workers got a fair share in the fruits of production, and a measure of job security. The transformation of a crude industrial production machine into something approximating social citizenship is an immense achievement, not to be sacrificed lightly on the altar of "free trade." It took one depression to show that wage cuts are no route to recovery. Will it take another to show they are a poor formula for competitiveness? Well-paid workers, after all, are consumers.

NO

Michael Kinsley

KEEP TRADE FREE

Free trade is not a religion—it has no spiritual value—and Bob Kuttner is right to insist, as he did in TNR two weeks ago, that if it is no longer good for America in practical terms, it is not a sensible policy for liberals anymore. He and I would also agree that a liberal trade policy ought to be good for working people in particular (including people who would like to be working but aren't). The question is whether free trade is just a relic from two happier eras—the period of liberal clarity two centuries ago when Adam Smith and David Ricardo devised the theories of free enterprise and free trade, and the period of American hegemony after World War II when we could dominate world markets—or whether it is still a key to prosperity.

Kuttner argues that Ricardo's theory of "comparative advantage"—that all nations are better off if each produces and exports what it can make most efficiently—no longer applies. Local factors such as climate and natural resources don't matter much anymore. As a result, "most basic products . . . can be manufactured almost anywhere" with equal efficiency. This means, Kuttner says, that the only ways one nation (e.g., Japan) gains comparative advantage over another (e.g., us) these days are through low wages or "government action." Either of these, he says, makes nonsense of Ricardo's theory. In addition, Kuttner says, Ricardo didn't account for the problem of "idle capacity"—expensive factories sitting unused.

"Idle capacity" is an argument against any competition at all, not just from abroad, and has a long history of being carted out whenever established companies (the airlines, for example) want the government to prevent newcomers from horning in on their turf. If you believe in capitalism at all, you have to believe that the temporary waste of capital that can result from the turmoil of competition is more than outweighed by the efficiency of competition in keeping all the competitors on their toes. A capitalist who builds a plant knowing (or even not knowing) that it is less efficient than a rival abroad deserves whatever he gets. As for older plants that are already built—that capital is sunk. If the cost of running those plants is higher than the cost of buying the same output from abroad, keeping them running is more wasteful than letting them sit idle.

This brings us to the real problem; not sunk capital but sunk lives. The middle-class living standard achieved by much of the United States working class is one of the glories of American civilization. Yet Kuttner says, "semi-skilled labor overseas is producing advanced products for the U.S. market at less than a dollar an hour. Who really thinks that we should lower American wages to that level in order to compete?"

We shouldn't, of course. But importing the products of cheap foreign labor cannot lower American living standards as a whole, and trade barriers cannot raise living standards. This is not a matter of morality: it is a matter of mathematics. If widgets can be imported from Asia for a price reflecting labor costs of $1 an hour, then an hour spent making widgets adds a dollar of value to the economy. This is true no matter what American widget makers are being paid. If foreign widgets are excluded in order to protect the jobs of American widget makers getting $10 an hour, $1 of that $10 reflects their contribution to the economy and $9 is coming out of the pockets of other workers who have to pay more for widgets. Nice for widget makers, but perfectly futile from the perspective of net social welfare.

After all, if this economic alchemy really worked, we could shut our borders to all imports, pay one another $1,000 an hour, and we'd all be rich. It doesn't work that way. In fact, as a society, we're clearly better off taking advantage of the $1 widgets. The "comparative advantage" of cheap Asian labor is an advantage to *us* too. That's why trade is good.

But what about the poor widget makers? And what about the social cost of unemployment? If former widget makers aren't working at all, they aren't even adding a dollar's worth to the economy. Protec-

tionism is, in effect, a "make work" jobs program—but a ridiculously expensive one, both directly and indirectly. The direct cost, in this example, is $9 an hour. The indirect cost is in reducing the efficiency of the economy by preventing international specialization.

If the disparity between American and foreign wages is really that great, Americans just shouldn't be making widgets. We could pay widget workers at $8 an hour to do nothing, and still be better off. We could put them to work at their current wage doing anything worth more than a dollar an hour. We could spend the equivalent of $9 an hour on retraining. And we owe it to widget workers to try all these things if necessary, because they are the victims of a change that has benefited all the rest of us by bringing us cheaper widgets (and because, as Lester Thurow points out, doing these things will discourage them from blocking the needed change). To protect them while they keep on making widgets, though, is insane.

These suggestions are, of course, overt tax-and-spend government programs, compared to the covert tax-and-spend program of protectionism. In a period of political reaction, the covert approach is tempting. But hypocrisy is not a sensible long-term strategy for liberals, nor is willfully ignoring the importance of economic productivity.

In many basic industries, American wages are not all that far out of line, as Bob Kuttner seems to acknowledge in the case of autos. Modest wage adjustments can save these jobs and these industries for America. It is uncomfortable for a well-paid journalist to be urging pay cuts for blue-collar workers. On the other hand, steelworkers (when they are working) make more than the median

American income. Protectionism to preserve wage levels is just a redistribution
of national wealth; it creates no new
wealth. Nothing is wrong with redistribution, but in any radical socialist
redistribution of wealth, the pay of steelworkers would go down, not up. So it's
hard to see why the government should
intervene to protect steelworkers' wages
at the expense of general national prosperity. This is especially true when millions are unemployed who would happily
work for much less, and there is no jobs
program for them.

But Bob Kuttner believes that protection can be good for general national
prosperity even apart from the wage
question, in an age when other nations'
"comparative advantage" comes from
government policies that include protectionism. It is important to separate different strands in the common protectionist
argument that we have to do it because
Japan does it. Many politicians of various
stripes, and William Safire in a recent
column, argue (on an implicit analogy
between trade war and real war) that
only by threatening or building trade
barriers of our own can we persuade the
Japanese to dismantle theirs and restore
free trade. Kuttner, by contrast, thinks
that the idea of free trade is outmoded;
that the Japanese are *smart* to restrict
imports and we would be smart to do the
same as part of an "industrial policy."

Both Safire and Kuttner assume incor-
rectly that free trade needs to be mutual.
In fact, the theory of free trade is that
nations benefit from their own open borders as well as the other guy's. This may
be right or wrong, but the mere fact that
Japan is protectionist does not settle the
question of what our policy should be.

Certainly, it's worth looking at Japan
for clues about how to succeed in the

world economy, and certainly one key to
Japan's success seems to be a govern-
ment-coordinated industrial policy. (The
current vogue for "industrial policy" is
assessed by my colleague Robert Kaus in
the February *Harper's*—forgive the plug.)
But why must such a policy include trade
barriers? One reason Japan thwarts imports is a conscious decision to reduce
workers' living standards in order to
concentrate national resources on industrial investment. I presume this isn't
what Kuttner and other liberal trade revi-
sionists have in mind. Kuttner and others
include protectionism in their "industrial
policy" for two other reasons. First, as a
sort of bribe to get unions to go along
with sterner measures—possibly necessary, but not a case for protection on its
own merits. Second, to give promising
industries a captive market in which to
incubate and gather strength before taking on the world.

The trouble with this "nurture" argument is that there's no end to it. Kuttner
himself says that it's "not unreasonable"
to "treat every emerging technology"
this way, and also says that "most of
America's major industries can be winners" with the right treatment. After you
add the few hopeless loser industries
where we must allegedly create barriers
to save American wages, you've got the
whole economy locked up, and whether
this will actually encourage efficiency or
the opposite is, at the very least, an open
question. And if every major country
protects every major industry, there will
be no world market for any of them to
conquer.

Kuttner's model for "managed trade"
is the Multi-Fiber Arrangement, an international agreement that restricts imports
of textiles. This, according to Kuttner,
permitted the American textile industry

to modernize and become productive, to the point where exports exceeded imports—a less impressive accomplishment if you recall that the M.F.A. *restricts* imports.

Kuttner concedes that, despite the productivity gains, textile prices are higher than they would be without protection from cheap foreign labor. (Indeed, the current situation in the textile industry, as Bob Kuttner describes it, seems to vindicate Luddites, who got their start in textiles; human beings could do the work more efficiently, but machines are doing it anyway.) So what's the point? According to Kuttner, "The benefits include not only jobs, but contributions to G.N.P., to the balance of payments, and the fact that investing in this generation's technology is the ticket of admission to the next." Yet Kuttner does not challenge the "alegbraic manipulations" he cites that show how each job saved costs the nation "several hundred thousand dollars" in higher textile prices. The only "contribution to G.N.P." from willful inefficiency like this can be the false contribution of inflation. The balance of payments is a measure of economic health, not a cause of it; restricting imports to reduce that deficit is like sticking the thermometer in ice water to bring down a feverish temperature. As for the suggestion that the *next* generation of technology will bring the *real* payoff—well, they were probably promising the same thing two decades ago when the Multi-Fiber Arrangement began.

Kuttner also worries that "without some limitation on imports," Keynesian fiscal policies don't work. This is like the monetarists who worry that financial advances such as money market funds will weaken the connection between inflation and the money supply. Unable to make their theory accord with life, they want the government to make life accord with their theory. There *is* a world economy—which Bob Kuttner seems to recognize as a good thing—and this means Keynesian techniques will increasingly have to be applied internationally. . . .

There can be no pretense that domestic content legislation has anything to do with "industrial policy"—improving the competitive ability of American industry. It is protectionism, pure and unadorned, and each job "saved" will cost other American workers far more than it will bring the lucky beneficiary. Like most protectionist measures, far from aiding America's adjustment to world competition, it just helps put off the day of reckoning.

POSTSCRIPT

Should the United States Protect Domestic Industries from Foreign Competition?

Kuttner argues two basic points in his essay. First, he contends that the world that English economist David Ricardo modeled in 1817 is starkly different than the world we know today. He describes our world as "a world of learning curves, economies of scale, and of floating exchange rates." It is a world where comparative advantage "is created not by markets but by government action." Second, he maintains that although free markets will lead to factor price equalization—that is, wage rates in developing countries will rise and U.S. wage rates will fall as long as there is a differential—we should not, and cannot, allow this to happen. He asks us: Do we want wage levels in the United States to fall to a dollar an hour? Should we allow some nations to exploit their workforce so that we Americans can consume cheap goods and services?

Kinsley does not believe that free trade is a "relic" from the past. He maintains that Kuttner has just forgotten the lessons from his introductory economics course. After looking at the simple mathematics of Kuttner's proposal, Kinsley contends: "Protectionism is, in effect, a 'make work' jobs program . . . a ridiculously expensive one, both directly and indirectly." He believes we can achieve the same end without sacrificing the benefits of "international specialization." Kinsley goes on to argue that when "every major country protects every major industry"—the natural consequences of Kuttner's national industrial policy—"there will be no world market for any of them to conquer." He contends that we will return to the isolationists' world, a world that is poorer than it need be.

As in the case of the Kuttner essay, the plea for protection is often coupled with a plea for an "industrial policy." Robert Reich of the Kennedy School at Harvard clearly articulates this view in a two-part article that appeared in *The Atlantic Monthly* in March and April of 1983, and in his book entitled *The Next American Frontier* (Times Books, 1983). The conservative response is equally well articulated. See, for example, Walter Olson, "Don't Slam the Door," *The National Review* (March 4, 1983); John Hein, "A New Protectionism Rises," *Across the Board* (April 1983); and, Richard W. Wilcke, "The Protection Racket," *Inquiry* (April 1983).

ISSUE 17

Can the Third World Pay Its Debt Without U.S. Help?

YES: Peter Bauer, from "Ethics and Etiquette of Third World Debt," *Ethics and International Affairs* (1987).
NO: Bruce Stokes, from "A Long, Uphill Climb," *National Journal* (April 15, 1989)

ISSUE SUMMARY

YES: Economics professor Bauer insists that, unless they are pressed, Third World countries will not pay the debt that they have a moral obligation and a fiscal capacity to pay.
NO: Bruce Stokes, a journalist who specializes in international trade issues, replies that, even with generous concessions, the economic well-being of Third World countries is so fragile that any one of many negative events will result in massive defaults.

It is interesting to trace historically the development of the crisis posed by the debt owed by Third World countries. It began innocently enough in the 1960s. As in all free-market transactions, both sides of the market—the suppliers or lenders and the demanders or borrowers—willingly entered into the financial contracts that form the basis of this crisis. The Third World countries were in desperate need of foreign funds to underwrite capital investments to sustain the level of economic growth they had experienced in the post–World War II period. The banks, on the other hand, stood ready to supply these funds.

The system worked reasonably well. The funds that were borrowed were used to build new plants and to purchase new equipment. Investment in primary industries, such as steel and oil, leaped forward. Industrial output increased; Gross Domestic Product (GDP), which is comparable to the U.S. Gross National Product (GNP), tripled from 1960 to 1980; and the sale of exports provided enough foreign currency to pay the interest on their foreign debt. Both the borrowers and the leaders were pleased with the system.

The energy shock of 1973-1974 served to accelerate the borrowing process. Both the number of loans and the size of the loans made to the governments and corporations of Third World countries increased markedly. The international banking community had excess dollars to lend. It must be remembered that as oil prices skyrocketed upwards from $2 a barrel to $20, $30 and $40 a barrel, the oil producing countries could not spend their export earnings fast enough; therefore, many of the dollars we spent on oil produced by the Organization of Petroleum Exporting Countries (OPEC) were ultimately deposited in the large international banks. On the other hand, corporations and the governments of Third World countries were in serious need of loans. In many cases these countries were affected more directly and more severely than developed countries. They not only had to pay higher prices for the energy they imported, but they also were faced with escalating fertilizer prices, since most fertilizers are petrochemicals. However, even in the face of the 1973–1974 energy shock and the second round of energy price increases in 1978, the system continued to work.

But note, to keep the system viable, the debtor nations had to increase their exports so that they could earn the dollars that were needed to service their ever-expanding debt obligations. When North America and Western Europe sank deeper and deeper into recession in the late 1970s and early 1980s, the demand for the exports produced by Third World countries began to fall dramatically. This reduction in spending was coupled with a growing protectionist mood. As a result of these two forces, total world trade began to decline for the first time in 30 years. Remember now, that the Third World was using its earnings to pay the international banks. Without exports there were no earnings and no way to pay even the interest on their debt.

Unfortunately, this is not the end of this tale of woe. At the very time that their export earnings were falling, the United States and the rest of the developed world began to raise their interest rates. In 1979, the prime rate was about 11 percent, by 1981 it had jumped to more than 20 percent. Since the interest rate Third World debtors were obligated to pay was linked to the prime rate, their interest costs nearly doubled overnight. This happened just as their ability to pay their debt obligations fell because of falling export earnings. The net result was that many, if not all, debtor nations were unable to pay their debt obligations. The debtor nations turned to the International Monetary Fund (IMF) and the international banking community. They asked the banks to "reschedule" their loans—spread the loans out over a longer repayment period—and to loan them new money to pay for the interest owed on their old debts. The banks had no choice. They postponed the repayment of the debt by making only the interest due and then loaned the debtor nations the money to pay that interest.

No one denies that this slight-of-hand works in the short turn. But no one believes this ruse can be continued indefinitely. The question for us is: Have export earnings risen sharply enough and interest rates fallen far enough to make it economically and politically possible for Third World countries to repay their international debt? Professor Bauer has no reservations about the ability of the debtors to meet their international financial obligations. All that is needed is for pressure to be applied by the financial community. Bruce Stokes is far less optimistic. He argues that, even with generous concessions to Third World countries, the financial community will need a great deal of luck to avoid the pitfalls that lie before them.

YES

Peter Bauer

ETHICS AND ETIQUETTE
OF THIRD WORLD DEBT

Third World debt may seem a doubtfully appropriate subject for a publication given over to ethics and international affairs.[1] Does it not belong to the realm of finance and perhaps of power politics, rather than to that of morality or the comity of nations? In what follows I shall try to dispel such doubts. The background to Third World debt, the attitudes reflected in differing policy prescriptions and also encouraged by them, and the effects of different policies on millions of people all extend well beyond the world of finance. They raise issues well within the legitimate purview of those whose focus is on the ethical dimensions of international relations.

I shall argue that Third World debtors could readily meet their obligations but that they would be foolish to do so as long as they are not being pressed to honor their obligations. The realities are often ignored, possibly because this suits the purposes of the powerful political and commercial interests both in the West and in the Third World.

I

Third World debt under discussion is sovereign debt, owed or guaranteed by governments. Sovereign debt has two distinct characteristics. First, the debtors could always pay since governments can tax their citizens. They also normally have substantial marketable assets, and they can requisition the assets of their citizens. Second, sovereign debts cannot be enforced in the courts. Payment is therefore a matter of willingness of the debtor governments, which in turn depends on the political and economic consequences of their decision for themselves and their countries. Servicing sovereign debt implies political and economic costs. Governments will try to avoid these routes unless the consequences of default outweigh these costs. The most important adverse consequence would be the failure to secure further external finance, which could result in economic breakdown. Such an

From Peter Bauer, "Ethics and Etiquette of Third World Debt," *Ethics and International Affairs*, vol. 1 (1987). Copyright © 1987 by the Carnegie Council on Ethics and International Affairs. Reprinted by permission.

outcome is improbable in the contemporary climate, so the debtors are under no great pressure to pay.

The inflow of new funds to a number of debtor countries has already declined substantially. The debtors are paying more to the creditors than they are receiving as new money. This relationship is often described as a perverse resource transfer from the poor to the rich. Such statements ignore the initial supply of resources to the debtors. Is it perverse to service one's debts? The net transfer of funds from debtors to creditors reflects the reduction of the inflow of new money, largely as a result of the conduct of the debtors. This sequence encourages further and more open default because the debtors feel that they do not have so much to lose.

The statistics bandied about on Third World debt sound frightening: hundreds of billions of dollars, even a trillion. But without qualification, they are misleading. For instance, it is rarely made clear whether the figures are gross or net, that is, whether they allow for the financial assets of the debtors, let alone for other marketable assets. Again, it is often left unspecified what debts are being discussed. Some statistics refer to debt to the banks; others include debts to Western governments and international organizations. The latter include debts to the International Development Association (IDA). These are unindexed loans of fifty-year maturity with ten-year grace periods at zero interest. Although termed loans, they are effectively grants, yet they are included in Third World debt. (If official foreign aid is thought desirable, it should take the form of outright grants rather than grants disguised as loans.) Debts owed to Western governments are usually subsidized loans under foreign aid programs. They are often scaled down or written off by the creditor-donors.

II

If a debtor does not meet his contractual obligations, i.e., defaults and says he cannot pay, one normally asks about his assets. This question is rarely asked in polite international society. Even the large liquid assets of debtors are rarely brought into discussion. In many cases these assets run into billions of dollars. A year or two ago Petroleos de Venezuela, the Venezuelan state oil monopoly, was reported to have billions of dollars in U.S. financial instruments. The government of Peru, an intransigent debtor, has recently refused to pay a few million dollars of interest on its external debts. Its foreign reserves are about $1.2 billion.

Liquid reserves apart, the major debtors have large marketable assets. In calendar year 1983 Pemex, the state-owned Mexican oil monopoly, earned $5.3 billion. It is widely believed that if it were managed privately the earnings would have been much larger. But even at $5.3 billion the capital value of Pemex could then be conservatively valued at between $35 and $40 billion. The sovereign debt of Mexico was then around $80 billion. The sale or pledge of part of Pemex might well have averted the Mexican debt crisis, as it would have shown the readiness of the government to meet its obligations. Much the same applies to most of the other debtors.

It is often said that the sale or pledging of assets of the debtors would infringe national sovereignty. Why should the use of assets to honor obligations arising from the inflow of resources have this effect? In both World Wars the British government pledged some of its own securities and requisitioned those of its citizens for sale or pledging abroad without this being regarded as infringement of its sovereignty.

III

What has happened to the many billions borrowed by the Third World debtors? This question again is rarely asked in polite society. The Third World problem debtors have spent hugely on prestige projects, on unviable industrialization, on politically motivated subsidies, and on other purposes designed to keep the rulers in power. This does not invalidate the argument that the debtors could pay if they wanted to, but it is pertinent to the merits and prospects of proposals for helping the debtors.

In assessing the resources of Third World governments it is pertinent that these governments severely restrict the inflow of equity capital. Most, possibly all, debtor governments reserve for themselves or their nationals a large part or the whole of the equity in most economic activity outside the informal sector. For instance, in Brazil, Mexico, Ethiopia, Ghana, Nigeria, and Tanzania—all debtor nations—foreign participation is totally banned over most of the economy. These restrictions are maintained or even extended amidst rescheduling negotiations and the pleas of debtors about their inability to pay. The restrictions on the inflow of equity have promoted reliance on bank finance and official foreign aid. They also obstruct the inflow of enterprise, know-how, and skills which often accompany the inflow of equity.

As I have already said, the statistics of Third World debt in public discussion are often confusing rather than informative. However, World Bank statistics suggest strongly that as a percentage of GNP neither the total outstanding sovereign debt of the major borrowers nor the interest and principal payments are particularly high by historical standards. In 1983 the GNP of the major Third World debtors was more than three times their sovereign debt, without allowing for reserves. Interest on the debt was about 2.3 percent of GNP and total debt service about 3.9 percent. As a percentage of export earnings, interest payments were about 12.9 percent and total debt service about 22 percent. Most of these ratios are significantly lower than they were, say, for Canada and Argentina on the eve of World War I, when these countries were rated first-class debtors.[2] Statistics on the huge indebtedness of Third world countries are prominent in public discourse: $80 to $90 billion for Mexico, $95 billion for Brazil. The GNP of these countries is a multiple of these figures.

It is also pertinent that the real burden of Third World debt has been much diminished by the worldwide rise in prices since the loans were contracted. As I have already noted, much of Third World debt represents soft loans, or practically gifts, as in the case of IDA loans. Some soft loans have been written off, as were British loans to Africa in 1978.

The major debtor governments are those of middle-income countries. They often preside over some of the most prosperous Third World economies. According to World Bank statistics, the per capita income of Mexico in 1984 was over $2,000, that of Brazil over $1,700, and that of Venezuela over $3,400. In 1985, often cited as a critical year for Brazil, the largest Third World debtor, automobile sales there were about a million units, a near all-time record. In the same year both the earnings and the dividend of

Petrobras, the state-controlled oil monopoly, were also very high—almost certainly all-time highs—with the dividend raised greatly.

Default by governments of middle-income Third World countries is not novel. Since the 1950s there have been numerous instances of scaling down, postponement, and write-off of sovereign debt of middle-income countries, including Argentina, Brazil, Chile, Peru, and Turkey. These various statistics do not suggest that full servicing of debt would impose hardship on the peoples of the debtor countries.

Moreover, there are ways of finding resources for debt service without measures even remotely resembling policies of austerity. They include the sale or pledging of some state-owned or -controlled companies, often loss-making enterprises, in their entirety or in part; the lifting of restrictions on the inflow of equity capital; and the adoption of more market-oriented policies. Reduction of the more extravagant forms of public spending would also set free resources without hardship to ordinary people, least of all the poor. The cost of the construction of Abuja, the new capital of Nigeria being built from scratch, exceeds the total sovereign debt of that country. The same is almost certainly true for Brasília and for Dodoma in Tanzania. Under these various headings there is clearly ample scope for finding resources for debt service without imposing austerity measures.

Altogether, much simple and readily available information on the incomes and assets of debtor countries makes plain that the Third World debt problem or crisis is one of liquidity, not of solvency. The liquidity problem has arisen from the well-founded apprehension of lenders about the readiness of the debtors to honor their commitments, even if they could do so. Reluctance or refusal to honor obligations raises moral issues. The issue is obfuscated in current discourse, in which attempts to make debtors honor commitments, rather than the failure of debtors to do so, have come to be regarded as immoral.

IV

The debt-service ratio, that is, interest and amortization payments as a percentage of export earnings, is now the widely accepted and officially endorsed measure of the capacity of Third World governments to service their debts. This is not a sensible criterion for the simple reason that export earnings depend critically on the policies of debtor governments. Of course these policies also affect GNP and its growth, but not as immediately and decisively as they do export earnings. The dependence of these earnings and also of the current-account balance on government policies is at times recognized in the context of macroeconomic financial policies, including exchange-rate policies. But the relevance of government policies in this context extends far beyond macroeconomics.

Governments can, and at times do, restrict exports directly in order to increase domestic supplies and reduce the price of politically sensitive commodities. For instance, in recent years the Indian government periodically restricted the export of tea for this reason. Again, the state-monopoly buying agencies of debtor governments have for many years paid farmers far less than market prices both for products for the home market and for export crops. Such policies reduce output, depress export earnings, and often increase the need for imports. Such policies have been pursued in many Third World countries, notably in Africa. Other policies which depress export earnings in debtor less developed countries (LDCs) include suppression of trade, forced collectivization, establishment of state trading monopolies, maltreatment of productive groups, diversion of resources from export, and many others.

V

Have there not been adverse external changes which would warrant substantial concessions to the debtors and even enable transfers to them? Adverse terms of trade in the Third World, slow growth and import restrictions in the West, and high interest rates are usually instanced in this context. Until 1985 the appreciation of the dollar also figured prominently, but for obvious reasons this is no longer heard. It is occasionally replaced by its opposite, namely that LDC export earnings denominated in dollars have been reduced in real terms. Let me now consider some wider implications of this type of reasoning.

Adverse economic change, notably changes in prices, is a familiar hazard. It is obviously improvident to assume that a country will never encounter economic setbacks. A prudent government would plan accordingly and accumulate foreign-exchange reserves in good times to meet its commitments in bad times. Much current discussion suggests that Third World governments can be expected to behave like children with no thought for the morrow, or like some pop stars who promptly spend all they earn.

The possibility of setting aside reserves in prosperity is rarely mentioned in these discussions. The major debtors, including Mexico, Brazil, and Venezuela, among others, enjoyed sustained prosperity from 1945 through 1980. Why have they not set aside reserves for less favorable times? Contrast this with, say, Hong Kong and Taiwan, whose governments have managed their affairs more prudently and have honored their obligations, while at the same time, their people have enjoyed much-improved living standards.

Incidentally, while it is widely and often rightly assumed that Third World governments are improvident in their financial affairs and in particular take short views in their financial conduct, this is by no means true of their citizenry. For instance the readiness of people in Southeast Asia, Africa, and Latin America to take a long view is evident from the very large locally owned acreage under tree crops such as rubber and cocoa.

The specific assertions of the deterioration of external conditions are also insubstantial in their own right, so to speak. To take the terms of trade first, the Third World debtors are a highly diverse aggregate; the terms of trade of individual countries move quite differently and often in the opposite direction. Mexico, Venezuela, and Nigeria are large oil exporters, while Brazil is a large oil importer. A fall in oil prices damages the former and benefits the latter. By choosing particular years, commodities, and countries, it can always be suggested that the terms of trade of debtors have deteriorated. In the 1970s the *rise* in oil prices was used as an argument for more aid, more lending, and debt write-offs for LDCs; in the 1980s the *decline* in oil prices is used to support the same argument.

Since World War II the commodity terms of trade of most Third World countries, including the problem debtors, have been highly favorable by historical standards. They were especially favorable in the late 1970s and early 1980s, that is, just before the debt crisis. Changes in more relevant indicators have been even more favorable, that is, indicators that allow, for instance, for changes in the real cost of exports, the improvement in the range and quality of imports, and the huge expansion in the volume of trade.[3] And to repeat, governments can in any case anticipate fluctuations in the terms of trade by accumulating and drawing down foreign-exchange reserves.

Import restrictions in the West adversely affect many LDCs. But they are not significant in their effects on the debtor countries. This is evident from the massive and rapid progress of such Far Eastern economies as South Korea, Taiwan, and Hong Kong, which are affected by these restrictions far more than such debtors as Mexico, Venezuela, Brazil, and Nigeria. In the face of the slowdown in recent years, the West still offers huge markets for the Third World debtors. The exports and export earnings of the debtors are affected far more by domestic policies than by such external factors as import restrictions or changes in rates of growth in the West. This is evident from the comparative performance of different exporting countries. The Western economies and those of the major debtors grew extremely rapidly through most of the postwar period, but this did not bring about prudent management of resources and reserves by the debtors.

Interest rates have risen since the 1970s. But it is clearly imprudent to borrow for short terms or at floating rates without allowing for the possibility of higher interest rates. This is especially so at times when interest rates are very low, as they were in the 1970s.

VI

Before turning to policies, let me draw attention to three episodes which epitomize the anomalies of much current discussion of Third World debt. In the fall of 1972 Dr. Sumitro, then Indonesian minister of trade, complained in an interview with the *Financial Times* (London) that the full servicing of the external debt of his country would be so burdensome as to be immoral, an opinion quoted approvingly by the paper. By the spring of 1974, after the huge rise in oil prices in 1973, an article in the same paper argued that it would be foolish for Indonesia to use the oil windfall to repay debt because most of the debt had arisen from soft loans and Indonesia could make a profit by postponing repayment.[4]

Here is the second example. The debt crisis erupted with Mexico's default in August 1982. In the same months the World Bank published a volume entitled *IDA in Retrospect*.[5] I have already mentioned this World Bank agency, which provides very soft loans—grants, in reality—to Third World countries. The preface of that volume, signed by A. W. Clausen, then World Bank president, was dated July 1982. The document points with pride to the fact that in 1982 Mexico and Brazil contributed substantially to IDA. Thus the Mexican government supported IDA at the same time that it defaulted on its contractual agreements.

Third, towards the end of 1985, Argentina, Brazil, and Venezuela, three problem debtors, agreed to supply substantial aid to Bolivia under a U.N. program: $20 million, $15 million, and $35 million, respectively.

VII

It is not the case, however, that regardless of the shortcomings of currently canvassed arguments, there are compelling reasons for large concessions to the Third World debtors and for the transfer of additional funds to them? Four reasons are often heard in support of this position. First, to ask the debtors to pay in full would impose morally unacceptable hardship on their peoples; second, attempts to make them pay would result in political and social upheaval which would bring to the fore populist or communist governments damaging to the West; third, without major concessions and further transfers to the debtors, their plight would endanger the Western banking and financial system; and fourth, without such concessions and transfers the Third World would buy less from West which would put at risk exports and jobs. This type of reasoning means that the West has no choice and must support debtors regardless of their conduct. Let me examine this position.

As I have already argued, the debtors could readily service their obligations without hardship to their peoples, least of all hardship to the poorest. The major debtors are middle-income countries. They also enjoy considerable current prosperity as shown, for instance, by the level of the sales of durables such as automobiles in Brazil in 1985, which I have already instanced. And, as I have already argued, the debtors have a range of options to acquire additional resources for debt service without restricting domestic incomes or activity, as, for example, by admitting more foreign equity.

The emergence of populist, communist, or other governments hostile to the West does not depend on the level of income or its rate of change. This is evident from experience in the Far East, the Middle East, and Africa. Moreover, the notion that concessions and transfers to Third World debtors are necessary to avert political changes damaging to the West opens the door to indefinite blackmail by Third World governments abroad and by commercial banks at home because the argument could be used for transfers quite unrelated to debt service.

Some formulations of this argument are both insubstantial and distasteful. In 1983 the chairman of a large U.S. financial conglomerate said that unless smaller communities in the U.S. support the bailing out of Third World debtors by banks, they might see their young men conscripted as a result of the rise of populist governments in Latin America.

If the banks' solvency is threatened by the bad and doubtful Third World debts, how can they still declare large profits and pay substantial dividends? If their capital base were insufficient, should they not strengthen it by reducing their dividends and calling for more capital instead of lending more to Third World debtors, thus throwing good money after bad? And if it were thought necessary to rescue banks with taxpayers' money, should this not be done directly rather than by laundering the money through Third World governments which may not use the funds to service their debts and are indeed unlikely to do so?

Even acknowledged default by Third World debtors would not threaten the Western financial system. Western governments can ensure that bank losses should not endanger the depositors (as distinct from the stockholders or the management), let alone the financial system. The governments could insist that the banks build up their capital base by reducing dividends and seeking new capital. The governments could also purchase loans at market value and/or take over some of the banks and sell them as going concerns after writing down the balance sheets. The oft-heard references to the experience of the 1930s are misleading. There was then a collapse of the money stock, which governments could certainly avoid now.

Are transfers to debtor governments required to protect economic activity and jobs in the West? They are not. If more government spending prompted economic activity and employment, this could be achieved more effectively by more domestic spending. Exports bought with money provided by taxpayers are in effect given away. To argue that this benefits the West is like saying that a shopkeeper prospers by giving away goods.

VIII

. . . In recent months (August-October 1986) the rescheduling or rescue program for Mexico was intensively discussed. According to press reports its main outlines are already set. The package is said to involve substantial deferment of repayments and easing of the debt service; considerable additional lending by the World Bank, the IMF, and the commercial banks; and provision for further deferral and possible reduction of repayment if the price of oil falls below $9 a barrel, or if the country's growth rate declines below a reasonable rate defined, I believe, as three percent per annum. Such provisions imply that a government need not set aside reserves for adversity and that a country's fortunes are determined al-

most exclusively by external forces. Concessions to the government if the growth rate falls below a specified level are particularly anomalous. This result can always be brought about by manipulating government policies or by the judicious use of statistics.

Preferential treatment of defaulting debtors directly rewards imprudence and dishonesty. Debtors who do not pay are treated better than those who do. There is some analogy here with the operation of foreign aid. A low level of per capita income is the primary criterion in the allocation of major categories of official Western aid, that is, government-to-government wealth transfers. It is the primary criterion of IDA aid. To support the rulers on the basis of the poverty of their subjects rewards policies of impoverishment. Preferential treatment of defaulting governments rewards the incompetent and dishonest. By what ethical standard is such perverse activity to be justified?

IX

The process of Third World debt negotiations has become politicized. According to press reports in Britain, it is now the politicians rather than the bankers who are in charge. This situation creates domestic and international tensions which should be avoided. There could be various ways of moving toward a depoliticization or privatization of this process. The banks could sell off part of their loan portfolios at a discount. They may be able to negotiate with debtors for acquiring equity participation in local enterprises. Such measures, together with steps to increase their capital bases, would promote confidence in the banks. A bank may have to be liquidated in the course of this process, but this need not endanger the banking system, though, as previously noted, it may be painful to some stockholders and managements. Even if some government funds were injected into this process, which is almost certainly avoidable, this would still be cheaper than the supply of further funds to Third World debtors.

The dominant view of the debt problem reflects the activities and opinions of powerful interest groups. These interest groups include: major banks that wish to avoid or postpone overt losses on their portfolios and also wish to continue and extend their profitable activities with least risk; the World Bank and the IMF, which seek to expand their roles at a time when the grounds for their existence are increasingly questionable; Third World governments that understandably press for more resources to keep themselves in power, reinforce their grip over their subjects, and persist in their policies; and the aid lobbies who welcome the most widely canvassed proposals because these envisage further transfer of resources from the West to Third World governments, a result the lobbies welcome. Moreover, transfers to the major debtors set up potentialities for yet further transfers. This is so because help to governments of middle-income countries and to Western banks can be adduced readily in support of further aid to governments of poorer countries, especially in Africa and South Asia.

The likely outcome of current discussions and proposals is the continued rescheduling and scaling down of existing debts and the injection of further funds into the Third World, especially the Third World governments. This outcome will give succor to those who disregard their obligations; increase the moral hazard of lending to Third World governments; expand the role of the World Bank and the IMF; lead to a further waste of resources; and also reinforce the politicization of life in the Third World.

NOTES

1. This paper is a revised version of a lecture given at an Ethics and Foreign Policy Seminar at the Carnegie Council on Ethics and International Affairs, New York City, on October 17, 1986.

2. These figures are taken from "The International Debt Quagmire," in *Friedberg's* (April 20, 1986), a bulletin issued by C. C. Friedberg & Co., a Canadian firm of commodity brokers. This article presents a convenient summary of some World Bank statistics. There are also informative data on this subject in two articles by Professor Deepa Lal, in *The Times* (London) (May 8, 1983), and in the *Wall Street Journal* (April 27, 1983), respectively. Professor Lal argues convincingly that the indebtedness of the major Third World debtors is quite modest by historical standards.

3. In many LDCs, especially in Africa, the producers benefited little from these conditions because a large proportion of export proceeds were taxed away by the state export monopolies.

4. The first of these articles was entitled "Debt Obligations Could Hit Indonesia's Economic Hopes." It appeared in October or November 1972. I have a Xerox copy but I cannot date it precisely. There is no index of the *Financial Times* for that year, and its library could not provide me with the date. The second article, entitled "What to Do with a Windfall," appeared on March 14, 1974.

5. *IDA in Retrospect* (Washington: The World Bank, 1982).

NO

Bruce Stokes

A LONG, UPHILL CLIMB

PEOPLE IN DEBTOR COUNTRIES HAVE BEEN "DYING OF THIRST," SEN. PAUL S. Sarbanes, D-Md., said at a recent Senate hearing, describing the Third World debt problem and U.S. efforts to deal with it. "[Former Treasury Secretary] Donald Regan said to them: 'Don't be thirsty.' [Former Treasury Secretary James A. Baker III] put a glass in front of them. He thought he'd be able to get water into the glass, but it didn't work."

And now, Sarbanes said, the Bush Administration has "come with a glass and with a concept that will put some water in it. But the question is, how much water?"

Since March 10, when Treasury Secretary Nicholas F. Brady broke with past U.S. policy and unveiled the outlines of a new American plan to reduce the $529 billion debt owed by some of the world's poorest countries, debt relief, long a taboo in Washington, suddenly seems inevitable.

Members of Congress, commercial bankers, international monetary officials and journalists have been scrambling to fill in the details of Brady's scheme: Like Sarbanes, they want to know how much water will be in the new glass.

But this preoccupation with the specifics of the Brady plan is a dangerous diversion, some Third World experts say, because it is based on a false assumption that a modicum of debt relief is all that indebted nations need to jump-start their long-sputtering economies. "Easing the debt burden is necessary but not sufficient," warned an economist at the World Bank.

The nearly decade-long debt crisis has profoundly debilitated the societies of many developing countries. They have strayed from the industrialization path they were following in the 1960s and 1970s, and now they face a long journey back.

To re-ignite Third World economic growth and keep it going, development experts say, savings and investment must increase, exports must expand, inflation must be controlled and government deficits must be reduced.

Brady, in portions of his speech that were largely ignored by the news media, acknowledged the importance of such traditional development efforts to the success of his initiative. In fact, some observers say that the fate of the Brady plan will be determined not by the nature and scope of the debt relief it provides but by whether it successfully leverages other needed reforms.

That will not be easy. Baker tried to spur such reforms, but with only mixed success. These are long-standing, deeply rooted problems that are likely to remain even if debt problems are brought under control.

Development experts fear that industrial country governments and commercial banks, despite their best intentions, will end up using the Brady plan to rid themselves of the cloud of debt that has hung over the world economy—and that the creditors may then turn away from the Third World's other problems.

Recent events suggest that such a course could prove dangerous. The Brady plan has raised Third World expectations of a debt-free future. The February rioting in Venezuela, in which 300 people died while protesting debt-induced austerity measures, could be a harbinger. "Desperation mixed with expectation is a volatile brew," said William D. Rogers, a partner in the Washington law firm of Arnold & Porter and a former undersecretary of state for economic affairs. Rogers, who represents a number of Latin American governments, said at a Washington conference on Third World debt, "I cannot recall a more ominous time for the hemisphere since the onset of the debt crisis in 1982.'

Avoiding such trouble, development experts say, requires changing the focus of the current debate—from the details of debt relief to the broader goal of using debt reduction to improve the lot of debt-ridden countries. Then the question might be not how much water is in the glass, but how much water is needed to quench the thirst of the poor.

For all the hoopla it has engendered, Brady's initial proposal, made at the Washington conference on Third World debt, was strikingly bare-boned. "The creditor community—the commercial banks, international financial institutions, and creditor governments—should provide more effective and timely financial support [to debtors]," he said. He urged commercial banks to voluntarily forgive a portion of both the principal owed by Third World debtors and the interest charges they pay.

To make this possible, Brady proposed that banks waive clauses in their loan agreements that keep them from striking deals with individual debtors unless all creditors agree.

Brady also suggested that the International Monetary Fund (IMF) and the World Bank use a portion of their funds as collateral for debt-reduction and interest-reduction schemes. And he called on Japan and other wealthy nations to offer new loans to debtor countries.

Additional details have since emerged. The Treasury Department has acknowledged that Brady's proposal could cut debtor payments to banks by an average of about 20 per cent. And Treasury officials have suggested that some countries, such as Mexico, could realize far greater savings by giving their creditors equity interests in such things as hotels and industries in exchange for debt reductions. Overall, Treasury estimates that the plan should lead to a debt reduction of about $70 billion.

The department has let it be known that it expects both the World Bank and the IMF to put up about $4 billion a year each for the next three years to underwrite the plan. And Japan has announced its willingness to contribute $4.5 billion over the next few years to help with debt reduction.

Many of the plan's specifies are likely to be nailed down in negotiations between debtor countries and their creditors, and the particulars are likely to change from case to case. The first such exercise may come in creditors' talks with the Philippines, where Japan is eager to move rapidly. But the real test may come over the next few months in discussions with Mexico.

By June, the Mexican government expects its foreign currency reserves to be running dangerously low because of a slowdown in export growth. At the end of that month, some of the nation's foreign debt will come up for rescheduling. And Mexico's current wage and price freeze—which has helped to curb runaway inflation, keep interest rates and the peso relatively stable and maintain domestic tranquility—ends this summer.

The Brady plan has already won support, with only minimal dissent, from the finance ministers of the major industrial nations, who met in Washington early this month. By the July economic summit in Paris, most experts expect the Administration to have a debt reduction blueprint ready for approval by the leaders of the industrial world. And by the time of the IMF-World Bank annual meeting in Washington this fall, the plan may get its first report card.

But analysts agree that it will be years before it would be possible to assess the plan's impact on the broad problems facing indebted countries.

LOST DECADE

"The Baker approach bought time for the creditors," said Richard E. Feinberg,

vice president of the Overseas Development Council, a Washington think tank. "The Brady plan is attempting to buy time for the debtors" to retool the engines of economic growth in their countries.

That will be no simple task. And the obstacles that the debtors face could negate or largely offset many short-run economic benefits that they may realize as a result of the Brady initiative.

Debtor countries, spurred by the industrial world's commercial banks and by unforeseen global economic changes, dug their economies into a deep hole in the 1980s. In the 17 most-indebted countries, the per capita gross national product, a rough measure of personal well-being, which had been growing at 4 per cent per year from 1965–80, declined by an average annual rate of 1.3 per cent from 1980–87, according to World Bank figures. Today, in real, inflation-adjusted terms, the average person in a debtor country is about 7 per cent poorer than in 1980. . . .

But the true personal costs of the debt crisis are even greater when measured against the projected incomes that people would have attained if per capita economic growth had continued on the upward path established before 1980. Because of this "lost decade," said Stuart K. Tucker, a fellow at the Overseas Development Council, people in debtor countries "are really a third poorer than they would have been otherwise."

Climbing out of this hole will be difficult if not impossible. In calculations performed for *National Journal*, Tucker estimated that with 4 per cent average economic growth per capita, the debtor countries could get per capita incomes back to 1980 levels in about two years. This would be no mean feat, considering that 4 per cent per capita growth would require over-all economic growth of more than 6 per cent, because of current rates of population growth. (Japan's economy grew by an average annual rate of 5.2 per cent during the 1970s.)

The more daunting challenge, Tucker said, is to bring people's incomes up to where they would have been if their nations had kept growing, for only then will the debt crisis truly be behind them. But even with booming economic growth of 6 per cent per capita, it would take until the year 2007 for individuals in debtor countries to regain their lost incomes, according to Tucker's estimates. A more achievable 5 per cent growth per capita would delay the catchup point for two decades, until 2027. And at 4 per cent per capita growth, people will never catch up.

This dismaying prospect leads most economists to conclude that the incomes that the poor might have had are irrevocably lost. "That [pre-1980 growth] path was a temporary aberration," said William R. Cline, a senior fellow at the Institute for International Economics, a Washington think tank. "You have to get back where you were [in 1980] and grow" from that starting point.

Even that will be an uphill climb. The most recent IMF *World Economic Outlook* estimates that the economies of the 15 most heavily indebted countries grew by only 1.1 per cent in 1988 and will grow by no more than 4.2 per cent per year by the early 1990s. Yet, to ensure economic recovery, the indebted countries should grow by a minimum of 5 per cent per year, concludes *The Road to Economic Recovery* (Priority Press, 1989), written by a task force on international debt. The group was assembled by the Twentieth Century Fund, a New York City-based research foundation. . . .

GROWING OUT OF DEBT

Attaining the IMF forecasts or the more ambitious Twentieth Century Fund goal is a formidable challenge because of the number and complexity of economic factors that must mesh.

The first task, the Twentieth Century Fund says, should be to increase net capital inflow to debtor countries from 1.6 per cent of their aggregate domestic economies, the level in the mid-1980s, to 4 per cent, the level achieved from 1978–81.

This would require stemming the outflow of capital: Latin American debtor nations now pay $30 billion to their creditors each year. Under the Brady plan, that might be achieved by cutting a country's debt and the interest rates that it now pays and by increasing capital inflow with new loans, more foreign investment and larger trade surpluses.

Robert D. Hormats, vice chairman of Goldman Sachs International Corp., a New York City investment firm, said, "The question is, can you really get the magnitude of debt reduction [through the Brady plan] that will make a sizable impact?" Mexico, for example, seeks to reduce its debt by at least a third and by as much as a half, depending on how much additional money it can borrow. And most debt analysts agree that debt reductions of similar magnitudes are needed for Brazil and Argentina.

Experience to date underscores the difficulty of bringing down the Third World's debts. Buying back debt requires dollars, which are hard to come by for developing countries. And as buy-backs progress, the value of existing debt will rise, as prospects improve that countries can pay back existing loans, thus increasing the cost. This is where IMF and World Bank funds would come into play, but there are questions about whether they are sufficient. "By the time Mexico and Venezuela are taken care of, the pot will be exhausted," Cline said.

In 1987, Mexico tried exchanging debt for bonds guaranteed by U.S. Treasury bonds purchased with Mexican foreign reserves. But that deal did not include guaranteed interest payments, and so it had few takers. The Brady plan envisions IMF and World Bank guarantees of interest rate payments to make such deals more attractive. Because the potential costs of such guarantees would be quite high, the industrial nations' finance ministers withheld endorsement of that aspect of the U.S. proposal, raising doubts about its implementation.

Despite its recently announced $3.6 billion loan to Mexico, the IMF is likely to move slowly because of its avowed need for increases in contributions made by member nations. The World Bank is worried that if it overextends itself in heavily indebted nations, that would harm its work in other countries and would risk its blue-chip bond rating. And Congress is wary of using the international financial institutions in this way. "After the savings and loan crisis," a Senate staff aide said, "we are going to be extraordinarily reluctant to transfer risk from the private sector to the public sector."

Finally, debt-equity swapping, apparently a cornerstone of Brady's proposal, is in disrepute. Mexico has suspended most such undertakings because of their inflationary impact. And other Third World nations strenuously resist it.

As a result of such problems, voluntary debt reduction has sliced only 4 per cent off the debt of the 15 most heavily indebted countries since 1984, according to the IMF.

Capital flows from creditors to debtors must also be increased. New loans by commercial banks are problematic, however: Since September 1985, commercial banks have lent the 15 most-indebted countries only $20.3 billion while receiving more than $20 billion in interest in 1988 alone, according to Morgan Guaranty Trust Co. of New York City.

Administration officials argue that major U.S. banks have a long-term self-interest in operating in Brazil or Mexico and can be counted on to increase their lending. But that is not what the banks are saying. "Demand for bank financing exceeds the capacity and willingness of banks to supply it," a banking industry representative said. "Moreover, banks are seeking new lines of business" outside the Third World.

Whether banks will go along with debt reduction and new lending is an open question. If banks drag their feet on the Brady initiative, banking experts on Capital Hill talk of resurrecting an unenforced provision of the 1983 International Lending Supervision Act that requires banks to build up their reserves against Third World loans. And "the Administration has a lot of favors it can bestow if commercial banks cooperate," Feinberg of the Overseas Development Council said. But so far, the Treasury Department has shot down suggestions from Federal Deposit Insurance Corp. chairman L. William Seidman and others to use tax deductions or major regulatory reforms to prod banks to write off Third World debts.

Export earnings can supplement new lending, but it is tricky business. If a positive trade balance is achieved by maintaining an artificially low exchange rate, making imports expensive and exports cheap, an inflationary spiral becomes almost inevitable. If a trade surplus is built up by shrinking imports, as indebted countries did in the early 1980s, capital is generated to pay debts at the expense of imported industrial goods needed for economic growth. If a trade surplus is the result of increased exports (the most-indebted countries increased their exports 26 per cent from 1986–88, according to IMF estimates), Third world nations risk triggering protectionism in industrial nations. Trade liberalization by Western Europe, Japan and the United States in the current round of multi-lateral trade talks would help alleviate many debtors' export problems. But trade experts say it is highly doubtful that indebted nations will ever return to the halcyon 1970s, when the value of their exports was rising 17 per cent per year.

INCREASING INVESTMENT

Greater investment is also needed in debtor countries to prime the economic pump. The Twentieth Century Fund suggests an investment goal of 24 per cent of the gross domestic product (GDP), up from 19.4 per cent in 1987. Some of this money can come from abroad. The IMF estimates that there was $8 billion worth of direct foreign investment in the most-indebted countries in 1988, up from $3.1 billion in 1984. But this represents only about 1 per cent of their GDP. Debtor governments are trying to increase this proportion. Mexico is drafting more liberal foreign investment regulations. And Brazil more than doubled its foreign investment, from $0.9 billion in 1987 to $2.2 billion in 1988, according to the Central Bank of Brazil. Yet because much of this foreign investment growth was the result of discredited debt-equity swaps, the IMF estimates that direct investment will fall in 1989 to $6.1 billion.

If foreign deep pockets are not the answer, much of the needed investment would have to come from savings within the high-debt countries. The Twentieth Century Fund suggests a savings target of 20 per cent of GDP, roughly equivalent to the average from 1978–81.

The first task, economists say, is to stem capital flight and try to repatriate domestic savings that have already gone abroad. The prescription for recapturing that money is the same as the prescription for increasing domestic savings, development economists say—a slowing of inflation, a return to positive real interest rates and capital market reforms. But these remedies will take time.

Thus, "a large part of additional public savings will have to come about at the expense of government expenditures," World Bank economists Marcelo Selowsky and Herman G. van der Tak wrote in an article in *World Development* in September 1986, or by raising taxes, argues Rudiger Dornbusch, a debt expert at the Massachusetts Institute of Technology. "The budget is the key issue," Dornbusch said. "And solving the debt crisis is not going to solve the budget crisis," which Dornbusch and others think eats up too much domestic savings in indebted countries, crippling private investment.

To balance budgets, development experts recommend reductions in subsidies for public enterprises and regional governments, privatization of state enterprises, regulatory reform and tax reform. "You cannot tell the U.S. taxpayer to pay [for debt reduction] when the Argentine taxpayer won't," Dornbusch said.

OUT OF THEIR HANDS

How much of this is feasible remains to be seen. "The debtors are being asked to liberalize financial markets, remove barriers to inward investment, deregulate the economy," Jesus Silva Herzog, the former Mexican finance minister, recently told London's *Financial Times*. "This may be economically sound, but for the most part, it is politically impossible."

While debtor governments hold much of their fate in their own hands, the Brady proposal's Achilles' heel could turn out to be the economic variables over which indebted countries have no control.

"One of the biggest obstacles to [debtor] recovery is what is going on in the U.S. economy," said Pedro-Pablo Kuczynski, chairman of First Boston International and a former Peruvian minister of energy and mines. Financing the U.S. current-account and trade deficits keeps interest rates high, adding to the cost of capital for debtors and enticing capital flight from Latin America.

The threat of recession that hangs over the global economy could also wreak havoc with debt relief plans. The IMF estimates that a 1 percentage point slowdown in annual economic growth in industrial countries would hamper expansion in debtor nations by 0.5 per cent, as the industrial world slows its buying of Third World products. Put another way, "a slower one-half of 1 percentage point growth in industrial countries would wipe out the benefits of a 20 per cent cut in Mexican debt," Tucker of the Overseas Development Council pointed out.

Debtor economies are also vulnerable to swings in volatile commodity markets. The recent rise in the price of oil has helped oil-exporting indebted countries, such as Mexico and Venezuela, offset other economic problems. Still, oil prices are only about half what they were when the debt crisis started. Even that is a mixed blessing. Oil-importing debtors, such as Brazil, now face significantly larger energy bills.

Finally, interest rate trends could make or break the Brady plan because as much as 70 percent of Latin American debt is pegged to variable interest rates. Debtor nations generally pay commercial banks a rate that is 1 percentage point higher than the current London interbank offered rate (LIBOR).

Using the rule of thumb that a 1-point movement in LIBOR is equivalent to a 10 per cent change in debt, the Brady plan, with its general goal of a 20 per cent debt reduction, would simply "offset the effects of the interest-rate rise in the last few years," observed First Boston's Kuczynski, author of *Latin American Debt* (Johns Hopkins University, 1988). "So all we will have achieved after putting ourselves through this painful exercise is to be back where we were a year ago, and that wasn't such a great situation."

The IMF forecasts that LIBOR, which in early April was at 10.4 per cent, will fall to 9.2 per cent in 1990, which should ease the problem somewhat. And no analyst forsees a return to the extremely high rates of the early 1980s. Even so, Shafiqul Islam, a senior fellow at the Council on Foreign Relations in New York City, argues that debtors "should try to maximize their fixed-rate exposure" to hedge against interest-rate spikes, because "countries don't know how to manage interest-rate risks." But commercial banks, which must raise money amid the market's ups and downs, have resisted such suggestions in the past. And both Brazil and Mexico have rejected similar proposals because of the high upfront cost of converting debts from floating rates to fixed rates.

Debtor countries might buy interest-rate caps, which ensure borrowers that they will never pay more than a given amount. But caps command an expensive premium.

The IMF, at Baker's suggestion, created a Compensatory and Contingency Financing Facility in late 1988. Through this new entity, countries facing balance-of-payments shortfalls can, for a short period of time, draw on a line of credit based on their IMF capital subscription.

Critics question whether the facility is adequate for the interest-rate movements the world is now experiencing, however. They point out that no major debtor has ever tested the system. And the critics also note that the IMF program was never intended to be more than a stopgap measure.

NOT MUCH TIME

Despite all the problems involved in debt relief and the difficulties of restarting economic growth in indebted countries, most economists agree that the Brady plan is a breakthough. "The political logjam [around Third World debt] has been broken," a World Bank official said in a recent interview. "There is now a willingness of all the political actors to visualize a broad number of [debt relief] measures. All somebody has to do is bang heads together to make sure it happens."

But "we don't have much time," Hormats said. "We need to move quickly to preserve the momentum." Televised images of the Venezuelan riots are seared into policy makers' minds, and there is a clear consensus that there can be no turning back. "I don't think Secretary Baker will be able to have a positive, constructive U.S. foreign policy in some areas of the world if [that policy] doesn't have a debt dimension to it," Sarbanes said.

But Brady's proposal involves what may be a fatal contradiction. Debtors want immediate relief to stem the outflow of their capital and to satisfy public expectations. Development experts argue, however, that a phased reduction would be more likely to leverage the domestic economic reforms that are necessary to get economies growing again.

The task of reform is further complicated by the Latin American election calendar. Argentina chooses a new president in May. If the left-leaning candidate of the Peronist Justicialist Party, Carlos Saul Menem, wins, creditors worry that he will take a hard line against debt repayment. And whoever wins, the Argentine electoral college does not meet until September, promising an inconclusive summer. Brazil elects a president in November, effectively putting major debt negotiations with that government on hold until then, and congressional and state elections are scheduled in Brazil for the fall of 1990. . . .

These factors will only delay debtors' efforts to recapture the economic wellbeing they lost over the past decade. And development economists warn that if debtors are to have a chance of ever regaining a modicum of prosperity, they must be sure that the process of solving the debt crisis gets them firmly back on the economic development path.

"It was surely a lost decade," Kuczynski said of the 1980s. "But it may not have been [totally] lost if it convinces governments that there is a definite way to do things better."

POSTSCRIPT

Can the Third World Pay Its Debt
Without U.S. Help?

The crushing debt that is borne by the Third World can no longer be ignored. Each year it grows bigger and becomes more ominous. The problem is simply stated: Third World countries do not have enough export earnings to even pay the interest they owe on their debt, let alone pay the principal. Consequently, as the months and years pass, the back interest owed is added to their original debt obligation. These debtors fall further and further behind.

At some point they begin to believe that they are trapped by their debt. A greater and greater share of their export earnings must be diverted from economic development projects to pay the interest on this debt. That is, they cannot pay their debt without expanding their economies, but they cannot expand their economies if all their earnings go to paying their debt. Something has to give.

The presence of this growing debt is also ominous for the developed world. If these debts must be written off as uncollectable, this could cause ruinous damage to those commercial banks that have extended large loans to developing countries. Would U.S. taxpayers have to bail out those commercial banks, as happened with U.S. savings and loan institutions (see Issue 15)? Remember, we are not dealing with inconsequential sums. The amount owed U.S. banks is fast approaching $200 billion, and the amount owed Canadian banks is edging ever closer to $50 billion.

Because of the dire consequences that this debt poses for both developing and developed countries, we are obligated to learn more about this problem. One place to begin is to read Cheryl Payer's essay "Causes of the Debt Crisis." Her work appears in *The Imperiled Economy*, published by the Union for Radical Political Economics in 1987. Payer not only provides a radical reformist view of this problem, but she also traces the historical roots of this problem. More conventional views of the events leading up to the current crisis are found in Robert D. Sloan's "The Third World Debt Crisis," *The Washington Quarterly* (Winter 1986) and in John Williamson's, *Voluntary Approaches to Debt Relief*, a publication of the Institute for International Economics (1988). Finally, it might be interesting to review the annual reports of some large commercial banks. As these banks adjust to the changing reality of Third World debt, they must justify their corporate decisions to shareholders.

ISSUE 18

Can Strict Economic Sanctions Help End Apartheid in South Africa?

YES: Robert G. Mugabe, from "Struggle for Southern Africa," *Foreign Affairs* (Spring 1988)

NO: Helen Suzman, from "The Folly of Economic Sanctions," *Business and Society Review* (Spring 1986)

ISSUE SUMMARY

YES: The prime minister of Zimbabwe, Robert Mugabe, argues that economic sanctions will raise the "cost of maintaining apartheid" and, as a consequence, hasten the demise of this "obnoxious system."

NO: Helen Suzman, who was a long-time member of the Progressive Federal Party in the South African Parliament and a vocal critic of apartheid, warns that economic sanctions will ruin the South African ecomomy and destroy the "inheritance that blacks inevitably will one day share."

In a democratic country such as the United States, it is hard to imagine the reality of a constitutional government that explicitly excludes 73 percent of its population from its protections. Yet this is what exists in the Republic of South Africa. Daily we are reminded of the evils that are associated with South African apartheid, which include the enforcement of more than 300 racially motivated laws that systematically deny blacks the right to vote, to live where they choose, to seek employment where they want, to attend schools that are reserved for white children, and to live in decent housing.

Perhaps because of its economic success—its ability to raise living standards for all members of the South African population, its regional importance for the economies of its neighbors, and its significance as an export market for many countries in the developed world—the Western world has taken great care in responding to the obvious and intolerable practices of the South African government.

An activist economic strategy was not devised by U.S. opponents to apartheid until the late 1960s and early 1970s. In those years, church leaders joined college students and civil rights groups to pressure the banking community to withhold loans to the Republic of South Africa. These early tactics had relatively little effect on the loans made to South Africa, but they did prepare the way for the widespread use of stockholder resolutions that called for disinvestment in South African operations.

The prospect of the devastating economic impact of these resolutions if they became fully implemented have prompted a more moderate response from the business community. One hundred and twenty-seven of the 200 U.S. firms with operations in South Africa have endorsed a code of business conduct that is popularly known as the Sullivan Principles. (The Reverend Leon H. Sullivan is a black Philadelphian minister and a member of the General Motors Corporation's Board of Directors. In consultation with twelve other U.S. firms, he drafted these guidelines in 1977.) These principles required firms operating in South Africa to: (1) provide color-blind eating, comfort, and work facilities; (2) follow equal and fair employment practices for all; (3) provide equal pay to all employees doing equal or comparable work for the same time period; (4) initiate and develop training programs to prepare blacks, coloureds, and Asians (the official minority classes in South Africa) for management and skilled positions; (5) increase the number of blacks, coloureds, and Asians in management and supervisory positions; (6) improve the standard of living of employees, such as improving their housing, transportation, schooling, recreation, and health facilities; and (7) "support the ending of all apartheid laws." (This guideline was added in 1985.)

For ten years the Sullivan principles provided the middle ground between those who would disinvest and those who would not meddle in the affairs of this African state. However, after ten years the Reverend Sullivan withdrew his endorsement from the code of ethics that carries his name. In a June 3, 1987, news conference, he stated that although his principles have been "a tremendous force for change," in the end they have "failed to undermine apartheid." Thus he called on all United States firms to disinvest in South Africa by March 1988 and for the United States to initiate an economic embargo of that state.

The Bush administration has rejected a policy of divestment and/or embargoes that would force U.S. firms to end trade relationships with South Africa and force U.S. companies and individuals to withdraw billions of investment dollars from the South African economy. Instead, the United States has pursued a much less aggressive policy of "constructive engagement." This policy applies some economic pressure in the form of limited trade restrictions, which the Administration can threaten to increase if progress is not made in dismantling apratheid.

Can the United States continue to pursue this relatively passive policy in the 1990s? If South Africa's new president, F. W. deKlerk, does not change the present course of affairs, will political pressures force the United States to impose economic sanctions? Who will win and who will lose if harsh economic sanctions are imposed by the United States and other world powers? These questions are addressed in this issue. How the United States and the other world power brokers respond to the answers given to these questions will play a significant role in determining the economic and political viability of South Africa.

YES

Robert G. Mugabe

STRUGGLE FOR SOUTHERN AFRICA

As the prime minister of a young and developing nation, I observe with sadness that several developing countries are locked in devastating conflicts. . . .

One such area of conflict now is southern Africa. I use the example of my own region because it presents a clear illustration of wanton destruction of lives and property, and of the danger posed to international peace and security.

Zimbabwe and the United States have mutual interests in bringing an end to the problem of apartheid in South Africa. Time has indeed run out, and South Africa now poses a threat to international peace and security that has implications far beyond the borders of the southern African region.

The Republic of South Africa is in the middle of a vicious and ugly civil war. The root cause of this crisis is the obnoxious system of apartheid which the majority of black people of South Africa do not want, as well as their own desire for freedom and independence in the land of their birth.

In the run-up to the general elections of May 6, 1987, we heard a lot of rhetoric about reform of apartheid from the ruling National Party, led by President P. W. Botha.* But that was soon proven to mean only cosmetic changes affecting pass laws, freehold title, trade unionism and aspects of social segregation. [South African] president Botha's regime is determined to maintain the two pieces of legislation that form the cornerstone of apartheid—the Population Registration Act, which color-codes people according to their race, and the Group Areas Act, which color-codes the places where they live. The structure of political power in the hands of a white minority remains intact, reinforced by the military. . . .

[T]he entire governmental apparatus is run in order to prosecute the civil war in defense of the interests and privileges of five million white South

---

*The President of South Africa is now F. W. de Klerk. Although there appears to be some moderation in apartheid policy, to date no fundamental changes have been made by the ruling National Party.—Eds.

From Robert G. Mugabe, "Struggle for Southern Africa," *Foreign Affairs* (Winter 1987/88). Copyright © 1988 by the Council on Foreign Relations, Inc. Reprinted by permission of *Foreign Affairs* (Winter 1987/88).

Africans. About half of the white population consists of Afrikaners, most of whom support the ruling National Party and its racist ideology of apartheid and discrimination, and half are descendants of British settlers. The May [1987] election saw an alliance of Afrikaners and English-speaking whites voting together for the security promised by P. W. Botha's National Party.

The representative organizations of the black majority, which numbers some 22 million indigenous people, are determined to overthrow the apartheid regime and establish a democratic government by a combination of internal armed struggle supported by economic sanctions and the material assistance that Africa and the international community are able to give. The balance of forces is shifting in favor of these organizations as more people get involved in the anti-apartheid struggle and the confrontation between black and white sharpens.

The African National Congress of South Africa was formed in 1912 and tried for almost half a century to negotiate the sort of society which we now have in Zimbabwe and are continuing to build. It was not until some 50 years later that the ANC decided that all peaceful options had been exhausted and there was no recourse but armed struggle. ANC leader Nelson Mandela, who has now been in jail for 25 years, explained in testimony during his trial on charges of subversion in 1964:

All lawful modes of expressing opposition to the [principle of white supremacy] had been closed by legislation, and we were placed in a position in which we had either to accept a permanent state of inferiority, or to defy the government. We chose to defy the law. We first broke the law in a way which avoided any recourse to violence; when this form was legislated against, and when the government resorted to a show of force to crush its opponents, only then did we decide to answer violence with violence.

The decision to fight for independence is not a phenomenon peculiar to southern Africa. Nor is the decision to fight for a nonracial society. Americans, more than most, must be aware of this, and also Europeans, who fought only 45 years ago to free their countries from Nazi occupation. Independence and the democratic right of the majority to decide their destiny is, or should be, a sacred principle to all of us.

Unfortunately, in South Africa the stage is set for a protracted and bloody conflict. It is one into which African states, the middle powers and the superpowers will be drawn, possibly on opposing sides, thereby setting the stage for a generalized war. . . .

South Africa, while at war with its own people, is waging an undeclared war against its neighbors. The combination of tactics varies from state to state, depending on the political, economic and military vulnerabilities of each, but at the heart of this policy of "destabilization" is the regular sabotage of the regional transportation system to ensure that all trade flows south through South Africa. In order to maintain this regional dependence Pretoria pursues a policy of aggression and destruction that has devastated neighboring economies and caused widespread suffering.

All of South Africa's neighbors have been subjected to direct incursions by the South African Defense Forces—attacks ostensibly aimed at members of the ANC,

but whose victims have always been in-
nocent citizens of the target state. Pretoria also relies extensively on the use of
the surrogate forces inherited from anti-
colonial struggles to its north, trained
and armed by the SADF to murder,
maim, rape and destroy on its behalf.

Why does South Africa do this to its
neighbors? It is certainly not because we
are a military threat. South Africa's motivation is in part economic, in part due
to the acquiescence of the international
community, and in part due to the deep-
seated knowledge of apartheid's rulers
that their system of racial segregation
and minority rule is doomed.

We are not militarily at war with apartheid, but apartheid is at war with us.
And militarily, economically and socially
we are paying an enormous price. Since
1980 the direct and indirect cost of South
Africa's destructive actions against its
neighbors has been well over $20 billion.
In the case of Mozambique alone the cost
from 1980 through 1985 is estimated at
between $5.5 billion and $6.5 billion.
And even these figures do not give a true
picture, for they exclude the vast amounts
of money we are forced to divert from
development to defense to protect our
hard-won sovereignty. . . .

What are the vital interests of the
United States in our region? More than
half of the United States' purchases of a
dozen minerals considered strategic or
critical are imported from South Africa.
Most of the strategic minerals, however,
can be purchased elsewhere in the region. For example, although South Africa accounts for about one third of the
world's production of chrome ore, my
country contains most of the known deposits of high-grade chrome ore. Zambia,
Zaíre and Botswana are also alternative
sources of some strategic minerals.

The United States is tied to the South
African economy by as many as 200 U.S.-
based multinational companies, which
have direct investments estimated at
billions of dollars. The pressure of the
anti-apartheid protest has forced several
companies to divest their shareholdings
in South Africa. It must also be noted
that these corporations' investments in
black Africa north of the Limpopo River
and south of the Sahara are much larger
than those in South Africa.

Another common excuse for the maintenance of U.S. relations with apartheid
South Africa is the protection of the Cape
sea route. This is an old excuse for policies of aggression in our region. The
British government used it as the main
justification for proposing to sell arms to
South Africa in 1971. But it is common
knowledge that modern air transport has
made the Cape sea route irrelevant as a
strategic point. The U.S. Secretary of
State's Advisory Committee on South
Africa, which published its report in January, concluded that "the active collaboration of the South African government,
whatever its ideology, is *not* an important
factor in protecting the Cape sea route."

These then are the cosmetic issues for
which there are alternatives and solutions. The Advisory Committee report
goes on to say: "A greater source of
danger to the West is the growth of
Soviet influence in the region, promoted
by white intransigence in South Africa,
growing political instability, rising levels
of racial violence, and armed conflict." . . .

We take note of the Reagan Administration's commitment to operate within
our regional consensus. But we remain
concerned that the main objective of the
Administration's policy planners is not
to stem Pretoria's regional aggression;
rather, their main fear is that the people

of the region may turn toward communism and the Soviet Union. We are cognizant of the fact that both superpowers are searching for friendly port and/or military facilities in the region, trying to expand their political and economic influence and to deny that influence to the other.

But it should be noted that, in keeping with our philosophy of genuine nonalignment and true independence, no country in the region has permitted military or naval base facilities to either superpower. . . .

The socialist countries of Eastern Europe and Asia are willing to give us weapons to defend ourselves against apartheid's onslaught. And when they do so there are those who question our nonalignment. This is mischievous and inaccurate. None of us fought for our independence to become the proxy of anyone else. Nor are we. The vast bulk of our trade is with Western countries, and they also provide most of our development aid, but this does not make us a proxy of the West any more than arms from the socialist countries make us their proxy. If it were not for apartheid's destabilizaton of our region, we probably would not need these arms.

Those who judge Africa in terms of East and West do us a grave disservice and they display deep ignorance. Those who see South Africa only in the context of "the whites" and "the blacks" display equal ignorance. We are not opposed to the whites in South Africa; neither are the liberation movements, as they have often stated. It is the policies of apartheid that we oppose and will continue to oppose with all the moral, political and diplomatic power available to us, in support of the oppressed people of South Africa.

We would like to take seriously the words of Secretary of State George Shultz, speaking to the Senate Foreign Relations Committee last year [1987]: "We want a democratic and prosperous South Africa, where all races participate politically and economically, at the center of a peaceful and rapidly developing southern African region."

These words must now be matched by deeds, and existing relations expanded to create mutual trust . . . by taking concrete steps to remove the source of violence in our region. Only when we have achieved this will the region be able to achieve its vast economic potential. The interests of the United States in peaceful development are eloquently presented in the Secretary of State's Advisory Committee report:

> As a nation with long-term interests in southern Africa and a fundamental commitment to the promotion of justice and democratic values, the United States cannot stand aside as a human tragedy of potentially immense proportions threatens to unfold in South Africa. The stakes are too high. At risk are the lives of thousands, possibly millions, of South Africans, black and white, the future political and economic viability of the entire southern third of the African continent, and history's judgment of the United States.

Against this background it is necessary for the U.S. Administration to condemn by concrete actions those enforcing the apartheid system and to support, again concretely, those struggling for freedom and justice. The U.S. Congress did pass last year [1987], over the Administration's veto, a package of limited sanctions. But the United States should give political, moral and material assistance to the majority who will sooner or later take their "rightful place in the governance of the country," and whose relations with the United States will be "strongly influenced by the links that are established during the period of the struggle."

The time has passed for engaging in dialogue with only the apartheid regime; the policy of "constructive engagement" is dead and has been committed to history. U.S. policymakers and leaders of other nations deeply involved in South Africa should encourage dialogue among all parties and promote compromise. I would add that African leaders from the region have played a positive role in this regard and will continue to do so. We have provided venues for informal meetings to encourage familiarization and communication that can lead to a better understanding between individuals on both sides of the problem. There is a vast barrier of culture and scarce or false information (the latter deliberately created) that must now be bridged. We emphasize the importance of these informal discussions. . . . It is urgent to convince Mr. Botha that it is in his interest to negotiate sooner rather than later. He and his colleagues must be persuaded of the need for a new political system, and that apartheid cannot be "reformed." He must be persuaded at the outset to extend basic human, legal and judicial rights to all citizens of the country, and to reintegrate the "homelands" into one country, to release political detainees and to lift the bans on individuals and political organizations.

When it comes time for negotiating, Mr. Botha must have . . . a powerful force standing over him to guarantee good faith in enforcing the decisions, because South Africa has amply proved its unwillingness to keep its word in international negotiations. It concluded its nonaggression Lusaka Accord with Angola and its Nkomati Accord with Mozambique in early 1984, but the report of the Commonwealth's "Eminent Persons Group," *Mission to South Africa*, confirms that "South Africa violated both these Accords from the very outset, giving the region further proof that it could not be trusted to honor even solemn Treaty obligations."

An atmosphere conducive to negotiation can be achieved with a combination of internal and external pressures that increase the cost of maintaining apartheid. Even the State Department's advisory report agrees that multilateral sanctions will have an effect in terms of signaling the termination of economic growth and political stability until apartheid is ended.

The Anti-Apartheid Act passed by the U.S. Congress a year ago was just such a signal. It banned the importation of South African coal, uranium, iron and steel, agricultural produce, textiles and krugerrands, and prohibited new U.S. loans, investments, credits and the sale of computer technology to the South African government and its agencies. It also terminated landing rights for South African Airways. Unfortunately, the thrust of the Anti-Apartheid Act has been blunted and watered down by the Pressler Amendment to the 1987 Appropriations Bill. As noted, the effect of this amendment is to deny financial resources to selected Frontline States, thereby making it difficult for them to participate in the sanctions program against South Africa.

Despite its pleading to the contrary, the United States has considerable leverage which has never been used, and sanctions are only part of this. It is the superpower to whom South Africa looks as an ally; it is a major trading partner and a member of many international organizations. There are material pressures which have never been used, or in some cases not enforced, in political, economic, cultural and military areas. It is true that only 200 U.S. corporations have, or had, direct investments in South Africa but these corporations wield considerable influence in Washington. If they are serious in their attempts to divest and distance themselves from apartheid, they must also use their political clout at home to bring apartheid to an end as quickly as possible.

The [British] Commonwealth has been active in the international campaign to end apartheid, both in imposing its own limited sanctions and earlier leading the way in promulgating the international arms embargo.

Sanctions relating to military, economic, cultural and sporting activities isolate the regime; they are one method of raising the cost of apartheid both economically and psychologically. South Africa has been taking serious steps for a decade to prepare for this eventuality and to minimize the effect on the economy and the military machine. However, that is no reason to exclude sanctions from the list of pressure points, nor is the excuse that sanctions will destroy the economy.

The opponents of sanctions say, in the first place, that such measures will hurt the blacks in South Africa the most. This is a spurious argument. In South Africa, the black response has been clear and categorical: if sanctions will play a part in terminating the suffering, they must be imposed. The Anglican archbishop of Cape Town, Desmond Tutu, has put this point most eloquently:

> For goodness sake, let people not use us as an alibi for not doing the things they know they ought to. We are suffering now, and this kind of suffering

seems to be going on and on and on. If additional suffering is going to put a terminus to our suffering then we will accept it.

A second argument is that sanctions against South Africa will hurt the neighboring majority-ruled states. But we are already suffering, as I have clearly illustrated earlier, and if additional suffering is necessary, we are also ready to pay the price. For several months the Frontline States consulted each other on whether to impose the Commonwealth package of sanctions, which was agreed upon at the Bahamas summit. It became clear that some Frontline States are not able to impose sanctions because their economies are tied into the South African economy like Siamese twins. This is true of those countries in the South African Customs Union as well as others. But although unable to do so themselves they urge those who can—especially the big powers—to adopt sanctions.

A third excuse used to argue against sanctions is that they do not work, the case of Rhodesia being cited as an example. But no single government, not even South Africa, could give formal recognition to the Rhodesian regime as long as it remained the target of comprehensive U.N.-sponsored mandatory economic sanctions. They worked in limited, but important and costly ways. Rhodesia was forced to sell its products at below-market prices and buy its imports at a premium.

The time for easy and comfortable choices in South Africa has run out.

This is the conclusion of the Secretary of State's Advisory Committee on South Africa, and it is a conclusion that we, the inhabitants of southern Africa, heartily agree with. We now expect those who wield power in the United States to understand the magnitude of this conclusion and seize the opportunity to retrieve their moral credibility by actively seeking a solution that can bring peace and justice to our region and allow us to invest our resources in the development of our people instead of defense. This should be the priority of U.S. policy toward the region.

The U.S. Administration should accept the value of sanctions as a means of raising the cost of maintaining apartheid, and should persuade its allies to adopt them. The United States should broaden its contacts with South Africans of all races and political persuasions in an effort to bridge the credibility gap widened by previous policies. This assumption of a more open, less rigid position applies also to its political and economic influence elsewhere in the region, which can be enhanced considerably by increasing assistance to the SADCC member countries and ending aid to UNITA bandits in Angola.

The United States and its allies have the capacity to play the role of power brokers in initiating negotiations toward a just, equitable society in South Africa and the participation of all its citizens in the democratic process. This is a process which we in southern Africa understand very clearly, for precedents abound within our region.

We in Zimbabwe saw how our armed struggle and our political mobilization, coupled with sanctions and other international pressure on [the whites, who ruled our country and brought them] to the bargaining table and ended the intransigent position of no majority rule "in a thousand years." There is now the example of Zimbabwe's reconciliation, our nonracial society and our agro-industrial economic base by which to judge the future of a black-ruled South Africa.

Zimbabwe is also an example by which to judge the enforcement of a cease-fire; one in South Africa could end the spiral of violence that has sucked the children of the townships into its vortex. When the cease-fire was declared in Zimbabwe the guns were laid down, and despite provocations from our adversaries, our people did not pick them up again but went to the polls in peace and cast their ballots and chose their government. Our circumstances in the region are not easy, and we have made mistakes as well as achieved successes, but I think people will agree that our transformation from a state of war to a country in which people of all races participate fully offers some hope for the future of our misguided and restive neighbor.

It goes without saying that in South Africa such negotiations cannot take place from prison cells, and therefore political prisoners and detainees must be released and bans on individuals, organizations and political parties lifted, so the representatives of the people can take their places at the bargaining table. The alternatives, in the words of Mr. Botha's predecessor, the late Mr. John Vorster, more than a decade ago, "are too ghastly to contemplate." Civil war is already upon us. The Commonwealth's Eminent Persons Group presented the reality clearly to the international community in their report, published more than a year ago:

The blacks have had enough of apartheid. They have confidence not merely in the justice of their cause, but in the inevitability of their victory. The strength of black convictions is now matched by a readiness to die for those convictions. They will, therefore, sustain their struggle, whatever the cost.

Time has run out. Serious choices must be made now. Just as the leaders of the United States over a century ago chose to try to overcome their house divided and use the strength of freedom, equality and human dignity to build a powerful nation, we must make the choices necessary to assist South Africa in shortening this difficult period in its history and getting on the road to prosperity and peace. We must do this, not only in the interest of regional peace and security, but in the interest of global peace and stability, giving due and careful consideration to the future of our small planet.

NO

Helen Suzman

THE FOLLY OF ECONOMIC SANCTIONS

Recently at the Students Union at Oxford University, Dr. Chester Crocker and I opposed the motion "that economic sanctions are necessary for the abolition of apartheid." Not surprisingly, the vote on the motion went against us. But the important point is that the students at Oxford were prepared to listen to the argument. It is doubtful whether this would be the case on any campus in the United States, for there the issue has been reduced to a simple equation—if you are against sanctions you must be for apartheid—you must be a racist.

It should be made clear that the ultimate aim of the motion—the abolition of apartheid—was not at issue. There was consensus that there is no valid argument against the abolition of a system that has so much inherent cruelty and oppression. It was on the means to that end, on the strategy to be employed, that there was a difference of opinion.

Whether criticism of Pretoria constitutes outside interference with domestic affairs, whether there are double standards, or whether expediency is implicit in the strong sentiments presently evident in U.S. public opinion is irrelevant. It would be a sad day if countries like the United States, which cherish human rights as their basic philosophy, allowed apartheid to go unprotested. As for double standards, while it is true that many countries that practice oppression worse than that of the apartheid regime escape the wrath of the world, South Africa claims to belong to the community of Western democracies and therefore must expect to be judged by those standards and not by those observed behind the Iron Curtain or in some Third World countries.

Certainly, there is expediency in the opposition to apartheid in the United States and elsewhere. No doubt, Citibank and Chase Manhattan pulled the financial plug on South Africa at the beginning of August 1985 because of threats of withdrawal by depositors rather than because of moral strictures against apartheid. And no doubt, too, the presence of black voters in their constituencies encouraged many U.S. congressmen to leap onto the anti-

From Helen Suzman, "The Folly of Economic Sanctions," *Business and Society Review* (Spring 1986). Copyright © 1986 by *Business and Society Review*, 870 Seventh Avenue, New York, NY 10019. Reprinted by permission.

apartheid bandwagon. Why not? Here was one of those rare occasions in politics when expediency and morality coincide.

Nevertheless, the two main factors that motivate people to support the imposition of sanctions are the moral factor and the punitive factor. Both are understandable. The moral aspect is a healthy impulse that makes one want to have nothing to do with the country that implements the repulsive system of apartheid—the "clean hands" syndrome. And that is fine, until it is realized that by divesting or disinvesting, which are two forms of sanctions, any influence that might have been exercised inside South Africa, such as setting an example to others regarding adherence to fair employment practices and exercising their social responsibilities, also disappears. The desire to punish South Africa, to use punitive measures like sanctions against the apartheid regime, is certainly understandable.

But retribution, when it comes, is not selective. Indeed, it falls more heavily on those it is meant to help than on those it is meant to punish. True, white South Africans would certainly feel the impact of sanctions, as indeed they are feeling the impact of the bank freeze and the drastic decline in the value of the rand. Businessmen in particular are now much more vocal than ever before in their opposition to apartheid. But business lobbies have far less influence, far less clout, with the government in South Africa than do their counterparts in the United States. It is not the businessmen who put the National Party regime in power. Most of them support the official opposition, the progressive Federal Party. The government is kept in power by civil servants, programmed over forty years to implement apartheid. About 40 percent of gainfully occupied whites are directly, or indirectly, in government employ in South Africa. Many of them are likely to turn their backs on the government and veer right if it deviates too far from existing policy. The regime is also kept in power by the white artisan class, such as the mine workers and other skilled workers in industry, who are hardly to the forefront of the struggle for black advancement, and by the rural white electorate which is notoriously reactionary.

The brunt of such measures would be felt by blacks at home and in the heavily dependent neighboring countries in South Africa. Whatever harm is done to South Africa's economy will certainly harm the economies of the neighboring black states, all of which are dependent to a greater or lesser degree on South Africa for jobs, markets, and transportation. The former High Commission Territories of Botswana, Lesotho, and Swaziland are part of a Customs Union with South Africa and belong to the rand monetary area. South Africa's Escom is an important source of power for these countries.

They depend entirely on routes through South Africa for trade. Malawi, Zaire, Zambia, and Zimbabwe are also heavily dependent on South African transport and ports for their imports and exports. Trade between South Africa and the rest of Africa is substantial. Alternative sources of supply could only be found at greater cost.

Over a quarter of a million foreign blacks work in South African mines alone, earning $1.1 billion per annum, half of which is repatriated. A further 70,000 blacks are employed in other occupations in South Africa, plus an estimated 1 million "illegals."

At home, blacks are always the first to get fired during economic recession. Unemployment is no light matter in a country like South Africa, which has no social security safety net. A visit to Port Elizabeth, once a thriving industrial town in the Eastern Cape, would be instructive. Today, Port Elizabeth is dying, in the most painful manner. Ford and other assembly plants have closed down. Unemployment among black workers is up to 60 percent. The townships are in ferment; they are occupied by police and the army. Daily there are reports of shootings and tear gassing. Black-on-black violence is horrific, with kangaroo courts meting out rough justice. Eight murders in a week are not unusual. Transfer this scene throughout the country and anarchy results, with blacks the main victims of the strategy of making the country ungovernable.

To all this the response is usually, "But blacks say they don't care. They say they are suffering so much already, that more suffering, more unemployment, will not matter." Well, generally blacks who say they don't care either have nothing to lose, or they are already unemployed. The second category—those who will lose nothing—are in sheltered employed: their jobs are not in jeopardy. And those in the third category—those who want everyone to have nothing—hope that unemployment will spur on the revolution and will lead to a swift transfer of power to the black majority.

COLLAPSE FEASIBLE?

There is little point in entering into arguments about the first two categories, but the third category deserves some attention. If it were feasible that sanctions would do the trick, the sanctions would bring down the Pretoria regime instantly, or, at worst, within weeks rather than months, to borrow Harold Wilson's famous prediction regarding the demise of Ian Smith's government in Rhodesia (a demise, incidentally, that took a further fifteen years to be accomplished, and with it the death of some 30,000 people), if sanctions would swiftly rid South Africa of the system of apartheid and replace it with a nonracial democracy, no reasonable person could fail to back such action to the hilt.

But this proposition is, in fact, not feasible. The euphoric idea that the Pretoria regime would collapse within a short time following the imposition of sanctions shows a woeful ignorance of the intransigence of the nationalist Afrikaaner character, and indeed one might say also of many English-speaking South Africans and their determination to retain, as long as possible, the status quo of white domination. They will agree to, and indeed already have accepted, incremental change, some of it more than cosmetic. But the total dismantling of apartheid and removal of its foundation stones, such as the Group Areas Act, the Race Classification Act, and the Land Acts, are simply not on the cards in the foreseeable future. Nor is transfer of political power to the black majority.

The Pretoria regime will not fall because of sanctions. It will make the changes it intended to make, which will fall far short of what it believes is demanded of it by the undefined expression "dismantling apartheid and sharing power." Thereafter, if continued pressure is put on it, the Pretoria regime will retreat into the *laager*, bringing with it an even more oppressive system than has been experienced up to now in South Africa.

This is not just a gesture of defiance; it is to the Afrikaaner nationalist the essential for survival. He has no motherland to return to; he represents 75 percent of the white electorate that put him in power to implement the policy of apartheid, and he has formidable military and police forces to back him up. Indeed, part of the 75 percent has already been eroded by the white political parties to the right of the National Party, which oppose any deviation from the old Verwoerdian, pure apartheid dicta.

There is no swift capitulation in sight. There is no possibility that the South African saga will have a rapid and happy end, if only sanctions are imposed. Nor is there any guarantee that a total transfer of power to a black majority will result in the replacement of the existing regime by a democratic nonracial government that will respect the rule of law and ensure a free press, free association, and free elections. The basic premise, that sanctions are necessary for the abolition of apartheid, implies that nothing else will do the trick. This is not true.

INTERNAL FACTORS

Although external factors have played an important role in promoting change, internal factors are likely to be more effective in the future. It is not only defections to the right that are eroding the National Party's power structure. There are also an increasing number of white South Africans, among them Nationalist M.P.s, who realize that apartheid is the disaster that has caused turmoil at home and isolation abroad. In South Africa, it is fashionable these days to say that white politics are irrelevant. On the contrary, white politics are very relevant, because whites are in power. Parliament remains an important forum from which to hold the government accountable for its actions and from which to propagate alternative policies through the press gallery.

South Africa does not consist of only radical blacks on the one hand and pro-apartheid whites on the other. There are hundreds of thousands of white South Africans who abhor apartheid. At the last general election, 20 percent of the white electorate voted for the Official Opposition, which advocates universal adult franchise, the repeal of all racially discriminatory laws, and a bill of rights within a geographic federation.

In addition, within South Africa there are extraparliamentary organizations whose actions could be very effective through black trade union action and black consumer boycotts. Both weapons will be much more effective when blacks dominate the skilled labor market and have increased their consumer power. Blacks will acquire this enhanced economic muscle only in an expanding economy, not in a shrinking market for black manpower induced by sanctions or disinvestment. It never seems to occur to the advocates of such punitive measures that success in their implementation would undermine the most significant power base that blacks could acquire.

The question may well be asked, "Why disapprove of disinvestment and sanctions and not of strike action and consumer boycotts, which are also a form of sanctions?" The reply is that strikes can be settled and called off, and consumer boycotts can be discontinued. They do not destroy the economy permanently. Repeal of mandatory sanctions can be vetoed by one vote at the U.N. Security Council. And once investors have withdrawn, they do not come back, as the experience in black African states has demonstrated.

SELF-DEFEATING SANCTIONS

Sanctions and other punitive measures are, in fact, self-defeating, for they blunt the cutting edge of the real weapons that blacks ultimately will be able to use against apartheid with which to make demands that will have to be accommodated. All this is long term, and it is manifestly true that blacks, especially young blacks, are demanding liberation *now*. "Liberation before the next school term" was one slogan heard toward the end of last year. Indeed, among the worst of the side effects created by outside pressures for sanctions is the delusion among young blacks that the transfer of power is imminent. Nothing is further from the truth, yet that sort of false impression has kept the unrest at fever point, has kept hundreds of thousands of black pupils out of school for months on end, and has led to the death of more than 1,000 black people over the last sixteen months, some through vicious vigilante gang wars, some through gruesome "necklace" murders, and most by police action.

People living 6,000 miles away from the scene who think they can judge the situation accurately have no idea whatsoever of the strength and ferocity of the police and military inside South Africa. Indeed, not only is victory not around the corner, it is not even within sight. Not only is the transfer of power not imminent, it isn't even under consideration. Change, however, is. And that is what should be encouraged—attainable objectives—as a forerunner to creating a climate for negotiation about the total dismantling of apartheid and black participation in the political power structure.

The Western democracies should keep up condemnation of apartheid; they should keep up pressure against apartheid, by all means, but not pressure that will lead to chaos and the wrecking of the economy. That is the strategy of despair—destroying the inheritance that blacks inevitably will one day share.

The system of apartheid—legally sanctioned racial discrimination—is an affront to people concerned with civilized values throughout the world. The eradication of apartheid would be an important gain for the civil rights movement and would increase the sum of human freedom, worldwide, but it should not be at the cost of more deaths, more poverty, more misery, more starvation, and more oppression.

POSTSCRIPT

Can Strict Economic Sanctions Help End Apartheid in South Africa?

The debate over economic sanctions against South Africa is not a debate over the morality or wisdom of a system of apartheid. Apartheid is simply indefensible. The more than 300 laws that are used to enforce apartheid (the African word for separate development) are cruel, inhumane, and too at odds with democratic notions of self-determination to be accepted in the modern world. Rather, those who debate economic sanctions against South Africa debate the costs and the benefits of this policy. Will those who we intend to help, the disenfranchised South Africans, bear all the costs and receive none of the benefits of this policy?

Certainly the position taken by Helen Suzman suggests that black Africa has underestimated the costs of divestment and sanctions for the following reasons: (1) Western firms will lose the ability to influence policies such as pay equity and job security for black workers; (2) neighboring black states such as Botswana, Lesotho, Swaziland, Malawi, Zaire, Zambia, and Zimbabwe would all suffer if the economy of the strongest country in the region was damaged; and (3) the white Pretoria regime will fight on for control of the government no matter how many sanctions are imposed, and in the process they will bring into being "an even more oppressive system than has been experienced up to now in South Africa."

If Suzman is correct, one country that will be immediately hurt by these sanctions is Zimbabwe. Yet the president of that country, Robert G. Mugabe, argues for sanctions. He tells us, "Time has run out." Mugabe goes on to remind us that he is not alone. Not only are South Africa's neighbors willing to pay the price for peace in their region, but the leadership of the black community within South Africa is willing to endure whatever the costs. In the words of the Anglican archbishop of Cape Town, Desmond Tutu: "For goodness sake, let people not use [this suffering] as an alibi for not doing the things they know they ought to. We are suffering now. . . . If additional suffering is going to put a terminus to our suffering, then we will accept it."

The deteriorating economic climate in South Africa and the press of public opinion has led many U.S. corporations to withdraw their investments (see Kevin Danaher's *The Political Economy of U.S. Policy Toward South Africa* [Westview, 1985]). The debate over the wisdom of divestment is also well documented in the *Wall Street Journal*. Back issues of this newspaper chronicle the struggle of firms to come to grips with this changing economic and political reality. Finally, several dozen articles, including Helen Suzman's essay, are found in the Spring 1986 issue of the *Business and Society Review*.

PART 4

Problems for the Future

As we look ahead, what are some of the key economic issues that will shape life in the United States? Two issues that have received close attention from economists are the size of the middle class and the state of the manufacturing base of the United States—both thought to be driving forces in economic growth.

Is the Middle Class Shrinking?
_____

Is Manufacturing Alive and Well and Living in the United States?

ISSUE 19

Is the Middle Class Shrinking?

YES: Katharine L. Bradbury, from "The Shrinking Middle Class," *New England Economic Review* (September/October 1986)

NO: Frank Levy, from "The Middle Class: Is It Really Vanishing?" *The Brookings Review* (Summer 1987)

ISSUE SUMMARY

YES: Federal Reserve Bank of Boston economist Bradbury believes that the middle class is shrinking; that is, there was a decline in the percentage of families with middle class incomes between 1973 and 1984. In looking for the causes of this decline, she concludes that demographic changes do not fully account for the shrinking and, therefore, the shrinking of the middle class was not "illusory or temporary."

NO: University of Maryland economist Levy sees substantial stability in the distribution of income over time: "The middle three-fifths of families has received between 52 and 54 percent of all family income in every postwar year." Although there was little income growth between 1973 and 1984, the U.S. has been "able to maintain 'the middle-class dream' through demographic adjustments."

What is the American dream? People respond in different ways to this question, but part of the American dream involves economic considerations. One dimension to the economic component of the American dream is an equitable distribution of income. This means that the economic rewards, or the income that individuals receive, depend on their economic contributions, their efforts in the workplace, and not on such factors as age, sex, race, or religion. A second dimension is the expectation of a steady reduction in the number of poor persons. A third dimension is that each succeeding generation should enjoy a higher standard of living—that there be an increasingly larger middle class enjoying an increasingly higher standard of living.

Is the economic component of the American dream a reality? Consider first the question of equity. Government statistics indicate that certain racial groups receive only a fraction of the income enjoyed by the typical individual or family. In 1985 the median income of white families was $29,152, while the median income of black families was $16,786. Racial minorities also experience higher unemployment rates: in 1986 the white unemployment rate was 6 percent while the black unemployment rate was 14.5 percent. Similar statistics indicate substantial differences in the incomes of male and female workers: the median income of year-round full-time male workers 14 years and older in 1985 was $24,999, while the corresponding figure for females was $16,252. Although there is agreement on the existence of these disparities, there is disagreement as to why they exist. Different racial and sexual groups differ in a number of ways, including age composition, geographic distribution, occupational distribution, and levels of job experience. The income and unemployment data need to be adjusted for these differences before any conclusions regarding discrimination can be made.

As for the ability of individuals and families to obtain the necessities of life, the usual measuring rod is the government's poverty count. In 1960 there were approximately 40 million poor persons. By 1969 the number of poor was significantly lower; because of economic growth and the creation of a number of programs to aid the poor, the number of poor persons was estimated at a little more than 24 million. However, in 1979 there were more poor people than in 1969, about 2 million more. During the early part of the 1980s the poverty count continued to increase, reaching a high of more than 35 million in 1983. Again, there are disagreements regarding the lack of progress in reducing poverty.

This issue is about the third component of the American economic dream: the status of the middle class. Is the size of the middle class increasing? Is the standard of living enjoyed by the middle class increasing? These questions are addressed in the following readings. To answer these questions certain problems must be resolved. One problem is an appropriate definition of the middle class. Clearly the reference is to those persons and families who are neither rich nor poor, but where exactly should the lines be drawn to separate the various groups? Another problem arises when it is recognized that, even if the size of the middle class remains unchanged, the standard of living or real income enjoyed by the middle class may have changed. A third problem involves explanations of changes in either the size or the standard of living of the middle class. Suppose the size of the middle class remained unchanged, what forces were at work to prevent the size of the middle class from expanding? Or worse yet, suppose the size of the middle class was decreasing while the size of the poverty class was increasing, how should one explain the failure of the economy to realize this part of the American dream?

In the debate that follows, Bradbury and Levy try to determine what is happening to the size of the middle class and its standard of living, and they try to ascertain the forces at work that generate the reported results. Bradbury and Levy use different definitions of middle class and this, in part, explains why they reach different conclusions about its size. They *both* suggest, however, that between the years 1973 and 1984 the middle class became worse off. As for the causes of the patterns they identify, both concentrate on demographic changes—changes in the characteristics of the population and of families and their behavior.

YES

Katharine L. Bradbury

THE SHRINKING MIDDLE CLASS

The perception is widespread that the American middle class is shrinking. Reports of more families in poverty and increased media attention to the relatively high-income "yuppies" are cited as evidence. Hypotheses about the causes of the decline abound. Some blame demographic changes: shifts in the age distribution caused by the baby boom, more families headed by women, and the rising proportion of two-earner families. Others point to changes in the national economy. Increases in employment in services and high technology manufacturing, for example, have reportedly replaced the high-wage blue-collar jobs of traditional manufacturing with a two-tier mix consisting of many low-skill, low-paying jobs and a few highly paid professional and technical experts.

The general perception of a shrinking middle is correct. Over the last decade or so, real family income has declined, and its distribution has become more unequal. This study examines changes in the distribution of family incomes in the United States from 1973 to 1984, and relates these changes to shifts in family types and sizes, the labor force status of wives, the age distribution of family heads, the regions in which families live. The analysis thus focuses on demographic changes affecting families rather than on changes in the economy. It finds that demographic changes were not the major reason for the decline in the percentage of families with middle-class incomes from 1973 to 1984.

I. RECENT INCOME PATTERNS AND TRENDS

The incomes of American families rose fairly steadily in real terms from at least 1949 to 1973, pausing only briefly during recessions and reaching new heights during each expansion.[1] Since 1973, however, the ground lost in recessions has not been recovered in the ensuing expansions. Median family income in constant dollars was slightly lower in 1979 (before the 1980 recession) than in 1973 (the year before the 1974–75 recession). It was lower still in 1984, the latest year for which data are available. While family incomes probably rose in 1985, the general stagnation of median income in the 1970s and 1980s to date stands in marked contrast to the experience of the 1950s and 1960s.

The distribution of family income has also changed in the past 10 or so years. Both the fraction of families with incomes below the poverty level and the fraction with incomes over $50,000 (in 1984 dollars) were higher in 1984 than in 1973. Recent increases in poverty stand in sharp contrast to steep declines during the 1960s and early 1970s and moderately stable poverty incidence during the second half of the 1970s.[2] At the other end of the distribution, the proportion of families with incomes over $50,000 (in constant 1984 dollars) continued rising more than enough during expansions to offset recession declines. High-income families were apparently less affected by rising unemployment and other adverse economic trends than those with low incomes. . . .

II. WHAT IS THE MIDDLE CLASS? AND IS IT SHRINKING?

. . . The middle class obviously comprises the "middle" of the income distribution and excludes the very richest and poorest members of society, but any more quantitative definition must be arbitrary. The family income range from $20,000 to $49,999 in 1984 dollars is used to define the middle class in this study. This choice implies that about one-half of families are in the middle class, about one-third have lower incomes, and the remainder (roughly 15 percent) have higher incomes. Changes over time in these fractions are the major focus of the study.

The use of simple money income cutoffs to define the middle class has several limitations. For example, families of different sizes have different income requirements for the same standard of living. Also, costs of living differ across regions. No good data exist to develop measures of family income that reflect cost variations associated with either family size or regional location. Dividing family income by the number of family members would fail to capture economies of scale in consumption—the fact that "two can live as cheaply as one."[3] Although variations in family size and regional living costs cannot be incorporated into the definition of the middle class, this study does consider how shifts in size and family locations have affected the measured size of the middle class.

The use of constant dollar cutoffs as a definition disregards cultural aspects of being middle class. Young couples raised in middle-class homes may well consider themselves members of the middle class before their current incomes are high enough to support a middle-class lifestyle. Similarly, formerly middle-class families who have raised their incomes to upper-class levels may continue thinking of themselves as part of the middle class. More broadly, the apparent focus of American culture (especially television programming and advertising) on the middle class makes people prone to define the middle class in such a way that they are included. The dollar definitions used here cannot reflect these special circumstances; rather they attempt to embrace the bulk of families that most people would consider to be enjoying a middle-class living standard.

Another complication in defining the middle class is the sizable and growing fraction of the American population that does not live in families (defined as two or more related people sharing living quarters). People living alone or with nonrelatives comprise 27 percent of all households in 1984 (and about 12 percent of the population), up from 20 percent of households in 1973. Partly because economies of scale in consumption reduce the comparability between incomes of single people and those of families, and partly because the cultural view of the middle class seems to focus on families, this analysis includes only family units. . . .

The income measure used by the Bureau of the Census to report family incomes introduces a final complication in defining the middle class. Census money income estimates reflect all cash income before taxes and other deductions. They include wages and salaries, self-employment income, government and private cash transfer payments (including welfare and pensions), and other "unearned" income such as dividends and interest, but not capital gains and other one-time payments. The primary difficulty is that the estimates reflect the addition to incomes of governmental cash transfer payments but not the reduction in incomes resulting from taxes or the additions due to noncash income such as

Medicare and employer-provided health benefits. Thus the measured distribution of income differs from the distribution of income after taxes and transfers. . . .

Defining the middle class as all those families with Census money incomes between $20,000 and $50,000 yields the patterns shown in Table 1. Using this definition, the fraction of families with middle-class incomes did indeed decline between 1973 and 1984, from 53 percent to less than 48 percent. Most of the decline in the middle-class share was picked up by the lower income class which increased from 32 percent of families to 36 percent; the upper income class grew slightly, from 15 percent to 16 percent of families. (The "middle-class" share also declined over the period according to other definitions of the middle class. For example, the fraction of all families with incomes between $15,000 and $40,000 declined from 52 percent in 1973 to 48 percent in 1984, with virtually all of the loss picked up by the lower income group.)

The total number of families increased by about 8 million (15 percent) between

Table 1

Distribution of Families by Income

Income Class[a]	Number of Families (thousands)		Percent of Families			Percent of Families		
	1973	1984	1973	1984		1973	1984	Change
Below $10,000	6,356	9,332	11.5	14.8	Below	32.1	36.4	+ 4.3
$10,000–20,000	11,319	13,704	20.6	21.7				
$20,000–30,000	12,458	13,224	22.6	20.9				
$30,000–40,000	10,366	10,246	18.8	16.2	Middle	53.0	47.9	− 5.1
$40,000–50,000	6,354	6,837	11.5	10.8				
$50,000–75,000	6,006	6,961	10.9	11.0	Above	14.9	15.6	+ 0.8
$75,000 and above	2,186	2,928	4.0	4.6				
Total	55,045	63,232	100.0	100.0		100.0	100.0	
Median Income	$28,048	$26,000						

[a]Income in 1984 dollars

Source: U.S. Bureau of the Census, Current Population Survey. March 1974 and March 1985, machine-readable data files.

1973 and 1984, so the number of middle-class families actually increased about 1.1 million, even as the middle-class fraction of families declined. But if the fraction of families with middle-class incomes had been the same in 1984 as it was in 1973, 3.2 million more families would have been middle class—2.7 million from below the middle and another one-half million families from above.

The fact that American society has become less "middle-class" would not be a source of concern if the families were generally becoming richer. The long history of rising real incomes in the United States has undoubtedly been accompanied by gradual upward revisions in the definition of the middle class. But increasing affluence was not the general case between 1973 and 1984. Thus many families may have been unable to achieve the living standards they had expected to attain at their current stage in life.

Whether anything should be done about the decline of the middle class, and what, depends on what has caused the shrinkage. If demographic changes are to blame, the problem may be transitory. For example, shifts in the income distribution caused by a skewed age distribution may correct themselves as members of the baby boom generation reach middle age and earn the middle-level incomes typical of those years. The problem may even be illusory—families may not be worse off if the decline in median family income simply reflects a decline in average family size or relocations to areas with lower living costs. On the other hand, if rising unemployment underlies the decline, the economy may grow out of the problem on its own or changes in macroeconomic policies may be called for. If inequality of educational preparation has played a critical role, the remedy might require changes in education and training institutions or individuals' career decisions. Alternatively, if shifts in the mix of occupations and industries are responsible, then the merits of training programs of "industrial policies" to protect or augment middle-class jobs warrant consideration.

III. THE IMPACT OF RECENT DEMOGRAPHIC CHANGE ON THE DISTRIBUTION OF INCOME

Some researchers have hypothesized that changes in family size, the age distribution of family heads, and the mix of family types have been major sources of the recent decline in the size of the middle class and average family income levels. The increasing labor force participation of wives is also thought to have reduced the size of the middle class by lifting a sizable number of middle-class families to higher income levels.

Many of these demographic changes are not exogenous—that is, they may have occurred in response to other demographic or economic changes. For example, a decline in men's average earnings is likely to cause an increase in the labor force participation of wives, which may, in turn, contribute to declines in average family size. Whether exogenous or not, however, demographic shifts are likely to be associated with changes in income. The analysis that follows quantifies the effects of these shifts on the distribution of family incomes between 1973 and 1984 and finds these effects small. The fraction of families with middle-class incomes declined within virtually all demographic groups, however defined. Thus the ultimate sources of the decline in the middle class apparently are not demographic changes. Nevertheless, demographic shifts have altered the characteristics of the middle class in important ways.

The method used to quantify the effects of demographic change is a shift-share analysis that divides the total change (in median income or the fraction of families with middle-class incomes) into two parts: that attributable to changes in the mix of families across demographic groups and that attributable to changes in income patterns within each demographic group. . . .

Interregional Differences in Income

Although income levels differ noticeably among the regions, the extensive movement of population to the West and South has had very minor consequences for the nation's overall distribution of income. Family incomes are below the national average in the South and the Mountain states of the West. Thus one might be tempted to attribute some of the decline in the national median family income to the rapid population growth in these areas. Since living costs are also lower in most of these areas—certainly in the South—a decline in well-being might not be implied.

In fact, median family income declined in all regions, as did the fraction of families with middle-class incomes. If the interregional population shifts had not occurred, the nationwide changes in the distribution of family income would have been only slightly smaller than they actually were, other things equal. Thus, although the purchasing power of $20,000 to $50,000 differs across the regions, interregional population shifts do not mask any underlying increase in the fraction of families with middle-class purchasing power. . . .

Smaller Families

The size of the average family in the United States fell from about $3^{1}/_{2}$ persons in 1973 to $3^{1}/_{4}$ in 1984, continuing a decline that began a decade earlier. The decline was largely attributable to a decrease in the number of children.

Since large families have higher average incomes than small families one might expect a decline in average family size to be accompanied by a decline in average family income (and vice versa). But small families need less income than large families to attain any given living standard, so a decline in average income combined with smaller family sizes might not imply a decline in living standards. The question is whether actual levels of well-being and the fraction of families enjoying middle-class living standards were rising even as the median family income and measured size of the middle class were declining.

It seems not; average living standards did decline between 1973 and 1984, although they declined somewhat less than median family income declined. First, the shift-share analysis implies that the decline in average family size accounted for only one-fifth of the decline in median family income that occurred between 1973 and 1984, assuming the average (real) incomes of families of each size were unchanged between the two years. (Declining family sizes account for a negligible fraction of the decrease in the size of the middle class.) Second, for each family size group both the median income and the fraction in the middle class declined between 1973 and 1984. . . .

Third, income per family member did not show an improvement—the median family's income per family member was about the same in 1973 and 1984. Small families have above-average income per family member. If this higher income per member meant that small families had a higher level of economic well-being than large ones, on average, then the shift toward smaller families might raise the average standard of living even as well-being declined for each family size. But because of economies of scale, the same income per family member implies a lower living standard for a small family than for a large one. Hence the observed decline in average family size accompanied by very little change in average income per family member implies a decline in average well-being.

The Baby Boom Generation

The incomes tend to be highest for those families with heads age 35 to 54. Consequently, some observers have hypothesized that the slippage of the median and the decline in the middle class are attributable to shifts in the age distribution. In particular, the baby boom generation is thought to have swelled the ranks of younger families whose incomes are relatively low. It turns out, however, that changes in the age distribution of family heads between 1973 and 1984 had an effect opposite to that hypothesized, raising the median income slightly and augmenting the middle-class fraction of families. A sizable decrease in the number of family heads under age 25 (whose families have very low incomes) coupled with rapid growth in families with heads age 35 to 44 more than offset the income decline associated with increases in the elderly (who have the lowest median income) and decreases in the number of families with heads age 45 to 54, the group with the highest median income.

The explanation for such contrary results is that, by 1984, the baby boom generation was no longer dominated by the very young. Most definitions of the baby boom say it began in 1946 and ended around 1964. By 1984 baby boomers ranged in age from 20 to 38, and many had therefore reached the age when family incomes are relatively high. Moreover, the age groups most heavily influenced by the baby boom generation—families with heads age 25 to 34 and 35 to 44—have the highest proportions in the middle class. The young and the elderly have much larger proportions of lower income families while those 45 to 54 and 55 to 64 have larger proportions of high-income families. . . .

The Growing Importance of "Nontraditional" Families

Many believe that the decline of the "traditional" middle-class family, consisting of a husband, wife, and perhaps some children, is responsible for the shrinkage of the middle class. Married-couple families accounted for 85 percent of all families in 1973 and fewer than 80 percent by 1984, continuing a pattern of decline that began about a decade earlier. Single-parent families, especially those headed by women, expanded rapidly, their numbers increasing by over 50 percent between 1973 and 1984.

Husband-wife families are concentrated in the middle class, while almost two-thirds of single-parent families have incomes below middle-class levels. Thus one might expect the decline in the number of husband-wife families to have a powerful effect on the size of the middle class. But it did not. If the only change occurring over the 1973-84 period had been the decline in the husband-wife fraction of all families, the middle-class share of all families would have fallen less than $1^{1}/_{2}$ percentage points, not the actual 5 percentage points. Thus the decreasing proportion of husband-wife families contributed more to the decline in the middle class than the shifts in family size, age, and region just discussed, but the effect was still only a small part of the overall change. The key change was not the decline in husband-wife families but rather the decline in the fraction of husband-wife families with middle-class incomes—from 57 percent to 52 percent. In addition to its effect on the middle class, the decrease in married-couple families contributed to the decline in median family income, accounting for more than one-third of the total change.

The proportion of husband-wife families with middle-class incomes would have fallen even more if the labor force participation of wives had not increased. Spouses were working or looking for work in 42 percent of husband-wife families in 1974 and 54 percent in 1985; families with wives in the labor force were much more likely than single-earner husband-wife families to attain middle-class incomes, even though they were younger, on average. Thus the increasing labor force participation of wives actually served to increase the size of the middle class, contrary to the popular perception that the increasing labor force participation of women has increased inequality. . . .[4]

The Changing Status of "Ozzie and Harriet" Families

As supportive evidence that the overall decline in the middle class is not solely attributable to shifts in the composition of American families, the preceding discussion noted that the fraction of families with middle-class incomes declined within most demographic subgroups. But interaction effects may complicate this argument; for example, shifts in family size could underlie the decline in the middle-class fraction of families with heads aged 35 to 44, or shifts in the age mix of family heads might be responsible for some of the decline in the fraction of husband-wife families with middle-class incomes. These concerns can be set aside when examining how the situation changed for more narrowly defined demographic subgroups. How did the stereotypical middle-class family—headed by someone age 35 to 44 with nonworking spouse and two children—fare?

The fortunes of these "Ozzie and Harriet" families shifted in parallel with those of families in general between 1973 and 1984. The median income of 35- to 44-year old husband-wife families with two children declined by 7.4 percent in real terms over the period, from $34,200 to $31,600. And the fraction of these families with middle-class incomes, while higher than for other types of families (65 percent in 1973), declined by a greater amount—almost 8 percentage points compared to a 5 point decline for all families. Just as for all families, the bulk of the middle-class decline for this group translated into increased numbers of families with incomes below middle-class levels; the fraction with above middle-class incomes rose by 1 percentage point. Thus, Ozzie, Harriet, David, Ricky and their peers were particularly hard hit by whatever (nondemographic) changes assailed the middle class in the 1973-84 period. More generally, insufficient disaggregation does not appear to be masking a demographic explanation for the decline in the size of the middle class.

Summing Up the Effects of Demographic Change

Of the demographic shifts just examined, only the increase in single-parent families contributed measurably to the decline in the fraction of families with middle-class incomes between 1973 and 1984, an effect offset by the increasing labor force participation of wives. Decreases in both average family size and the fraction of families headed by married couples accounted for a sizable part of the observed decline in median family income, but again, these contributions were offset by increases in family income attributable to the increasing labor force participation of wives.[5]

If the labor force participation of wives had not increased, the fraction of families with middle-class incomes and median family income would have declined even more. As it was, with these increases offsetting the effects of other demographic shifts, the income changes to be explained by other factors are almost as large as the total changes that occurred.

The Changing Character of Middle-Class Families

The decreased presence of nonworking wives is one of the most important changes in the composition of the middle class. By 1984, husband-wife families with wives not in the labor force accounted for only one-third of middle-class families, down from one-half in 1973. Changes in the working patterns of women are probably also part of the reason that smaller families with fewer children comprised a greater fraction of the middle-class and upper-income group in 1984 than in 1973: families with three or more children declined as a fraction of all families, but declined disproportionately as a fraction of families with middle class and higher incomes.

The importance of wives' incomes to the middle class can be interpreted in another light: for an increasing number of families, attainment of middle-class living standards required both spouses to work.[6] The income of wives accounted for 26 percent of the incomes of middle-class families in 1984, a sizable increase from 16 percent in 1973. While increases in work thus prevented more precipitous declines in the standard of living attained by many families, the observed income declines may understate the decline in living standards since they do not take account of the costs of increased labor force participation, including out-of-pocket work expenses and reduced time available for "home production" and leisure. A recent study released by the Joint Economic Committee summarized, "We have gone from a nation where virtually all families could expect increased purchasing power to one in which few can maintain purchasing power even with increased participation in the labor force."[7]

IV. CONCLUSION

The proportion of American families with middle-class income levels declined between 1973 and 1984, while the fractions with higher and lower incomes increased. Over the same period, the real income of the median family in the United States fell. These changes have raised concern that real economic well-being in the nation is on the decline, and even that the fabric of society, dependent on a strong middle-class core, is threatened.[8] In the past, new government policies to redistribute income have been undertaken after each spurt in inequality.[9] But the choice of a policy remedy, if any, depends on the causes of the problem. In particular, if demographic changes, such as shifts in family size, composition, and age, were to blame the difficulty might be illusory (not implying any actual decline in well-being) or temporary.

The analysis of this paper, however, indicates that demographic changes are not responsible for the bulk of the 1973–84 decline in the size of the middle class or in median family income. An increase in single-parent families played some role, but was offset by increases in the labor force participation of wives. Thus it seems that the dwindling of the middle class is real and probably not transitory.

A number of alternative explanations for the decline in the middle class have been advanced. Some commentators have argued that the middle class has become smaller because of shifts in the occupational and industrial mix of jobs in the U.S. economy, specifically the decline of traditional smokestack industries such as autos and steel combined with secular growth in employment in services and the expansion of high technology manufacturing.[10] Others have found that inequality is growing within industry and occupation groups,[11] implying that shifts among these groups cannot be the full explanation for increased inequality in the economy as a whole and that something broader is occurring. Macroeconomic changes occurring during the 1973–84 period have also been cited,[12] including a slowdown in productivity growth, rising unemployment, swings in inflation, several recessions, and alterations in government income maintenance policies.

This study eliminates demographic change from the list of major causes of the decline of the middle class. Further research is needed to understand the importance of competing explanations and to identify appropriate remedies.

NOTES

1. Following methods used by the Bureau of the Census, this study uses the consumer price index to convert all data to 1984 dollars. If the GNP price deflator were used instead, "real" median family income would appear to have been about the same in 1984 as in 1973, after several decades of steady increase. Use of the GNP price deflator would not, of course, change the relative shapes of the income distribution in the two years.

2. The poverty level varies with family size and other family characteristics, and is adjusted from year to year using the consumer price index.

3. One approach sometimes used to adjust incomes for family size and economies of scale divides family income by the poverty line, which reflects how subsistence food costs vary with family size. However, variations in food costs across family size groups for the very poor may bear little relation to how living costs vary across family sizes for those with much higher incomes. Interregional variations in living costs were measured by the Bureau of Labor Statistics "Urban Family Budgets," but this series was discontinued after 1981.

4. Sheldon Danziger and Peter Gottschalk also find that wives' increased labor force participation has reduced inequality. See "How Have Families With Children Been Faring?" Institute for Research on Poverty Discussion Paper 801–86, January 1986.

5. These estimates are not strictly additive since the calculations of the effect of each shift do not control for simultaneous changes in the other factors, but the relative magnitudes are comparable.

6. Richard A. Easterlin argues that increased labor force participation and decreased childbearing among young adults "reflect chiefly the grim struggle of the baby boom generation to maintain their relative economic status" in "The Struggle for Relative Economic Status," December 1985, paper presented at the Conference on Non-Replacement Fertility, Hoover Institution, Stanford University, November 7–9, 1985, revised December 1985, mimeo, University of Southern California, p. 1.

7. "Family Income in America," prepared for the Joint Economic Committee, 99 Cong. 1 Sess., November 28, 1985, p. 8.

8. See Lester Thurow, "The Disappearance of the Middle Class," New York Times, February 2, 1984; and Robert Kuttner, "A Shrinking Middle Class Is a Call for Action," Business Week, September 16, 1985.

9. See Lester Thurow, "New Punishment for the Middle Class: The Hidden Sting of the Trade Deficit," The New York Times, January 19, 1986, and "A General Tendency Toward Inequality," paper prepared for annual meetings of the American Economic Association, December 1985, mimeo, Massachusetts Institute of Technology.

10. See, among others, Barry Bluestone and Bennett Harrison, *The Deindustrialization of America* (New York: Basic Books, Inc., 1982); Bob Kuttner, "The Declining Middle," *The Atlantic Monthly*, vol. 252, no. 1 (July 1983), pp. 60–72; Bruce Steinberg, "The Mass Market is Splitting Apart," *Fortune*, November 28, 1983, pp. 76–82; Lester Thurow, "The Disappearance of the Middle Class," *New York Times*, February 5, 1984, and "A General Tendency Toward Inequality," paper prepared for annual meetings of the American Economic Association, December 1985, mimeo, Massachusetts Institute of Technology.

11. Analyses of earnings by occupation and industry generally focus on individual workers rather than on family incomes. Peter Henle and Paul Ryscavage found increasing inequality in the distribution of earnings among men in most industry and occupation categories from 1958 to 1977; see "The Distribution of Earned Income Among Men and Women, 1958–77," *Monthly Labor Review*, April 1980, pp. 3–10. Robert Z. Lawrence provides evidence that the distributions of earnings in high technology and services do not differ much from that for manufacturing as a whole; the basic change stems from a decline in the percentage of workers with middle-class earnings *in all sectors* rather than from shifts among sectors ("Sectoral Shifts and the Size of the Middle Class," *The Brookings Review*, Fall 1984, pp 3–11). Martin Dooley and Peter Gottschalk found increases in earnings inequality between 1968 and 1979 for men within labor force cohorts even after controlling for education, experience, and unemployment in "Earnings Inequality among Males in the United States: Trends and the Effect of Labor Force Growth," *Journal of Political Economy* (1984), vol. 92, no. 1.

12. Frank S. Levy and Richard C. Michel argue that economic stagnation is largely responsible for the increasing "inequality of prospects for achieving the American dream"; see "The Economic Future of the Baby Boom," Urban Institute Research Paper, December 1985.

NO

Frank Levy

THE MIDDLE CLASS:
IS IT REALLY VANISHING?

Inequality, a word used in conjunction with the poor during most of the postwar period, has taken on a broader meaning. Several analysts now argue that not only the poor but the middle class itself is in trouble.[1] There is no shortage of casual observation for this conclusion. Since 1980 perhaps 7 percent of all workers have been displaced, their plants closed or their jobs abolished. The majority are blue-collar workers, most of whom had to take substantial pay cuts. At the same time few days go by without another story about a young investment banker who is making $100,000 or more well before his or her 30th birthday.

When one moves from the individual example to economy-wide statistics, the evidence for a declining middle class is weaker. The U.S. Census Bureau has published annual estimates of the distribution of family income since 1947. They show a highly unequal distribution, but over almost 40 years this inequality has remained fairly stable. In 1984, for example, the richest one-fifth of families received $9.15 of income for every $1.00 received by the poorest one-fifth. But . . . this ratio never fell below $7.20 to $1.00, even in the boom of the late 1960s.[2] And the middle of the distribution has been more stable than the extremes: The middle three-fifths of families have received between 52 and 54 percent of all family income in every postwar year. How is this stability to be reconciled with fears of a vanishing middle class?

An answer begins with a point of perspective. It is easy to imagine the richest one-fifth of families—the group that received 42.9 percent of all family income in 1984—as a group of real estate moguls and arbitrageurs, all with at least six-figure incomes. The image is misleading. In 1984 the richest one-fifth included all families with incomes of $45,300 or more, a standard that counts income from husbands, wives, and all other family members.

If this number seems low, it says something about reference groups. The United States today contains 64 million families headed by a wide variety of people: lawyers, computer repairmen, single 19-year-old women, 68-year-old retirees in Oregon, and so on. When we judge our own incomes, we often

From Frank Levy, "The Middle Class: Is It Really Vanishing?" *The Brookings Review* (Summer 1987). Copyright © 1987 by The Brookings Institution, Washington, D.C. Reprinted by permission.

think in terms of our immediate peers—for example, young-to-middle-aged professionals; the top quintile of this group today begins at something closer to $65,000.

BEHIND THE STATISTICS: STAGNANT INCOMES . . .

The surprisingly low starting point for the richest quintile also provides the first clue in discovering whether the middle class is really shrinking: In recent years the incomes of U.S. workers and families have stagnated badly. Viewed in terms of income growth, the post-World War II years can be divided into two periods. From 1945 through 1973 real wages and salaries grew 2.5–3.0 percent a year. In 1953 the average 40-year-old man made $15,500 (all income figures are in 1984 dollars). In 1973 the average 40-year-old man made $28,120. Then the steady wage growth stopped.

At the end of 1973 the Organization of Petroleum Exporting Countries substantially raised oil prices. The effect was to transfer a large piece of U.S. purchasing power abroad, and by 1975 real U.S. wages had fallen by about 5 percent. More important, the oil price increase marked the beginning of a dramatic slowdown in the growth of U.S. productivity—output per worker. Rising productivity is the ultimate source of rising wages. For most of the postwar period, worker productivity grew 2.5–3.5 percent a year. But in the decade after 1973 productivity grew at only 0.9 percent a year, a development that even now is not completely understood.

The income loss from the 1973–74 oil shock followed by slow-growing productivity meant that real wages did not regain their 1973 levels until 1979. Then the Iranian revolution and the second OPEC price increase began the cycle again. The result was more than a decade of declining wages. Had incomes continued to grow moderately after 1973, the average 40-year-old man in 1984 would have earned about $35,000. In fact, he earned $24,600—$3,620 less in real terms than the average 40-year-old man in 1973. Other age groups experienced similar income losses.[3]

Family incomes did not suffer as much as the incomes of individual workers. Between 1973 and 1984 the median income of a 40-year-old men fell by 13 percent, but median family income—the income at the "center point" of the family distribution—fell by only 6 percent, from $28,200 to $26,400. This more moderate decline reflected two demographic trends. One was the big increase in the number of working wives and in families that depended on two incomes rather than one. The second trend was the rapid rise in age at first marriage, which kept many young people from forming what would have been moderate-income families.[4]

A third trend (of which young singles were a part) was the continuing decline in the birthrate, which began in the mid-1960s. Fewer children did not affect family incomes directly, but they increased income per capita within families by lowering the number of capitas that had to be fed. (The issue of birthrates is discussed below.)

Nonetheless, the decline in median family income over a sustained period was something new—and unexpected—in post-World War II America. In 1947 median family income stood at $14,100 (in 1984 dollars). It grew fairly smoothly for the next 26 years, doubling to $28,200 in 1973, before it began its slow drop.

This decline helps explain why the middle class appears to be shrinking.

Being "middle class" has always had several meanings. One meaning involves being in the middle of the income distribution. A second meaning involves being able to afford a middle-class standard of living as the term is defined and redefined. Between 1945 and 1973 the two meanings were almost interchangeable. The middle of the income distribution got a slightly larger share of the pie but, more important, the pie itself grew rapidly. The whole distribution moved to higher incomes, and families in every quintile experienced substantial economic progress.

Since 1973 the middle share has deteriorated to the level of the late 1940s, *and* average incomes have declined. As a result the bottom five-sixths of the income distribution have lost ground absolutely as well as relatively. Being in the middle of the income distribution no longer guarantees a middle-class lifestyle as it has come to be defined. The middle of the income distribution is not getting much smaller, but it is growing a little poorer—despite more two-earner families.

. . . AND CHANGING DEMOGRAPHICS

Declining incomes are one explanation for fears of a vanishing middle class. A second explanation involves shifting demographics in the income distribution's lower half. Over the past 15 years the average position of elderly families has improved, moving significant numbers of them from the bottom of the income distribution to the lower middle. Younger families took their vacated places.

The improved position of the elderly reflects, in large degree, the effect of Social Security. In 1972 Congress tied Social Security benefits to the Consumer Price Index to guarantee protection against inflation. At that time workers' wages had increased faster than inflation for almost three decades. Giving the elderly an indexed benefit seemed an equitable and inexpensive proposition. Congress could not know that one year later, inflation-adjusted wages would begin more than a decade of decline. In the context of this decline, indexed Social Security benefits (and greater private pension coverage among more recent retirees) meant that successive waves of the elderly had modestly increasing incomes.

At the same time the position of many younger families worsened. Part of the deterioration reflected changes in family structure. The proportion of families under age 65 headed by a woman rose from 12 percent to 16 percent. Among families with children under age 18, the proportion headed by a woman rose from 15 percent to 21 percent. As husband-wife families increasingly relied on two earners, these single-parent families were at a big economic disadvantage. Today fully one-half of them are in the distribution's bottom quintile. Since 1980 significant numbers of two-parent families who were hurt by the 1980–82 recession and its aftermath have also fallen to the bottom of the income distribution.

These movements compounded by two other trends, later marriages and lower birthrates, had a profound effect on children. Throughout the 1950s and 1960s the poorest one-fifth of families included 15–17 percent of the nation's children. In 1984 those families contained 24 percent of the children. Children's downward slide in the distribution reflected both the numbers of moderate-income young people who did not have children and the economic troubles of the families who did.[5]

In one sense, these rearrangements of groups within the income distribution affected our perceptions of inequality more than the level of inequity itself. Poor children are more visible in day-to-day life (and in the media) than recent retirees who are doing all right. We see more of what is going wrong than of what is going right, and we draw too pessimistic a conclusion.

In a different sense, these rearrangements do work to increase inequality, not in any one year but on a "life cycle" basis. Imagine, for example, a young husband and wife who begin married life with income in the lower middle of the distribution. As they reach their peak earning years, their family income increases relative to other families, and they move toward the higher end of the distribution. When they retire, they move toward the bottom of the distribution. If all families followed this pattern, income inequality in any one year would have less meaning.

Mobility within the income distribution was never this perfect, but the rearrangements at the bottom of the income distribution have diminished it further. When a middle-class family retires, private pensions and indexed Social Security now keep it from falling as far down in the distribution as it once might have. Conversely, in today's economy, families at the bottom of the distribution—particularly families headed by single women—have weak prospects for income growth that would move them up in the distribution. For both groups, future income is more closely tied to current income. Long-run inequality has increased correspondingly.

In sum, census estimates of a relatively stable income distribution obscure the way in which the middle-class is changing. Family income equality has never been a strong point of the American economy.[6] Nonetheless, rapidly rising incomes and, to a lesser extent, mobility within the income distribution enabled large numbers of families to enjoy a middle-class living standard for at least part of their lives and served as a substitute for greater economic equality. But since the 1973–74 oil price increase, income growth has stagnated while mobility within the income distribution has diminished. To this point, we have been able to maintain "the middle-class dream" through demographic adjustments—more two-earner couples, postponed marriages, and low birthrates. These adjustments can take us only so far. If we do not return to a healthy economy with rising real wages, the middle class, and with it, the nation's social fabric, will come under increasing strain.

NOTES

1. See, for example, Bob Kuttner, "The Declining Middle," *Atlantic*, July 1983, pp. 60–72, and Katherine L. Bradbury, "The Shrinking Middle Class," *New England Economic Review*, September/October 1986, pp. 41–45.

2. Income equality reached its post-World War II high point in 1968–69 when the unemployment rate for adult men stood at a little over 2 percent. Since 1973 the unemployment rate for adult men has averaged slightly over 6 percent.

3. This 13 percent drop (from $28,120 to $24,600) may be slightly overstated in two ways. The calculation is based on inflation adjustments using the Consumer Price Index, a widely used measure that until recently put too much weight on the cost of new housing and so overstated inflation in the post-1973 period. In addition, over the 1970s workers received an increasing portion of their compensation in fringe benefits (including increasingly expensive health insurance), and so the money-only figures in the text understate total economic gains. These factors together might reduce the 13 percent drop to perhaps a 5–6 percent drop over 11 years. Before 1973, a 25–30 percent rise would have been expected over a similar period.

4. The incomes of single persons (unrelated individuals in census parlance) are tabulated in a

separate income distribution. The rapid rise in the age of first marriage helped give a false impression of young people's affluence. Many young people had high discretionary income (despite low incomes) because they had no mortgage to pay or children to feed.

5. This relative decline in children's positions within the income distribution coupled with absolute decline in median family incomes explains the rapidly increasing child poverty rates mentioned by Gary Burtless.

6. Such estimates as exist for the pre-1947 period suggest that the top quintile of families received over 50 percent of all income in the 1920s and that current patterns reflect a leveling that took place during the Great Depression and World War II.

POSTSCRIPT

Is the Middle Class Shrinking?

Economist Bradbury believes that the middle class shrank between 1973 and 1984. Defining the middle class as those families with incomes between $20,000 and $50,000 (measured in 1984 dollars), the percent of middle class families declined from 53 percent of all families in 1973 to less than 48 percent in 1984. To make matters worse, there was a decline in real family income. Bradbury examines five different demographic changes to determine if they can account for the decline in the relative size of the middle class: interregional differences in income; smaller families; the baby boom generation; the growing importance of "nontraditional" families; and the changing status of "Ozzie and Harriet" families (families with two children and a nonworking spouse and headed by someone aged 35 to 44). Here she concludes that these demographic factors "are not responsible for the bulk of the 1973–84 decline in the size of the middle class or in median family income."

Levy believes that the middle class is not disappearing. Defining the middle class as the middle three-fifths of families in the distribution of income (so that 20 percent of all families have less income and 20 percent of all families have more income than the middle class), the middle class receives about the same percentage of income as it did in the past. Levy admits that while the distribution of income has remained constant, real median family income fell between 1973 and 1984; measured in 1984 dollars, median family income fell from $28,200 to $26,400. Levy also examines the characteristics of the population and families to achieve a better understanding of why the economy produced these results. He concludes that the American economy has been "able to maintain 'the middle class dream' through demographic adjustments—more two-earner couples, postponed marriages, and low birthrates."

The two selections presented here have been shortened considerably, especially the article by Bradbury; the original articles present much more detail in support of their arguments. Levy's article is drawn from his book *Dollars and Dreams: The Changing American Income Distribution* (Russel Sage/ Basic Books, 1987). Other articles that support the notion of a declining middle class include Robert Kuttner's "A Shrinking Middle Class Is a Call for Action," *Business Week*, September 16, 1985, and "The Disappearance of the Middle Class," by Lester Thurow, *New York Times*, February 2, 1984. For an interesting article regarding the controversy over wealth distribution, see "Scandal at the Fed?" in the April 1987 issue of *Dollars and Sense*. For government statistics on income and income distribution, see *Money Income of Households, Families, and Persons in the United States* (U.S. Bureau of the Census, Current Population Reports, Series P-60).

ISSUE 20

Is Manufacturing Alive and Well and Living in the United States?

YES: Molly McUsic, from "U.S. Manufacturing: Any Cause for Alarm?" *New England Economic Review* (January/February 1987)

NO: Nicholas S. Perna, from "The Shift from Manufacturing to Services: A Concerned View," *New England Economic Review* (January/February 1987)

ISSUE SUMMARY

YES: Former Federal Reserve Bank of Boston researcher McUsic examines the behavior of output, employment, and productivity in U.S. manufacturing. She finds that manufacturing has maintained its relative share in U.S. total production and argues that the decline in the number of manufacturing jobs reflects the growth of manufacturing productivity. She concludes that the recent changes in the structure of the U.S. economy do not signal the demise of manufacturing, nor have they brought about a reduction in living standards.

NO: General Electric economist Perna is pessimistic about recent changes in the structure of the economy. He identifies several symptoms of ill health in manufacturing: (1) imports of durable goods have been rising rapidly; (2) the rate at which manufacturing's share of employment has been declining has accelerated; (3) productivity growth in U.S. export industries has lagged behind that of similar industries in other countries; and (4) "industry analysis shows that the U.S. employment mix has shifted towards lower paying jobs, particularly since the 1960s."

In addressing the idea of a transformation in the American economy, some economists speak of the deindustrialization of the American economy, of the demise of manufacturing. They are concerned about U.S. manufacturing because they believe that the high standard of living enjoyed by most Americans is the direct result of a growing and prosperous manufacturing base; therefore, if manufacturing is dying, then Americans may face an erosion of their living standards.

How important is manufacturing to the U.S. economy? If importance is measured by size, then for some time now manufacturing has not been the most important sector of the economy. Back in 1946, manufacturing generated fewer jobs than did the service sector (e.g., transportation and public utilities, wholesale trade, retail trade, real estate)—14.7 million as opposed to

24.4 million. In 1987, manufacturing employed 19.1 million people, and service employment totaled 77.5 million. As McUsic indicates, the percent of total production accounted for by manufacturing has been very stable, ranging between 20 and 22 percent since 1947. Although this might suggest that manufacturing is relatively unimportant compared to services, many still believe that a healthy manufacturing sector is the key to the overall health of the economy.

Assessing the health of a particular sector of the economy is no easy task. A major problem is that the economy is always in a state of change. Some of these changes may be temporary as the economy responds to a variety of impulses. One example is the changes the economy undergoes each year as the seasons change: agricultural output expands during the harvest season; there is an influx of students into the labor market as summer vacations begin. Because these seasonal patterns are well known, many economic statistics are adjusted accordingly and carry the note, "seasonally adjusted."

Another type of change reflects the business cycle: the repeated pattern of business expansion followed by business contraction that is a part of the history of capitalist economies. The U.S. economy experienced cyclical contractions in 1980 when total production fell by $5 billion from the previous year, and in 1982, when the fall in production was much greater, some $80 billion. If an assessment of the health of the manufacturing sector were restricted to contractionary periods only, the diagnosis would be that the patient was indeed ill.

In addition to seasonal and cyclical changes there are structural changes. The best example here, and one that is referred to in the following readings, is the transformation of the American economy from an agricultural society to an industrial or manufacturing-based society. Farm employment in 1947 exceeded 10 million workers, but by 1986 farm employment had fallen to just slightly more than 3 million. If you contrast farm employment with total employment you find that in 1947 about one out of every five jobs was a farm job, while in 1986 only one of every forty jobs was a farm job. Even as farm employment fell, however, because of productivity advances, farm production doubled.

The difficulty for economists is to separate these various kinds of change. If the changes are temporary, there is no cause for concern. A seasonal problem is like a winter cold: both create mild discomfort that will pass. A cyclical downturn is more serious and can be likened to a broken arm, which is certainly more of a problem than a cold, but with time the patient will heal and resume normal activity. A structural change might be considered a major illness like lung cancer. You may or may not survive.

So is U.S. manufacturing alive and well? McUsic sees only minor symptoms of ill health. All things considered, she believes that manufacturing has been performing quite well. Perna thinks that the kind of evidence that McUsic uses is too simplistic and that a more detailed analysis reveals significant problems.

YES

Molly McUsic

U.S. MANUFACTURING:
ANY CAUSE FOR ALARM?

To the laid-off GM employees in Flint, Michigan, who were not called back to work after the recession, the laborers in Gary, Indiana, who can no longer find work in the steel industry, and the patriotic consumer in Boston who cannot find an American-made VCR, U.S. industry appears somehow to be failing. This perception has been amplified by published reports that the United States is not manufacturing enough, that productivity is low, and that jobs are being lost to firms in other countries. The prospect of our manufacturing industries losing their competitive edge suggests a concomitant lowering of living standards to those who fear that this country is losing its capacity to produce tradeable goods.

This article examines the output, employment and productivity of U.S. industry. The study concludes that the recent course of industrial development in the United States corresponds closely with long-standing historical trends here and in other industrialized countries. In many respects our goods-producing industries appear to be faring remarkably well, in view of the rapid development of industrial capacity in other industrialized countries and in newly developing countries. Since at least 1960 manufacturing output has consistently accounted for about one-fifth of GNP in the United States. Although U.S. industrial growth slowed during the 1970s, every indicator of industrial strength recovered during the 1980s. The slump—frequently attributed to high energy prices, high inflation, and a growing proportion of younger, less experienced workers in the labor force—appears to have been only temporary.

In the 1980s the United States has performed as well as other developed nations in every category of industrial growth, and by most measures its level of productivity and standard of living remain the highest in the world. The trend toward services employment, which is consistent with many theories of economic development, appears to be no more rapid here than in other developed nations, and it does not appear to have accelerated significantly during the last decade.

From Molly McUsic, "U.S. Manufacturing: Any Cause for Alarm?" *New England Economic Review* (January/February 1987). Copyright © 1987 by the Federal Reserve Bank of Boston. Reprinted by permission of *New England Economic Review*.

In general, U.S. goods and manufacturing industries are performing as expected, given global and historical trends.[1] The structural shifts that are occurring—such as the decline in manufacturing's share of employment or the decline in our share of world output—are influenced greatly by worldwide patterns of economic development as well as by changing incomes in the United States. These shifts do not appear to be caused by any intrinsic problem with the U.S. industrial base.

I. OUTPUT

The alleged shift from goods to services has dominated recent discussions about the course of economic development in the United States.[2] Many fear that our economy is producing fewer goods and that a society that survives on services will inevitably slip into decline. Output data provide no clear evidence that the United States is shifting to a service economy; perhaps more importantly, it is not evident that such a shift would be a sign of economic decline. . . .

The breakdown of output by industry shows that it is not manufacturing but the agriculture, mining and construction industries whose relative share of output has declined since 1960, as services' share has risen. Manufacturing industry output has remained a remarkably constant share of GNP, not fluctuating much beyond 20 to 22 percent of total output since 1947.

The recent growth in manufacturing's share of output also follows long-standing historical patterns. Although manufacturing output has expanded at about the same rate as GNP when measured over long intervals, during business cycles its

growth has been more volatile. . . . From 1960 to 1985 manufacturing output grew at an average annual rate of 4 percent. It grew 5.3 percent from 1960 to 1973 and then slowed to 2 percent from 1973 to 1980.[3] In the most recent recovery, the expansion of manufacturing output has been particularly robust, faster than GNP growth alone would suggest.

Other industrialized nations have experienced many of the same economic trends as the United States. All the developed countries had lower growth in industrial production during the 1970s than in the 1960s. . . . Only Japan has had greater growth than the United States during the 1980s, due primarily to U.S. recession from 1980 to 1982. Since its economic recovery, the United States has had the highest growth in industrial production.

As a share of world industrial output, U.S. production has declined steadily since the end of World War II. In the late 1940s, the United States produced more than 60 percent of world manufacturing output. By 1983 it produced about 31 percent of developed nations' output.[4] As Germany rebuilt in the early postwar period, as Italy and Japan developed in the 1960s, and as other Third World nations have recently emerged as competitors, it was inevitable that the United States' *share* of output would decline even as its *level* grew. Once the European and Japanese economies were rebuilt, manufacturing accounted for a constant or even declining share of their economic activity also. Only in the newly industrializing countries is manufacturing output's share of GDP growing.

As countries develop, their economies shift from agriculture to manufacturing and then from manufacturing to services.[5] As more developing nations move from agrarian economies to manufacturing, many U.S. industries will have to cope with stiffer competition and will continue to lose market share. Unless economic growth in the United States exceeds that of the rest of the world, our share of world output will continue to decline as other nations catch up with our technology, skills, and living standards. However, this does not imply that the U.S. standard of living will stop rising. Since World War II our share of world output has declined, yet our standard of living has risen. As long as the world economy is growing sufficiently rapidly, U.S. output and living standards will continue to expand.

While goods have accounted for a constant share of GNP in the United States until now, services' share ultimately may increase as the economy continues to develop. Such a shift toward service output would occur not because our manufacturing industries can no longer compete but because society wants more services.

As countries develop, their residents acquire an increasing stock of machines, factories, consumer durables, schools and roads. A given stock of goods, in and of itself, creates a need for services. For example, the purchase of one car requires years of repair service. The demand for services, therefore, will tend to grow along with an expanding stock of goods. The production of new goods also depends on the stock of existing goods. New production supplies enough goods to replace those that have worn out, to meet the needs of an increasing population, and to satisfy each person's demand for additional belongings. With slower population growth and with increasing affluence, the rate of growth of the stock of goods may decline in the United States. As a result, the demand

for newly produced goods would fall relative to the demand for services.[6] . . .

The increasing number of two-earner families will also continue to contribute to the rising demand for services. The larger income attained by two-earner families generates an increase in demand for both goods and services. Initially the demand for housing, consumer durables and clothing increases with income, but at higher levels of income families increasingly value services. Families with growing incomes can afford to increase their quality of life through leisure, education and health services. With rising affluence, the demand for services will eventually increase faster than that for goods. The growth of services also increases as work previously performed by a stay-at home spouse and not included in the GNP accounts becomes purchased services—restaurant meals, laundry service, housekeeping—and is valued as national output. If the trend toward more two-earner families continues, the demand for services may tend to increase relative to goods.

A greater share of services in national output would be a rational market response to continuing economic development. In a maturing economy factors such as rising incomes, changing composition of the labor force, and a mounting stock of goods per person foster a greater need for services relative to goods.

II. EMPLOYMENT

While goods production still accounts for a constant share of GNP, employment in goods-producing industries has long been a declining share of total employment. In 1960, 45 percent of private nonagricultural workers were in goods-producing industries; by 1985 that number had fallen below 31 percent. The share of total non-agricultural private employment in manufacturing has dropped from 37 percent in 1960 to 24 percent in 1985. This shift is not a recent phenomenon. Since at least 1900, service industries have employed more people than manufacturing, which achieved its largest share of total employment around 1920. Moreover, this shift toward service employment is likely to continue. Employment in manufacturing is not expected to grow more than 0.6 percent annually from 1984 to 1995, and because overall employment is expected to grow more quickly, manufacturing's share will decline to an estimated 21 percent by 1995.[7]

Much the same pattern can be found in other industrialized countries. Furthermore, this decline in the share of manufacturing employment is expected to continue abroad as well. In Japan forecasts project an additional 10 million jobs in services during the next 15 years accompanied by a loss of 2.6 million jobs in manufacturing.[8] Only in the newly industrializing nations, where manufacturing is of rising consequence in GNP, is its share of total employment increasing.

It is not just manufacturing's relative share of employment that is declining in the United States, but the absolute number of people employed in manufacturing as well. In 1969 employment in manufacturing reached 20.2 million persons, a level not surpassed until almost 10 years later. In 1979 employment peaked at 21 million persons, after which it declined until 1983 and then recovered slightly to its 1985 level of 19.4 million.[9]

These figures probably underestimate the number of people who work for manufacturing industries, however. Employment in business services has soared from 871,000 in 1960 to 4,612,000 in 1984,

and this rapid growth is expected to continue.[10] Formerly many of these business service jobs were done within the manufacturing industries and categorized as manufacturing. Now the jobs are done by outside consultants and classified as services. When a textile company hires an outside security force, or an electronics manufacturer brings in engineering consultants, employment in manufacturing is lower than if the same work had been done by the manufacturer's employees. If even one-third of the business service jobs were done by manufacturers, there would have been no drop in "manufacturing employment."

Even a decrease in manufacturing employment is not a sign of U.S. deindustrialization. Manufacturing employment is an inadequate measure of the health of either manufacturing industries or the total economy. Due to the complex relationships between output, employment and productivity, one measure cannot suggest the whole story.

The error in overemphasizing employment figures is most easily illustrated by agriculture. Between 1929 and 1985 the agricultural sector suffered an absolute decline in employment of 70 percent. According to the employment figures alone, farming was distressed. In fact, over that period farming was a success story. Technological advances enabled fewer farmers to produce more, thereby increasing the non-agricultural work force and helping to advance U.S. living standards to the highest in the world. . . .

The relationships among output, employment and productivity in manufacturing are similar. In the past five years output in manufacturing has grown 3.3 percent per year but productivity grew more quickly, so employment dropped by 0.9 percent annually. As the U.S. economy matures, demand for manufactured goods is not expected to grow as rapidly as it once did. With limited growth in demand and increasing productivity, manufacturing employment will not rise as it did in the 1960s.

The recent decline in manufacturing employment has not meant a decline in total employment or the standard of living. Overall, the United States has been successful in providing jobs for its population. The civilian labor force has risen from 59 percent of the population in 1960 to 65 percent in 1985. Civilian employment, a measure dependent on the business cycle, has also risen, from 56 percent of the population in 1960 to 60 percent in 1985. During the 1970s, despite the slower average growth in output, the economy was able to absorb a large number of new workers. Civilian employment actually grew more quickly in the 1970s than in the 1960s or 1980s. Employment has not grown so rapidly in Europe and Japan, and employment as a proportion of population has declined there as well.

The U.S. standard of living, measured as gross domestic product per capita, has risen throughout the past four decades, although its rate of growth slowed in the 1970s as it did in other countries. Between 1960 and 1984 average GDP per capita in Europe and Japan increased more rapidly than in the United States. Because living standards here still appear to exceed those prevailing in other countries, the growth of GDP per capita abroad will tend to exceed that in the United States as living standards converge across all nations.[11]

III. PRODUCTIVITY

Throughout U.S. history, high productivity has enabled domestic industries to pay high real wages while remaining competitive in world markets. Since 1973 the growth of productivity in the United States has slowed considerably, and many now fear that our products will no longer be competitive and our standard of living will decline. With the considerable public attention paid to productivity measures has come misunderstanding. Productivity measures have valid uses to both engineers and economists, but used alone they are not a clear indicator of the health of industry.

From 1960 to 1973 productivity in nonfarm business, measured as output per hour, grew at an annual rate of 2.4 percent. From 1973 to 1985 it grew only 0.6 percent per year. Growth in manufacturing productivity declined from 3.2 percent between 1960 and 1973 to only 2.2 percent between 1973 and 1985. These broad intervals obscure important variations, however. Productivity growth depends on economic growth. In early stages of recovery, real output expands faster than employment, increasing labor productivity. As the recovery continues, firms begin hiring new workers and the rate of growth in labor productivity declines. Late in the business cycle, productivity begins to fall as output declines but employers are reluctant to lay off workers immediately. The nature of the recovery also is important. If capacity utilization remains low during the expansion, productivity does not increase as rapidly.

The influence of recessions and recoveries may be minimized by comparing productivity growth during periods between cycle peaks.[12] From 1973 to 1980 nonfarm business productivity grew only 0.3 percent, while from 1980 to 1985 it grew 1.0 percent per year and after 1982 growth accelerated to 1.6 percent annually. Manufacturing productivity grew

1.2 percent from 1973 to 1980, while between 1980 and 1985 it increased 3.7 percent per year. After 1982 manufacturing productivity increased at a rate of 4.7 percent annually. Another way to reduce cyclical effects in the comparisons is to consider productivity growth over the last five recoveries. The results show that manufacturing productivity growth has been higher in the current recovery than in any recent recovery period.

Productivity growth in the United States since 1980 compares favorably with the expansion of productivity elsewhere in the world. From 1960 to 1973 and again from 1973 to 1980 this country had the lowest rate of productivity growth of the seven largest OECD countries, measured both by output per hour in manufacturing and by GDP per employed person. This reflected to some extent the high level of productivity already enjoyed by the United States. As U.S. technology dispersed, it was inevitable that productivity would grow more quickly abroad than in the United States. Since the last recession, however, U.S. productivity growth has been higher than almost any OECD country and the overall level of manufacturing productivity remains the highest in the world.[13]

This slowdown in productivity growth in the 1970s was not a structural problem caused by the shift of employment from goods to services. If service industries had a lower productivity level or slower productivity growth than the goods-producing industries, an increase in service employment relative to goods might be expected to decrease overall productivity growth. However, in the last 25 years service productivity has not depressed total productivity.[14]

Not all service industries are labor-intensive, low-productivity industries. On average, services tend to be more capital-intensive than goods industries, and historically the range of their productivity growth rates has not been significantly narrower than that of the goods-producing industries.[15] During the period of greatest productivity slowdown, from 1973 to 1980, productivity grew more in services than in the goods-producing industries, and the increasing share of employment in services apparently has had a negligible effect on the economy's overall productivity growth.[16]

Whatever the productivity trends, it is not clear whether productivity data should be seriously considered as an indicator of U.S. industrial decline or growth, since there are serious problems both in measuring and in interpreting productivity data. Declining productivity is not synonymous with a loss of efficiency or an erosion of competitiveness. For example, as a result of rising energy prices in the 1970s, many industries used less capital and more labor. This adjustment tended to lower labor productivity as these firms adopted the most economical mix of more labor-intensive inputs to produce their output most efficiently. In the medical service industry the rise in the number of employees and the accompanying drop in productivity was at least partly the result of highly skilled professionals conserving their time by transferring some of their responsibilities to less skilled employees or to laboratories. Such an increase in efficiency would tend to be accompanied by a drop in measured labor productivity.[17]

Improvements in quality of output, unless reflected in a price change, also are not shown in productivity measurements. In the past 10 years electronic products such as computers and calculators have undergone vast technological improvements. Since their relative prices and therefore their value in the GNP accounts have decreased, the measured productivity of the industries making these products has declined despite the improvements in quality.

Comparisons of measures of productivity for different nations can be especially misleading. Different methods of national accounting, different measures of hours (hours worked vs. hours paid) and various levels of sophistication in collecting and reporting the data, increase the degree of unreliability. The Bureau of Labor Statistics, which publishes the most dependable series, adjusts foreign data for greater consistency with U.S. measures but differences in statistical concepts and methods remain. . . .

IV. INDUSTRY SPECIFICS

The data for individual U.S. industries provide a more detailed view of the relationships between output, employment, and productivity in the U.S. economy. . . .

Output in most manufacturing industries grew from 1973 to 1980 and again from 1980 to 1984, with two-thirds enjoying a higher rate of growth in the 1980s. As in the aggregate, employment growth slowed for most manufacturing industries in both periods. Since 1980 employment has increased only in a few manufacturing industries—furniture and fixtures, electric and electronic equipment, motor vehicles and other transportation equipment, rubber and miscellaneous plastic products, and publishing and printing—and even in these industries, except for printing and publishing, employment declined until 1983. The motor vehicle industry had especially robust employment growth recently, 8 percent from 1982 to 1983 and 14 percent from

1983 to 1984. Productivity grew for most manufacturing industries in both periods and accelerated between 1980 and 1984. Only in petroleum and coal refining, which had to adjust to volatile pricing of inputs and changing demand, did productivity actually decline. . . .

Service industries in general experienced greater growth in employment and output than manufacturing industries, but lower productivity growth. Output in nearly half of the service industries grew more slowly during the 1980s than in the 1970s, but output actually decreased from 1980 to 1984 only in transportation, where rising output in air transportation was offset by large declines in intercity trucking and bus and railroad transportation.

Employment has risen in every service industry since 1973 except for the telephone and telegraph industry, where productivity grew more rapidly than output. The two industries were output grew most, credit agencies and financial brokers, and business services, also had the largest growth in employment. The brokerage industry combined employment growth with productivity growth, while business services experienced a productivity decline.[18] . . .

V. CONCLUSION

In 1938 Alvin Hansen told the American Economic Association that "The economic order of the western world is undergoing in this generation a structural change no less basic and profound in character than . . . the Industrial Revolution. We are passing . . . over a divide which separates the great era of growth and expansion of the nineteenth century from an era which no man . . . can as yet characterize with clarity or precision."[19]

In 1961 Robert Theobald wrote, "Despite the continuing increase in manufacturing, the number of people employed in this field appears to have reached a peak, at least in the United States."[20] In 1983 Representative Stan Lundine wrote, "In the last three and a half years, the United States has lost over three million jobs in manufacturing alone. Old factories sit like tombstones in the graveyard of industrial America. . . . There are people who will never return to their old jobs, factories that will never reopen."[21] The current publicity is not the first alarmed report about the prospects for U.S. manufacturing.

During the 1970s, U.S. industrial output, employment, and productivity grew more slowly than in the 1960s, but it is not obvious that the 1970s were a blueprint for the future. Since the recovery in 1982, U.S. manufacturing output has risen faster than its historical trends, overall employment has reached new peaks, and manufacturing productivity has been increasing more quickly than in the 1960s.

The fears of a rising service economy, with barber shops and laundromats replacing steel mills and auto plants, are greatly exaggerated. Since the 1940s both manufacturing and goods have accounted for a constant share of output. Employment declined in most manufacturing industries but the cause was growth, not deindustrialization: productivity grew so quickly that falling employment accompanied increasing output. Eventually services may account for a larger share of output in the United States, but this alone would not be an omen of decay or loss of competitiveness. Instead, it may be a natural adjustment of our maturing economy to the accumulating affluence of its residents and the inevitable development of our trading partners.

While that data reviewed in this article do not show that all U.S. industries are flourishing, they also reveal no evidence of profound economic ills. The courses of output, employment, and productivity today are consistent with long-standing historical trends that have prevailed both in the United States and in other industrialized nations.

NOTES

1. One area, of course, in which U.S. manufacturing has been faring badly is international tread. While it is beyond the scope of this article to examine the possible causes behind the deterioration in the U.S. merchandise trade balance, the data discussed here reveal no support for the theory that the U.S. trade deficit is either causing or caused by a "deindustrialization" of America. For a detailed survey of the causes and composition of the U.S. trade deficit, analyzed by geographic source and major commodity category, see Norman S. Fieleke, "The Foreign Trade Deficit and American Industry," *New England Economic Review*, July/August 1985. Fieleke concludes that the causes of the trade deficit are not to be found in an analysis of industry-by-industry competitiveness and that rising import competition is not an accurate indicator of industrial health. He reached similar conclusions in a more recent article that focused on New England: "New England Manufacturing and International Trade," *New England Economic Review*, September/October 1986.

2. Goods-producing industries include agriculture, mining, construction, and manufacturing. Service-producing industries include transportation, public utilities; wholesale and retail trade; finance, insurance and real estate; and other services.

3. The equation % $\triangle$IP = $-2.98 + 2.28\triangle$ % GNP was estimated using annual data from 1960 to 1985. IP is the Federal Reserve Board's industrial production index for manufacturing. GNP is measured in constant 1982 dollars. Robert Z. Lawrence estimated the same equation for 1960 to 1973 and found that the percent change in industrial production was 2.24 times the percent change in GNP. See *Can America Compete?* The Brookings Institution, 1984, p. 21.

The periods—generally running from a business cycle peak to the subsequent peak—have been selected to reduce the influence of the business cycle on reported growth rates. The growth rates for manufacturing output are calculated using the Federal Reserve Board's industrial production index for manufacturing. For a description of this series see "A Revision of the Index of Industrial Production," *Federal Reserve Bulletin*, July 1985, pp. 487–501. The deflated manufacturing output series from Table 6.2 of the *Survey of Current Business*, produced by the Bureau of Economic Analysis, usually shows lower growth rates: 3.4 percent for 1960 to 1984; 4.8 percent for 1960 to 1973; and 1.0 percent for 1973 to 1980.

4. The estimate of U.S. share of world manufacturing output in the late 1940s is from William H. Branson, "Trends in United States International Trade and Investment since World War II," in Martin Feldstein, ed., *The American Economy in Transition*, 1980, p. 183.

The 1983 share estimate was calculated by adding together the manufacturing output in Canada, the United States, Japan, Australia, Austria, Belgium, Denmark, Finland, France, Germany, Greece, Italy, Netherlands, Norway, Sweden, Turkey and the United Kingdom using constant 1980 prices and 1980 exchange rates. The output figures were published in the OECD *National Accounts, Vol. II, 1971–1983*. The U.S. output share figure in 1983 would have been smaller if the newly industrializing countries' manufacturing output had been included.

5. See Colin Clark, *The Conditions of Economic Progress*, Macmillan & Co., 1951, and Victor R. Fuchs, *The Service Economy*, NBER #87 General Series, 1968.

6. Suppose goods decay at the rate d, that the population grows at the rate n, and that the stock of goods per capita grows at the rate g. Then the production of goods equals (d + n + g)G, where G is the stock of goods. Suppose that the demand for services per unit of accumulated goods is s, then the ratio of service production to GNP is s/(d + n + g + s). This ratio will rise if s should rise or if d, n, or g should fall. The level of s could be increasing because a set amount of goods requires more servicing (people own their cars longer, for example, so more service is required) or because services themselves create a need for more services. See Lynn E. Browne, "Taking in Each Other's Laundry—The Service Economy," *New England Economic Review*, July/August 1986.

7. Valerie A. Personick, "A Second Look at Industry Output and Employment Trends through 1995," *Monthly Labor Review*, November 1985, p. 34.

8. Leslie Helm, "Will Japan Really Change?" *Business Week*, May 12, 1986, p. 58.

9. These figures are from the U.S. Bureau of Labor Statistics Current Employment Statistics Program (survey of business establishments). According to the Current Population Survey, also

one by the BLS, manufacturing employment was 20,746,000 in 1970, 22,459,000 in 1979 and 20,879,00 in 1985. All U.S. employment figures are taken from the Establishment Survey because of its more detailed breakdown by industry. For international comparisons the U.S. data were taken from the Current Population Survey because these data are most comparable to those of other nations. Roughly speaking, the Establishment Survey uses data from payroll records and is a count of jobs and workers. The Current Population Survey is a household survey and is a count of persons including the self-employed, unpaid family workers and private household workers. For a more detailed description see *Handbook of Labor Statistics*, March 1984, p. 174. Although the two survey results differ quantitatively, they show the same trends in manufacturing and goods employment.

10. Valerie A. Personick, "A Second Look," p. 278.

11. Other published figures show that GDP per capita in other nations exceeds that of the United States. These alternative figures are calculated using market exchange rates rather than purchasing power parity exchange rates, which are the number of currency units required to buy goods and services equivalent to what can be bought with one unit of United States currency. The measures using purchasing power parity exchange rates are more accurate, because market exchange rates seldom reflect only the relative purchasing power of currencies. See R. D. Norton, "Industrial Policy and American Renewal," *The Journal of Economic Literature*, March 1986, p. 28.

12. The years 1960, 1973 and 1980 were peaks in the business cycle. In 1960, 1980 and 1985 manufacturing capacity utilization was about 80 percent but in 1973 capacity utilization was 87 percent. Although some differences in the selected years do exist, examining growth rates over these periods should tend to reveal underlying trends.

13. GDP per employed person is unpublished data from the Bureau of Labor Statistics. The figures are based on purchasing power parity exchange rates in U.S. 1984 dollars and OECD price weights. Manufacturing productivity growth rates were calculated from the productivity indexes published by the BLS. Relative manufacturing productivity levels are a series constructed by the author. The measure of productivity in various countries is crude but can provide a rough comparison. Manufacturing output is for 1983, taken from the OECD *National Accounts Vol. II 1971–1983* deflated to 1980 dollars using purchasing power parity exchange rates from the Bureau of Labor Statistics. Hours are calculated using number of employees multi-

plied by average hours. Numbers of employees and average hours data are also from the Bureau of Labor Statistics.

Other authors have differing estimates of productivity levels, although most agree that the United States still maintains a lead. A. D. Roy in "Labor Productivity in 1980: An International Comparison," *National Institute Economic Review,* no. 101, August 1982, p. 29, quoted in Robert Z. Lawrence, *Can America Compete?* p. 33, estimated that in 1980 U.S. output per employed worker-year was 16 percent higher than Japan, 21.7 percent higher than Germany, and 31.3 percent higher than France.

Robert Z. Lawrence in *Can America Compete?* p. 33, reported that the Japanese Ministry of International Trade and Industry estimated the value-added labor productivity in Japanese manufacturing to be about 17 percent below that of the United States in 1980.

William J. Baumol and Kenneth McLennan got different results by extrapolating the Japan Productivity Center's 1977 productivity level estimates. They estimated that in 1981 the level of manufacturing productivity in the U.S. and Japan was virtually identical. See their chapter "U.S. Productivity Performance and Its Implications, in Baumol and McLennan, eds., *Productivity and U.S. Competitiveness,* 1985, p. 15.

Martin Bronfenbrenner in "Japanese Productivity Experience" in the same volume, p. 70, calculated that in the late 1970s American productivity remained well above the Japanese in most major industries.

14. See Ronald E. Kutscher and Jerome A. Mark, "The Service Producing Sector: Some Common Perceptions Reviewed," *Monthly Labor Review,* April 1983, pp. 21–24; also Edward F. Denison, "The Shift to Services and the Rate of Productivity Change," *Survey of Current Business,* October 1973, pp. 20–35.

For a complete review of sources on both sides of the issue see Edward N. Wolff, "The Magnitude and Causes of the Recent Productivity Slowdown in the United States: A survey of Recent Studies," in Baumol and McLennan, eds., *Productivity and U.S. Competitiveness.*

15. The average capital intensity (capital stock in billions of dollars divided by hours paid) of goods is .029 compared to .039 for services. From 1973 to 1980 productivity growth rates in goods industries ranged from -8.87 to 3.67. In services the range was -3.2 to 6.6. The average growth rate was .15 for goods and .28 for services. From 1980 to 1984 the range for goods was -3.3 to 13.9 and -4.5 to 4.8 for services. The average growth rate for goods was 3.3 and services 0.6.

16. This analysis is similar to that used by Kutscher and Mark, "The Service Producing Sector," pp. 21–24.

Productivity was measured as the gross product originating in goods and services divided by hours worked with each sector weighted by its share of total hours. Productivity growth was separated into three components: (i) productivity growth within goods industries and within service industries; (ii) productivity growth due to the change in service share of total hours; (iii) an interactive effect. The interactive effect was divided evenly between (i) and (ii).

Hours worked (U.S. Bureau of Economic Analysis) was used rather than hours paid because it is a more accurate measure of productive time. Productivity growth measured as output per hour paid also showed little effect from the increased importance of services. See Krent Kunze, "New BLS Survey Measures Ratio of Hours Worked to Hours Paid," *Monthly Labor Review,* June 1984, p. 3 for an explanation of the differences between hours paid and hours worked.

17. The medical service industry example is from Denison, "The Shift to Services," pp. 20–35.

18. Although productivity growth has fallen for business services it is unlikely that this has depressed overall productivity growth. Presumably companies hire business services because management believes that those who provide business services are no less efficient than the company's own employees.

19. Alvin H. Hansen, "Economic Progress and Declining Population Growth," *American Economic Review,* March 1939, quoted in R. D. Norton, "Industrial Policy and American Renewal," p. 5.

20. Quoted in James Fallow, "America's Changing Landscape," *The Atlantic,* March 1985.

21. Stan N. Lundine, "Industrial Strategy Yes," *Challenge,* July/August 1983, p. 17.

NO

Nicholas S. Perna

THE SHIFT FROM MANUFACTURING TO SERVICES: A CONCERNED VIEW

I. SUMMARY AND CONCLUSIONS

The benign view of the changing U.S. industrial structure tells us "not to worry." Manufacturing has been doing just fine and has performed well during the current recovery. Its share of GNP has been stable for years, and the declining proportion of jobs in manufacturing is simply the continuation of a long-term trend that reflects superior productivity. The shift to services is just normal economic evolution, very similar to the earlier move out of agriculture that raised U.S. living standards. Furthermore, plenty of high-paying service jobs are available. The United States is not in danger of becoming a nation of fast-food franchises.

An alternative view says that things may not be so rosy and certainly are not so simple. During the current recovery, manufacturing has not climbed nearly as far above its previous peak as it did in earlier cycles. Moreover, it is important to recognize the special difficulties of measuring long-term economic trends. Each time the U.S. Department of Commerce changes the base year used in calculating real GNP it alters the manufacturing share of the U.S. economy. Recasting the historical data gives the impression of long-term stability. However, because of these measurement problems, we cannot be sure whether manufacturing's share of GNP has remained stable. The alternative view holds that in reality the manufacturing share of GNP has declined sharply during the postwar period. A large part of this decline can be found in the compression of profit margins in the wake of slowing economic growth and intensifying international competition. Interestingly, U.S. *consumption* of durable goods has risen as a share of GNP while the *production* share has fallen due to rising imports. This is not consistent with the view that the shift away from goods is a simple matter of maturity, affluence, or income elasticities.

From Nicholas S. Perna, "The Shift from Manufacturing to Services: A Concerned View," *New England Economic Review* (January/February 1987). Copyright © 1987 by the Federal Reserve Bank of Boston. Reprinted by permission of *New England Economic Review.*

Manufacturing's share of jobs has been decreasing at an accelerating rate since the late 1960s and early 1970s. This decline reflects *nonmanufacturing's* inferior productivity combined with its faster output growth more than it reflects the superior efficiency of U.S. manufacturing, however. Labor productivity growth has stagnated in nonmanufacturing for more than a decade, requiring that extra output be obtained entirely through more labor input. This also helps explain the slowdown in overall productivity growth in the United States and the virtual disappearance of real wage gains. Multifactor productivity data, which take the contributions of both capital and labor into account, tell the same tale.

International comparisons of overall manufacturing levels can also be misleading, especially with respect to the industrialized nations. Data for Japan indicate that productivity in some major export industries is probably well ahead of that in the United States even if Japanese overall manufacturing efficiency is not. As for the newly industrializing countries, their productivity *growth* rates are so far above those in the United States that it will not be long before their productivity levels equal or surpass ours. Meanwhile, their shortcomings in productivity are offset by lower wages. Lack of overall productivity growth will make the adverse shift in the terms of trade that is currently underway all the more difficult for the United States to digest.

While there are many high-paying nonmanufacturing jobs and numerous low-paying manufacturing jobs, industry analysis shows that the U.S. employment mix has shifted towards the lower-paying jobs, particularly since the late 1960s. Also, the historic drift from farm to factory may not be the relevant analogy, since that movement was from low-productivity farming to higher-productivity industrial work. The current movement may well be in the opposite direction.

Finally, manufacturing plays a very important role in U.S. international trade. Much of our rather small potential for services exports is in areas where other countries may have (or soon acquire) significant advantages: that is, services that benefit from highly skilled labor and low capital costs.

The issue is not whether eventually we will all cook each other's hamburgers, do each other's washing, manage each other's financial portfolios, or nurse each other's illnesses. Rather, will productivity in hamburgers, laundries, financial and medical services rise fast enough to keep overall real incomes growing at an acceptable pace? Is productivity growing fast enough in manufacturing and in services to enable the United States to export more of both and to redress our growing balance of payments disequilibrium without sizable reductions in living standards? Again, recent record gives cause for continuing concern.

II. THE BENIGN VIEW OF U.S. MANUFACTURING

The position of those supporting the benign view of the changing U.S. industrial structure[1] generally takes the following form: 1) *Share of GNP:* The manufacturing share of real GNP has not declined, nor has the goods share. Factory output in the current recovery has been strong relative to past cycles. 2) *Share of Jobs:* The manufacturing share of jobs has been falling, but this trend is decades old. It reflects manufacturing's superior productivity as well as the mature stage of economic development in an affluent society. This development is quite similar to the earlier decline in agriculture's share of the U.S. economy, which was accompanied by sharply higher U.S. living standards. 3) *Further Issues and Implications:* The effects of these changes in interindustry mix are probably positive or at least neutral. The shift to services has not retarded the overall rate of productivity gain, nor has it reduced average wage levels. Just as there are ample domestic opportunities for the growth of services, there must be plenty of opportunities for exporting them.

III. U.S. MANUFACTURING: A COUNTERVIEW

Manufacturing has grown less than in previous expansions but about in line with real GNP when quarterly data are used to capture cyclical movements.[2] However, it is important to keep in mind that manufacturing previously underwent a long and steep slide that dated back to 1979 and by mid-1986 the amount by which manufacturing exceeded its past peak was still much less than in previous cycles. GNP did a somewhat better job relative to past cycles.

Measuring Manufacturing's Relative Share of the U.S. Economy

Defining manufacturing's real share of the U.S. economy poses some major measurement problems. For one thing, value added by manufacturing is calculated by subtracting deflated purchases of materials and services from deflated sales, yielding a residual with a potentially wide error margin.

The second difficulty is a more fundamental index number problem: the size of manufacturing's share is very sensitive to the particular base year used in calculating real GNP.[3] The more recent the base year, the smaller the manufacturing share of real GNP. For 1969, moving the base from 1958 to 1982 reduced the manufacturing share from 31 percent to 22 percent. The same thing happens to the goods share of GNP when the base years are shifted. Very much the same issues arise in connection with the Consumer Price Index. When the market basket becomes obsolete, the Bureau of Labor Statistics updates it. However, in contrast to the GNP, the historic data are not recast to reflect the new weights. That is because the 1980s proportion of consumer spending is no more relevant for the 1950s than the 1950s basket is for the 1980s. The problem exists whether one looks at GNP from an industry vantage point (for example, manufacturing) or from a product point of view (for example, goods). The further one gets from the base period, the less representative it is of the economy's actual structure.

Current-dollar value added may well be a better measure of manufacturing's share of GNP, or at least an important additional gauge. It avoids both measurement problems described above, while indicating changes in the major components of value added. The compensation share has declined by one-fourth between 1968 and 1985. The profits share plunged by two-thirds during the same period while profits plus depreciation have dropped by more than one-third. One explanation may be the combination of slow growth and intense international competition.

There is a third measurement problem. Some observers claim that a sizable amount of manufacturing employment and output has really been transferred to the service sector as, for example, business consultants take over for corporate staffs and factories hire workers from service sector firms specializing in temporary help.[4] There does not appear to be more than anecdotal support for this claim. McKenzie and Smith cite the decline in value added as a percentage of manufacturing shipments, as evidence of such contracting out. They recognize, however, that this could also reflect the shift towards increased use of imported components. Recent analysis of occupational patterns within various industries does not provide evidence of large volume of contracting out.[5] Rather, one must look elsewhere for explanations of the rapid growth of business services employment.

Production versus Consumption
U.S. consumption of manufactured goods has risen much faster than U.S. production. Consumption of durables of all types (consumer goods, capital goods, defense hardware) has been rising rapidly as a percentage of GNP since World War II and particularly after 1978. This does not support the view that a declining "goods" share of GNP is a virtually inevitable by-product of rising affluence and the higher income elasticities for services than for goods. The production share has fallen since 1978, as a growing fraction of domestic consumption is being met through imports.

Manufacturing's Declining Share of Jobs
Manufacturing's declining share of jobs is not simply the continuation of a long-term trend. The "rate of decay" has accelerated: -0.9 percent annual average decline between 1948 and 1968; -2.1 percent between 1968 and 1978; and -2.5 percent between 1978 and 1985. Thus the annual rate of decline between 1978 and 1985 was nearly triple that of the 1948–68 period.

Relationship to productivity.
Arithmetically, most of manufacturing's falling job share reflects the faster growth in labor productivity in the manufacturing sector than in nonmanufacturing. However, this does not indicate a superior record in manufacturing so much as it reflects the lower productivity in nonmanufacturing. Productivity gains in nonmanufacturing were almost on a par with those in manufacturing between 1948 and 1968, but they have since turned negative. Manhours growth has accelerated in nonmanufacturing despite the slowing growth in real output, because productivity has become so poor. Although services productivity poses measurement problems, it is not clear that the net result is an understatement of gains. For example, one reason for the rapid rise of gasoline station productivity is the spread of self-service pumps. Here, customer labor has been substituted for employee labor, or equivalently, quality has deteriorated.

The most important comparisons for U.S. manufacturing are not with U.S. nonmanufacturing, but with foreign competitors. U.S. manufacturing productivity growth is below that of our most important global competitors, particularly the newly industrializing countries. While the level of productivity is important for competitive comparisons, it is not the level of overall manufacturing productivity that is relevant. This is affected by the mix of industry output as well as by goods that are not traded internationally. Much more critical is the productivity level of those industries that sell in global markets. Here the available data go back to 1982, but are illuminating, nonetheless.

Japanese manufacturing productivity was below the overall U.S. average but with considerable dispersion around the average. The Japanese were considerably below the United States in domestically oriented industries such as food processing and publishing but above it in important export industries such as motor vehicles and electrical machinery.

Productivity is growing so much faster in the developing countries than in the United States that it will not take long to erase any existing U.S. advantage. In the meantime, the productivity level disadvantages of the developing countries are more than offset by significantly lower levels of labor compensation.

Comparison with agriculture.

The current shift in the U.S. industrial structure and employment mix is very different from the decline in the farm share of U.S. jobs from about 50 percent in the 1880s to 3 percent in 1980s. That shift raised living standards as workers moved from lower productivity farming jobs to higher productivity manufacturing jobs, pulling up the average. The current movement appears to be in the opposite direction, from high productivity manufacturing to lower productivity non-manufacturing, thereby lowering the average.[6]

IV. FURTHER ISSUES
AN IMPLICATIONS

Impact of Nonmanufacturing on Productivity Growth

Some statistical studies conclude that the current shift towards services is not reducing the productivity growth of the economy.[7] The index number problem discussed above may affect these calculations. Since the decline in the manufacturing share is understated, the effect of the changing mix on productivity may also be understated.

. . . [T]he slowdown of productivity growth in nonmanufacturing must have lowered the overall average, as manufacturing productivity continued to grow at about the same rate as before. The picture for nonmanufacturing productivity has gotten progressively worse, from a slowdown between 1968 and 1978 to an outright decline from 1978 to 1985.

The U.S. Bureau of Labor Statistics series on multifactor productivity, which attempts to capture the contributions of both capital and labor, tells the same tale: that multifactor productivity in the overall private nonfarm sector and in manufacturing rose at about the same rate from the late 1940s to the early 1970s. Since then, private nonfarm productivity has been essentially flat; this, again, reflects declining productivity in nonmanufacturing.

The consequences of this overall slowdown are also straightforward: real wage gains have shrunk in the wake of dwindling labor productivity improvements.[8] The decline in the rate of real wage growth provides independent corroboration that the United States has, in fact, been experiencing a productivity slowdown and not simply a productivity measurement problem.

Effect of Changing Industry Mix on Average Incomes

Average annual employee compensation ranges widely within manufacturing and across other industries (Table 1). But overall, manufacturing pay is one-fourth higher than nonmanufacturing pay and almost double the pay in retail trade.

Table 1

**Average Annual
Employee Compensation in 1985[a]**

All Industries	$25,294
Manufacturing	29,992
High: Petroleum and Coal Products	56,665
Low: Apparel and Other Textile Products	15,559
Nonmanufacturing	24,108
Transportation and Public Utilities	34,725
Railroads	46,052
Air Transportation	39,663
Electric, Gas and Sanitary Services	39,542
Communication	40,270
Telephone and Telegraph	42,125
Radio and TV Broadcasting	31,784
Wholesale Trade	28,874
Retail Trade	15,516
Finance, Insurance, Real Estate	27,658
Banks	25,559
Security and Commodity Brokers	55,711
Services	21,401
Auto Repair	18,377
Health Services	24,296
Legal Services	34,488
Educational Services	17,496
Private Households	11,924
Government	28,075

[a]Per full-time equivalent employee
Source: U.S. Bureau of Economic Analysis.

Some of the highest nonmanufacturing pay is to be found among the more "industrial" services: railroads, electric and other utilities. In many ways, these are a lot more like manufacturing than services. For example, producing electricity and running a refinery are both highly capital-intensive, continuous-flow operations. Yet electricity is counted as a service, while oil refining is included in nondurable manufacturing. The compensation data shown in Table 1 have advantages over some of the more familiar series. They include forms of pay that have become increasingly important but are not included in the average hourly or weekly earnings series: fringe benefits as well as lump-sum and profit-sharing payments.

Has the changing industrial composition of the U.S. economy raised or lowered average incomes? Neil Rosenthal of the U.S. Bureau of Labor Statistics has found that the occupational mix of the work force has been moving towards higher-paid jobs.[9] However, this movement has been even more pronounced within manufacturing than in nonmanufacturing. Rosenthal's article really does not attempt to assess the impact of changes in the industrial mix of the U.S. economy. Marvin Kosters found that the changing mix of U.S. industry accounts for some of the real wage slowdown, but that the preponderance is due to the productivity problem.[10]

My analysis, using data from the U.S. Bureau of Economic Analysis on compensation and the number of full-time equivalent workers, shows that industry mix has had a negative effect on average compensation since the late 1960s.[11] The shift in the industrial composition of jobs has reduced average compensation by about 1 percent relative to 1978 and 3 percent compared with 1968. The methodology is straightforward: 1985 compensation per worker for each of the roughly 70 industry classifications was weighted by the job mix of earlier years, to show what 1985 average compensation would have been if the earlier industry mix had prevailed. The job share of other high-pay sectors (mining, transportation and public utilities) has also declined, but manufacturing has had the largest negative impact on average pay. Furthermore, some of the decline in those other sectors is linked to manufacturing; for example, there is less need for U.S. electricity when imports of manufactured goods replace domestic production.

In an important sense this approach may understate the impact of the shift in the industrial composition of jobs, since it examines only the movement from high-wage to low-wage employment to no-wage unemployment. On the other hand, this analysis does not take into account the extent to which faster growth of compensation outside of manufacturing may have offset the effects of the declining weight of manufacturing on average pay levels. In any event, more research is needed in this area.

Services and the Balance of Payments
There is a reason to worry about how and when U.S. international payments will be brought into equilibrium.[12] How will the United States service its huge foreign debt? Manufacturing now accounts for roughly two-thirds of merchandise exports.

The potential for stepping up exports of services is surprisingly limited relative to the magnitude of current trade deficits. Over 60 percent of services exports is investment income; that is, interest, dividends, and corporate retained earnings. While this percentage is likely to grow in the future, so will the comparable outflows, reflecting earnings on increased foreign investment in the United States. Travel and transportation, which amount to about 20 percent of services exports, are running a sizable deficit. There is likely to be only modest improvement in this deficit over the next few years, mainly because the real dollar exchange rate has declined very little when weighted to reflect travel rather than trade patterns.[13] Exports of telecommunications, business consulting, and the like are relatively small. Even very rapid growth won't make much overall difference for the trade deficit five years from now. More-

over, there is every reason to expect increased imports of services, particularly those that are labor-intensive and those provided by countries with lower capital costs than the United States.

NOTES

1. See Molly McUsic, "U.S. Manufacturing: Any Cause for Alarm? *New England Economic Review* January/February 1987), and, for example, Michael F. Bryan, "Is Manufacturing Disappearing?" Federal Reserve Bank of Cleveland, *Economic Commentary*, July 15, 1985); J. Baxter, "Please, No More Myths About the Decline of U.S. Manufacturing," *Iron Age* (Oct. 18, 1985); and Ronald E. Kutscher and Valerie A. Personick, "Deindustrialization and the Shift to Services," *Monthly Labor Review* (June 1986) pp. 3–13.

2. This statement is at odds with John A. Tatom's findings in "Domestic vs. International Explanations of Recent U.S. Manufacturing Developments," Federal Reserve Bank of St. Louis *Review* (April 1986), pp. 5–18. His equation relating real manufacturing output growth to real GNP growth underpredicted actual growth by 2 percentage points from 1980:4 to 1985:4.

3. A succinct but nontheoretical discussion of how shifting the base period affects the growth rates of real GNP and the GNP deflator as well as the relative shares is given in "A Note on the Effect of Shifting the Base Period," in "Revised Estimates of the National Income and Product Accounts of the United States, 1929–85: An Introduction," *Survey of Current Business* (December 1985), p. 14. In general, when an item's relative price falls (when its price rises less than other prices), then its relative share of the total GNP will fall as the base year is moved forward in time. The issues are covered quite thoroughly by Robin Marris in his *Economic Arithmetic* (London: Macmillan & Co., 1958), Chapter 9, in the context of measuring real income.

4. Molly McUsic, "U.S. Manufacturing," and, for example, Richard B. McKenzie and Stephen D. Smith, *The Good News About U.S. Production*, Publication No. 72 (St. Louis, MO: Washington University Center for the Study of American Business, 1986).

5. Bobbie H. McCrackin, "Why Are Business and Professional Services Growing So Rapidly?" Federal Reserve Bank of Atlanta *Economic Review* (August 1985), pp. 14–28.

6. In making these interindustry productivity comparisons, it is important to exclude the effects of the imputation for owner-occupied housing in the GNP. In 1985 this amounted to $106 billion and was allocated to the GNP originating

in the real estate sector. Since there is no employment associated with this imputation, the net result is to overstate productivity in real estate and, thus, productivity in services.

7. See Ronald E. Kutscher and Jerome A. Mark, "The Service-Producing Sector: Some Common Perceptions Reviewed," *Monthly Labor Review* (April 1983), pp. 21–24.

8. The relationship between productivity and real wages is defined by Allen M. Cartter in *Theory of Wages and Employment*, (New York: Irwin, 1958).

9. Neil H. Rosenthal, "The Shrinking Middle Class: Myth or Reality?" *Monthly Labor Review* (March 1985), pp. 3–10.

10. Marvin H. Kosters, "Free Markets Bring Change and Growth," prepared for the 40th Anniversary Symposium of the Joint Economic Committee of Congress and reprinted in *Challenge* (March/April 1986), pp. 55–64.

11. *Survey of Current Business*, July 1986, Tables 6.4B to 6.7B.

12. See Paul R. Krugman and George N. Hatsopoulos, "The Problem of U.S. Competitiveness in Manufacturing," *New England Economic Review* (January/February 1987).

13. Bruce Kasman, "Prospects for the U.S. International Travel Deficit," *Federal Reserve Bank of New York Quarterly Review* (Summer 1986), pp. 44–46.

POSTSCRIPT

Is Manufacturing Alive and Well and Living in the United States?

McUsic assesses the status of U.S. manufacturing by examining patterns of change in output, employment, and productivity. With respect to output she finds that, since 1947, manufacturing's share of the Gross National Product has been quite constant, between 20 and 22 percent. She also finds that during the 1980s U.S. industrial output grew more rapidly than that of any other industrialized country, with the exception of Japan. She goes on to note that although the U.S. share of world output has declined, this decline was to be expected and the U.S. standard of living has increased in spite of this decline. Employment data reveal a decline in manufacturing jobs, both in terms of absolute numbers and in terms of the percentage of total jobs. But this result should not be alarming. It is a pattern found in other industrialized countries and it indicates that manufacturing productivity has been increasing. Turning specifically to productivity, McUsic is optimistic. She finds that productivity growth as been higher since the 1982–1983 recession than it has been in recent recoveries. She also finds that U.S. productivity patterns for the 1970s were due to special circumstances that have subsequently disappeared. She concludes: "While the data reviewed in this article do not show that all U.S. industries are flourishing, they also reveal no evidence of profound economic ills."

Perna's examination of the data regarding U.S. manufacturing suggests that "things may not be so rosy." He lists several reasons to be worried about U.S. manufacturing. First, the United States has satisfied an increasing demand for durable goods by expanding imports rather than expanding domestic production. Second, the number of jobs in manufacturing, expressed as a percent of the total number of jobs, has been falling much more rapidly in the 1978–1985 period than in the 1948–1968 period. Third, the belief that the shift from manufacturing to service jobs is like the shift from agricultural to manufacturing jobs is fundamentally incorrect. The agriculture to manufacturing shift was from lower productivity jobs to higher productivity jobs, while the manufacturing to service shift is from higher productivity jobs to lower productivity and lower paying jobs. Fourth, when productivity patterns are compared across countries, other countries have been outperforming the United States in the production of those commodities in which there is international competition. Fifth, the lack of performance in the manufacturing sector combined with the prospect of increasing international competition in service exports suggests that the United States will be unable to achieve a balance in its international payments.

For readings that are consistent with the position taken by McUsic, see "Is Manufacturing Disappearing?" by Michael F. Bryan, *Economic Commentary*, Federal Reserve Bank of Cleveland, July 15, 1985; "Please, Please No More Myths About the Decline of U.S. Manufacturing," by J. Baxter, *Iron Age*, October 18, 1985; "Deindustrialization and the Shift to Services," by Ronald E. Kutscher and Valerie A. Personick, *Monthly Labor Review*, June 1986; "Why Has Manufacturing Employment Declined?" by John A. Tatom, *Review*, Federal Reserve Bank of St. Louis, December 1986; "Is Manufacturing Dead?" by David L. Birch, *Inc.*, June 1987; and "The Growing Share of Services in the U.S. Economy—Degeneration or Evolution?" by Mack Ott, *Review*, Federal Reserve Bank of St. Louis, June/July 1987.

For readings that are more consistent with the position taken by Perna, see "The Problem of U.S. Competitiveness in Manufacturing," by Paul R. Krugman and George N. Hatsopoulos, *New England Economic Review*, January/February 1987; "The Service Sector's Productivity Problem," by Alan Murray, *Wall Street Journal*, February 2, 1987; and *Why Manufacturing Matters: The Myth of the Post-Industrial Economy*, by Stephen S. Cohen and John Zysman (Basic Books, 1987). Other interesting readings include "Taking in Each Other's Laundry—The Service Economy," by Lynn E. Brown, *New England Economic Review*, July/August 1986; and *Can America Compete?* by Robert Z. Lawrence (Brookings Institution, 1984).

CONTRIBUTORS
TO THIS VOLUME

EDITORS

THOMAS R. SWARTZ was born in Philadelphia in 1937. He received his B.A. from LaSalle University in 1960, his M.A. from Ohio University in 1962, and his Ph.D. from Indiana University in 1965. He is currently a professor of economics/college fellow at the University of Notre Dame and the director of the Notre Dame Center for Economic Education. He writes in the areas of urban finance and economic education. He and Frank J. Bonello are often coauthors. The coedited *Alternative Decisions in Economic Policy* (Notre Dame Press, 1978) and *The Supply Side: Debating Current Economic Policies* (Dushkin Publishing Group, 1983). His most recent book is *The Changing Face of Fiscal Federalism*, which he edited with John E. Peck, to be published by M. E. Sharpe Press in 1990.

FRANK J. BONELLO was born in Detroit in 1939. He received his B.S. from the University of Detroit in 1961, His M.A. from the University of Detroit in 1963, and his Ph.D. from Michigan State University in 1968. He is currently associate professor of economics at the University of Notre Dame. He writes in the areas of monetary economics and economic education. This is his seventh book.

STAFF

Marguerite L. Egan   Program Manager
Brenda S. Filley   Production Manager
Whit Vye   Designer
Libra Ann Cusack   Typesetting Supervisor
Juliana Arbo   Typesetter
Jean Bailey   Graphics Coordinator
Diane Barker   Editorial Assistant

AUTHORS

STEVEN ALTMAN is president of the University of Central Florida at Orlando and former provost of Florida International University in Miami. He is a past president of Texas A & I University.

PETER BAUER is emeritus professor of economics at the London School of Economics. He is a Fellow of Godwin Caius College at Cambridge University and a Fellow of the British Academy.

STEVE BARTLETT is a member of the U.S. House of Representatives from Texas. He serves on the Banking, Finance, and Urban Affairs Committee, and on the Education and Labor Committee.

BARRY BLUESTONE is a professor of political economy at the University of Massachusetts at Boston and a senior associate of the John W. McCormack Institute of Public Affairs.

KATHARINE L. BRADBURY is assistant vice president and an economist at the Federal Reserve Bank of Boston. She is a former research associate for The Brookings Institution.

STEPHAN CHAPMAN is a columnist and editorial writer for the *Chicago Tribune*.

KENT CONRAD is a U.S. senator from North Dakota. He has served on the Budget Committee and the Energy and Natural Resources Committee.

DOLLARS & SENSE is a monthly magazine edited and produced by a collective of economists and journalists offering interpretations of current economic events from a socialist perspective.

BYRON DORGAN is a member of the U.S. House of Representatives from North Dakota. He has served on the House Ways and Means Committee.

LOU FERLEGER is an associate professor of economics and associate dean of arts and sciences at the University of Massachusetts at Boston.

MILTON FRIEDMAN is currently a senior research fellow at the Hoover Institute at Stanford University, where he has been since 1977. He was for many years on the faculty of the University of Chicago. He was awarded the Nobel Prize for Economics in 1977.

JOHN KENNETH GALBRAITH is an internationally renowned economist who, before his retirement in 1975, was Paul M. Warburg Professor of Economics at Harvard University.

ROBERT S. GAY is a senior economist and vice president at Morgan Stanley & Co., Inc. He served for eight years on the research staff of the Federal Reserve Board in Washington, D.C.

TERESA GHILARDUCCI is assistant professor of economics at Notre Dame University in South Bend, Indiana.

ALAN GREENSPAN is the chairman of the Board of Governors for the Federal Reserve System.

CLIFFORD HACKETT served in the Foreign Service and on the staffs of congressional committees involved in foreign affairs.

GERALD L. HOUSEMAN is a professor of political science at Indiana University. He is currently teaching comparative and world politics in Malaysia under a cooperative program with Malaysia and the University of Indiana.

ROBERT W. KASTEN, JR., is a U.S. senator from Wisconsin. He is active in the Appropriations Subcommittee on Foreign Operations.

MICHAEL KINSLEY is a senior editor for the *New Republic.*

BOB KUTTNER is a columnist for the *New Republic* who writes on social and political subjects.

FRANK LEVY is on the faculty of the University of Maryland's School of Public Affairs. In 1987 he was a Guggenheim fellow on leave at The Brookings Institution, as a visiting fellow in economic studies.

JAY R. MANDLE is a professor of economics at Temple University in Philadelphia, Pennsylvania.

DAVID McCURDY is a member of the U.S. House of Representatives from Oklahoma. He serves on the House Select Committee on Intelligence.

RICHARD B. McKENZIE is a professor of economics at the University of Mississippi in Oxford, Mississippi. He is widely published and is known for his research and writings on the economics of public choice.

MOLLY McUSIC is a former senior research assistant at the Federal Reserve Bank of Boston.

LAWRENCE M. MEAD is an associate professor of politics at New York University. He has conducted extensive research on federal welfare and employment programs.

JOHN MILLER is an associate professor of economics at Wheaton College in Massachusetts. He is a member of the National Steering Committee of the Union for Radical Political Economics.

CHARLES R. MORRIS writes frequently about national affairs. He is the author of *Iron Destinies, Lost*

Opportunities, a history of the arms race.

ROBERT G. MUGABE is the prime minister of Zimbabwe.

THOMAS MULLIGAN is an assistant professor of management and marketing at the Brock University School of Business Administration in St. Catharines, Ontario, Canada. He has also taught at Duke University.

NATION'S BUSINESS is a publication of the U.S. Chamber of Commerce that reports on a wide range of business-related issues.

RUTH NEEDLEMAN is associate professor and coordinator of labor studies at Indiana University Northwest in Gary, Indiana. She is a member of the Industrial Relations Research Association, and the University and College Labor Education Association.

JOHN D. PAULUS is a managing director and the chief economist at Morgan Stanley & Co., Inc. Before joining Morgan Stanley, he was a financial economist for Goldman, Sachs & Co. and director of research for the Federal Reserve Bank of Minneapolis.

NICHOLAS S. PERNA is manager of economic analysis at General Electric Company.

DONALD W. RIEGLE, JR., is a U.S. senator from Michigan. He has been active on the Senate Banking, Housing, and Urban Affairs Committee, the Budget Committee, and the Finance Committee.

WILLIAM SIMON was secretary of the U.S. Treasury; he writes widely on economic issues and public policies.

MORTON H. SKLAR served as legal counsel and director of Jobs Watch, a public interest project providing information and support services related to unemployment.

BRUCE STOKES is a staff correspondent for the *National Journal.* He covers trade and international economics.

HELEN SUZMAN has been a member of the South African Parliament since 1953. For thirteen years, 1961–1974, she was the sole member of the opposition Progressive Federal Party in Parliament.

THOMAS TAUKE is a member of the U.S. House of Representatives from Iowa. A former newspaper reporter and editor, he serves on the Education and Labor Committee.

MURRAY L. WEIDENBAUM writes widely in the area of government regulation. He is the director of the Center for the Study of American Business at Washington University.

INDEX